Acceptance and Change:

Content and Context in Psychotherapy

Acceptance and Change:

Content and Context in Psychotherapy

Editors:
Steven C. Hayes
Neil S. Jacobson
Victoria M. Follette
Michael J. Dougher

4

Acceptance and Change: Content and Context in Psychotherapy / edited by Steven
C. Hayes, Neil S. Jacobson, Victoria M. Follette, and Michael J. Dougher

272 pp.   Paperback. ISBN 1-878978-19-5

Hardback. ISBN 1-878978-20-9

© 1994 CONTEXT PRESS
933 Gear Street, Reno, NV 89503-2729

Printed in the United States of America

Contributors

- Andrew Christensen, *University of California - Los Angeles*
- James V. Cordova, *University of Washington*
  Michael J. Dougher, *University of New Mexico*
- Albert Ellis , *Institute for Rational-Emotive Therapy, New York City*
- Victoria M. Follette, *University of Nevada*
- William C. Follette, *University of Nevada*
  Elizabeth V. Gifford, *University of Nevada*
  Karen Griffee, *University of New Mexico*
  Leslie Greenberg, *York University*
  Joseph R. Haas, *Northern Nevada Child and Adolescent Service*
- Steven C. Hayes, *University of Nevada*
- Heidi L. Heard, *University of Washington*
- Neil S. Jacobson, *University of Washington*
- Kelly Koerner, *University of Washington*
  Barbara S. Kohlenberg, *Reno Veteran's Administration Medical Center*
- Robert J. Kohlenberg, *University of Washington*
- Marsha M. Linehan, *University of Washington*
  Joseph LoPiccolo, *University of Missouri*
- G. Alan Marlatt, *University of Washington*
  Christopher McCurry, *University of Nevada*
  Carol W. Metzler, *Oregon Research Institute*
  Susan M. McCurry, *University of Washington*
  Amy E. Naugle, *University of Nevada*
  Robert F. Peterson, *University of Nevada*
  Melissa A. Polusny, *University of Nevada*
  Hank Robb, *Pacific Institute for RET, Lake Oswego, Oregon*
  Amy Schmidt, *University of Washington*
  Kelly G. Wilson, *University of Nevada*
  Edelgard Wulfert, *The University at Albany, State University of New York*
  Robert D. Zettle, *Wichita State University*

About the Conference

This book is the result of the *Nevada Conference on Acceptance and Change,* held in Reno at the University of Nevada in January of 1993. The conferences was part of the Nevada Conference Series, a program designed to bring together applied workers and academics to consider important and controversial aspects of research and practice in psychology and related fields. The *Nevada Conference on Acceptance and Change* was supported by the Clinical Psychology Program in the Department of Psychology, the College of Arts and Science and the Graduate School at the University of Nevada, and by CONTEXT PRESS.

Table of Contents

Preface 10

Section 1 - General Issues

Chapter 1 13
Content, Context, and the Types of Psychological Acceptance
Steven C. Hayes, *University of Nevada*
Discussion of Hayes 33
The Elusive Nature of Acceptance
Joseph R. Haas, *Northern Nevada Child and Adolescent Service*

Chapter 2 37
The Act of Acceptance
Michael J. Dougher, *University of New Mexico*
Discussion of Dougher.. 46
On the Use of Acceptable Language
Robert D. Zettle, *Wichita State University*

Section 2
Acceptance and Approaches to Intervention

Chapter 3 53
Acceptance in Experiential Therapy
Leslie Greenberg, *York University*
Discussion of Greenberg 68
Acceptance, Experience, and Choice
Robert F. Peterson, *University of Nevada*

Chapter 4 73
Acceptance and Change: The Central Dialectic in Psychotherapy
Marsha M. Linehan, *University of Washington*
Discussion of Linehan 87
**The Experiential Acquisition of Acceptance: Clinical
Supervision as a Laboratory**
Barbara S. Kohlenberg, *Reno Vetern's Administration Medical Center*

Chapter 5 91
Acceptance in Rational-Emotive Therapy
     Albert Ellis , *Institute for Rational-Emotive Therapy, New York City*
     Hank Robb, *Pacific Institute for RET, Lake Oswego, Oregon*
     Discussion of Ellis and Robb 103
     The Nature of Acceptance in Rational-Emotive Therapy
     Niloofar Afari, *University of Nevada*

Chapter 6 109
Emotional Acceptance in Integrative Behavioral Couple Therapy
     Kelly Koerner and Neil S. Jacobson, *University of Washington*
     Andrew Christensen, *University of California - Los Angeles*
     Discussion of Koerner, Jacobson, and Christensen 119
     Acceptance in Couples Therapy
     William C. Follette and Melissa A. Polusny, *University of Nevada*

Chapter 7 125
Acceptance and the Therapeutic Relationship
     James V. Cordova and Robert J. Kohlenberg,
       University of Washington
     Discussion of Cordova and Kohlenberg 141
     Reorientng and Tolerating
     Christopher McCurry, *University of Nevada*

Section 3 - Acceptance and Approaches to Specific Problems and Populations

Chapter 8 149
Acceptance and Broad Spectrum Treatment of Paraphilias
     Joseph LoPiccolo, *University of Missouri*
     Discussion of LoPiccolo 171
     The Overt-Covert Link
     Kelly Koerner, *University of Washington*

Chapter 9 175
Addiction and Acceptance
> G. Alan Marlatt, *University of Washington*
> Discussion of Marlatt 198
> **Mindfulness and Recovery from Substance Dependence**
> Kelly G. Wilson, *University of Nevada*

Chapter 10 203
Acceptance in the Treatment of Alcoholism: A Comparison of
Alcoholics Anonymous and Social Learning Theory
> Edelgard Wulfert, *The University at Albany, State University*
> *of New York*
> Discussion of Wulfert 218
> **Setting a Course for Behavior Change:**
> **The Verbal Context of Acceptance**
> Elizabeth V. Gifford, *University of Nevada*

Chapter 11 223
Acceptance and the Family Context
> Karen Griffee, *University of New Mexico*
> Discussion of Griffee 234
> **The Costs of Non-Acceptance**
> Carol W. Metzler, *Oregon Research Institute*

Chapter 12 237
Acceptance, Serenity, and Resignation in Elderly Caregivers
> Susan M. McCurry and Amy Schmidt, *University of Washington*
> Discussion of McCurry and Schmidt 252
> **Caregiving in Context**
> Amy E. Naugle, *University of Nevada*

Chapter 13 255
Survivors of Child Sexual Abuse: Treatment Using a
Contextual Analysis
> Victoria M. Follette, *University of Nevada*
> Discussion of Follette 269
> **Acceptance and Sexual Abuse Survivors:**
> **The Cultural and Therapeutic Context**
> Heidi L. Heard, *University of Washington*

Preface

The modern area of empirical applied psychology is not very old. Controlled outcome investigations, good measures, careful specification of treatment, assessment of treatment integrity, and the many other characteristics of modern applied research, have only been popular for a very few decades. There are many, many applied approaches that have had very little empirical scrutiny of this kind — including approaches that are reasonable and promising.

The nearly exclusive focus on direct, change-oriented techniques within this brief first wave of empirical clinical investigation is gradually being widened to include these other procedures. There is a new wave of applied research into contextual, acceptance-based approaches as a result.

Acceptance-based approaches are not new. They are represented outside of psychology in traditions as old as Buddhism, and within psychology by some of the least empirically-oriented wings, such as Gestalt or existential therapy. Surely not everything that goes under the banner "acceptance" will prove to be useful. But it is already clear that there is something of considerable value here. Some of our most intractable clients are now being moved; roadways are being laid across some of the widest intellectual bogs in applied psychology.

If acceptance methods are not really new, why should we be excited? Because now the theoretical and methodological skills of modern empirical psychology are being applied to these issues. Researchers are doing basic analyses, developing new techniques, developing assessment methods, and writing therapy manuals. Acceptance methods will be enhanced by this and made more accessible to clinicians everywhere. In so doing, the entire field may be changed in some significant ways. This *is* new, and it is very exciting.

Steven C. Hayes
Neil S. Jacobson
Victoria M. Follette
Michael J. Dougher

October, 1994

Section 1

General Issues

Chapter 1

Content, Context, and the Types of Psychological Acceptance

Steven C. Hayes
University of Nevada

I have six major points to make in this chapter. First, *applied psychology has been too interested in changes in content at the expense of changes in context.* A large majority of procedures and techniques in applied psychology attempt to modify or eliminate psychological reactions such as undesirable thoughts, feelings, bodily sensations, memories, attitudes, behavioral predispositions, and the like. When the form or the frequency of these psychological events change in a "positive" direction we usually believe we have met the goal of psychological intervention.

There is nothing inherently wrong with this approach, but it has come to be implicitly viewed as the only way to produce a positive psychotherapeutic end. Changes in the context of psychological problems are equally important, if not more so. Such changes have been given relatively more weight by the non-empirical traditions within applied psychology. It is only quite recently that a number of empirical researchers have turned to the serious investigation of these methods.

My second point is that *psychological acceptance is one of the most important contextual change strategies.* The meaning of psychological events is found in the relationship between those events and their psychological context. The dominant context within which the mere presence of certain kinds of psychological events is held to be "a problem" is that of deliberate manipulation and control. In that context, apparently uncontrollable events can be much more threatening than they would be otherwise and unsuccessful control efforts can be extremely distressing.

These same psychological events in another context are no longer "the same psychological events." Their actual nature changes qualitatively when context changes. By establishing a posture of psychological acceptance, events that formerly were taken to be inherently problematic, become instead opportunities for growth, interest, or understanding. In other words, attention shifts from problems of historical content to problems of current functioning.

My third point is that *acceptance is of different types, and not all of them are psychologically healthy.* Sometimes, first-order change efforts, that is, a deliberate change in content, is quite desirable. As in the Serenity Prayer of Alcoholics Anonymous, the point is not so much to be committed to change or to acceptance, but rather to have the wisdom to know when these different approaches are applicable.

My fourth point is that *we can derive from learning principles when psychological acceptance is likely to be most useful.* By carefully focusing change efforts in those areas where deliberate change is useful, and by using emotional acceptance methods in areas in which they are most applicable, we can look forward to greater psychotherapeutic success with a greater number of people. Many of our so called treatment failures are, I believe, failures of first-order change efforts being applied where they do not belong. First-order change efforts are dominant within the psychotherapeutic culture. When clients have had multiple treatment failures, a careful examination of their therapy histories often shows that all of these treatment failures are in fact failures of first-order change strategies. For that reason, acceptance-based procedures have particular relevance to clients who have failed to improve despite their best efforts in several treatment regimens.

My fifth point is that *the barriers to all forms of acceptance are verbal barriers.* In adults, conscious, deliberate, and purposeful change efforts are always guided by verbal rules. Such verbal involvement is part of why we label behavior with terms like "deliberate" or "conscious." Even being able to see that there is an alternative to deliberate change requires some loosening of the normal language system which overwhelms the psychology of most individuals. In the context of a panoply of interpretations, evaluations, plans, and verbal purposes, it is often hard to find room for or awareness of the simple human act of becoming more fully present with the psychological events unfiltered by these verbal entanglements.

My final point is that *radical forms of acceptance require a manipulation of verbal processes, but that less obtrusive forms of acceptance are possible.* Many of the acceptance procedures that have been developed are quite dramatic and intrusive. They can be quite helpful. But acceptance methods also apply in very short term or limited settings, such as very brief therapy, or in primary care settings.

The Overemphasis of Content-Oriented Change

There are several problems with first-order change efforts in psychotherapy. This is particularly so when the focus of these change procedures are the private psychological reactions of the individual (thoughts, feelings, and so on), rather than their overt behavior or their circumstances. These private events are perhaps the dominant focus of change-oriented procedures in psychotherapy. It is much more common to have a client complain of too much anxiety or too much depression, or disturbing thoughts, than it is for a client to complain of a skills deficit or of overt response accesses or deficits.

Why Private Events are the Usual Suspects

Private events are a reflection of our history. What humans feel when they have "feelings" is the past brought to bear on the present by the current situation. We are enculturated to talk about our history primarily in emotional terms. A person with a difficult or traumatic history is likely, of course, to feel feelings called things like "anxiety" or "sadness." Because aversive histories produce "negative" emotions, there is a kind of logical error that is easy to commit.

The error goes something like this. If one's history were different, one's reactions would be different. Some reactions are conventionally more desirable than others: anxiety is bad, for example. If one's history were different, one's emotional reactions might be "better" than they are now. If they were better, that would be desirable. Therefore, the focus of therapy should be on these desirable changes.

The error in this kind of thinking is to equate the reactions normally produced by one's history with that history. Merely having positive psychological reactions *does not mean that the negative effects of a difficult psychological history have been removed.* We can see this in the extreme with clients whose psychopathology is in fact bound up in an attempt to achieve first-order change of these negative private events. The drug addict "feels better" when he or she is stoned. But this feeling is not the same as having a better history. When the drug wears off, the client is back where they started from, except now with the additional problem of a growing drug habit and of the loss of self-esteem associated with this form of psychological coping.

It is a reasonable goal to build a more positive history from the present forward. If this is done, the person might feel more pleasant things. But the key issue is not the emotional reaction. Indeed, the process of building a more positive history might over the short term produce considerable emotional discomfort.

The culture can be very supportive of repressive first-order change practices. For example, it is not uncommon for a person facing the sadness associated with a death in family to be told to think about something else, to "get on with life," to focus on the positive things, to try to pour themselves into work, or to otherwise avoid the aversive properties of an inherently aversive event. This kind of advice has the negative side affect of decreasing the ability of the individual to be present with their own psychological reactions in difficult circumstances. Grief is not an enemy of healthy living, even though it can be unpleasant to a gut-wrenching extreme.

The Costs of Non-Acceptance

The overemphasis on first-order change efforts by empirically-oriented psychotherapies inadvertently supports a kind of mass cultural illness, in which a main goal (often *the* main goal) of life is to have good feelings rather than bad feelings. Many healthy things in life do not feel good. There are natural tragedies in everybody's life; persons who are building intimate relationships will almost always find themselves facing feelings of vulnerability; the pervasiveness of human misery is not something that people can feel good about. Doing good and living good is not the same as feeling good. There are too many ways to take a shortcut to "good feelings" that are done at a cost of healthy living. Indeed, many forms of psychopathology are, at their core, these very short cuts. What is a phobia but a way of escaping fear? What is depression but a way of avoiding hurt, anxiety, or anger? What is drug abuse but a way of producing one emotion instead of having another?

An emphasis on first-order change as applied to private psychological reactions *encourages people to live somewhere other than in the present*. Humans have the capacity to construct verbally futures that have never been directly experienced. They can compare their present circumstances to a verbalized ideal or a verbalized conception of what is normal. They can then respond strongly to the lack of presence of an ideal, as opposed to the inherent aversiveness of what is actually present. All first-order change efforts contain within them an extended future that includes so called positive outcomes. When a person tries to get rid of anxiety and replace it with relaxation, for example, the person is interacting with the present moment in the context of a verbal plan that is tied to a verbal future that is quite different than the present. This future is not *literally* present of course. The past is no longer here, and the future is yet to come. What is present is not the past or the future, but the present verbalizations of the past and the future. What is present is the construction of another time frame than what is going on in the present moment. When the person enters into these temporal constructions, they can easily loose contact with what is actually happening now. Instead, the issue seemingly becomes what *will* happen, or what *has* happened—and both of these as literally conceived.

It is this entanglement with language that deadens and dulls contact with the present moment. Language has been the focus of the mystical wings of every major religious tradition. It is not by accident that monks chant, or repeat mantras, or try to answer inherent unanswerable koans, or are silent for years at a time, or practice non-analytic forms of meditation. All of these mystical and contemplative practices have as their central goal the loosening of the dominance of evaluative languaging about the past and the present. To the extent in psychotherapy that we encourage this domination of the constructed past and future over the experienced present, we have supported practices that limit the growth and health of individual human beings.

The result of improper application of first-order change efforts is needless trauma. In physical medicine "trauma" is the result of actual damage to the structure of the organism. Metaphorically, in a psychological sense, trauma occurs when events seemingly have created actual damage to the psychological life of the individual. Nothing can be more traumatic than the apparent life threatening quality of an intensely negative psychological event. When it appears as though one is about to be overwhelmed psychologically, trauma is likely. When pain or confusion or sadness appears in an intense way in the psychological life of an individual, and their only form of responding is to attempt to change these events, or to simply tolerate them without abandoning the change agenda itself, the individual has constructed the content of psychological event as a kind of threat to their survival. If I must not be anxious, and yet I am anxious, then something dangerous or even invalid has occurred. The trauma this causes goes far beyond the direct experience of the anxiety itself. This "should not be happening."

It is this combination of the *context of control* and the *presence of undesirable content* that creates much of the psychological trauma that individuals then struggle with.

If a person experiencing intense anxiety knew to experience it without struggle, they would find that the negative content is not inherently trauma producing. Pain is not equal to trauma. If someone exercises every day, very often they will feel aches and pains. This does not mean that they are doing something that is physically damaging. Similarly, if someone is open to the richness of their own psychological life, very often they will feel pain, but this does not mean that they are creating psychological damage by their psychological openness.

To the contrary, the real damage comes from people trying not to feel, think, or remember what they already feel, think, and remember anyway. That puts them in the untenable position of experiencing something, while at the same time holding that experience to be in some way inherently threatening to them and their survival as psychological being. That is the essence of psychological trauma.

Finally, I am concerned that the overemphasis on first-order change has *needlessly increased our failure rates.* Some of the everyday change efforts that the culture encourages us to engage in are harmless enough when people are facing fairly normal situations, and have fairly normal histories. There is nothing wrong with a little bit of relaxation, or a little bit of distraction when someone is feeling a little bit of anxiety. But someone with the more difficult history, who has experienced intense form of anxiety, can sometimes be caught in a downward spiral by these seemingly innocent change efforts.

For example, the person who responds to an initial panic attack by trying to make sure that the panic does not reoccur, is but a hair away from a downward spiral into panic disorder. One sure way to reduce the likelihood of anxiety is to avoid situations in which they occur, or to ingest alcohol, or tranquilizers, or to try to distract oneself or ignore one's own psychological reactions. If anxiety is bad enough to have to be avoided, anxiety is bad enough to be anxiety provoking.

The vigilance of the panic disordered person watching out for the least signs of anxiety, and responding to a normal twitch or twinge with a rush of panic, is an example of how normal change efforts can spiral people down into what we call psychopathology. Similarly, the obsessive compulsive person who tries not to think a thought, is not doing something fundamentally different than what the so called normal person does routinely, when they distract themselves or routinely think of something else. But for someone who *must not* think a negative thought, they *must* contact a verbal rule that is normally designed to help the person avoid the thought, but in fact produces it. It's not possible to follow a rule "do not think of X", without also thinking of X.

The paradox is this. If the need for first-order change efforts is not too great, they can occur in the realm of private psychological events without too much danger. But it is precisely when they are seemingly really needed psychologically, that persons have a hard time implementing them. And it is then that their failure causes needless trauma.

Some of our most intractable and challenging clinical cases can be thought of as challenging not the therapist, but this very system of first-order change. Yet, we seem to have a hard time getting the lesson. Instead, empirical clinicians usually then try ever more elaborate and intense ways of producing first-order change. Whatever good these procedures do, the massive number of clinical failures that we know exist show that there is a serious problem in the widespread applicability of these methods.

It's time for the empirical clinical psychologists to face the likelihood that some of their cherished beliefs are in fact part of the problem. This present volume presents an alternative to that tradition. Admittedly, the data are not completely in. But those data that do exist suggest that many of our most difficult cases will respond if we take an entirely different approach. This different approach, however, is linked to an entirely different clinical agenda. This makes the alternative difficult to explain and initially difficult to understand, both for our clients and for empirical psychotherapists interested in learning it. But that very difficulty underlines that this alternative truly is *different*. This recognition is itself positive. Since the best predictor of future behavior is past behavior, our most difficult clients are unlikely to respond positively to more of the same.

2. Acceptance as a Contextual Change Strategy

In content oriented approaches the basic focus is that there is a problematic event, and that therefore our efforts should be to change the event itself. In context oriented approaches the formulation is still that there is a problematic event leading to efforts to change the event, but that very formulation is seen to be applicable only in a particular psychological context. Clinical efforts are focused then on changes in that context itself.

I will have more to say later about the nature of the context that supports deliberate change efforts. For now what I want to do is to show that acceptance versus first-order change are two different contexts, in which the formula "problem event therefore change the event" can exist (see Figure 1).

Consider a set of psychological events. Suppose we are dealing with the following: strong feelings of fear, intense physiological arousal, thoughts such as "I am going to die," and behavioral responses associated with escape or defense. This entire set of events can be glued together, verbally, under the label of a "panic attack" or "intense anxiety." In a context in which these events are taken to be problems, and in which change efforts are focused upon them, it is likely that these events will be construed in exactly that way. But in other contexts, very similar or even identical events (defined formally or topographically) will have different psychological functions. For example, if a person likes going to some of the most modern roller coasters, they are very likely to experience intense periods of fear, strong bodily sensations, thoughts such as "I'm going to die," and some of the behavioral precursors of escape or defense. Yet, people pay significant amounts of money for these psychological experiences.

There is little in the private psychological reactions of anxious, depressed, angry, or confused persons that need to be changed before a healthy and successful life can be lived. A posture of psychological acceptance, in which the goals of the individual is to get more fully present with what they feel and think and remember, *and* to bring

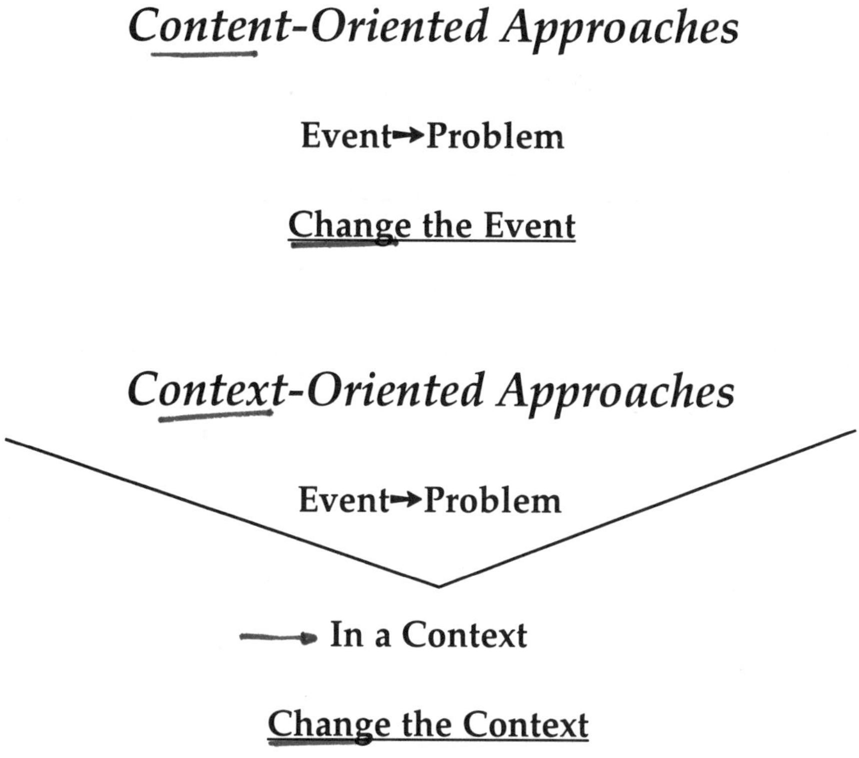

Content-Oriented Approaches

Event→Problem

Change the Event

Context-Oriented Approaches

Event→Problem

──► In a Context

Change the Context

Figure 1. The difference between content and context oriented approaches.

all of that with them into a successful pattern of adjustment in an overt behavioral sense, changes the negative content functionally, without having to change it topographically or situationally. It is not necessary for a person who is having a panic attack, to have fewer panic attacks, or to have less intense panic attacks. What is most important is that the person drain the trauma out of these so called panic attacks and begin living a valued life. If the person had a different purpose, namely that of psychological openness and healthy living, "panic" need not be viewed as one's own enemy, or an indication of the failure of one's life.

The paradox is this. In the context of deliberate change, fearsome content is inherently fearsome. In other words, in the context of deliberate change, difficult content is supported in its destructive function—all in the name of changing its form or frequency. In the context of psychological acceptance, fearsome content is changed functionally, even if no change occurs in its form or its frequency. When one deliberately embraces the most difficult content, one has transformed its stimulus function from that of an event that can cause change or avoidance, to that of an event that causes observation and openness. The paradox is that as one gives up on trying to be different one becomes immediately becomes different in a very profound way.

③ Types of Acceptance

There are several domains of acceptance, psychologically speaking. We can break these down into personal domains on the one hand, and social or situational demands on the other. It is not appropriate to embrace acceptance efforts in all of these domains. Psychological acceptance is not the same as stoicism or rationalized helplessness.

ⓐ Personal History

Within the personal domains we can distinguish four areas: personal history, private events, overt behavior, and self. Accepting personal history is the only sensible thing to do. Time is but a measure of change, and change goes in one direction. It goes from now to now. The nervous system similarly goes in only one direction. It too goes from now to now.

Because of the ability of language to produce that which has never been experienced and to categorize events and ways that allow them to be compared to conceptualized ideals, it is easy for humans to get caught in the idea that there is something *wrong* with their history, or that something *needs to change* in their history, before they can live a happy, committed, and successful life.

We are historical organisms. Our psychological problems always emerge from our history in interaction with the current circumstances. Thus, it is the most natural thing for people looking at their problems, to imagine that if their history had been different that their problems would have been different. In some sense, this is literally true. It is also completely useless since all changes are additive—never subtractive. No one has found a way to live a different childhood or to have a different set of experiences than one has already had.

Time and the human nervous system always goes "forward," in the sense that what comes after includes the change from what went before. The only thing we can do is to build our history from here. Our history from here can of course be quite different than the history that brought us here. But even then, all we will be doing is adding to the development of the individual. We will never subtract from one's development.

A person who has been raped, or who has had his or her parents die, or who has been the object of cruelty, naturally wants to have this history in some way removed. It is natural, because we as verbal organisms can compare these set of circumstances to a conceptualized ideal. But there is no way to accomplish this end, and if there were, there would be nothing to prevent all humans from having nothing but sugar sweet histories without the depth and humanity that comes from suffering. Life asks a question of all of us: whether or not we are willing to contact more fully the psychological reality of our own history.

Any efforts to diminish that can be inherently damaging, because it suggests that the person cannot start from where they are. It suggests that there is something inherently "wrong" with the individual and the individual's history. That is an extremely damaging place from which to work with people who have psychological difficulties. A much more secure place to work, is a place from which details of one's history are valid, meaningful, important, and embraceable, no matter how difficult the content.

Private Events

A second area is that of private events, such as emotions, thoughts, behavioral predispositions, and bodily sensations. Here, the picture is more complex. Some private events surely can be changed deliberately, and it might be quite useful to do so. For example, a person might feel weak or ill, and by going to a doctor discover the source of these difficulties and ideally have them treated successfully. But psychologically produced private events very often do not work in this way. Deliberately trying not to think something is usually a fool's end. Deliberately trying not to feel something can often set up conditions that produce more of that exact emotion. In a later section we will try to distinguish the learning principles that suggest when change efforts and acceptance efforts are most likely to be useful in this domain.

Overt Behavior

A third domain is overt behavior. Most often, but not always, deliberate change efforts are useful and reasonable in this domain. There is nothing in psychological acceptance strategies that suggests that we should "accept" our own maladaptive behavior. Psychological acceptance is not about justifying or explaining away difficulties. In fact, the whole purpose of psychological acceptance is to harness the person's capacity for deliberate change to the domains in which this effort is useful by not tying them to areas in which it is not.

Sense of Self

The fourth area is the area of self. Because we are dealing with issues of acceptance and change, the only senses of "self" that are relevant here are those that involve knowing by the person involved. We cannot avoid or accept that which we do not know. This puts aside many meaningful senses of the term "self" such as self as integrated repertoires of behavior, or self as a physical body. When limited in this way, there are three senses of self: self as the content of knowing, as the process of knowing, and as the context of knowing.

The conceptualized self. The ability to engage in derived relational respond-ing, which is the essence of human verbal behavior (as will be discussed later), means that we can derive relations between our ongoing unified stream of behavior and a panoply of categorical concepts. We can evaluate, interpret, predict, explain, rationalize, and otherwise interact verbally with our own behavior.

The set of verbal relations of this kind is what I mean by "self as content." This is our "conceptualized self." We try verbally to make sense of ourselves and to put our own histories, behaviors, and tendencies into a conceptual scheme. Because we have a history of applying verbal concepts in systematic ways (e.g., we learn to be "right," "correct," and "coherent") as we conceptualize ourselves we enter into a conspiracy to distort the world to fit these conceptualizations. If a person believes him or herself to be "confident," there is less room to contact directly instances of behavior that could more readily be called "insecure." To admit to contradictory evidence as readily as confirmatory evidence would be not to care about whether one is correct. Because that is unlikely, it is not possible to believe a "conceptualized self" without an associated tendency toward self-deception.

The conclusion this leads to is ironic. Clients come to us with a story about their problems and the sources of those problems. If this story is accepted by the client as the literal truth, it must be defended, even if it is unworkable. "I am a mess because of my childhood" will be defended even though no other childhood will ever occur. "I am not living because I am too anxious" will lead to efforts to change anxiety even if such efforts have always been essentially unsuccessful.

Direct contact with the events in the present is not possible in the presence of a defended set of verbal beliefs. It is also not possible in the context of literal disbelief, since disbelief too must be defended and justified verbally. I will have more to say about this shortly.

Acceptance of a conceptualized self, held as a literal belief, is not desirable. If the story is negative, accepting it is tantamount to adopting a negative point of view that, furthermore, is to be defended. If the story is positive, facts that do not fit the tale must be distorted. In either case, the effects are negative. In Acceptance and Commitment Therapy (Hayes, 1987; Hayes & Wilson, 1993, in press) we suggest that clients should "kill themselves everyday"—meaning that literal evaluations and categorization about oneself are better left to die as fast as they pop up.

Self as a process of knowing. Self as the process of knowing is necessary for humans to live a civilized life. Our socialization about what to do in life situations is tied to the process of verbal knowing.

Emotional talk is perhaps the clearest example. Consider, for example, the training that goes on in forming equivalence classes between the fuzzy set of bodily sensations, behavioral predispositions, thoughts, environmental situations, and the arbitrary name for a "emotion." Human emotion is a complex set of events tied together by strands of verbal behavior. Humans have emotions that non-verbal organisms would not know to have.

When the verbal community wants to know about a person's history and response tendencies, the requested information is largely in emotional terms: "are you thirsty?" or "are you upset about something?" Such conditions emerge from complex and largely unknown histories, but their common emotional effects have fairly consistent response implications. A person who is not able on an ongoing basis to describe and categorize their own behavior has difficulty linking their socialization about what to do in life with the highly individualized and changing circumstances they find themselves in.

A person who has had a deviant history that did not give rise to self as an ongoing process of knowing will have a hard time living a successful life. For example, suppose a young girl has been sexually abused for many years by her father. Suppose expressions of emotion associated with the aversiveness of this experience are consistently reinterpreted, ignored, or denied. The person would have a hard time "knowing what she was feeling" and as a result would have a hard time telling others how to treat her. A similar effect occurs when, as described above, people are unwilling to have certain reactions. Suppose a person is unwilling to feel feelings called anger (e.g., because "people who get mad explode and act destructively. I don't get mad."). Such a person will distort their process of knowing so that even when a verbal category applies by social convention (i.e., the person could readily call their responses "anger") they will fail to apply it ("no, I'm not angry at all. I'm just amazed by what you are saying.") The end result is that the person has little effective guidance from the verbal community about how to behave, and is unable to guide those around them about their own histories.

It is inherently constraining to take the *content* of one's verbalizations to be who you are. An effective human life requires a healthy sense of self as an on-going process of knowing oneself. This includes being fully in contact with conceptualized selves, not as content but as process (i.e., "now I am saying x, y, and z about my self" instead of "I am x, y, z").

Self as context. The final aspect of s elf–self as the context for knowing– is the one that is most often ignored. In order to have the ability to report events verbally, it is necessary to develop a sense of perspective or point of view. If I ask you what you did yesterday, I have to be able to trust that the report is made is from a perspective or point of view that is consistent and predictable.

Very young children have a hard time with this. If a very young child is asked what someone else in the room sees, the child would likely report what he or she sees. The child has not yet learned to imagine having some other perspective or point of view and has not thereby learned to be clear about one's own perspective or point of view.

If I ask many, many questions of a person, the only thing that will be consistent is not the *content* of the answer, but the *context* from which the answer occurs. "I" in some meaningful sense is the location that is left behind when all of the content differences are subtracted out. Children learn this sense of perspective, and learn to label it "I." When you close your eyes, this enculturation produces a sense of location behind your eyes, for example. It is a kind of pure consciousness–a place from which events are known independently of the specific content of events.

This is the sense of self that is most closely related to concepts of spirituality or transcendence (Hayes, 1984). It has these qualities, because consciousness is not thing-like for the person being conscious. All things have limits–that is how they are distinguished from anything else. But one can be conscious of the limits of everything except one's own consciousness. For that reason, the sense of perspective or self as a place from which things are observed does not change once it emerges around the age of three or four. It is everywhere you have ever been so far as you know. It has no limits you have been able to knowingly experience directly. Thus, it is not thing-like, but instead is everything (that without limits) or no-thing (also that without limits). "Spirit" is a perfectly reasonable term for the experience.

It is not too difficult to help clients experience the essential connection between the person they are today and the person they were last summer, and the person who was once a teenager, and the person who was once four. People literally can remember "being behind my eyes" in each of these ages and situations. This sense of self as pure consciousness, or of self as context, is critical, because it means that there is at least one stable, unchangeable, immutable fact about oneself that has been experienced directly, and is not just a belief or a hope or an idea.

The only sensible thing to do with self as context is to accept it, since any verbal behavior is based upon it and we cannot function as nonverbal organisms. If I try to become unconscious to get rid of this sense of self as context, a conscious "I" will be aware of this very attempt. Sometimes very disturbed people try to get rid of self as context by splitting or by dissociation. This is a form of emotional avoidance so massive that it has profoundly negative consequences. If I cannot integrate one moment with another under a continuous "I" as a location (e.g., as in a multiple personality disorder) I cannot readily access my own history verbally.

Self as context is important for another reason. It is self as context that permits other important forms of acceptance. It is the stability and constancy of self as context that allows a client to enter into the pain of the maelstrom of their own life and their own difficulties, knowing in some deep way that no matter what comes up, they will not be changed.

Social and Situational Domains

Social and situational domains present some of the same complexities in personal domains. When we are considering the domains relevant to other persons, we can consider the acceptance of other's personal history, private events, overt behavior, or sense of self.

Once again, acceptance of others' personal history seems to be the only reasonable course available, since history is not changeable except by addition to what is. It is only changeable *from now*, not *to then*. In the area of private events, acceptance of others' emotions, thoughts, behavioral predispositions, bodily sensations, memories and so on, is the defining characteristic of a loving stance towards other people. Nonacceptance of others' private events is an inherently non-validating position, a point long made by experiential and humanistic psychotherapies (Perls, 1969, 1973; Rogers, 1951, 1961, 1965).

In the work that we do in ACT we often attempt to make this point by creating in imagination examples of the person's own children, or of other children who are having undesirable private events. For example, the person may imagine their child standing in front of them afraid. Usually, the person is ready to be loving and accepting. If asked "can you love this child even though the child is afraid?" the answer is usually "yes." Most adults are prepared to believe that it is wrong to punish a child for being afraid or for having self doubts. Yet, when it applies to themselves as adults, they may be quite ready to do exactly that. If themselves as adults were standing their afraid, the usual initial response is rejecting and critical.

Acceptance of others' overt behavior is sometimes called for, but often change is equally appropriate. Acceptance is called for when the efforts to change overt behavior of others undermines other features of the relationship which are important, and when the behavior itself is unimportant. For example, it may not be worth the effort it would take to prevent a spouse from leaving underwear on the bathroom floor. But it is also possible to error on the other side of this issue when the behaviors are not trivial, as when we support other people in doing things that are not workable for them in the name of "relationship." Often the decision not to try to change the overt behavior of others even when change is called for, is a kind of emotional avoidance. For example, a spouse may be unwilling to face their own emotional reactions or their emotional reactions associated with their spouse's emotional reactions, if legitimate efforts were made to change the other person's behavior. Often this avoidance is in the name of the relationship, but in fact it contributes to a dishonest relationship.

In the area of situations, change is usually a reasonable context from which to work. The exception, of course, are situations that are inherently unchangeable. A person dealing with a assuredly fatal disease (such as a person with AIDS), or with the death of a spouse, is dealing with an unchangeable situation, and acceptance is the only reasonable course of action. When situations are changeable, however, first-order change efforts are usually called for. Ironically, these are made more difficult because they may require acceptance of one's own reactions to the change efforts. People are far less powerful in their manipulation of their situational constraints in part because they would have to face issues of embarrassment or fear of other psychological issues in order to confront these changeable situations.

When Acceptance Is Likely to Be Useful

The times when acceptance or change is most likely to be useful can be derived in part from learning principles. It is useful to distinguish six different situations as is shown in Figure 2. In column 1 are nonverbal processes that are similar to classical conditioning. In the right hand column are those verbal and nonverbal processes that are similar to operant conditioning. There are three rows consisting of one row in the nonverbal domain and two rows for speaker and listener functions in the verbal domain.

In the nonverbal domain we are talking directly about normal classical and overt conditioning. The verbal domain requires a bit more discussion. In several recent articles I have argued that the essence of verbal behavior is the learned ability to relate events bidirectionally and combinatorially, and to transform the stimulus functions of related events in terms of the derived stimulus relations they participate in (Hayes & Hayes, 1989, 1992b; Hayes, 1994).

Types of Psychological Adjustments: Some Examples

		Two-term Contingencies	Three-term Contingencies
Direct		Normal Classical Conditioning	Normal Operant Conditioning
Derived	Speaker	Verbal associations	Rule-formulation; Problem-solving and reasoning
	Listener	Verbal elicitation	Rule-following; Believing

Figure 2. Six types of psychological adjustments

The process begins in very early childhood. Children are taught that a name stands for an object, and an object is called the name. This simple bidirectional relation between a "word" and an event is trained many thousands of times with many thousands of different examples. Data from our laboratory (Lipkens, Hayes, and Hayes, 1993) show that children as young as sixteen months have acquired a generalized relational ability such that stimulus directions taught in one direction are derived in the other. For example, if the novel object is given a novel name, even sixteen month old babies will then be able to orient towards the object given the name, *without additional training.*

These derived stimulus relations become increasingly elaborated with experience. For example, very young children will learn that if a novel name is used, it probably refers to a novel object rather than a familiar object. In the study just mentioned, we were able to show that before two years of age, children would take advantage of this learned ability to perform a bidirectional relation between a novel name and a novel object such that the child not only knows that the name probably refers to the novel object, but the child will also begin to call the novel object by that name. By three years of age, these bidirectional "relational frames" can be combined to form networks of relations and stimulus functions given one related event will be available, transformed by the underlined relation, to all the members of that network. For example, children will smile at positive descriptions and cry at negative descriptions of events, even though nothing positive or negative has ever happened directly in association with these descriptions, and even if the descriptions are related only through several verbal intermediaries to the actual events that have positive or negative functions.

Not only does the ability to construct extended networks increase, but the kinds of underlying relations increase as well. Children learn relational frames of cause and effect, or comparison, or time, and the effects of the increasingly verbal world they live in are transformed accordingly. For example, very young children can be told that after a particular task, a particular consequence will immediately follow, and this instruction, quite apart from any direct experience with the described contingency, can control behavior for a brief period of time. Older children can have the same kind of description made with events that are much more remote in time and more probabilistic. As a result, present behavior becomes related to increasingly abstract, derived, remote, and probabilistic consequences.

This thumb nail sketch of a behavior analytic approach to verbal knowing, or "cognition," has a large body of literature supporting the basic concepts (see the following book length reviews: Hayes & Chase, 1991; Hayes, 1989; Hayes & Hayes, 1992a; Hayes, Hayes, Sato, & Ono, 1994). The big impact of these derived stimulus relations occurs when stimulus functions are transformed through derived stimulus relations because it means that ones verbal history transforms the functions of the nonverbal world. For that reason, the bottom rows in Figure 2 are distinct from the top two.

We can divide verbal functions into speaker and listener aspects. In the speaker verbal functions that are like classical conditioning we find verbal associations—in this case an element in a verbal network is present because of a direct history with related events. For example, if a person raised in the United States were to hear the words "Mary had a little," it's very likely that what they will say or think of is "lamb." This reaction in some sense is automatic.

I sometimes ask my clients to try to think of something other than lamb in association with "Mary had a little." I then say "Mary had a little," and people answer various kinds of things, such as "guitar", or "Volkswagen." When you ask whether or not they successfully accomplished the job, they find that even when they have been thinking about guitars or Volkswagens, they first had to think the word "lamb."

In the case of the listener, similar things occur. If I say the word "lemon," a person is likely to think of a sour fruit. Thinking of a sour fruit in association with he word "lemon," is on some sense not a voluntary or operant behavior. Once it is well established, it's automatic. In the operant column, speaker functions consist of relational activity that is controlled by its consequences. Problem solving and reasoning are two examples. On the listener's side it includes following rules because of the consequences associated with rule following. It also includes acts of belief based on the logical (relational) nature of the rule.

This three by two diagram divides the world in a way that allows us to ascertain when acceptance or change methods might be called for. In general any conscious, deliberate or purposeful attempt to regulate or change anything is an instance of speaker and listener verbal functions that emerge from the operant side of this diagram. Deliberate change efforts involve operant speaker and listener functions, and they can usually be applied to operant behavior or its verbal correlates.

Classical conditioning processes are much less likely to be successfully governed by the *consequential aspects* of verbal rules. These processes are not "purposive." The problem is described above in the example of "Mary had a little lamb." Verbal associations, verbal elicitation, normal classical conditioning processes are not matters of operant choice.

Simply put, the left hand column is much less likely to yield to first-order change efforts in any simple or direct way, as compared to the right hand column. The problem for verbal organisms, however, is that any content quickly becomes verbal content. When anything happens to people they are likely to talk with themselves or others about it. They are likely to apply verbal categories to these events. Thus, any content becomes verbal content, and any verbal content can cue deliberate verbal regulatory processes. Thus, any of the nonverbal or verbal respondents that are represented in the left hand column can become entangled in verbal rules about what is good or bad or what is desirable or undesirable—and change efforts can quickly be directed towards these conceptualized events.

Some Examples of Times When Acceptance is Useful

Acceptance seems called for when one of five things occurs. First, *the process of change contradicts the outcome*. Much as one cannot earn a lasting peace through the means of war, it is not possible to earn self acceptance by criticism and deliberate change, or to learn peace of mind by rejecting negative thoughts, or to eliminate disturbing thoughts by thinking about how to get rid of them. If a person tries to earn self acceptance by change, a paradox is created. The person may believe that they will be an OK person when they change, but the very fact that they need to change reconfirms the fact that they are not an OK person.

The second instance when acceptance is called for is when *change efforts leads to a distortion, or unhealthy avoidance of, the direct functions of events*. For example, a person may construct their childhood as a happy one, even if it means that they cannot recall the events of their childhood clearly. To recall them clearly might challenge the verbal categorization.

A third situation in which acceptance is called for is one in which *social change efforts disrupts the social relation or devalues the other*. Even though the specific event might be changeable in principle, it may undermine the very reason why the person would be interested in seeing the other person change. That is, sometimes it is better just to let go of being right about trivial matters in the larger interest of supporting the relationship with another person.

A fourth situation is one in which the *outcome ultimately cannot be rule governed*. It is not possible to be experienced merely by following rules. Many things have to be learned by doing. Hitting a baseball, or falling in love are very unlikely to be successful if the actions are too heavily rule governed.

The final situation occurs when the event is unchangeable. It may not be fair that one's father was killed, but no amount of attempting to change it will be successful.

Barriers to Acceptance Are Verbal

There is nothing in the top row not to accept when we are dealing with the personal domains in nonverbal organisms. It does not seem possible for a dog or a cat to fail to accept their history or their emotions or memories—even though they have all of these. When events become verbal, their truth or falsity becomes involved. Any literal belief to some degree demands either change or defense—that is, it demands something other than what we mean by acceptance. But since a verbal organism can bring verbalizations to bear on everything in the personal domain, it seems that acceptance is difficult or impossible without an alteration of verbal processes. Essentially, to achieve acceptance in a radical sense we have to find a way of moving some of the lower rows in a verbal organism into a state that is somewhat more like the upper row in a nonverbal organism.

Some of the verbal barriers to acceptance include reason giving, evaluation and literality. In the case of reason giving, some sort of story is formulated explaining one's own behavior. This leads to nonacceptance, because of the larger history that we have of giving good reasons for what we do. If acceptance would make room for bringing into the present events that would contradict one's own stories about one's life, then acceptance would mean that one's reasons are in some sense invalidated. Similarly, any action of belief or disbelief, or evaluation in terms of good and bad or right and wrong, suggests a polarity that cannot be held simultaneously. What is true rejects that which is false; what is right rejects that which is wrong; what is good rejects that which is bad. But since verbal categories can be applied arbitrarily, even the most coherent and sensible story or evaluation excludes, and must exclude, many of the verbal formulations that could be applied to any event.

The problem can be seen in Figure 3. As one moves up onto a continuum of belief or disbelief, or truth or falsity, one moves away from direct contact with the

Belief and Experiential Openness

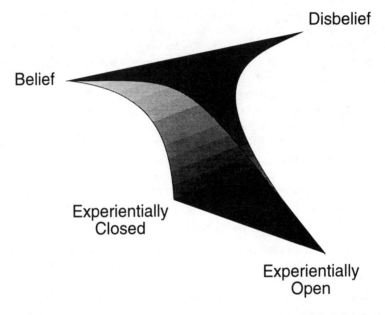

Figure 3. The relation between behaving on the basis of literal belief-disbelief and relative openness to direct experience. This figure argues that in order to be more fully open to the direct functions of events, the dominance of their verbally derived functions must weaken.

present moment and all of its complexity. In other words, the degree to which we are fully open to our own experiences must suffer. I sometimes ask my clients to describe something that is happening now. Whatever is described, however, was happening a moment ago, not now. Most talk does not even pretend to be in the present, as when we busily evaluate the past and consider our future. The ongoing verbal process is always in the present but the literal verbal content is never in the present. Thus, acting purely on the basis of the literal verbal functions of events necessarily moves human out of contact with the here and now.

A final barrier is worth mentioning. In addition, our stories and evaluations are used to manipulate the behavior of others. Thus, another barrier to its acceptance is that acceptance essentially lets others off the hook or opens oneself up to an inability to manipulate others through our verbal tales.

The Nature of Acceptance

In a nontechnical sense, psychological acceptance involves experiencing events fully and without defense, as they are and not as what they say they are. In a more technical sense, it involves making contact with the automatic or direct stimulus functions of events, without acting to reduce or manipulate those functions, and without acting on the basis solely of their derived or verbal functions. When this action is put into the context of meaningful choices about behavior, it is a means to an end. When accept in order to live a more vital life.

There is a continuum of acts of acceptance. At the lowest level, resignation and toleration are initial steps along the continuum, but they are heavily contaminated by a context of change, and by the literal meaning afforded to the events. At a higher level, acceptance involves the deliberate abandonment of a change agenda in situations in which that agenda does not work. At another level, acceptance involves emotional or social willingness, that is, the openness to one's own emotions or the experience of being with others. At an even higher level, acceptance involves de-literalization: the defusion of the derived relations and functions of events from the direct functions of these events. As one moves far enough along the continuum into the domains of emotional willingness and deliteralization, it is possible to begin to stay in the present, and to do what works even with all of the psychological events that one has been previously struggling with and trying to change.

Thus, radical forms of acceptance require a manipulation of verbal processes. Less intrusive forms are possible, however. It is still meaningfully an acceptance strategy to allow a mate to engage in behaviors that one finds to be a minor irritation. A more radical form of acceptance in this case would require manipulation of verbal processes, such that a person was able to be more fully present with their own sense of irritation in association with the habits and patterns of their loved one. But it is not necessary in all cases to work heavily on the defusion of individuals from their thoughts or with the active embracing of previously difficult emotional or other psychological material.

These lower forms of acceptance are the kinds that are readily available for time limited circumstances. I have been surprised how often people who have had a very first panic attack, or who have had a tragedy in their life, are open to acceptance-based strategies long before they develop the signs and symptoms of a psychopathological condition that is full-blown. The panic attacks need not turn into panic disorder, and tragedies need not turn into depression. We can intervene early and effectively with fairly limited acceptance strategies. Often simply opening up the option of feeling what one feels, thinking what one thinks, and putting one foot in front of the other so as to do what needs to be done is a revelation to clients. Clients come in thinking that they have to win the war with their own psychology. They simply have not known how to do so. Often it is a relief when they find out that no one else knows how to do so either, and furthermore, winning war is unnecessary.

Conclusion

This chapter has not covered the many techniques that are available to achieve psychological acceptance. We have worked for nearly fifteen years on such procedures (see Hayes, Strosahl, and Wilson, in press for a detailed description of ACT. Shorter descriptions are available in Hayes, 1987; Hayes & Wilson, 1993, in press; Kohlenberg, Hayes, & Tsai, 1993). Other chapters in this volume show some of the clever ways that acceptance methods are being used. My point in this chapter has been that it is time to take these methods seriously, and to achieve a better balance in the empirically oriented psychotherapies between acceptance and change.

References

Hayes, L. J. & Chase, P. N. (1991). *Dialogues on verbal behavior.* Reno, NV: Context Press.

Hayes, S. C. (1984). Making sense of spirituality. *Behaviorism, 12,* 99-110.

Hayes, S. C. (1987). A contextual approach to therapeutic change. In Jacobson, N. (Ed.), *Psychotherapists in clinical practice: Cognitive and behavioral perspectives* (pp. 327-387). New York: Guilford.

Hayes, S. C. (Ed.). (1989). *Rule-governed behavior: Cognition, contingencies, and instructional control.* New York: Plenum.

Hayes, S. C. (1994). Relational frame theory: A functional approach to verbal events. Chapter in S. C. Hayes, L. J. Hayes, M. Sato, & K. Ono (Eds.), *Behavior analysis of language and cognition* (pp. 9-30). Reno, NV: Context Press.

Hayes, S. C. & Hayes, L. J. (1989). The verbal action of the listener as a basis for rule-governance. In S. C. Hayes (Ed.), *Rule-governed behavior: Cognition, contingencies, and instructional control.* (pp. 153-190). New York: Plenum.

Hayes, S. C. & Hayes, L. J. (Eds.). (1992a). *Understanding verbal relations.* Reno, NV: Context Press.

Hayes, S. C. & Hayes, L. J. (1992b). Verbal relations and the evolution of behavior analysis. *American Psychologist, 47,* 1383-1395.

Hayes, S. C., Hayes, L. J., Sato, M. and Ono, K. (Eds.). (1994). *Behavior analysis of language and cognition.* Reno, NV: Context Press.

Hayes, S. C., Strosahl, K., & Wilson, K. G. (in press). *Acceptance and Commitment Therapy.* New York: Guilford Press.

Hayes, S. C. & Wilson, K. G. (1993). Some applied implications of a contemporary behavior-analytic account of verbal events. *The Behavior Analyst, 16,* 283-301.

Hayes, S. C. & Wilson, K. G. (in press). Acceptance and Commitment Therapy: Altering the verbal support for experiential avoidance. The Behavior Analyst.

Kohlenberg, B., Hayes, S. C., & Tsai, (1993). Behavior analytic psychotherapy: Two contemporary examples. Clinical Psychology Review, 13, 579-592.

Lipkens, G., Hayes, S. C., & Hayes, L. J. (1993). Longitudinal study of derived stimulus relations in an infant. *Journal of Experimental Child Psychology, 56,* 201-239.

Perls, F.S. (1973). *The Gestalt approach and eye witness to therapy.* Palo Alto, CA: Science and Behavior Books.

Perls, F.S. (1969). *Gestalt therapy verbatim.* Lafayette, CA: Real People.

Rogers, C.R. (1951). *Client-centered therapy.* Boston: Houghton-Mifflin.

Rogers, C.R. (1961). *On becoming a person.* Boston: Houghton-Mifflin.

Rogers, C. R. (1965). *Client-centered therapy: Its current practice, implications, and theory.* Boston: Houghton Mifflin.

Preparation of this chapter was supported in part by a grant from the National Institute on Drug Abuse, #DA08634.

Discussion of Hayes

The Elusive Nature of Acceptance

Joseph R. Haas
Northern Nevada Child and Adolescent Service

In the preceding paper, Steve Hayes describes a very elusive phenomenon from both the perspective of practical clinical intervention and basic scientific theory. This is no easy task, and this paper makes several strong inroads towards an integrated account of acceptance.

Defining Acceptance

Defining acceptance was a critical issue discussed throughout this volume. Hayes' definition is particularly interesting to me because it has strong appeal at both a clinical and a theoretical level. The definition is as follows: "Psychological acceptance involves experiencing events fully and without defense, as they are and not as they say they are." This statement seems to be both a definition and a goal. As a definition, it has the same face validity as definitions offered for processes such as defense mechanisms. As a goal, the statement represents what many practicing clinicians would endorse as a "psychologically healthy" stance with respect to life. Intuitively, the full experiencing of events would seem to lead to much more effective actions with respect to these events. At a practical level, this definition/goal seems to be a solid bridge between theoretical contextual approaches and mainstream psychological therapies. This bridge is especially important in view of the gap between theoretical/research oriented psychologists and practicing psychologists. Hayes' paper and the scope of this entire volume has been to embrace an essentially clinical term and attempt to deal with it in a theoretically and empirically credible manner. However, like most clinical terms, acceptance intuitively makes sense, but is difficult to pin down. From a scientific/empirical perspective clinical terms are elusive. Acceptance seems to be no exception. Hayes' definition may prove more troublesome to clinical researchers than it does to practicing clinicians. Clinicians seem more comfortable with elusive phenomena. The goal of science is to reduce elusiveness. A standard scientific approach would most certainly raise the question as to how one would decide when another was engaging in acceptance. Hayes' definition does not meet the criteria for the type of operational definition commonly associated with methodological behaviorism and practical behavioral research. Its just not that kind of definition. Hayes' handling of the theory behind his use of the term acceptance is a prime example of an operational definition from a radical behavioral perspective (Skinner, 1945). Acceptance is theoretically defined in terms of core principles of behavior analysis.

For Hayes, acceptance in humans occurs when operant and classical conditioning occur in pure form. Acceptance is a nonverbal process. Non-acceptance occurs in humans when principals of relational responding (Hayes, 1991) are involved in the control of behavior. Non-acceptance involves verbal processes. Hayes views verbal behavior as involving relational principles as opposed to operant and classical conditioning principles in pure form.

The definition stated above does not capture the theoretical underpinnings as they are richly described in this paper. Perhaps an addition might read. "The verbal community talks about acceptance when nonverbal processes control behavior. The term non-acceptance is talked about when verbal processes override control by nonverbal processes." Notice that this style of definition does not define a state called acceptance. It may lead to a better understanding of acceptance but does not increase our likelihood of identifying it when it is happening in the natural setting. Acceptance remains elusive.

The fact that acceptance is defined functionally as opposed to formally may be a barrier to the "acceptance" of this definition by the mainstream clinical research community. Standard psychological research relies exclusively on topographical definitions of responding. Research is based on measurable changes in problems. Hayes captures this issue nicely in his discussion of first order versus contextual (second order change).

The question arises as to what the scientific study of acceptance would look like. Process oriented research on acceptance would need to clearly identify contexts in which derived relational control overrides direct operant and respondent control. Behaviors or outcomes associated with the presence of accepting will need to be identified as well. This is not an easy task. Even if laboratory demonstrations are achieved, the observation and manipulation of accepting in the natural environment still remains elusive.

Skinner's (1957) analysis of verbal behavior stands as an example of an interpretive analysis based on functional terms that has inspired relatively little direct study of human verbal behavior in its natural setting. An inherent difficulty, for naturalistic research based on functional as opposed to formal analyses, is finding measurement technologies that demonstrate the key aspects of the functional analysis as they occur naturally. Interpretations based on a functional analyses and backed by basic laboratory studies have historically not been accepted by the mainstream research community. The analysis presented here must still overcome the same difficulties associated with Skinner's accounting of verbal behavior. It is very difficult to make the leap from interpretation to empirical study. This difficulty is at the heart of why the bulk of clinical psychology research focuses on first order as opposed to contextual change.

Acceptance as it Relates to Contextual Change

I find Hayes' distinction between first order and contextual change to be a novel approach to the age old clinical distinction between content and process. It also illustrates precisely why contextual accounts have not become mainstream and remain somewhat elusive. For Hayes, a psychology focusing on first order change finds itself in the business of identifying problems and proceeding to attempts at eliminating problems. However, a clinical approach focusing on acceptance sees this first order change effort as being the problem. If I understand Hayes point, contextual change involves contextual manipulations that would stop efforts at first order change. This specifically involves short circuiting verbal behavior (i.e. derived relational responding) that maintains first order change efforts or nonacceptance. According to Hayes (1991), "All non-acceptance is based on derived relational responding."

As I read Hayes, I find myself tempted to adopt a simple maxim: "All verbal behavior is bad and nonverbal behavior is good!" However, this is an evaluation that according to Hayes would lead me down the primrose path of non-acceptance. In lieu of this black and white approach, an interesting area for further study would be identifying types of derived relational responding that would lead to increased acceptance. This approach gives rise to several questions. Are there verbal contexts which enhance acceptance? Can acceptance be instructed? Do different types of derived relations discourage acceptance more than others?. What would a verbal community sound like if verbal behavior was geared towards enhancing acceptance?

Summary

This paper begins a very hard look at acceptance from a contextual behavior-analytic approach. It presents an account that is appealing from both practical/clinical and scientific/empirical perspectives. However, acceptance still seems elusive by nature. Contextualistic analyses such as this are not unlike Zen koans. I am tempted to say that if you meet an accepting Buddha on the road it would be a good idea to kill him.

References

Hayes, S. C. (1991). A relational control theory of stimulus equivalence. In L.J. Hayes and P.N Chase (Eds.), *Dialogues on verbal behavior: Proceedings on the first international institute on verbal relations*. Reno, NV: Context Press.

Skinner, B.F. (1945) The operational analysis of psychological terms. *Psychological Review, 52*, 270-277.

Skinner, B. F. (1957). *Verbal behavior*. New York: Basic Books.

Chapter 2

The Act of Acceptance

Michael J. Dougher

University of New Mexico

As I look over the contents of this volume and see acceptance implicated in the cause and treatment of virtually every human ailment this side of world hunger, it seems that it might be useful to spend some time discussing some basic issues related to acceptance. In particular, I think it would be useful to discuss the meaning of acceptance, its clinical relevance, how we can know what to accept and what not to accept, the sources of influence that interfere with acceptance or breed unacceptance and the implications of acceptance for clinical research. Now, each of these is an important and complex issue, and it will not be possible to deal exhaustively with them given the present time limitations. Moreover, it is unlikely that there will be agreement among us concerning these issues. However, my purpose is not to provide a definitive account of acceptance or to try to forge some consensus. Rather it is to try to get some clarity about what constitutes acceptance and to begin a dialogue on its clinical relevance.

The Meaning of Acceptance

Assuming along with Wittgenstein and other semantic functionalists (e.g., Skinner, 1957) that the meaning of a term is to be found in its use, we can turn to the literature on acceptance to see how the term is used. Two things become clear. First, there is some disagreement about whether acceptance is an act of an individual, i.e., a behavior, or whether it is best seen as cognition (see Jacobson, 1992). The position taken here is that acceptance is most usefully seen as an act or a behavior. That is, acceptance is something one does. This position is based on the contention that we are philosophically and pragmatically better off if we do not take the common dualistic position of dividing human action and experience into the behavioral and the mental. But, this is neither meant to be an appeal to reductionism or operationism, nor is it intended to strip the term of its semantic complexity. When I say acceptance is a behavior, I am not, as is commonly done when referring to behavior, restricting it to publicly observable motor movements. I am taking as the definition of behavior anything and everything an integrated organism does. Acceptance is something an organism does; it is, therefore, behavior.

Taking a behavioral approach to the issue of acceptance requires that the act be understood not in terms of its topography or form, but in terms of its function. Thus, it matters little what the structure or formal nature of acceptance is. What matters in terms of its definition is what it does. And this can be determined only by understanding acceptance in relation to the context in which it occurs.

The second thing about the term acceptance that becomes clear from a reading of the relevant literature is that acceptance is typically defined negatively. That is, it is generally defined by what it is not. As an example both Hayes (1987) and Jacobson (1992) refer to acceptance as giving up or letting go of the struggle to change or to control. In some sense, acceptance is really doing nothing, and that makes it difficult to define positively or in terms of the occurrence rather than the absence of certain acts. Reasonable synonyms for accepting might be "having" or "allowing." Regardless, it would be helpful to our understanding of acceptance to specify the contexts within which acceptance is likely to be beneficial.

As it is used here, context refers to the entire constellation of continuously evolving influences operating on behavior at any particular time. A useful way of talking about behavioral contexts is in terms of contingencies of reinforcement. To simplify matters, these involve the situations that evoke or occasion behavior, reactions to those situations, including our public and private verbal and emotional responses (i.e., our thoughts and feelings), and the consequences that result from these actions. Taking this perspective, acceptance would involve *not* attempting to avoid, control, or change any element of the relevant contingencies operating at a particular time. Thus, occasioning events, the actions and reactions they engender, and the consequences that result are allowed to occur and no attempt is made to avoid, control or change them. The context and reactions to it are simply experienced. To accept, then, is to have or allow situations and events and the reactions that result.

The Clinical Relevance of Acceptance

Having defined acceptance in this way, the question arises as to its clinical significance. Quite obviously, simply accepting the world as it is is not the road to Nirvana. Many things in the world can and should be changed. So we are confronted with several questions. Specifically, in what contexts is acceptance clinically relevant? What role does unacceptance play in clinical problems? Assuming that some things can and should be changed, how does one determine when and what to accept and when and what not to accept?

Starting with the issue of the context within which acceptance is clinically relevant, it seems to me that acceptance has clinical relevance only in those situations that constitute conflict. In behavioral terms, this can be described as behavior under the control of competing contingencies. Either incompatible behaviors are evoked or a given behavior results in both reinforcing and punishing consequences. In these situations, behavior has a cost. Take as an example a social situation where one individual finds another attractive and is contemplating initiating a verbal interaction. Now, there are at least two sets of contingencies operating simultaneously. On one hand, one has to do with the reinforcing or desirable consequences attendant to approaching the other person and engaging in social discourse. These would include whatever immediate consequences are inherent in a potentially pleasant social interaction and the possibility of further development of the relationship, intimacy, partnership, shared experiences, etc. On the other hand, there are those undesirable consequences associated with rejection. These include the possibility of an unpleasant interaction, and the aversive thoughts and feelings that typically follow an unreceptive reaction. If there were no competing contingencies in this situation, i.e., no conflict, it would not be clinically relevant, and acceptance would not be interesting. That is, if there was no threat of rejection or if rejection itself did not constitute an aversive or undesirable state of affairs, one individual would simply approach the other and there would be little more to it. There would be no fear, no dread, no stream of self-deprecating statements, no catastrophizing, no clinical issue. In addition, if there was no positive contingency in this situation, that is, if the consequences of initiating a social interaction are not potentiated as reinforcers, there can be no conflict, and thus, no clinical relevance.

Now, if the present definition of acceptance is applied to this hypothetical situation, and this situation does, in fact, involve conflict, some interesting issues and questions emerge. First, it becomes apparent that a person cannot literally accept the entire context and all of the responses it engenders because, by definition, the context evokes incompatible behaviors. At the very least, the overt actions evoked by the positive contingency, approach, would preclude those evoked by the negative contingency, avoidance. One cannot simultaneously approach and avoid another person. So acceptance cannot literally mean accept the context as it is.

From this perspective, it is easy to see that acceptance inevitably involves choice. One cannot act in accord with competing contingencies. In fact, in a conflict situation, one *must* struggle against the influences, at least some of the influences of one set of contingencies. In the hypothetical social situation described above, as one person approaches the other, he or she is struggling against the influence of the contingency that would steer him or her away from the social interaction. But, from a clinical perspective, we know exactly how we would want the individual to act. We would want to see approach behavior. The reason for this is because acting in line with one of the competing sets of contingencies is *better* from a clinical perspective. It is *better* for the long-term effective functioning of that individual.

On what basis can we make this claim? Ultimately it comes down to a question of values. Most clinicians would argue that, in the long run, it is better to strive for intimacy than it is to try to avoid rejection. It is, after all, better to have loved and lost than never to have loved at all. The point is that acceptance, by itself, is neither a sufficient nor possible clinical goal. It has to be considered in a larger context. In particular, acceptance must be considered in a context of other therapeutic goals. In the absence of such a context, acceptance is simply an abstract term; it has no clinical relevance.

Goals and Values

Only by having clear therapeutic goals can we address the issue of choice and the question concerning what aspects of a context are to be and not to be accepted. But the issue of therapeutic goals inevitably involves a discussion of values because goals are directly derived from values. Admittedly, a discussion of values is difficult. After all, there is no final justification for any set of values, and any attempt to defend them ultimately boils down to a kind of dogmatism (Hayes & Hayes, 1992). But that does not mean that the issue should be eschewed or that values and goals should not be made explicit. In fact, there is no way to avoid the issue at least implicitly. All therapeutic goals, regardless of how circumscribed or justifiable, are derived from values.

Take, for example, the treatment of an agoraphobic client. The client is housebound, and his or her attempts to venture outside typically result in severe anxiety often punctuated by full-blown panic attacks. It is clear that no therapist would accommodate the client's request to become more comfortable with his or her confinement, and rightly so. Instead, at least one treatment goal would be to get the client outside of the house precisely because of the value placed on living a fuller and richer life than can be realized in the confines of an individual's home.

The role of values in the determination of therapeutic goals is perhaps more conspicuous with clients whose problems are less circumscribed. For example, when clients present with such amorphous and difficult to operationalize issues as interpersonal alienation, lack of meaning in life, identity confusion, self-doubts, and existential angst, treatment goals are less clearly specified and therapists' values play a more conspicuous role in the formulation of treatment plans. As an example, let's return to the hypothetical example described above and add a little more information. The individual is actually an adult male client. In the described situation he opted to avoid the opportunity for social interaction and, in fact, left the context feeling depressed, confused, and lonely. As it turns out, this is characteristic of this client, who, in general, describes his life as isolated, lonely and empty. He reports that he wants to develop relationships, but is terrified of rejection. After several unsuccessful attempts to develop social relationships, he is wondering if it wouldn't be simpler and less painful to learn to cope with his loneliness.

As was stated earlier, however, it is clear that the clinically beneficial choice, what every clinician would have hoped for in this example, is that the client would have taken the risk and initiated a social exchange. And the reason is that, implicitly or explicitly, relationships, especially intimate relationships are valued. They are indicative of psychological health and well-being. Most clinicians would argue that social relations should be pursued even at the risk of rejection and the pain it entails. These values, then, determine the goals of treatment and the choices to be made. In the context of acceptance, they suggest what contingencies are and are not to be accepted.

Understanding the relation between values and acceptance is helpful because it provides a framework for understanding the general benefits of acceptance and the adverse effects of unacceptance. From a clinical perspective, values would seem to stem from whatever view the therapist takes of psychological health or well-being. That is, clinicians value that which is in accord with and facilitates psychological health. Accordingly, acceptance is ameliorative when it facilitates psychological well-being. Conversely, unacceptance causes problems when it interferes with psychological well-being. At this point, it might be helpful to talk a bit about what is meant by psychological well-being.

Psychological Well-Being

The whole notion of psychological health or well-being might seem a bit odd in a paper written from a behavior analytic perspective (see, however, Follette, Bach & Follette; 1993, for an expanded discussion). After all, the received view of behaviorism is not highly correlated with a concern over such seemingly unscientific and humanistic issues. Moreover, the field of behavior therapy has been conspicuously silent on the issue. Actually behavior analysis does have a good deal to say about the issue of values, but that discussion is beyond the scope of this paper. Nevertheless, the issue cannot be ignored forever, especially because it is essential to get clear about our view of psychological health so that we can get clear about our treatment goals and values.

Borrowing heavily from the humanistic and existential psychotherapy literatures (because these are the literatures that have mostly directly addressed the issue), let me propose the following list of characteristics of psychological well-being:

> Commitment to Values
> Openness to Experience
> Intimacy
> Genuineness
> Acceptance of Self and Others
> Generativity
> Productive Work

Although there is certainly room for disagreement about what should be included in this list, it is safe to say that most would agree that individuals displaying these characteristics would be defined as psychologically healthy. Regardless, the point here is not to establish the defining characteristics of psychological health. It is to discuss these general characteristics in the context of acceptance.

What is interesting about these characteristics is that each entails conflict. That is, they represent sets of competing contingencies. In addition, each requires acceptance and suggests how acceptance might be incorporated in a course of treatment. Take, for example, commitment to values. What is meant here is a willingness to act in accord with one's values even when there are short-term contingencies for not doing so. If, for example, one values the consequences associated with achievement, then a commitment to achievement requires that one act accordingly even though there is the real possibility of failure. This goal defines acceptance as a willingness to have the experiences associated with the threat of failure that is inherent in the struggle for achievement.

Commitment to values goes hand in hand with the second characteristic, openness to experience. By definition, this requires that experiences be accepted as they occur and that no attempt be made to avoid, control, or change them, even when they are aversive. This would include the anxiety one feels in social situations, the self-defeating thoughts that occur when one tries their hand at something new, or the disappointment that results when expectancies are not met. The conflict here is obvious. It is simply less aversive to attempt to control unpleasant experiences than it is to have them. From many theoretical perspectives, however (see for example, Greenburg, this volume), the denial, warding off, or distortion of experience is the defining characteristic of psychological disorders (see also Hayes, 1987). This goal defines acceptance as the willingness to have all of the experiences associated with living life in line with one's commitments.

Intimacy with other individuals clearly involves risk in that one simply cannot be intimate without being vulnerable. To struggle against vulnerability is to directly interfere with intimacy. Thus, one must accept vulnerability in order to be intimate. Without taking the time to address each of the other characteristics individually, it can be said they all serve to provide a basis for selecting specific therapeutic goals and, thus, give meaning to acceptance as an integral part of a therapeutic effort.

Unacceptance, i.e., the struggle against that which is inherent in the pursuit of psychological well-being, not only interferes with psychological well-being, it creates problems in its own right. For example, unacceptance of the behavior of a partner in an intimate relationship not only interferes with intimacy but also creates additional conflict (Jacobson, 1992). Similarly, emotional avoidance, or the struggle against one's own thoughts and feelings, not only leaves one closed to experience, it causes more distress. As Hayes (1992) and others (e.g., Linehan, 1993) have pointed out, the attempt to control emotions often serves to distort and exacerbate them. Just such a process is clearly implicated in clients with obsessive-compulsive disorders who engender the very thoughts they try to avoid by trying so hard to avoid them. It is the attempt to control that is the very target of those therapies with a focus on increasing acceptance (e.g., Hayes, 1987; Jacobson & Christensen, this volume; Linehan, 1993). From this perspective, it appears that unacceptance plays an important role in the development of clinical disorders. If this is true, it seems useful to explore the sources of unacceptance.

Sources of Unacceptance

At least three sources of unacceptance can readily be identified. The first is a history of reinforcement associated with attempts to solve problems by identifying the source of the problem and removing or modifying it. Western culture, in general, has a long history of reinforcement for identifying and modifying the causes of problems. In particular, science and technology have progressed by gaining control over physical forces and modifying them in ways that are intended to enhance our environments. Illness is remedied by the identification and elimination of its underlying cause. Machines are repaired by identifying faulty parts and replacing them. This approach to problem solving has a long history of success, and individuals within our culture are encouraged from a very young age to solve problems in this way. Given this history, it would seem to make good sense that people would try to solve their problems in living in much the same way as they solve their mechanical problems—they identify the causes and seek to eliminate them. However, it is generally the case that what people identify as the causes of their problems and what they seek to eliminate or modify are their thoughts and feelings. This stems directly from the culture's view of private events and their relation to public behavior. I would argue that this view of private events is the second source of unacceptance.

Beginning early in life, children are taught that thoughts and feelings are causes of behavior and acceptable reasons for actions. When asked for explanations for their behavior, children are virtually required to respond by naming the accompanying thoughts and feelings. As an example, when asked why they have acted aggressively toward another child, children typically respond first by saying they don't know. This honest response is generally unacceptable, and the interrogation continues until an acceptable response occurs. Acceptable answers typically include a statement of how the child felt at the time of the assault. These can be generated by selecting an appropriate private event (e.g., mad, scared, sad, tired, embarrassed, confused, uncertain, etc.) and inserting it into the blank to complete the following sentence: "I did it (didn't do it) because I was ___ ." In this way, children quickly come to see their thoughts and feelings as the causes of their actions. Given this history, it is quite reasonable that individuals would struggle to modify their private events as solutions to their problems in living.

The third source of unacceptance is the culture's portrayal of the good life, at least as it is typically depicted in the popular media. A reasonable abstraction of this portrayal is that those who attain the good life not only enjoy an abundance of resources and diversions, they are characterized by the absence of self-doubts, fears, apprehensions, anger, sadness, jealousy, remorse, etc. In fact, the very presence of these negative private events is indicative of psychological disturbance.

This rather vacuous ideal is reinforced by both "pop-psychology" and some forms of professional psychology. As an example, a quick perusal of the "psychology" sections of many bookstores reveals a virtual plethora of strategies to rid oneself of those pesky negative thoughts that make us feel bad and stand in the way of the good life. New and improved methods of self-enhancement and their associated jargon replace yesterday's methods as rapidly as new fashions replace old. Buzz words like "co-dependence" and "inner child" replace old buzz words like "erroneous zones" in the vocabularies of those who desperately search for the causes and remedies of their angst. What seems remarkable is that after cycling through various remedies like hypnosis, relaxation, meditation, massage, strategically placed crystals and pyramids, valium, thought stopping, positive affirmations, effective communication training, and recovery programs, the search for new "solutions" does not extinguish. In fact, entering therapy is often just a link in the chain of attempts to eliminate distressing private events. Clients presenting complaints are generally described in terms of unwanted thoughts and feelings, and they are typically seen as inherently problematic obstacles to effective change (Zettle & Hayes, 1986). However, given the sources of unacceptance inherent in the culture, maybe this persistence is not so remarkable after all. It would probably be more surprising if it occurred to most of us that the culture's view of the good life is an advertiser's creation, and that the struggle against negative thoughts and feelings is itself pathogenic.

The Heart of Acceptance

At the heart of acceptance-oriented therapies is a different view of private events and a different view of psychological health. If thoughts and feelings are seen as behaviors, then it is easier to understand that they too are the products of a particular history. That is, they are just something one does; they have no special status. They are neither the causes of suffering nor obstacles to change. This is often a startling discovery for clients who have been led to believe that their thoughts are somehow true reflections of reality and that the simple occurrence of negative thoughts and feelings is indicative of psychological disturbance. If, however, thoughts and feelings are understood as nothing more than the results of a particular history, then there is no need to fear them, react to them, struggle against them, control them or change them. They simply do not have to be modified in order to change behavior.

This does not mean, however, that acceptance is some kind of applied nihilism which seeks to have clients simply tolerate the suffering inherent in that miserable form of existence we call human life. There is a critical distinction to be made between the occurrence of a thought or feeling and an individual's reaction to that thought or feeling. It is one thing to feel anxious, and quite another to react to that anxiety. Similarly, it is one thing to think, "I'm a failure," and a different thing to react negatively to that thought. This distinction is made because it is the reaction to certain thoughts and feelings, not the thoughts and feelings themselves, that leads to distress and suffering. In particular, it is the unacceptance of thoughts and feelings or the struggle to control them that is the source of distress and suffering. It is possible, and this is the goal of many acceptance-based therapies, to have the thoughts and feelings attendant that result from living in the world, understand them for what they are, and get on with the pursuit of the experiences which gives one's life meaning and richness.

Implications for Psychotherapy and Research

This view of acceptance has some implications for psychotherapy research. If one takes an acceptance approach, then the goals of treatment entail helping clients learn to take a different perspective on their thoughts and feelings, to give up the struggle against them, and to pursue those experiences and interactions that give richness and meaning to their lives. Accordingly, measures of the effectiveness of acceptance-based therapies are likely to be different from those measures that characterize the current psychotherapy research literature. It is not unfair to say that the current literature is marked by a relative emphasis on the alleviation of negative thoughts and feelings (e.g., Barlow, Rapee, & Brown, 1992). Much less emphasis is placed on the assessment of change in clients' functioning that might be considered indicative of increased psychological health. With acceptance-based therapies, the emphases are likely to be reversed. Instead of the elimination of distressing thoughts and feelings per se, outcome measures would focus on degree of acceptance and the extent to which clients make desired changes in their lives. Treatment success would be determined not by the relative proportion of positive and negative thoughts and feelings, but by the extent to which clients live their lives in accord with their values and experiences. In addition to reductions in scores on depression scales or fear surveys, increases in scores on scales that measure such things as openness to experience, involvement in pleasurable and enriching activities, and interpersonal intimacy would be routinely included in results sections. These are the kinds of changes many clinicians actually emphasize and assess more informally. Psychotherapy research with this type of focus might be more relevant to practicing clinicians and may help close the scientist-practitioner gap.

References

Barlow, D. H., Rapee, R.M., & Brown, T. B. (1992). Behavioral treatment of generalized anxiety disorder. *Behavior Therapy, 23*, 529-550.

Follette, W. C., Bach, P. A., & Follette, V. M. (1993). A Behavior analytic view of psychological health. *The Behavior Analyst.*

Hayes, S. C. (1987). A contextual approach to therapeutic change. In Jacobson, N. S. (Ed.), *Psychotherapists in clinical practice: Cognitive and behavior perspectives* (pp. 327-387). New York: Guilford.

Hayes, S. C., & Hayes, L. J. (1992). Some clinical implications of contextualistic behaviorism: The example of cognition. *Behavior Therapy, 23*, 225-250.

Jacobson, N. J. (1992). Behavioral couples counseling: A new beginning. *Behavior Therapy, 23*, 493-506.

Linehan, M. (1993). *Cognitive behavioral treatment of borderline personality disorder: The dialectics of effective treatment.* New York: Guilford.

Skinner, B. F. (1957). *Verbal Behavior.* New Jersey: Prentice-Hall.

Zettle, R. D., & Hayes, S. C. (1986). Dysfunctional control by client verbal behavior: The context of reason giving. *The Analysis of Verbal Behavior, 4*, 30-38.

Discussion of Dougher

On the Use of Acceptable Language

Robert D. Zettle
Wichita State University

There can be little doubt that a specification of what acceptance is (and is not) is critical to any subsequent discussion of its role in the initiation, maintenance, and modification of clinically relevant behavior. In what follows, selective comments stimulated by Dougher's paper, in particular, and the larger conference, more generally, will be offered on the nature of acceptance and the implications associated with differing ways of thinking and talking about acceptance.

Dougher suggests that acceptance is most meaningfully viewed as an act or behavior. Undoubtedly, some will take exception to such a behavioral perspective and it is beyond the scope of this commentary to present a detailed argument in favor of regarding acceptance as behavior. Suffice it to say that this writer also views acceptance as behavior because it seems useful to do so.

There would appear to be several advantages associated with conceptualizing acceptance as behavior. One implication concerns the language and terminology to be used in talking about the phenomenon in question. Discussion and debate about verbal behavior often are dismissed as matters of "mere semantics," as if the issues involved were trivial. Subtle distinctions in the language of acceptance, however, may have important implications in our efforts to understand acceptance as behavior.

Acceptance or Accepting?

If acceptance indeed is to be conceptualized as behavior, it seems curious that "it" is talked about as a noun (acceptance) rather than as a verb (accepting), especially by radical behaviorists whose own verbal behavior typically is more tightly controlled. There may be several sources of support for speaking of acceptance as a noun-like thing or entity. The term "acceptance" itself is not a scientific one and commonly is used by the wider verbal community in a variety of contexts. Moreover, the lay public often speaks of behavior more generally by using noun-like language (e.g., "I have an idea."). Of more critical importance, however, for the current discussion is that psychologists also routinely engage in similar verbal behavior. One might even argue that this tendency is so common and insidious that it is even embedded in the definition offered by psychologists for their own discipline. Psychology is regarded as the science of behavior rather than the science of behaving. Why this is the case is unclear but it may result from the study of static entities or things seeming to be more scientific than the investigation of a "moving target" inherent with a dynamic subject matter.

Before more fully discussing the specific implications of focusing upon accepting rather than acceptance, it should be acknowledged that others, from seemingly disparate vantage points, also have raised concerns about using nouns in place of verbs in psychological discourse. Roy Schafer (1976), for instance, has argued for a new action language for psychoanalysis to replace the traditional one of metapsychology:

"In doing so, one uses verbs and adverbs to describe the person doing things. One renounces both the use of mentalistic nouns, such as structure, function, force, and drive, and the use of adjectives that qualify those nouns, such as weak, strong, autonomous, and rigid" (1978, p. 187).

The tendency within psychology to transform verbs into nouns also has been decried from an interbehavioral perspective. The study of attention, perception, memory, and cognition, for example, more appropriately are regarded as matters of attending, perceiving, remembering, and thinking (Kantor & Smith, 1975). Kantor, in commenting further on word misuse in psychology, noted that, "The errors begin with the rhetorical substitution of nouns for verbs as grammarians would say and then making constructs into events" (Observer, 1981, p. 603). Reification results and the focus of psychology is diverted away from the study of behaving.

The Nature of Accepting

Dougher points out that "acceptance is typically defined negatively," and he regards doing so as clearly unsatisfactory unless the context in which acceptance occurs also is taken into account. Accepting also may be defined primarily by what it is not. This stance does not appear to be particularly troublesome for radical behaviorists provided that "what it is not" also involves other behaviors. Indeed there is precedent for an analogous practice within the behavior analytic literature. Despite some questions about their distinctiveness (Woods, 1983), both DRO (e.g., Reynolds, 1961) and DRI schedules (e.g., Patterson, 1965) have been used to effectively strengthen behaviors incompatible with other actions.

Dougher's assertion that acceptance has clinical relevance only in conflict situations suggests several behaviors which may be incompatible with accepting. Foremost among these actions are avoiding and escaping. Avoiding and escaping are incompatible with accepting, and these actions also are incompatible with approaching. Indeed conflicts typically are characterized as situations in which contingencies supporting avoiding/escaping coexist with other contingencies supporting approach behavior. This, however, does not mean that accepting is synonymous with approaching. While it seems meaningful to regard accepting as not avoiding or escaping, the same cannot be said about approaching. To appreciate why this may be the case requires more careful consideration of "what" is avoided in conflict situations.

What is commonly held to have been avoided or escaped under such circumstances are the aversive contingencies which participate in an approach-avoidance conflict. Clinically, however, this analysis seems incomplete unless it also is recognized that avoiding and escaping may occur in reaction to other behaviors occurring in conflict situations. These other behaviors may consist of thinking and feeling and more typically are characterized as "unwanted private events" (e.g., obsessive thoughts and/or anxious feelings).

Deliberate efforts to escape from or avoid particular thoughts and feelings, however, often appear to be counterproductive. In particular, the act of suppressing specific thoughts paradoxically often results in increased thinking of the very sort to be avoided (Lavy & van den Hout, 1990; Wegner, Schneider, Carter, & White, 1987). The futility of attempting to control obsessional thinking is underscored further by the general ineffectiveness of thought stopping (Masters, Burish, Hollon, & Rimm, 1987; Reed, 1985). Instead, it may be more useful clinically to take measures to dissuade clients from attempting to suppress, control, avoid, or escape from their own private events. It is in this sense that it appears meaningful to speak of accepting in terms of what it is not. Alternatively, accepting also might be thought of as the behavior of "just noticing" or tacting ones own thinking and feeling (Hayes, 1987).

Implications of Behavioralizing Accepting

There would appear to be several implications associated with focusing upon accepting as a behavior rather than on acceptance as a noun-like thing. This forum obviously precludes an exhaustive discussion of all of the implications, and the comments which follow of necessity will be selective.

Perhaps most importantly, emphasizing acceptance as behavior makes explicit the need ultimately for a functional analysis of this action. Controlling variables which help shape and maintain accepting as behavior must be identified and, if possible, manipulated to assess their impact upon accepting. This endeavor obviously is not an easy one and a functional interpretation of accepting may need to precede an experimental or applied analysis of the variables of which accepting is a function.

There was considerable discussion and debate throughout the conference about whether acceptance is best regarded as an outcome or process. The language of acceptance appears to lead inherently to confusion over whether acceptance is best thought of as an outcome, a process, or both. Much of this confusion seemingly could be avoided by speaking instead of accepting. Accepting as a behavior is fluid and dynamic and more meaningfully viewed as a process rather than a static entity or steady-state responding. In this regard, it is perhaps tempting to think of acceptance as the outcome of accepting, the process. However, in doing so attending is diverted from behavior and, unfortunately as seen throughout psychology more generally, all too often leads to exclusive focus upon the outcome as a reified entity. Just as cognition and attention have supplanted thinking and attending as the subject matter of psychology, the same would likely occur with respect to acceptance and accepting.

The focus of this conference was upon both acceptance and change and, by implication, the possible relationship between the two. It would seem useful also to recast change in more explicit behavioral language as changing. The possible relationship between acceptance and change accordingly can be reframed as one between accepting and changing. This reformulation makes explicit that the relationship to be understood is between one behavior and another. A functional interpretation and analysis of changing as a behavior becomes necessary and, perhaps of even greater importance, an interpretation and analysis of the variables which would support a relationship between accepting and changing. Behavior analysts have not found it useful to regard a behavior as an initiating cause for yet another behavior by the same organism (Hayes & Brownstein, 1986). This is not to say that accepting has no role to play in changing. At best accepting may exert a controlling function over changing, but the context in which this occurs must be identified and understood.

Conclusion

Convening a conference on acceptance and change, in this writer's opinion, has the potential to create a fertile ground for collaboration among clinicians of diverse orientations and perspectives. Whether or not this potential is realized and results in more effective psychotherapeutic approaches, of course, remains to be seen. It is suggested that carefully considering the language to be utilized in this endeavor may itself be found to be useful.

References

Hayes, S. C. (1987). A contextual approach to therapeutic change. In N. S. Jacobson (Ed.), *Psychotherapists in clinical practice: Cognitive and behavioral perspectives* (pp. 327-387). New York: Guilford.

Hayes, S. C., & Brownstein, A. J. (1986). Mentalism, behavior-behavior relations, and a behavior analytic view of the purposes of science. *The Behavior Analyst, 9,* 175-190.

Kantor, J. R., & Smith, N. W. (1975). *The science of psychology: An interbehavioral survey.* Chicago: Principia Press.

Lavy, E. H., & van den Hout, M. A. (1990). Thought suppression induces intrusions. *Behavioural Psychotherapy, 18,* 251-258.

Masters, J. C., Burish, T. G., Hollon, S. D., & Rimm, D. C. (1987). *Behavior therapy: Techniques and empirical findings* (3rd ed.). New York: Harcourt Brace Jovanovich.

Observer (1981). Comments and queries: Words and their misuse in science and psychology. *The Psychological Record, 31,* 599-605.

Patterson, G. R. (1965). An application of conditioning techniques to the control of a hyperactive child. In L. P. Ullman & L. Krasner (Eds.), *Case studies in behavior modification* (pp. 370-375). New York: Holt, Rinehart & Winston.

Reed, G. F. (1985). *Obsessional experience and compulsive behaviour: A cognitive-structural approach.* Orlando, FL: Academic Press.

Reynolds, G. S. (1961). Behavioral contrast. *Journal of the Experimental Analysis of Behavior, 4,* 57-71.

Schafer, R. (1976). *A new language for psychoanalysis.* New Haven, CT: Yale University Press.

Schafer, R. (1978). *Language and insight.* New Haven, CT: Yale University Press.

Wegner, D. M., Schneider, D. J., Carter, S. R., & White, T. L. (1987). Paradoxical effects of thought suppression. *Journal of Personality and Social Psychology, 53,* 5-13.

Woods, T. C. (1983). DRO and DRI: A false dichotomy? *The Psychological Record, 33,* 59-66.

Section 2

Acceptance and Approaches to Intervention

Chapter 3

Acceptance in Experiential Therapy

Leslie Greenberg
York University

In this paper acceptance will be discussed from the point of view of humanistic/ experiential approaches to therapy (Rice & Greenberg 1993, Rogers 1952, Perls 1969). Acceptance has been a key component of this tradition from its inception. In discussing acceptance from this perspective, we will look at two very different aspects of acceptance, self-acceptance and acceptance of another.

Self-acceptance, addressed in the first part of this paper, will include a discussion of a paradoxical theory of change (changing to be "what you are" rather than what you are not) and of the role of emotion in change. These factors will be used to illuminate how acceptance enhances adaptation and problem solving. Specific models of the processes involved in different types of internal acceptance that result in therapeutic change will also be presented.

In the second part of the paper, interpersonal acceptance will be discussed. The nature and function of interpersonal acceptance will be explored and a stage model of how empathic affirmation of intense vulnerability leads to change will be presented. Finally the role of acceptance in enhancing intimacy in couples therapy will be discussed.

Self-Acceptance

In discussing self-acceptance we need first to provide an answer to the question, Acceptance of what? Any discussion of acceptance requires the specification of what it is that is being accepted. In talking about self-acceptance in the humanistic/ experiential view, it is ultimately acceptance of one's experience that is being referred to. Acceptance then applies to the domain of private subjective events and of tacit experience, rather than to the acceptance of explicit, overt behavior. Thus we are talking about acceptance of feelings, such as feeling sad or afraid, or acceptance of desires and wishes, such as sexual desires or longings for affection. In my view a key issue in helping understand how self acceptance is therapeutic is recognizing the central role of *experiencing* in human functioning.

Two central assumptions in this view therefore are that (1) there is a continuous ongoing automatic process of internal experiencing, a process that results from both external and internal dialectical interactions, i.e., from interactions between the organism and the environment, and from interactions between different parts of the organism with each other, and that (2) the experiencing process is automatic, not subject to conscious, deliberate control, yet is affected by conscious symbolization of it. Experiencing then is both a given of existence, has a certain structure and involves certain processes including such characteristics as being inchoate and as developing when symbolized. Experience then is seen as having both a nature and a directionality.

Self acceptance then involves acknowledgment in awareness of experience. We are beings who can either attend to and symbolize our experience in conscious awareness or cannot. As a human being I am at particular points in life faced with dilemmas such as: Can I accept my feelings of weakness, of anger or pain or of cruelty? Can I listen to myself and accept my experience, whatever it is? Or do I try to shape myself, and my experience, to be something other than what it is, to shape it up, to some standard or value. Can I allow myself to experience pain, shame, fear or dread? Or do I tighten up against it, stop breathing, avoid it, and try to focus my attention on something else?

One major alternative to acceptance is avoidance or denial of experience. Another alternative is self-manipulation or control of experience in order to attain an ideal. Although most people believe that avoidance or denial is unhealthy many hold the view that attaining goals through self-manipulation is desirable. They believe that one 'should' aim to push oneself to be where one is "not", in order to attain goals, or achieve excellence. People are always faced with the question of whether or not they should attempt to mold their experience to what they think it should be, to be what they or others think is best. In an achievement oriented society, striving for excellence is a much extolled virtue. How can one just passively "allow" their experience, and be content with their "rotten" old self. In this conflict between ideals or shoulds, and acceptance, people mistake "being" and "doing," and therefore believe that they can achieve and strive for ideals in the realm of what they feel, rather than in the realm of what they do. An overly strong goal orientation therefore often results in unremitting standards about how one should "be," rather than how one should "behave." Standards for experiencing replace standards for conduct. People begin to develop beliefs such as "I should be strong," "I shouldn't be angry or weak or cruel," and so on, and they try to feel certain feelings or they condemn themselves for what they do feel. From an experiential therapy view, letting go of unattainable goals, however, is as important in healthy living, as is striving towards attainable goals. Living a healthy life then depends not on self manipulation but on acceptance of ones experiencing.

The Primacy of Process

In resolving the dilemma between feeling and doing, it is important to emphasize the *primacy of process* in human experiencing. Change in experience over time is the natural order; stasis is what needs explanation. This view on the importance of the primacy of process in living is well captured by a story about King Solomon in which in giving counsel to people who come to him with a variety of troubles, he always ended his counsel by holding out his ring for them to kiss and told them to read the inscription on the ring. Written on the ring were the words "and this too shall pass" capturing that everything is subject change. This captures the paradox of acceptance and experiencing, i.e., that the more people accept themselves, in their full complexity, the more they change.

The Consequences of Acceptance

The affective consequences of acceptance are that people become more understanding and compassionate, both toward themselves and toward others. When people are aware of whatever feeling or reaction they currently experience, they are unified, integrated beings in that moment. Acceptance of experience thereby enhances internal cohesion and inner harmony. The behavioral consequences of self-acceptance are that once a feeling is fully in awareness and is fully accepted, then it can be coped with like any other situation. Acceptance therefore enhances coping and problem solving. Self-acceptance, however, does not mean acceptance of some "real" entity such as a real self. Rather, it refers to a *process*, the process of accurately symbolizing in awareness current experience.

Immediacy of Experiencing

Acceptance implies immediacy of experiencing. In general, therapeutic change, in the humanistic tradition has been seen as involving "experiencing" rather than "talking about experience." The process of experiencing involves moving to a greater sense of immediacy, in which feelings are *currently felt* rather than just being talked about in a conceptual way. Rogers (1961) in an attempt to describe how change took places in Client Centered Therapy defined seven process strands of change. Openness to experience and acceptance of feelings were central concepts in these process strands. From observations of clients in therapy, he found that change occurred by people moving from being distant from their experience to identifying with or owning their experience. Empathic attunement to, and understanding of people's feelings was seen as the major tool of intervention designed to facilitate people in this type of acceptance of their inner experience.

Perls (1973) also emphasized immediacy of experiencing. It is important to note that Gestalt therapists emphasize living "in the present," a process of awareness, as opposed to living "for the present," a process of impulsiveness. Living in the present involves being fully aware of what is occurring in the moment rather than living for the present which implies disregard for consequences. Gestalt has been referred to as a Western Zen because of its similarity to Zen in its emphasis on present awareness. Perls (1969) in his writings referred to the central importance of "is-ness" in creative adjustment and healthy functioning. He believed that much dysfunction in present society occurs because people have become experience-phobic, avoiding their feelings, particularly unpleasant ones. This produces phoniness as opposed to authenticity, numbness and deadness as opposed to lively sensing. The basic phobic attitude is characterized as being afraid to be who, and what, one is. Pathology in this view rather than being caused by repression of the immoral, as suggested by Freud, is caused by disallowing and avoidance of the painful and by lack of acceptance and suppression of the adaptive (Greenberg & Korman, 1993).

According to Perls (1969), attending and awareness are therefore the antidote to avoidance. A major class of interventions in the Gestalt approach then involve suggesting that people attend to and stay with their current feelings. To this are added a variety of in-session experiments to help people discover "*how*" awareness is blocked and how experience is avoided. In this awareness process, attention is turned to becoming aware of *how* one interrupts both ones internal experience and ones contact with the world. The goal is one of *owning* the interrupted experience and *expressing* it more contactfully in awareness.

According to both Rogers (1961), and Perls (1969), feelings therefore need to be *experienced* with immediacy, in the session as opposed to being avoided or only known conceptually. Both believed that when successful, clients in experiential therapy move toward being the process they inwardly actually are, that they move away from being what they are "not," and become more authentic. Rather than conceal, they begin to reveal their inner experience. In this process of "becoming" it is, however, not enough to accept something intellectually. Rather, experience needs to be "realized" i.e., made real in experience. The person needs to experience in the present what he or she is saying. The person then begins to feel what they are talking about and their language then reflects this. Thus a person will move from saying "it is upsetting" to "he makes me angry" to the direct expression of "I feel angry" or "I *am* afraid." Here the language moves from nonspecific and outer focused to more concrete and inner focused.

Paradoxical Theory of Change

These perspectives on acceptance have led to a view referred to by Beisser (1970) as the Paradoxical theory of change. Change occurs when one becomes what one is, not when one tries to become what one is not. The implication for therapy is that, by rejecting the role of "changer," therapists can help others to change. The therapist therefore encourages people to be "where" and "what" they are, to be fully invested in their current experience and positions rather than trying to influence, persuade or modify their behavior to help them achieve a change goal. In this perspective change involves, for the moment, "letting go" of the goal of what one would like to become, and becoming what one "is." The premise involves the view that one must stand in the place one is, in order to have a firm footing to later be able to move. One must arrive at a destination before one can decide to leave it or even possibly to stay.

This view of acceptance has set up a dichotomy in relation to intervention, a dichotomy between modifiers who push for change vs. facilitators who supposedly accept what is and don't aim for change. This of course is somewhat of a false dichotomy, more semantic than real. Facilitators focused on bringing out "what is," are concerned about a particular type of internal change, the change of overcoming avoidances and change to the allowing and accepting of previously avoided experience.

The facilitative tradition essentially recognizes that there is often conflict between getting to where one wants to be and being where one is, i.e., conflict between changing and not wanting to change and between what one should be and what one is. They suggest that in order to resolve this conflict it is helpful to fully invest oneself in one pole of this conflict at a time, identifying with each pole fully, accepting both parts, one at a time and owning both of them as oneself. For example in a conflict between "you should be strong" vs. "I feel weak," the person is invited to experience and express each side often enacting this in a two-chair dialogue (Greenberg, 1984; Greenberg, Rice, & Elliott, 1993). Identification with, and owning of, alienated fragments is then viewed as leading to integrative self-acceptance.

There are two important aspects of this view of conflict:

1. It is the disaffiliative relationship *between* aspects rather than the feelings as such that must change, i.e., the negative internal relationship between parts, particularly negative evaluation of one part by another, needs to change to a more affiliative positive relationship between parts.

2. It is the disowning or avoiding of experience that results in problems, and change occurs by re-owning and integrating. Thus once I say "I feel weak, vulnerable, angry, jealous" and I accept this experience. I integrate this experience and am changed.

The Role of Emotion in Acceptance and Change

Why does changing to be who one "is," lead to therapeutic change. It is here that the role of emotion in human functioning becomes important. Emotion helps to explain the paradoxical theory of change. In simple terms emotional disorder is often caused by the conflict between deliberate, conscious, conceptual processing and automatic, spontaneous, emotional processing (Greenberg, Rice, & Elliott, 1993). Crucial to the view of self-acceptance as curative is the view that emotions are not disruptive but rather organize people for adaptive action and provide feedback to people about their responses to situations.

Emotions give us information about our evaluations of the personal significance of events to us and organize us to act adaptively in response to these situations (Greenberg & Safran, 1986; 1989; Safran & Greenberg 1991; Greenberg, Rice, & Elliott, 1993). Emotions by evaluating the personal significance of situations and by providing feedback about our responses enhances orientation and problem solving. People then need to accept their primary emotional experience because it provides them with adaptive information and action dispositions.

Emotions give us this information about our responses to situations by means of a complex set of tacit information processing. This includes feedback about our evaluation of the significance events have for us. Emotion is an automatic rapid action response tendency system which has had adaptive evolutionary significance in the survival of our species. It enhances orientation and problem solving. This is not to say that emotions cannot be dysfunctional but to assert that even when emotions are dysfunctional they still need to be accepted in order for people to know how they are responding and to be able to move forward. People can either receive the information, allow and accept their automatic evaluations and reactions, and work with their emotions meaning as a part of the definition of reality; or they can avoid their feelings and thereby ignore their experience. Primary feelings which are avoided can become a major source of difficulty because their unacknowledged presence often interferes with orientation and problem solving. Not recognizing fear or anger leaves people disoriented and poorly situated to behave adaptively; they neither oganize to flee from danger nor protect themselves from boundary violations.

Once people accept their feelings, in addition to benefiting from the response tendency information inherent in them, a variety of other things also occur. Among these are: 1) They learn that their experience is *not as threatening* as it was the first time it occurred, when the avoidance began; 2) They learn that they *can experience* this aspect of themselves and not fall apart and expire. This builds confidence and a sense of efficacy; 3) People learn that they may now be able *to do constructive things suggested by feelings*, that they couldn't do before; 4) Allowing feelings may also *open up experiencing of other more positive* feeling that have been avoided; and 5) The *effort that was tied up in avoidance* now becomes available and people feel more energetic.

Models of the Change Processes in Acceptance

In our research program we have studied two major processes involving self-acceptance. One is the process of allowing and accepting painful experience (Greenberg & Korman, 1993; Greenberg, 1994), the other is the process of moving from negative self-evaluation to self-acceptance (Greenberg, et al., 1993). These will be discussed briefly below.

A Model of Allowing and Accepting Experience

A key process in accepting of experiencing is one of *allowing* the experience of previously disallowed painful experience. This means letting the tears come, feeling the feeling fully in one's body and letting it happen rather trying to control it. Our observation of the therapeutic allowing of painful emotional experiences such as hurt, vulnerability, and aloneness, often from separation and abandonment, reveals the following three necessary and sequentially occurring processes (Greenberg, 1994; Greenberg & Paivio, in press).

A change in internal relations involves a move from avoidance and negative evaluation of internal experience to an accepting stance. Painful, bad, and hopeless feelings are not "things as such," but products of internal relations. The very acts of approaching, attending to, and accepting or positively evaluating one's pain leads to its transformation. Often people may allow experiences of weakness or of feeling afraid but then, rather than accept these feelings, they will negatively evaluate them as unacceptable and shut down or feel dangerously out of control. It is the ability to breath, relax, and accept the feeling that is crucial in making the allowing process become a transformative experience.

Re-owning is the process of identifying, as one's own, the feelings and associated thoughts, memories, needs, and action tendencies that have been previously disowned and have been seen as being caused by others, or as belonging to others, or simply as not existing. Disowned experience, while not integrated into the dominant self-organization, still exerts influence on behavior. People tend to deal with the unacceptable by depersonalizing their feelings and not experiencing them as their own, thus weakening their self-organization. Therapy can be understood as not so much a process of bringing previously unconscious material into consciousness as it is one of reclaiming disowned experience. Gestalt therapists (Perls, 1973) use experiments of deliberate awareness to promote experiences "that is *me* who is thinking, feeling, needing, wanting, or doing this." People can distinguish between the conceptual processing of information in an intellectual way, and the experiential linking of that information to the self (Greenberg et al., 1993).

An increased sense of agency and volition and the feeling that one is the agent of one's experience comes along with re-owning. With a sense of agency in one's feelings there is an experience that one is no longer helpless or the passive victim of one's feelings. With the development of a coherent, agentic sense of self in relation to a particular domain of experience, hope develops together with the sense that "I can do something about this." While a sense of agency may not yet provide a concrete plan of action, there is a feeling of confidence that action is possible and that change can occur.

A Model of Integrative Self-Acceptance in Two Chair Conflict

An important aspect of self-acceptance is moving from negative evaluation of an aspect of self experience towards a more accepting stance of this same aspect of self-experience. An intervention derived from the practice of Gestalt Therapy, two-chair dialogue for resolving splits (Greenberg, 1984), has as its goal integrative self-acceptance. In this process the client begins with a split between two aspects of experience in which one aspect views another aspect of experience critically. The negative self-evaluations are global and stable, with the person judging him or herself for having failed to meet an all-important set of standards or requirements. While criticism and blame are directed inward, the client typically reacts in a dejected, helpless manner. There is generally an intense level of inner conflict surrounding the issue of what "should" be done. The self is viewed as unacceptable and is not to be trusted, is unworthy and is always at fault. However once acceptance is achieved, the relationship between the two sides changes and the aspects become more integrated.

Integrative self-acceptance can be described in the following manner. There is a clearer understanding of how various needs and goals of the personality can be accommodated, and how previously antagonistic sides of the self can be reconciled in a working relationship. There is now a high regard for the self as a trustworthy and as a responsible agent in the process of self-direction, and/or as being worthy of understanding and kindness. The person experiences a sense of wholeness and compassion for the previously despised aspect. Aspects of the self previously in conflict or discordant are now felt to be more harmonious and in unison. The previously critical part shows acceptance of previously disliked, rejected, or negatively evaluated aspects of the self. There is a sense of real listening, openness, and contact between the two parts, which are now combined in one of two ways: 1) within an affiliative relationship between the previously opposed parts, with expressions of caring and/or of feeling embraced in a close, comforting manner; or 2) with statements of a clearer sense of self-definition by one part which now feels stronger, more powerful, and freer to be, and/or an openess or flexibility from the other side, showing acceptance of this new-found sense of self-direction.

Based on our observation of experiences in therapy of integrative self-acceptance, people in this state feel a greater sense of either self-affiliation or self-autonomy. They use affiliative terms such as: embracing, understanding, accepting, caring, protecting, or loving the self, or of feeling cared for, protected, touched, comforted, or embraced. Autonomy-oriented expressions appear most in combination with affiliation in terms such as: new options, compromise, not stubborn, renegotiate, acceptance, separate, outlined, equal, stronger, courage, risking, and taking charge.

A measure of the six stages of resolution that we have observed in the process of moving from negative self-evaluation to integrative self-acceptance is given below with those aspects involving acceptance underlined for emphasis (Greenberg, Rice, & Elliott, 1993).

Degree of Resolution Scale - Splits

1. The client describes a conflict with which he or she is currently struggling *in which one aspect of the self is not in harmony with another aspect and is unaccepting or coercive toward the other part of the self.* The two aspects may not be clearly delineated, and the opposition between the two parts may not be the focus of the clients attention.
2. The client begins to *actively criticize or coerce the self in a negative fashion.* The two aspects of the self are clearly delineated and are brought into contact with each other highlighting the nature of the opposition between the two sides. *The criticisms, expectations,* or judgements of the self *are clearly expressed* in a concrete and specific manner and the self-reactions begin to be explored and expressed.
3. The clients underlying feelings in response to the criticisms emerge and are differentiated until a new feeling or felt sense of self is arrived at.
4. The needs or wants associated with the newly experienced sense of self are expressed clearly and challenge or throw into doubt the guiding standards and ideals that underlie the criticisms.
5. For the first time greater consideration is given to the expressed feelings and needs. Compassion concern or respect for the self may be shown. *The self is recognized and accepted as a trustworthy and responsible agent in the process of self-determination. The client genuinely accepts his or her experience.* The client

expresses either a caring or comforting type of self-embracement or describes a clearer, stronger sense of self and freedom to be.

6. There is a clear *understanding of how various needs and desires may be accommodated* and how previously antagonistic sides of the self may be *reconciled in a working relationship*. The discourse may involve some *negotiation* between the aspects an may involve planning how *to function in greater harmony*. The client may experience a sense of *wholeness or inner harmony as aspects* of the self previously in conflict are felt *to be more in unison*. There is sense of *real inner listening and of contact and openess to the self as it most fundamentally is.*

Interpersonal Acceptance

To truly accept another and his or her feelings is not easy. In accepting another I am often faced with some of the same dilemmas as in self-acceptance. Can I permit someone to feel angry or admiring toward me? Can I accept a persons weakness, anger or cruelty as a part of him or her? Can I accept differences in others, especially differences in someone with whom I am in an intimate relationship?

According to Rogers (1951) prizing or valuing others in therapy, as opposed to appraising or judging them, is a crucial ingredient of promoting therapeutic change. This is captured in the client-centered attitude of non-judgementalness or unconditional positive regard. If in therapy one really gets a feeling for what it is like to be the other person, acceptance and warmth almost always follow automatically. The therapist then experiences and can communicate warm, unconditional acceptance of the client. A positive sense is thus communicated that the client is a worthwhile person whose value does not depend on performing certain behaviors or having feelings. The term *prizing* (Butler, 1952) seems best to capture this stance. The therapist prizes the client, valuing and honoring the client just as he or she is now, because of being human, not simply because he or she is entertaining, hard-working, or in pain. Each person is unique and interesting, someone whose world one has the privilege of entering for a time. It is important to point out that prizing is not the same as offering reassurance, although it may have this effect on the client. Prizing is seldom expressed directly in words, but it can nonetheless be pervasively felt in a good therapeutic relationship. It comes through indirectly and nonverbally in voice (Rice & Kerr, 1986), manner, and perhaps most importantly, consistency.

The client benefits from the therapist's unfailing positive regard in two ways (Greenberg, Rice, & Elliott, 1993). First, the experience of being accepted and truly valued by another person is a unique learning experience, which helps to *counteract internalized conditions of worth* and negative self-evaluations and self-doubts. Second, by removing the need for interpersonal vigilance, it *frees up the client's processing capacity, increasing attentional breadth as well as access to memory.* This allows the client to engage more fully in inner exploration. Support of this type thus encourages the client to face more painful and anxiety-provoking material. The reduction of interpersonal anxiety allows the client to tolerate more intrapersonal anxiety in self-exploration, creating an optimal environment for engaging in the cognitive-affective and behavioral tasks of therapy.

Empathic attunement to and acceptance of clients' ongoing affective experience is a crucial aspect of the essential fabric of the therapist's involvement in acceptance. Empathic attunement to clients' feelings helps clients to *confirm* and *strengthen* their own sense of themselves. Their sense of themselves is not only passively accepted, it is also confirmed. Thus acceptance involves an active process of recognizing and affirming their truth, i.e., of validating their experience. This process of confirmation is similar to what occurs when children, with the support their caretaker, synthesize their own internal emotional responses to situations. With the support of the caretaker's empathic attunement to their experience, they are able to develop a stronger sense of their own selves (Stern, 1985). In a similar way, clients build a stronger sense of their own experience by having their experience recognized and validated to by their therapists. Having one's own feelings understood and accurately reflected back both verbally and nonverbally helps one to experience the feeling more fully and with increased confidence that "this is really what I am feeling." Feelings are often inchoate, emerging from a highly subjective, idiosyncratic, inner world for which there is no formal descriptive language. When the experience is symbolized and shared, it is confirmed as being what it is by the other's understanding of it. The process of empathic attunement and acceptance therefore leads to the building of a sense of confidence in one's own experience. Thus growth and the strengthening of the self occurs best in the context of empathy and acceptance.

Rogers' view of unconditional positive regard can be seen as being constituted by two components (Greenberg, Rice, & Elliott, 1993; Lietaer, 1991): acceptance and warmth.

Acceptance refers to a "baseline" attitude of consistent, genuine, noncritical interest, and tolerance for all aspects of the client (Rogers, 1957; 1959). In other words, prizing is not felt as contingent on being a good client. Accepting the client unconditionally requires an act of "letting go," not only of preconceptions and expectations for the client, but also of the therapist's personal values, preferences, and standards. Where a person might typically make judgments in other situations or relationships, the therapist in this situation waits with a genuine attitude of interest, without any impulse to evaluate. This unconditional acceptance comes easier if one has "unconditional confidence" in the human potential for self-understanding and change (Harman, 1990).

The second aspect of prizing, *warmth*, is a stronger, more active state that the therapist may experience at times in therapy. At particular times, the therapist experiences an immediate, active sense of caring, appreciating, feeling privileged, and valuing the client in the moment. Warmth also refers to desiring the best for the client, or valuing, or wishing him or her well, but without a sense of feeling responsible for "fixing" how the client is.

Acceptance then means a regard for the other as a person of unconditional self worth -- a person of value no matter what the person's condition. Acceptance requires the absence of judgment and criticism. Evaluation by another is a threat especially when it occurs in relation to areas of personal vulnerability. Negative evaluation always creates defensiveness, and often results in some portions of experience being denied to awareness. Being valued and prized on the other hand makes a person feel *safe* and this is an important element in any helping relationship. When a person feels accepted, they relax. Warmth on the other hand involves liking and concern for a person's behavior or feelings. The warmth and liking of the other reduces the fear involved in facing life and its pain and suffering. As noted previously, reduction of *interpersonal anxiety* brought about by the other's acceptance leads to an increased tolerance of intrapersonal anxiety. Acceptance by a therapist therefore both strengthens the person's sense of self by allowing the person to be him or herself with the accepting therapist, and simultaneously provides a safe working environment for completing further therapeutic tasks involving deepening and acceptance of inner experience.

Acceptance from, and being listened to, by the other leads to a greater ability to accept and listen to oneself. Rogers (1961) referred to acceptance and understanding as leading to the undoing of conditions of worth, those internalized attitudes of conditional self-acceptance such as "I'm only acceptable *if*--". Rogers' key hypothesis was that acceptance of the clients experience by the therapist would lead to an increased acceptance of self by the client. If the person is accepted with no judgment, met with only compassion and empathy, the individual will develop the courage to be, and to take risks. This undoing of conditions of worth can be thought of from a framework of interpersonal theory as a process of internalizing supportive interaction. By being accepted, the client is able to take the same stance towards the self as the one taken by the therapist and thereby becomes less evaluative and more accepting. Interpersonal learning thus occurs within the accepting relationship.

Finally, acceptance of another and nonjudgmentalness is not just a behavior but is a particular state of being which one enters. It involves listening to another in a fully absorbed, attentive state, and this parallels the nonjudgmental experience of the viewing of a beautiful sunset. In this state one values what one sees, as it is, and one does not say I wish there was a little more red on the right or that cloud would just move over a bit. One appreciates the sunset as it is. It is equally extremely rewarding to non-judgmentally accept another; and this form of acceptance of another produces a great feeling of relaxation and intimacy.

Empathic Affirmation of Intense Vulnerability

Some of the most powerful moments in therapy occur when therapists are able to convey acceptance to client's expressions of vulnerable, self-relevant emotions. Such emotions as deep hurt, intense shame, feelings of bitterness, despair about the future, or a sense of total isolation from others are felt as intensely personally defining. People feel extremely vulnerable about having these feelings. Moreover they are feelings that, in our culture, are often considered to be "abnormal" and unacceptable to others, or even to oneself. It is therefore crucial that the therapist recognize and empathically affirm the person's experience at these moments.

Clients often fear that if they reveal themselves and fully express these painful emotions, or other seemingly unacceptable aspects of themselves, that the therapist will judge them, feel alienated from them, or even reject them. They fear that they themselves will be viewed by the therapist as unacceptable, abnormal, defective, or even frightening. There is thus often an attempt to close down, or hold off, dreaded feelings or aspects of self and to avoid dealing with them. For some clients there is even the fear that if they fully acknowledge these dreaded negative feelings, these emotions will be bottomless and engulfing, and they will lose control and will, themselves, be overwhelmed by them. We have defined and constructed a preliminary model of an in-therapy change event involving the affirmation of intense vulnerability (Greenberg et al., 1993). This is described below.

A client's statement of intense vulnerability presents an important opportunity for an empathic and highly validating intervention by the therapist. This provides an affirming interpersonal experience with the therapist. For instance, the following two client statements represent statements of personal vulnerability at which validation by the therapist is therapeutic. In the first, the client expresses feelings of loss and a type of envy and bitterness related to the loss that she finds difficult to accept: "I wanted so badly to have a child myself, and I can't (sob). And now my sister is having one, and its terrible. I just *can't feel glad for her. I even have bad feelings toward the baby.*" In a further example, a client who had experienced a loss expressed a feeling of deep overwhelming emptiness: "Nothing seems to have any meaning any more. It's like I have no desire to carry on struggling." In both of these examples the clients express painful feelings that are difficult to assimilate, and in their voice and manner of expression there is a sense of intense vulnerability.

If one can fully express a feared, dreaded, unacceptable aspect of experience such as intense despair, and have it fully received by a therapist who is sensing the feeling in its full intensity, and is clearly valuing the client with no reservations, this can be a powerful experience that promotes change. The product of this event is the crucial interpersonal learning that one's experience is acceptable to another; and this validation leads to a stronger sense of self.

In this whole process, clients are confirmed by making contact and being accepted as they are. They are helped to become unique selves by the therapist's confirming them in their uniqueness. It is the existence of the self as a separate center of experience and *agency* that is *confirmed* by the therapist's empathic affirmation of the client's unique inner experience. Accepting clients as they are in their vulnerability or despair does not imply accepting them as forever stuck, nor does it imply that the therapist has given up hope for their change. Instead, the continuing empathic affirmation of the whole person while they are experiencing and revealing these painful aspect of themselves helps them to differentiate this aspect of self from the total self. They cease to feel as overwhelmed by the vulnerability and can see the feared aspect as a part rather than as all of themselves. The person feels stronger and more able to cope. This strengthened sense of self makes possible further changes and growth.

After the initial period of empathic prizing by the therapist at a vulnerability marker, the client may continue to be clearly disturbed by the intensity or depth of the feelings of fear, shame, or despair, as indicated by voice and manner as well as content; or the person may hold back in an effort to stifle the feelings. Empathic understanding and affirmation then leads: 1) to an intense expression of the negative self-experience, then; 2) to an expression of the most painful aspect of the experience, and finally; 3) to feeling calmer and more integrated.

As the emotional expression deepens and continues to be empathically received by the therapist, the client begins to feel that what was previously viewed as a totally unacceptable aspect of experience can be seen as an understandable, humanly acceptable feeling. The anxiety that has previously inhibited the full sharing of these experiences is reduced, and they can be expressed in their full intensity. It is as if going to the very bottom, fully feeling the experience and not being overwhelmed by it, enables the client to start up again and move toward personal growth. The client is now able to feel the whole experience in its full intensity, leading to a sense of relief and acceptance of the entire experience into his or her sense of self. Thus acceptance by the therapist leads to greater self-acceptance.

Acceptance in Couples Therapy

The role of acceptance in couples therapy will be reviewed briefly below. There are two components of acceptance of one partner by the other that appear to be important in close relationships and in couples therapy. One is acceptance and valuing of the partner's internal experience in a non-judgemental fashion, free of expectation of how they should be or feel about themselves, or what attitudes they should hold. The second is a non-coercive, tolerant attitude towards the others behavior. This latter form of acceptance involves a type of letting go of attempts to control or change the other's behavior. It results in ending the blame or criticism that generally follows the frustration of not being able to change the other. This type of acceptance also relates to the development of tolerance and understanding of the other as a different person with likes, dislikes, styles, and views all of his or her own. The two major contrasts to acceptance in marriage are criticism and control. Acceptance in couples then involves nonjudgementalness of the other's experience and noncontrollingness of the other's behavior.

Nonjudgemental acceptance of one's partner, particularly of one's partners innermost feeling and needs, without any attempts to change those aspects of the partner, provides the partner with the experience of being accepted and loved exactly as he or she is. This produces intimacy (Greenberg & Johnson, 1988).

This is a process which involves one partner's first disclosing his or her primary experience, then the other partner's accepting this. This process of disclosure of previously unexpressed feelings and needs is central to Emotionally Focused

Therapy for couples (Greenberg & Johnson, 1988). Acceptance of one partner by the other not only provides the experience of being heard or validated but also interrupts or prevents possible nag/withdraw, negative interactional cycles, or reactance responses from one's partner. Acceptance produces mutually affirming interaction and trust. Acceptance in relationships is the opposite of, and antidote to the poison of, intimacy, blame, and coercion.

Acceptance of one's partner's behaviors that one finds unacceptable, in our view, is often not an explicit therapeutic goal. Often dislike or lack of acceptance of the other's behaviors, such as being too untidy, procrastination, or being too talkative in social situation, is a function of unexpressed hurt feelings, such as feeling resentful or feeling lonely, that are unrelated to the behaviors focused on. When these feelings are expressed and accepted by the partner, the disapproval of the other's behavior often fades and disappears and tolerance emerges.

Development of attitudes of tolerance and development of the ability to let go of attempts to control, however, are also an important set of attitudes and abilities to attempt to promote more directly in couples therapy. These attitudes, however, probably flow most from the creation of intimacy and from feelings of love towards and security with one's partner. These feelings are best evoked by the creation of strong attachment bonds characterized by emotional accessibility and responsiveness (Greenberg & Johnson, 1988).

Conclusion

Acceptance is a crucial component of a variety of change processes. Self-acceptance results in the acknowledgment of internal experience and the attainment of greater internal harmony. Acceptance by and of another is a crucial biological inter-human process which results in greater harmony between people, the creation of intimacy between them, and the provision of a healing environment.

References

Beisser, N. (1970). Paradoxical theory of change. In Fagan & Sheppard II (Eds.), *Gestalt therapy now*. New York: Harper

Butler, J.M. (1952). The interaction of client and therapist. *Journal of Abnormal and Social Psychology*, 47, 366-378.

Greenberg, L.S. (1984). A task-analysis of intrapersonal conflict resolution. In L. N. Rice & L. S. Greenberg (Eds.), *Patterns of change: Intensive analysis of psychotherapy process* (pp. 67-123). New York: Guilford Press.

Greenberg, L.S., & Johnson, S.M. (1988). *Emotionally focused therapy for couples*. New York: Guilford Press.

Greenberg, L.S., & Korman, L. (1993). Assimilating emotion into psychotherapy integration. *Journal of Psychotherapy* and Integration, 3, 249-266

Greenberg, L.S., Rice, L., & Elliott, R (1993). *Facilitating emotional change*. New York: Guilford Press.

Greenberg, L.S., & Safran, J.D. (1987). *Emotion in psychotherapy: Affect, cognition, and the process of change.* New York: Guilford Press.

Greenberg, L.S., & Safran, J.D. (1989). Emotion in psychotherapy. *American Psychologist, 44,* 19-29.

Harman, J.I. (1990). Unconditional confidence as a facilitative precondition. In G. Lietaer, J. Rombauts, & R. Van Balen (Eds.), *Client-centered and experiential psychotherapy in the nineties* (pp. 251-268). Leuven, Belgium: Leuven University Press.

Perls, F.S. (1973). *The Gestalt approach and eye witness to therapy.* Palo Alto, CA: Science and Behavior Books.

Perls, F.S. (1969). *Gestalt therapy verbatim.* Lafayette, CA: Real People.

Rogers, C.R. (1951). *Client-centered therapy.* Boston: Houghton-Mifflin.

Rogers, C.R. (1961). *On becoming a person.* Boston: Houghton-Mifflin.

Safran, J.D., & Greenberg, L.S. (Eds.) (1991). *Emotion, psychotherapy, and change.* New York: Guilford Press.

Stern, D. N. (1985). *The interpersonal world of the infant: A view from psychoanalysis and developmental psychology.* New York: Basic Books.

Discussion of Greenburg

Acceptance, Experience, and Choice

Robert F. Peterson
University of Nevada

Experiential and Humanistic approaches to clinical problems have played a primary role in keeping the concept of acceptance alive in the clinical literature. Greenburg's paper, "Experiential/Humanistic Approaches to Acceptance," continues this tradition. Greenburg points out that there is a continual, automatic process of internal experience which is not subject to conscious control. The central issue is whether the individual remains open to this experience and allows it to continue without judging, conceptualizing, or changing it in some way.

Internal experience may often be negative, painful or just plain uncomfortable. As a result there is substantial motivation to escape, avoid, or diminish it. Other than the classic masochist, there is little in the histories of most individuals which would lead them to tolerate bothersome inner states, particularly since the control of both external and internal events is a hallmark of human behavior. For this reason, non-resistance or acceptance may be difficult to learn.

Experience may be divided into two dimensions: experience of the self and experience of the other. Self acceptance involves the acknowledgement of one's own experience and is a goal of most psychotherapeutic approaches. With the therapist providing a permissive environment, the client is encouraged to be "real" and express accurately and frequently the internal events he or she is aware of. Particularly important are the conflicts between what the individual feels he or she "should" be experiencing, what he or she "wants" to experience or do, and what is actually happening. Some clients avoid accepting current experience believing that such an action will lock in negative emotions and they will be forced to have the similar experiences in the future. While that may be true in the short run, the paradoxical result is that by not attempting to change anything, change often begins to occur.

Clinical lore suggests that there may be a reciprocal process between the acceptance of the self and of others. The more one can tolerate his or her own internal stimuli, the more likely he or she will accept the behavior of others. At the same time, the more accepted one feels by another, the more one may be able to acknowledge and accept aspects of their own experience. This raises an important therapeutic question: If one goal of therapy is to produce the maximum amount of acceptance of both self and other, should therapy be directed toward the former or the latter? Although empirical data on this question are lacking, therapists may wish to consider

whether the problem is an externalizing disorder such as aggression or an internalizing disorder like depression, and focus the direction of treatment accordingly.

One level up from the acceptance of self and other is acceptance as context.
When an individual has developed acceptance as context, responding continues in
the usual way. However, the consequences of such responding are tolerated without
resistance or excessive emotion. While behavior continues to be goal directed,
acceptance as context produces less concern over the attainment of the goal. The
spirit of this approach is captured in a statement by Zen Master Suzuki (1970) who
said:

> Our effort... should be directed from achievement to non-achievement.
> Usually when you do something, you want to achieve something, you
> attach to some result. From achievement to non-achievement means to be
> rid of the unnecessary and bad results of effort. If you do something in the
> spirit of non-achievement there is a good quality in it. So just to do
> something without any particular effort is enough.

Suzuki appears to suggest that: 1) behavior may be more effective if one does not try
too hard to achieve a particular outcome and, 2) that it is better to accept or not
become emotionally attached the consequences of a response, whatever the outcome may be. Such a view however, does not mean to act without conscience or
compassion. In Zen and other Buddhist traditions, compassion toward both self and
other is one of the highest values and a distinguished state of personal development.

Gestalt clinical approaches and Eastern meditation methods both seek the same
outcome in terms of the mindfulness of sensations, thoughts, feelings, and other
internal states. In this regard it is noteworthy that Greenburg refers to Gestalt
Therapy as "Western Zen." Both approaches argue for the benefits an expanded
consciousness. Among Gestalt therapists, the saying goes: "Jesus saves but awareness
heals," (R. Price, personal communication, Nov. 29, 1976). What is it about
awareness that might encourage psychological or physical healing? Could increased
awareness amplify or optimize natural psychological and physical regulatory processes? The literature on meditation suggests that this is possible (Carrington, 1977).
A greater awareness of stimuli emanating from the sympathetic (involuntary)
nervous system may also have effects on parasympathetic (voluntary) events. For
example, an expanded awareness of both external and internal events could lead to
alterations in behavior that prevent other problems from occurring. Thus sensing
that one is fatigued before it grossly interferes with performance may prevent future
mistakes.

Greenburg points out that the experience of internal states provides both
information about events as well as a direction for behavior. Directionality is often
experienced as an "urge" to behave in a particular fashion. From a Gestalt viewpoint,
observation and awareness of "urges" leads to behaviors which are more likely to be
real, true, or natural, given the specific history and the person and the current
environmental stimuli which function to produce the "urge". Psychological problems arise when the individual inhibits responses and seldom acts in accordance with

urges or feelings. At the same time, other problems are likely to arise if the individual shows little restraint and acts whenever an urge is experienced.

The awareness of internal states also raises the issue of the evolutionary importance of emotion and other subjective experience, an issue which has not been widely discussed in behavioral circles. Information about external stimuli alone may not be adequate to make the best possible decision in a given situation. There is likely to be a behavioral and perhaps even a survival advantage by utilizing information from internal stimuli as well. Restricting the range of one's awareness may result in a decrease in the number of possible responses or choices to a given situation. This in turn may reduce the likelihood of responding in ways which maximize reinforcers or avoids important aversive events.

One might question whether there is a state of awareness which represents an increase over baseline levels but still falls short of acceptance. "Knowing" about something, for example, may not be the same as experiencing it. The Gestalt tradition suggests that knowing per se, is not sufficient to bring about clinical change. Experience is more likely to do so. It is also possible that an individual might "allow" certain sensations into awareness without necessarily "accepting" the implications of the information received. In this sense, the word acceptance suggests that additional cognitive functions may be involved, compared to simple experiencing.

A major issue concerns the development of acceptance. Clearly there is an increased ability to "accept" as one moves from child to adult. What are the factors which cause this change? Also, what accounts for the vast differences in acceptance between age mates? Research directed toward answering these questions has floundered, largely because of the lack of objective measures of acceptance. Greenburg's call for increased empirical rigor in developing such measures should be heeded by clinician and researcher alike.

Once learned, what circumstances lead to acceptance? Although one may "choose" to accept a given feeling or event, just how does such a choice come about? Gestalt Therapy offers at least one technique to develop choice. The technique involves encouraging individuals to thoroughly experience the polarities or para-doxical aspects of an experience. As a result, the issues on both sides of a possible choice become heightened. After awhile, one side becomes figure and the other ground. This awareness frequently leads to a preference. The word choice not only implies the selection of a course of action but the existence of alternatives as well. Research suggests that many organisms prefer circumstances which contain more than one way of obtaining reinforcement when compared to a single method. (Voss & Homie, 1970; Catania, 1980). Knowledge of additional "choices" may contribute to an organisms survival.

Greenburg's paper also raises issues concerning the meaning of "choice", and conflicts with a deterministic view of behavior. Humans (including the most devout behaviorists) act as if they have choices even when embracing a deterministic view of the causes of behavior. If behavior is the result of a past history of reinforcement and current environmental stimuli, filtered through a particular physiological and constitutional matrix, how can one "choose" to do anything? The issue is sufficiently complex that it cannot be thoroughly addressed here. However, it may be argued that the feeling of being able to choose, while real, experientially, is actually an illusion. The variables which determine the choice are already in operation but the individual making the choice is simply not aware of them. Nevertheless, it is possible to learn to "choose" to accept more of one's experience. This acceptance may allow additional information into awareness and as a result permit other variables to exert causal influences which change or optimize responding.

References

Carrington, Patricia. (1977). *Freedom in meditation*. Garden City, N.Y: Anchor Press.

Catania, A. C., & Sagvolden, T. (1980). Preference for free choice over forced choice in pigeons. *Journal of the Experimental Analysis of Behavior, 34,* 77-86.

Suzuki, Shunryu (1970). *Zen mind, beginner's mind.* New York: Weatherhill.

Voss, S. C. & Homie, M. J. (1970). Choice as value. *Psychological Reports, 26,* 912-914.

Chapter 4

Acceptance and Change: The Central Dialectic in Psychotherapy

Marsha M. Linehan
University of Washington

The purpose of this paper is to describe a treatment that has as its core idea the balance of acceptance and change in the treatment of mental disorder. The treatment was named dialectical behavior therapy (DBT) to highlight the importance of balance and synthesis of polarities in psychotherapy. The most important polarity at every level of therapy is that between the need for both acceptance and change. This is the one that led originally to a focus on dialectics as a philosophical base for the treatment. The treatment was originally developed for people who came into therapy because they wanted to die. It subsequently evolved into a treatment for individuals with histories of repeated parasuicidal behavior (Linehan, 1984) and for those meeting criteria for borderline personality disorder (Linehan, 1987; 1993a; 1993b). Currently, it is being applied in a number of different areas, including treatment of dissociative disorders (Barley et al. 1993), drug abuse (Linehan, 1993c; in press), and inpatient psychiatric care (Swenson, 1992). Controlled treatment studies to date, however, have been conducted only by our University of Washington treatment group and by Barley and his associates. Thus, the extrapolation of the treatment to other disorders, while currently under investigation, is speculative.

The necessity of both therapeutic acceptance of the client and of helping the client accept him or herself is recognized by all therapy approaches. Historically, however, some therapeutic approaches have emphasized one side of the dialectic over the other. For example, both client-centered therapy (Rogers, 1965) and psychoanalytic treatments based on Kohutian self psychology (Kohut, 1977) have traditionally focused most heavily on therapeutic acceptance of the client as the proper stance of the therapist. In contrast, the historical linkage of behavior therapy with learning theory (which can be defined as change brought about by experience) has led to a strong emphasis in behavior therapy on the therapist as a change agent (Kazdin, 1977). Psychoanalytic treatments based on the theories of Kernberg share a similar emphasis on targeting change, although from quite a different theoretical base (Kernberg et al., 1989). Although even the most extreme acceptance or change based treatment must recognize the necessity of both acceptance and change within therapy, the relative emphasis on describing therapy in terms of both, varies across therapeutic schools. In the last few years, there has been a growing recognition among behavior therapists of the necessity of redressing the imbalance of change focused interventions over acceptance focused interventions (Goldfried & Davison, 1994). The presence of so many chapters by behavior therapists in this volume highlights this emerging interest.

The transformation of a traditional behavioral therapy intended to treat suicidal and borderline clients into dialectical behavior therapy was a result of pilot studies in the 1970s, applying a change focused treatment to these severely dysfunctional, and often traumatized, individuals only to have it repeatedly fail to engage clients in the treatment process itself. Over time a treatment that focuses essentially on the balance of acceptance and change was developed. This acceptance-change balance occurs in a number of areas within DBT. Two of these areas will be discussed in this chapter. The first has to do with the balance of acceptance and change as targets or goals of treatment. The second area is in the therapeutic strategies used by the therapist, i.e. the behaviors engaged in by the therapist. In this sense, the balance of acceptance and change is a principal treatment strategy, blending specific change strategies and acceptance strategies into a coherent therapeutic whole. Acceptance, at least when acceptance is viewed as an action rather than a state of the individual, cannot be discussed without simultaneously discussing change. However, because this book is about acceptance, and because the focus on change has, until very recently, been the topic of most therapy discussion, I will discuss here what I mean by acceptance and how it is interwoven into psychotherapy. I have discussed the process and strategies of change extensively elsewhere (Linehan, 1993).

Balancing Acceptance and Change as a Therapeutic Goal

In behavioral terms, treatment targets in most psychotherapy regimes can be conceptualized as the reduction of disordered or dysfunctional behavioral and emotional response patterns, and the increase of functional or skillful patterns. Exactly what these targets are in a particular case is usually an outcome of some combination of the theoretical persuasion of the therapist, the behavioral disorder(s) of the client, individual characteristics of the client, and the context of the disordered behavior. Change occurs by both accepting the presence of disorder in the current moment and by working actively to reduce it. In behaviorally based treatments, the approach is one of shaping; a behavioral concept very similar to that of harm reduction, an approach advocated most strongly by treatment researchers within the substance abuse field (Parry, 1989; Marlatt & Tapert, 1993). The relationship of harm reduction to acceptance is discussed extensively by Marlatt in this volume, and I will not discuss it further here.

A major outcome goal of psychotherapy with the borderline individual and those with other serious disorders is the reduction of dysfunctional behavioral patterns, such as chronic suicidality and self-destructive impulsivity, interpersonal patterns that contribute to interpersonal chaos and interference in the therapeutic relationship, high emotional reactivity and dysregulation, including problems with severe anxiety, depression, and anger, dysfunctional cognitive patterns, such as paranoia and dissociative episodes, and instability of a sense of identity (e.g., Kernberg et al., 1989). However, the reduction of dysfunctional response patterns, especially when they occur in response to stressful events, requires that the individual have a range of more functional or effective behaviors in his or her behavioral repertoire. Acquisition, strengthening, and generalization of functional response capabilities must be explicitly or implicitly addressed. Biological therapies remediate skills deficits (in their most general meaning) by direct modification of biological processes thought to limit capability for improved functioning. Psychological therapies rely on the therapeutic relationship and learning principles. In both cases, however, the practitioner needs to be clear on just what capacities are most important to improve. Capabilities or skillful behaviors can, of course, take many forms and attention to them can be either implicit or explicit in therapy.

Historically, in behavior therapy, attention to behavioral targets and skills has usually been explicit rather than implicit. The value of an explicit over an implicit approach, however, can be questioned (Rosenfarb, Hayes & Linehan, 1989). More recent behavioral approaches based on radical behaviorism (Hayes, 1987; Kohlenberg & Tsai, 1991) are based on implicit skill enhancement strategies, where although new behavioral skills are shaped, verbal instructions and description and categorization of skills to be acquired and practiced are limited. In contrast, in skills training approaches to treatment, specific sets of skills are identified to the client, instructions for each are given, and formal practice is implemented in sessions and assigned between sessions. In DBT, as well as other behavioral treatments such as relapse prevention (Marlatt & Gordon, 1985), both explicit and implicit capability enhancement are balanced within the therapy. In DBT, capability enhancement is usually implicit within individual psychotherapy and explicit in the formal skills training portion of the treatment, conducted either individually or in groups.

A broad set of skills can be identified that may be relevant to individuals who are suicidal or whose behavioral patterns are impulsive, are out of control, and/or fit the profile of BPD. In DBT, five classes of behavioral skills are identified. These skills can, in turn, be divided into those most closely related to change skills and those that most closely represent acceptance skills. Targeting skills for changing one's self is, of course, the hallmark of self-control therapies (Kanfer & Goldstein, 1991). A review of any behavior therapy textbook (e.g., Craighead, Craighead, Kazdin, & Mahoney, 1993) suggests that a wide variety of change skills have been promoted in various behavior therapy programs. In DBT, three sets of change skills receive emphasis: general self-management skills (based on application of learning principles), interpersonal effectiveness skills, and emotion regulation skills. Each of these sets of skills is drawn primarily from the very wide body of work in behavior therapy on both interpersonal and assertion skills, as well as the many behavioral and cognitive programs for modifying one's own behavioral and emotional reactions.

Acceptance of others and of self, as they are in the moment, is, of course, an important part of any self-management, interpersonal effectiveness or emotion regulation program. At a minimum, the realities of one's own functioning and of the context within which it occurs, as well as the limits inherent in each, must be acknowledged and addressed. Avoidance, denial, or refusal to acknowledge or accept these events precludes effective intervention. Beneficial change may occur inadvertently, but planned changes will be difficult to achieve. Thus, in all treatments targeting behavioral change skills there will of necessity be some emphasis on teaching acceptance. Because the basic intent of using self-management, interpersonal and emotion regulation skills is to effect some sort of change, the "acceptance so as to change" skills taught in this context are viewed primarily as themselves change strategies. Thus, I will not discuss them further here.

The acceptance skills can also be further divided. In our current DBT program two sets are emphasized, distress tolerance and radical acceptance skills, and mindfulness skills. In DBT these skills are implicitly, and sometimes explicitly, targeted in every mode of therapy (e.g., individual psychotherapy, group skills training, telephone coaching, milieu treatment) and are also explicitly taught in separate individual skills training modules. Because, as I noted, acceptance is so important for change, these skills are also interwoven into all other skills training. The formal acceptance skills taught in DBT are described below.

Acceptance Skills

Mindfulness

The increasing emphasis on mindfulness and mindfulness practices in Western psychotherapies (e.g., Marlatt, Chapter ; Kabat-Zinn, 1990) parallels the increasing practice of Eastern meditation within Western societies as a whole. An emphasis on mindfulness is central in Eastern philosophical and theological thought and meditation practice. Thich Nhat Hanh (1975) quotes from a third century translation of the Sutra of Mindfulness: "When walking, the practitioner must be conscious that he is walking. When sitting, the practitioner must be conscious that he is sitting. When lying down, the practitioner must be conscious that he is lying down.... No matter what position one's body is in, the practitioner must be conscious of that position. Practicing thus, the practitioner lives in direct and constant mindfulness of the body . . ." (p. 7). He goes on to add that mindfulness also requires consciousness of each breath, each movement, every thought and feeling, everything which has any relation to ourselves" (p. 8). From a more Western perspective, Langer (1992) has defined it as "a state of conscious awareness in which the individual is implicitly aware of the context and content of information . . . a state of openness to novelty in which the individual actively constructs categories and distinctions" (p. 289). This is "in contrast . . . [to] a state of mind characterized by an overreliance on categories and distinctions drawn in the past and in which the individual is context-dependent and, as such, is oblivious to novel (or simply alternative) aspects of the situation" (p. 289). Mindfulness, in her view, is in contrast to habit, rigid invariance, overlearning, and automatic (vs. controlled) processing.

The mindfulness skills in DBT are drawn primarily from Zen psychology and practice but are compatible also with Western definitions and practice. The Zen meditation practices that make up the mindfulness skills described here are translated from formal Zen meditation practice (zazen) instead of applied directly.

Although strict mindfulness meditation practice may be appropriate for individuals with some disorders (Kabat-Zinn, Lipworth, & Burney, 1985), many seriously disturbed individuals simply do not have the motivation and/or the capability to meditate in this manner. This difficulty is acknowledged by Zen masters (Kapleau, 1980) and is the source of the old Zen saying that Zen practice is for the strong of mind and strong of body (Reick, Jo-un An, personal communication, 1992). The mindfulness skills I discuss here were developed for these clients.

Clients are first presented with the concepts of "emotion mind," "reasonable (or rational) mind," and "wise mind." Emotion mind and reasonable mind are defined as states of being where thoughts, actions, and feelings are under the primary influence of concurrent high emotional arousal (emotion mind) or of non-aroused, highly intellectual and/or rational though (reasonable mind). Wise mind is a functioning which reflects a synthesis of contextual influence with balanced awareness of both events that are currently happening as well as of emotional responses to these events. In wise mind, realistic appraisals and constructions of events (both current and past) and logical inferences and thought as well as immediate emotional responses enter jointly in the pathway of influencing subsequent responses. Thus, right at the beginning clients are told that an important goal of therapy is to accept both their emotions as well as their (apparently contradictory) rational, cool, or "non-emotional" cognitive processes. Mindfulness skills are presented as the vehicles for balancing emotion mind and reasonable mind to achieve wise mind. "Going into wise mind" is presented as the conscious effort to take in the entire context that is relevant to a particular problem or moment as well as to become aware of one's immediate and primary response to that context. In contrast to some approaches to treatment which put very high value on rational thought, intuitive thought and responses are presented as equally valuable and trustworthy.

The formal mindfulness skills practice consists of six quite specific skills: 1) observing, 2) describing, 3) participating spontaneously, 4) being nonjudgmental, 5) being mindful or focusing attention completely and only on one thing at a time, and 6) focusing on what is effective in a given situation. These mindfulness skills are inherently integrated into most aspects of the other modules. For example, during the two modules focusing on change (interpersonal effectiveness and emotion regulation skills) clients must practice observing and describing interpersonal situations and single emotions, respectively.

The goal of mindfulness is to develop a life-style of participating with awareness. Participating without awareness, it is assumed, is a characteristic of impulsive and mood dependent behaviors. Self-conscious observing and describing of one's own behavior is usually only necessary when a new behavior is being learned or change is necessary. For example, beginning drivers pay close attention to the location of their hands and feet and might mentally check off or rehearse verbally aloud what they are doing, what other cars are doing, and what instructions they should follow as they drive. As skill improves, however, such observing and describing drop out.

But, if a habitual mistake is made after learning to drive, the driver may have to revert back to observing and describing until a new pattern has been learned.

Part of mindfulness is learning to observe internal and external events without necessarily trying to terminate them when painful or prolong them when pleasant. Rather than leaving the situation or trying to inhibit the emotion, the individual attends to experience no matter how distressing that attention may be. This focus on "experiencing the moment" is based both on Eastern psychological approaches to reducing suffering as well as on Western theories of non-reinforced exposure as a method of extinguishing automatic avoidance and fear responses.

A second mindfulness skill is that of verbally describing events and personal responses. Here, the focus is on learning how to differentiate literal events from thoughts and feeling about those events. Describing requires one to be able to "step back" from events, so to speak, and our emphasis on describing is very similar to the treatment strategies suggested by Steve Hayes in his Acceptance and Commitment Therapy (see "Comprehensive Distancing," Hayes, 1987).

Participating

Participating, in the context of mindfulness skills, is entering completely into the activities of the current moment, without separating one's self from ongoing events and interactions. A good example of mindful participating is the skillful athlete who responds flexibly but smoothly to the demands of the task with alertness and awareness but not with self-consciousness. Participating in this sense of the term requires acceptance of the moment; resistance is the antithesis of participating.

As taught in DBT, a nonjudgmental stance (the fourth mindfulness skill) requires the individual to take a non-evaluative approach, judging something as neither good nor bad. It does not mean going from a negative judgment to a positive judgment. The position here is not that clients should be more balanced in their judgments but rather that judging should, in most instances, be dropped all together. An old Zen saying is that "Every day is a good day." The meaning, here, would be the same as saying "Every day is a bad day." This point may be subtle but it is, nonetheless, a very important one. The idea is that if one can be worthwhile, one can always, in the next moment, become worthless. "Just being" avoids either possibility. From a nonjudgmental stance, a focus on the consequences of behavior and events replaces evaluations of good and of bad. A nonjudgmental approach observes painful or destructive events and consequences of events, and might suggest changing behavior or events, but would not necessarily add a label of bad to the behavior and events.

Mindfulness as a whole has to do with the quality of awareness that one brings to activities. A fifth mindfulness skill is "doing one thing at a time," or focusing the mind and awareness in the current moment's activity rather than splitting attention between several activities or between a current activity and thinking about something else. Such one-mindfulness requires control of attention. Like participation described above, one-mindfulness requires for its practice acceptance of the moment since a focus on change, i.e., on a different but changed moment, of necessity interferes with staying in the current moment. Often clients in therapy are distracted by thoughts and images of the past, worries about the future, ruminative thoughts about troubles, or current negative moods. They are sometimes unable to put their troubles away and focus attention on the task at hand. The desire to get out of the current moment or to repair the past is so great that staying in the present is nearly impossible. The focus of one-mindfulness practice is to teach the client how to focus attention on one task or activity at a time, engaging in it with alertness, awareness, and wakefulness.

The final mindfulness skill is labeled being effective or "doing what works." The focus on effectiveness within mindfulness is taken from the Zen practice of "using skillful means" and is directed at balancing the tendency to focus on what is "right" with a corresponding emphasis on doing what is needed to be effective in a particular situation. A central issue for many clients is whether they can indeed trust their own perceptions, judgments, and decisions; can they expect their own actions to be correct or "right." Taken to an extreme, an emphasis on principle over outcome can lead to disappointment and alienation of others. Clients often find it much easier to give up being right for being effective when it is viewed as a skillful response rather than as a giving up or giving in.

Distress Tolerance and Radical Acceptance

Representing a natural progression from mindfulness skills, distress tolerance skills represent the ability to experience and observe one's thoughts, emotions and behaviors without evaluation and without attempting to change or control them. Distress tolerance skills focus on both tolerating and radically accepting reality just as it is in the moment.

The focus in most standard behavior and cognitive therapies on ameliorating distressing emotions and events is balanced by a corresponding emphasis on learning to bear pain skillfully. The automatic inhibition and/or avoidance of painful emotions, situations, thoughts, etc., is viewed as an important component in psychological dysfunction and the prolongation of the very pain one is seeking to avoid. "The first truth . . . is that life is suffering. Avoidance of suffering leads to worse suffering.... we drink alcohol excessively to avoid that pain, thus causing more pain" (Aitken, 1982, p. 49). Tolerating distress does not imply "giving up" or necessarily approving of a situation, but it allows one to cope with pain in the moment to reduce long-term suffering. Indeed, the premise is that tolerance and acceptance of a situation as it is in the moment are prerequisites of any coherent and effective change strategy. Distress tolerance skills are aimed at tolerating distress - rather than impulsively acting to remove the pain without thought of whether the act will lead to more distress in the long run. Four sets of distress tolerance are taught: 1) distraction skills which focus on occupying the mind or the body with other sensations, perceptions, thoughts, activities, etc., 2) self-soothing skills which focus on comforting and encouraging one's self until the painful event is lessened or over, 3) "improving the moment" which includes imaginal and cognitive-verbal strategies for changing the "meaning" of an event until the stress is relieved, and 4) pros and

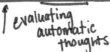

evaluating
automatic
thoughts

cons which require one to review the pros of tolerating versus the cons of not tolerating. The skills are taught as "crisis survival skills" and the task is presented much like the task of the individual in prison: if you have to stay in prison for 20 years, you might as well find a way to tolerate it while you are there rather than only fight to get out. *(which will likely lead to a longer stay)*

Radical acceptance has a number of characteristics. Most importantly, it is the fully open experience of what is just as it is. By fully open, I mean without constrictions, and without distorting, without judgment, without evaluating, without trying to keep it, and without trying to get rid of it. What's very important here is this notion of without adding judgment of good and bad. So, accepting is not necessarily evaluating positively. And, in fact, accepting is one thing and evaluating is another. Nor is acceptance necessarily the same as compassion or love. Another way of thinking about it is that radical acceptance is radical truth. In other words, acceptance is experiencing something without the haze of what one wants it to be and what one doesn't want it to be. Or, another way to think about it is that radical acceptance is an unrivaled entering into reality just as it is at this moment. "This one moment" is the crucial part of the statement. It is important to remember here that accepting "at this moment" says nothing about what's happening in the next. Acceptance "in this moment" is not necessarily saying anything about the next moment. So, you can radically accept reality in this moment and radically change or let it go completely in the next moment.

Radical acceptance is an act of the total person that's allowing of "this moment" or "this reality" in this moment. It is without discrimination. In other words, one doesn't go around choosing what to accept and what to reject or change. It's not a question about whether one is going to accept this or not accept it as if there are some things one should accept and other things one shouldn't. The notion of radical acceptance is that of "total allowance now." That means that radical acceptance is not simply a cognitive stance or cognitive activity; it is a total act. It is jumping off a cliff. You must keep jumping over and over because you can only accept "in this one moment." Therefore, you have to keep actively accepting, over and over again in every moment. If radical acceptance is jumping off a cliff into the deep abyss, then there is always a tree stump coming out of the cliff just below the top and the minute you fall past you reach out and cling onto that stump. And then you're on another cliff's edge, asking perhaps, "How did this happen?" Then, you jump off the cliff again. Radical acceptance is the constant jumping off, jumping off, jumping off and jumping off, yet again. Radical acceptance is also the nonjudgmental acceptance of the repeated grabbing onto the tree stump.

In some sense, people usually don't understand radical acceptance until they have some sort of experience where, possibly out of complete desperation, they simply "get it." People who have experienced the death of a loved one often speak of not being able to "accept" the death. In many senses, grieving is the process of "radically accepting" the reality that the person has died. Being stuck with a near fatal or fatal illness or with incurable pain, failure, or loss may also be the occasion for a person's first experience of "radical acceptance" in its most pure or experiencable form.

II. Balancing Acceptance and Change as Therapeutic Strategy

A core tension in the conduct and process of psychotherapy is that between the acceptance and change strategies used by the therapist. An emphasis on client change unbalanced by acceptance can lead, paradoxically, to refusal or inability to change. Focusing solely on client change - of motivation, capability or skill level, or of biological function - is very often experienced as invalidating by the client and precipitates resistance, rigidity, stagnation and noncompliance, and at times results in client withdrawal and early dropout from treatment. The emergence of paradoxical therapies is based on this premise. In a review of 29 outcome studies using paradoxical techniques, Hampton and Hulgus (1993) conclude that prescription of the symptom (rather than instructions to change the symptomatic behavior) tended to show the greatest durability of therapeutic effects. Research on reactance theory as related to psychotherapy (e.g., Worchel & Shackelford, 1991) suggests that such a reaction will be most likely in chronically disturbed individuals who experience themselves as threatened and out of control.

An emphasis on acceptance of the client, unbalanced by a focus on change, can also, paradoxically, lead to stagnation combined with hopelessness and demoralization. Unconditional acceptance and validation of client behaviors may prove at times equally problematic and can also invalidate. If the therapist only urges the client to accept and self-validate, it can appear that the therapist does not regard the client's problems seriously. Pure acceptance based therapies can appear to discount the desperation of the seriously disturbed individual since they offer little hope of change. The client's personal experience of the current state of affairs as unacceptable and unendurable is thereby invalidated. Exhortations to accept one's current situation offer little solace to the individual who experiences life as painfully unendurable. It is not inconceivable that suicidal behavior in some individuals at some times functions to "wake up" the environment, including the therapist, and get the environment to take the client's problems more seriously. "Taking more seriously" here would include such things as offering more nurturance, removing the client from stressful environments (e.g., by hospitalizing), or intervening to get more resources for the client or change others' reactions to the client (e.g., by more intensive case management or by talking to the client's significant others). Thus, balancing acceptance strategies with effective change strategies is, paradoxically, a necessary acceptance strategy.

Some support for the value of the dialectical aspect of DBT, i.e., the balance by the therapist of acceptance and change strategies within individual sessions, was found in a study by Shearin (Shearin & Linehan, 1993). Over 7 months of DBT treatment, weekly client diary cards of suicidal behaviors were collected from 4 clients along with weekly ratings of the therapeutic relationship using a short form of Benjamin's Structural Analysis of Social Behavior (SASB; Benjamin, 1974; 1988). The dialectical hypothesis, which was supported, was that suicidal behaviors would decrease in the week following sessions where the therapist was rated as simultaneously controlling, nurturing (change focused), and giving autonomy (acceptance focused). Further supporting the hypothesis, neither pure therapeutic acceptance nor pure change predicted subsequent suicidal behavior.

Beutler (Beutler, 1979; Beutler & Clarkin, 1990) has written about the necessity of providing prescriptive treatments to clients based on attention to various stable client characteristics. That is, treatment strategies are prescribed according to client characteristics measured at the beginning of therapy or at various points in the course of therapy. In contrast, similar to the emphasis in functional analytic psychotherapy (Kohlenberg & Tsai, 1991), DBT emphasizes attention to within session variability in client behavior patterns as the critical factor that needs attention. With many client populations, particularly the severely distressed clients, treatment strategies must be modified continuously within sessions as client behavior changes moment to moment. Specifically, the relative emphasis on acceptance based strategies versus those that are overtly intended to produce change, must be balanced within sessions in accord with the clients within session, changing behavior.

Although it is somewhat arbitrary, all treatment strategies in DBT are categorized as representing mostly strategic efforts to effect change or as representing mostly acceptance of reality as it is. The change strategies are drawn directly from usual behavior therapy techniques and procedures and include a broad list of strategies, including problem solving strategies such as behavioral analysis, solution generation and analyses, commitment strategies, use of contingencies, exposure techniques, cognitive modification, and, as noted above, formal and informal skills training procedures. With only a few exceptions, these strategies are pulled from current literature on behavioral treatments and I expect they will change as treatment technology improves. Contrasting with and balancing the "change technologies" are strategies which more fully encompass acceptance of the client, of the therapy and therapist, and of the contextual system in which each resides. As a whole, these strategies are called validating strategies. The expectation is that validation by the therapist - of both the client and the therapeutic relationship, permeates all change efforts. Similar to the change strategies, the validation strategies were also borrowed from a diverse set of sources, including both traditional Western psychotherapies and Eastern teaching practices common in Zen practice.

Validation

Elsewhere I have defined validation within psychotherapy as the following: The therapist communicates to the client that her responses make sense and are understandable within her current life context or situation. The therapist actively accepts the client and communicates this acceptance to the client. The therapist takes the client's responses seriously and does not discount or trivialize them. Validation strategies require the therapist to search for, recognize, and reflect to the client the validity inherent in her responses to events. (Linehan, 1993a, pp. 222-223).

The central idea of validation is to communicate to the individual that his or h behavior thoughts, feelings, and actions are "acceptable" as they are within the context that they occur. Valid action, beliefs, etc., do not need to be changed. Thus, validation balances change strategies. There are five levels of validation, each more completely accepting than the level before and each depending on the prior levels. The levels are: 1) active observing and listening without bias to the client's experience, 2) reflecting this experience back to the client, 3) verbalizing unverbalized experiences, emotions, thoughts and assumptions (i.e., "reading the client's mind," 4) active searching for and reflecting back to the client the validity of that experience or action in terms of past conditions, and 5) active searching for and reflecting back to the client the validity of that experience or action in terms of present conditions. The first three steps of validation are common to all psychotherapies, consisting of eliciting and accurately reflecting the client's feelings, thoughts and assumptions and providing accurate feedback about the client's patterns of behavior. This somewhat unstructured "making sense" of response patterns is an essential part of validation.

The fourth and fifth levels differentiate validation from ordinary (but also essential) reflection and empathic responding. It is the fifth level, however, that is essential to and defining of validation in its fullest sense. To illustrate the difference between levels four and five, imagine a new client in therapy who indicates that she does not trust the therapist. Compare a level four validation, "It makes sense that you do not trust me yet given the number of times you have been hurt by people you trusted," to a level five validation, "It makes sense that you do not trust me yet given that you have just met me and how could you know yet whether I am trustworthy or not." The philosophy of level five validation reflects an emphasis on the current moment, on searching for truth and on acknowledging that truth and the capability of discovering it are inherent within each person. In level five validation the therapist looks for that part of the client's response that is valid and reflects that validity or understandability. The therapist is not blinded by the dysfunctionality of the response, but finds the current contextual stimuli that support the client's behavior. When validating, the therapist communicates in a non-ambiguous way that the client's current and past behavior, thoughts or emotions make sense and are understandable within the context in which they occur. Suggesting that current behavior makes sense only in terms of previous events (but not in terms of current events) is not validating.

A paradox of validation is that as long as the therapist is mired in either validation or invalidation, the artificiality of the dichotomy is obscured. Behavior is neither valid nor invalid, neither good nor bad. Responses simply are. They arise within a context of causes and conditions that are both past and immediate, and that are both internal and external to the person. In turn, responses have consequences, which may either be desired or not. Thus, the therapist must adopt the nonjudgmental stance taught to clients. Bolling (unpublished manuscript, 1994) has labeled this level of acceptance as "getting rid of the construct of good and evil" (p. 5) and compares it to two other forms of acceptance. The first is acceptance, labeled

'e" by Bolling, connoting passivity, a stoical enduring of adverse
mplaint, and paying no heed to the actual consequences of
he second type of acceptance is that of being welcomed to a
......unty, or of "being accepted" by others. As Bolling notes, however, this second
form of acceptance usually also means that one meets the standards of the
community in behaviors relevant to the community. Bolling goes on to make a
compelling argument that both of these latter two forms of acceptance -- acceptance
as tolerance and acceptance as being welcomed, are forms of control and, thus, stand
in contrast to the radical acceptance that defines validation in DBT.

Radical validation requires that the therapist also maintain the stance of radical
acceptance of the reality of the therapeutic relationship and of themselves as
therapists who are fallible and limited in the ability to ameliorate the pain that many
clients experience. With the suicidal client, in particular, the therapist must radically
accept the possibility of suicide, i.e., that the therapy may simply not be effective
enough. The failure to accept this possibility is, in my opinion, a major factor in the
effectiveness of suicidal behavior at eliciting reinforcement from the therapeutic
community. Over and over one hears of treatment actions based more on a fear of
immediate suicidal behavior than a treatment plan designed to reduce the probability of suicidal behaviors over the long run.

(2) Environmental Intervention

Although case management strategies are often thought of as occurring outside
of the therapeutic interactions, DBT does include a set of strategies which address
the traditional concerns of case management. The bias in DBT is towards teaching
clients how to effectively interact with their environment, i.e., to change clients'
behaviors so that they can skillfully manage their own problems in the everyday
world. This approach (the consultant strategy) of teaching, coaching, encouraging,
supporting and generally refusing to manage the client's professional and/or
interpersonal network, is the core case management change strategy and is used
whenever possible. There are times, however, when intervention by the therapist is
needed. In general, the environmental intervention strategy is used over the
consultant strategy when substantial harm may befall the client if the therapist does
not intervene. The general rule for environmental intervention is that when clients
lack abilities which they need to learn, are impossible to obtain, or are not reasonable
or necessary, the therapist intervenes.

At first glance environmental intervention appears to be a change strategy since
the therapist is actively intervening in the life of the client. However, it is just the
reverse; environmental intervention is when the therapist accepts clients just as they
are in the moment and say, in essence, that in this one instance "rather than attempt
to change you and your behavior, we will change the environment." In environmental intervention, harm reduction is focused on aspects of the environment rather
than aspects of the client. The need for awareness and radical acceptance by the
therapist of both the client as he or she is in the moment and his or her current
environment is essential. Such awareness requires that the therapist has already

performed a comprehensive behavioral analysis. Because such analyses are done for the sake of change, they are included in the change strategies in DBT. It is this balance, between acceptance and change and the ever changing nature of each strategy depending on use and of point of view, that defines dialectical behavior therapy.

References

Aitken, R. (1982). *Taking the path of zen*. San Francisco: North Point Press.

Barley, W. D., Buie, S. E., Peterson, E. W., Hollingsworth, A. S., Griva, M., Hickerson, S. C., Lawson, J. E., & Bailey, B. J. (1993). The development of an inpatient cognitive-behavioral treatment program for borderline personality disorder. *Journal of Personality Disorders, 7*(3), 232-240.

Benjamin, L. S. (1974). Structural analysis of social behavior. *Psychological Review, 81*, 392-425.

Beutler, L. E. (1979). Toward specific psychological therapies for specific conditions. *Journal of Consulting and Clinical Psychology, 47*, 882-897.

Beutler, L. E., & Clarkin, J. (1990). *Differential treatment selection: Toward targeted therapeutic interventions*. New York: Brunner/Mazel.

Borkovec, T. D., & Inz, J. (1990). The nature of worry in generalized anxiety disorder: A predominance of thought activity. *Behavior Research and Therapy, 28*, 153-158.

Craighead, L., Craighead, W., Kazdin, A. E., & Mahoney, M. J. (Eds.) (1993). *Cognitive and behavioral interventions: An empirical approach to mental health problems*. New York: Allyn.

Goldfried, M. R., & Davison, G. C. (1994). *Clinical behavior therapy*. New York: Wiley.

Hampton, B. R., & Hulgus, Y. F. (1993). The efficacy of paradoxical strategies: A quantitative review of the research. *Psychotherapy in Private Practice, 12*(2), 5371.

Hanh, Thich Nhat (1975). *The miracle of mindfulness*. Boston: Beacon Press.

Hayes, S. C. (1987). A contextual approach to therapeutic change. In N. S. Jacobson (Ed.), *Psychotherapists in clinical practice: Cognitive and behavioral perspectives* (pp. 326-378). New York: Guilford Press.

Kabat-Zinn, J. (1990). *Full catastrophe living*. New York: Delacorte.

Kabat-Zinn, J., Lipworth, L., & Burney, R. (1985). The clinical use of mindfulness medication for the self-regulation of chronic pain. *Journal of Behavioral Medicine, 8*(2), 163-190.

Kanfer, F. H., & Goldstein, A. P. (1991). *Helping people change: A textbook of methods* (4th Ed.). New York: Pergamon.

Kapleau, P. (1980). *Zen: Dawn in the West*. New York: Anchor Press.

Kazdin, A. E. (1978). *History of behavior modification: Experimental foundations of contemporary research*. Baltimore: University Park Press.

Kernberg, O. F., Selzer, M. A., Koenigsberg, H. W., Carr, A. C., & Appelbaum, A. H. (1989). *Psychodynamic psychotherapy of borderline patients*. New York: Basic Books.

Kohlenberg, R. J., & Tsai, M. (1991). *Functional analytic psychotherapy: Creating intense and curative therapeutic relationships.* Plenum.

Kohut, H. (1977). *The restoration of the self.* New York: International Universities Press.

Langer, E. J. (1992). Matters of mind: Mindfulness/mindlessness in perspective. *Consciousness and Cognition: An International Journal, 1*(4), 289-305.

Linehan, M. M. (1984). *Dialectical behavior therapy: A treatment manual.* University of Washington, Seattle, WA.

Linehan, M. M. (1987). Dialectical behavior therapy for borderline personality disorder: Theory and method. *Bulletin of the Menninger Clinic, 51*, 261-276.

Linehan, M. M. (1993a). Cognitive behavioral therapy of borderline personality disorder. New York: Guilford Press.

Linehan, M. M. (1993b). Skills training manual for treating borderline personality disorder. New York: Guilford Press.

Linehan, M. M. (1993c). Dialectical behavior therapy for treatment of borderline personality disorder: Implications for the treatment of drug abuse. In L. Onken, J. Blaine & J. Boren (Eds.), *NIDA research monograph series: Behavioral treatments for drug abuse and dependence* (pp. 201-215).

Linehan, M. M. (in press). *Combining pharmacotherapy with psychotherapy for substance abusers with borderline personality disorder: Strategies for enhancing compliance.* NIDA monograph.

Linehan, M. M., & Kehrer, C. A. (1993). Borderline personality disorder. In D. H. Barlow (Ed.), *Clinical handbook of psychological disorders* (pp. 396-441). New York: Guilford Press.

Marlatt, G. L., & Gordon, J. R. (1985). *Relapse prevention: Maintenance strategies in the treatment of addictive behaviors.* New York: Guilford Press.

Marlatt, G. A., & Tapert, S. F. (1993). Harm reduction: Reducing the risks of addictive behaviors. In J. S. Baer, G. A. Marlatt & R. J. McMahon (Eds.), *Addictive behaviors across the life span* (pp. 243-273). Newbury Park, CA: Sage Publications.

Parry, A. (1989). Harm reduction [Interview]. *Drug Policy Letter, 1*(4), 13.

Rogers, C. R. (1965). *Client-centered therapy: Its current practice, implications, and theory.* Boston: Houghton Mifflin.

Rosenfarb, I. S., Hayes, S. C., & Linehan, M. M. (1989). Instructions and experiential feedback in the treatment of social skills deficits in adults. *Psychotherapy, 26*, 242-251.

Shearin, E. N., & Linehan, M. M. (1992). Patient-therapist ratings and relationship to progress in dialectical behavior therapy for borderline personality disorder. *Behavior Therapy, 23*, 730-741.

Swenson, C. (1992). Supportive elements of inpatient treatment with borderline patients. In L. H. Rockland (Ed.), *Supportive elements of inpatient treatment with borderline patients.* Guilford.

Worschel, S., & Shackelford, S. L. (1991) Groups under stress: The influence of group structure and environment on process and performance. *Personality and Social Psychology Bulletin, 17*, 640-647

Discussion of Linehan

The Experiential
Acquisition of Acceptance:
Clinical Supervision as a Laboratory

Barbara S. Kohlenberg
Reno Veterans Administration Medical Center

Marsha Linehan's discussion of the use of acceptance with severely disturbed clinical populations is noteworthy for several reasons. First of all, she offers not only a discussion of the philosophical and conceptual aspects of acceptance as a clinical strategy, she also offers specific, step by step modules designed to teach the therapist how to teach the behavior of acceptance to severely disturbed clients. Second, her innovative strategies have been developed for use with clients who are acknowledged by clinicians as being among the most difficult to treat (clients meeting the criteria for borderline personality disorder)–in part because progress is slow or nonexistent but most importantly because these clients tend to generate extremely aversive emotional reactions in their therapists. Finally, initial studies suggest that Linehan's treatment approach actually helps improve the lives of the clients her treatment team treats, more so than other standard treatments (Linehan, Armstrong, Suarez, Allmon, & Heard, 1991; Linehan & Heard, 1993). As with any new, developing treatment that shows promise, an analysis of the *actual* active ingredients--as opposed to the *stated* active ingredients, is in order.

What is Acceptance?

Linehan describes acceptance as being central to her approach to treatment. Acceptance is described as being an act of the total person, an act of "accepting what is". In addition, it is proposed that the act of acceptance in itself *is* behavioral change, and also can *lead to* behavioral change. These definitions can be confusing for several reasons. First, the move to reify the notion of acceptance ultimately does not promote clarity or understanding of the term. Second, acceptance described as both being and leading to behavior change (without an analysis of how this could be) confuses the issue.

A solution to these concerns may be found by considering the Skinnerian notion that a term is defined by appealing to the conditions that give rise to the use of the term (Skinner, 1945). This would legitimize the practice of describing acceptance both in terms of being a de facto example of behavior change, and as something that would lead to other behavior change that is distinct from the act of acceptance itself. In other words, the measurement of the presence or absence of acceptance would be tied to particular goals. Thus, the term "acceptance" could be occasioned by different circumstances--such as circumstances seen in the process and circumstances seen in the outcome measures of therapy.

In conducting psychotherapy with severely disturbed individuals, being able to measure "acceptance" by appealing to either process measures, or outcome measures (or both) would becritical. It is not difficult to imagine a client who acquires acceptance skills that are evident in the therapy relationship, and even out of therapy, and who also injures themselves or even suicides. Similarly, it is imaginable that one could obtain good outcome measures, while process measures might reflect instances of excessive control (e.g. passivity and over-compliance). Evidence of acceptance in both process and outcome measures would be most parsimonious, however, it is possible to imagine having one in the absence of the other. Given the often severe "punishment" experienced by therapists who treat severely disturbed clients, it would be critical for the therapist to learn to discriminate instances of acceptance as a process and acceptance as an outcome if the behavior of "doing therapy" with these individuals is to be maintained. Further progress in the treatment of these individuals is obviously contingent on the willingness of therapists to treat them, and this hinges on the reinforcement available for the therapist.

How is Acceptance Taught?

Linehan delineates some of the actual behaviors involved in teaching her clients the behavior of acceptance. She describes the core mindfulness skills that are central to the treatment. These skills involve "what" skills (observing, describing, and participating), and "how" skills (being non-judgmental, acquiring focused awareness, and acquiring the ability to be focused on effectiveness). Very specific behavioral programs have been developed and are suggested as ways to teach such skills. While these skills might appear to be related to acceptance and thus related to therapeutic gains, how these skills actually contribute to gains observed is not clearly understood.

Furthermore, it is the case that what might be called acceptance is seen in individuals who have not been exposed to the training procedures that Linehan describes. The question of how, naturalistically, acceptance is acquired, is an important issue in furthering our understanding of acceptance. How is it that some people survive severe trauma differently (and with more success) than others (e.g. survivors of the Holocaust, survivors of traumatic childhoods, survivors of combat related trauma). Commonalities in the acquisition and use of acceptance in these instances might enhance our understanding of acceptance in a generic and a specific sense.

It appears to be a critical point that the step by step skills training intended to in part produce the behavior of acceptance may be one route to that end. It is clear, however, that there are other routes to take toward acceptance. Thus, the specific skills training developed by Linehan might capture part of what produces acceptance, and there also might be other, more generic routes toward that end.

Clinical Supervision--The Shaping of Acceptance

Linehan clearly emphasizes the importance of clinical supervision in the treatment of the borderline. Supervision teams designed to support the therapist as the therapist and client are involved in treatment is regarded as a critical component of the treatment. Why might this be so?

Supervision can be an experiential learning process for the therapist. Linehan encourages therapists to bring up and work on their own therapy interfering behaviors, as well as those of their clients. It appears that the same processes of acceptance that the clients are to work on also are grist for the mill in supervision. These processes involve the practice of acquiring and dispensing support and acceptance in the face of emotional disregulation, as well as maintaining adherence to the treatment protocol. This process parallels that of the kinds of acceptance valued for the client. It could be that supervision shapes, via natural contingencies, the very behaviors in the therapist that the therapist then will attempt to shape in the client.

It is perhaps not a coincidence that other than Linehan, the primary providers of treatment for the borderline come from psychoanalysts. Psychoanalytic supervision is also intensive, experiential, and requires that the analyst focus on developing their technical skills and analytic ability, while also learning to work through their own resistances (Dewald, 1987; Fleming & Benedek, 1966; Weiss, 1987). It might be the case that the actual, generic, active ingredient in the teaching of acceptance lies more in the contingency shaping of acceptance that goes on in supervision which in turn is transmitted to the client. As the therapist struggles to be "present to what is" in supervision, perhaps they acquire skills that will increase their ability to discriminate relevant aspects of their client's struggle to do the same. Furthermore, "what is", when working with severely disturbed clients, can be disturbing feelings such as hopelessness, defeat, wanting to avoid the client, and so on. These feelings can be difficult for a therapist to reveal in a professional supervision situation.

Thus, the study of the give and take of the supervision process might reveal critical elements necessary for acceptance to occur. Further study and sensitivity to the contingencies found in the supervisor/supervisee relationship might reveal more precisely some of what is necessary to produce acceptance. While the techniques proposed by Linehan clearly are innovative and effective, it is important to continue to emphasize the active ingredients present in the therapy relationship itself, and on the conditions required to maximize the therapists ability to create the conditions necessary for acceptance to occur.

References

Dewald, P. A. (1987). *Learning Process in Psychoanalytic Supervision: Complexities and Challenges*. International Universities Press, Inc. Madison.

Fleming, J., & Benedek, T. (1966). *Psychoanalytic Supervision*. Grune & Stratton, NY.

Linehan, M. M., Armstrong, H. E., Suarez, A., Allmon, D., & Heard, H. L. (1991). Cognitive-behavioral treatment of chronically parasuicidal borderline patients. *Archives of General Psychiatry, 48,* 1060-1064.

Linehan, M. M., & Heard, H. L. (1993). Impact of treatment accessibility on clinical course of parasuicidal patients: In reply to R. E. Hoffman [Letter to the editor]. *Archives of General Psychiatry, 50,* 157-158.

Skinner, B. F. (1945). The operational analysis of psychological terms. *Psychological Review, 52,* 270-277.

Weiss, S. S. (1987). *The Teaching and Learning of Psychoanalysis.* Guilford Press, London.

Chapter 5

Acceptance in Rational-Emotive Therapy

Albert Ellis
Institute for Rational-Emotive Therapy, New York City

Hank Robb
Pacific Institute for RET, Lake Oswego, Oregon

Acceptance has been a key concept in Rational-Emotive Therapy (RET) since I (AE) first originated it in January, 1955. In fact, as I was formulating the basic principles and practice of RET in 1953 and 1954 and was doing a good deal of marriage therapy, I firmly advocated that married couples had better accept each other's sexual and other limitations and unangrily adjust to these limitations if they wanted to have a good relationship (Ellis, 1953, 1954).

Over the years, as RET developed, acceptance became one of the main cores of its theory and practice (Ellis, 1957, 1960, 1962, 1972a, 1973, 1977, 1985, 1988a, 1989b; Ellis & Harper, 1961a, 1961b). Where did I get this view? Mainly from early philosophers, especially from Epictetus (1890) and Marcus Aurelius (1890) and from more recent ones, especially Buber (1955), Niebuhr (Alcoholics Anonymous, 1976), and Russell (1965). Also, however, from my own experiences (Ellis, 1972b, 1990) and from working intensively with couples and families from 1943 onward (Ellis, 1949a, 1949b, 1949(, 1953).

The more I worked with couples and the more I applied the cognitive, emotive, and behavioral techniques of RET to their problems the more centrally important became my views of acceptance, until it has now become the most crucial aspect of RET-oriented marital and family (as well as individual) therapy. Let us, (AE and HR), in this paper, outline some of the main elements of therapeutic acceptance as epitomized in the work of RET practitioners.

Self-Acceptance

RET takes a position, along with that of Rogers (1961) and many other self theorists (Kohut, 1977; Lecky, 1943; Maslow, 1954), that unconditional self-acceptance is crucial to solid emotional and behavioral health and that happy marriage is possible, but not too likely, when it is significantly absent (Ellis, 1972a, 1973, 1976, 1985, 1988a, 1992). It is even more rigorous in this respect than Kohut (1977), Rogers (1961), and other self-esteem-oriented therapists because where they hold that people can *un*conditionally accept themselves when, and usually only when, a therapist or other significant person unconditionally accepts them, RET views this kind of self-acceptance as quite *conditional*. Why? Because if our clients accept themselves *because* we totally accept them, they are making their own acceptance *conditional upon* or *dependent upon* us and *our* accepting attitude. Obviously, if most other people-including their mates-only accept them conditionally, as will most likely occur, back to non-acceptance they will go!

RET tries to specifically define unconditional self-acceptance by giving people two clear-cut choices, one, philosophically inelegant and one more elegant. The first is: "I choose to thoroughly, unconditionally accept myself (though *not* some of my *behaviors*) *whether or not* I perform successfully and *whether or not* significant others approve of and accept me. I strongly *prefer* to do well and be loved by others—especially by my family members—but I don't *have to be*, and can accept myself as "good" or "worthy" just because I *exist*, because I am *alive*. because I choose to do so.

The trouble with this "solution" to the problem of unconditional acceptance is that it is pragmatic and workable but philosophically inelegant. For anyone could come along and object, "Your unconditional acceptance of yourself is practical but is also definitional or tautological. You choose to *define* yourself as 'good' or 'worthy' just because you are *alive* and because you choose to do so. Well, that will work pretty well because you won't have to worry about your possible 'badness' until you are dead. That's pretty safe! However, I choose to think that you are 'bad' and 'worthless' just because you exist, because you are alive, because you are human. In fact, I choose to believe that *all* humans, including myself, are worthless and that they shouldn't exist *at all*. Now which of us is right about your and my goodness?"

The answer seems to be: Neither of us is right or wrong. We just have different *definitions* of human worth and, from a purely definitional standpoint, are both entitled to our definitions of worthwhileness and worthlessness, even though yours will probably result in better results for you and for me than will mine. However, in taking this approach, we will have actually slipped from a discussion about self-*acceptance* to a discussion about self-*approval* because "conditional self-acceptance," as described above, is really definitional self-approval or self-disapproval. We have moved from "I *accept* myself *as* alive because I am, indeed, alive" to "I *approve* of myself *for being* alive because I am, indeed, alive.

The second, more philosophically elegant, choice of *un*conditional, and we might add *honest*, or *thoroughgoing*, self-acceptance that RET gives to mated (and other) people is: "I choose to rate or evaluate *only* my thoughts, feelings, and behaviors, so that I rate them as 'good' when they abet my main chosen goals and purposes (and those of my social group) and as 'bad' when they sabotage these same goals and purposes. But I refuse to rate my *self*, my *being*, my *totality*, my *essence*, or my *personhood* at all, because these processes are too complex and changeable to be given any global rating. I will try to perform well and be approved by others in order, in most instances, to enjoy my life more. But I refuse to see myself as a *good person* nor a *bad person*, but only as a *person who* at times *behaves* 'well' and at times *behaves* badly.' I sanely make this choice because it is literally impossible to nonarbitrarily rate someone's personhood. Thus, I refuse to attempt doing so myself and steadfastly reject the reports of others who claim, rather than demonstrate, they have done so."

The RET theory of *un*conditional self-acceptance is far removed from the usual theories of self-efficacy (Bandura, 1986) and self-esteem (Branden, 1970) for these theories state or imply that humans are only "good," or "worthy" *providing* that they function well and/or are socially approved and that they'd better like their *selves* for their good *behaviors*. RET holds that this concept of self-esteem mainly creates deep-seated feelings of anxiety-for even when you are doing "very well" today you almost inevitably worry about doing "poorly" tomorrow, and thereby you sink back to feelings of "worthlessness."

RET truly promotes self-*acceptance* rather than some form of self-*approval* because it steadfastly maintains that one's *personhood* cannot be rated. Most elegantly, it takes the position that one's personhood is simply not the sort of thing which is either approvable or unapprovable but only acceptable or unacceptable. As we shall see throughout, RET holds that we had better accept this particular aspect of the universe, namely our human personhood, for the same reason we had better accept all other aspects of the universe, because it, and they, exist. RET insists that refusing to accept what, in fact, exists is most probably the road to human folly and especially emotional disturbance. While some aspects of the universe are sensibly ratable and thus approvable or disapprovable, personhood, according to RET, is not one of them.

RET hypothesizes that people who conditionally–and especially, unconditionally–accept themselves tend also to conditionally approve others in the first instance and unconditionally accept others in the second instance, including their mates, and be less hostile, to others, including their mates. Two self-downers, of course, *can* have a good marriage, because they are what I (AE) call "love slobs," who think they *need* their partner's approval (Ellis, 1963, 1979). But there is a strong human tendency for humans to damn *both* themselves and others when they assess their and others' behaviors as "wrong" or "bad" (Ellis, 1957, 1985a, 1985b, 1985c). Why? Because humans are "natural" self-raters, of themselves and others, and by both nature and nurture *easily* jump from "because I *do* badly I *am* a bad person and from "because I *do* greatly I *am* a great person" (De Bono, 1990; Ellis, 1962; Korzybski, 1933; Lazarus, 1977). Consequently, they usually have to *train themselves*–and be often helped by therapists to do so–to fight against that tendency and make themselves significantly less evaluating of their own and of others' personhood (Ellis, 1972a, 1976, 1988a, 1988b, 1990a, 1990b, 1991a, 1991b,1992).

Effective individual, couples, and group therapists, says RET, had better, therefore, not only give clients unconditional acceptance but also actively-directively *teach* it to them, philosophically, emotively and behaviorally. They don't *have to* do this to significant help their clients. But they'd damned well better!

Acceptance of Others

As strongly pointed out in the first book on RET, How to Live With a Neurotic (Ellis, 1957). and as Jacobson (1992) has clearly recently reaffirmed, helping couples to change each other's obnoxious or annoying behavior is often beneficial-but often is not. Many marriage and family therapists—such as Ellis (1957, 1960, 1962, 1979), Ellis & Harper (1961), Erickson (1981), Haley (1991) and Satir (1967)—have reported success in this respect and several research studies have presented even more convincing evidence of desirable change (Jacobson, 1992). But even the best of these results are equivocal because many annoying partners simply refuse to change in spite of the most tactful, reinforcing, and persuasive help from their mates and their therapists.

What to do when an amicable divorce is not desirable or feasible? Fairly obviously, as several Western and Asian ancient philosophers pointed out, one partner can appreciably change his or her attitude toward the other and accept the other *with* her or his 'bad' behavior (Epictetus, 1890; Marcus Aurelius, 1890).

Probably the best way to do this, as suggested in the previous section of this paper, is for one partner to *un*conditionally accept, rather than rate, the other *whether or not* this other's behavior is "good" or "bad"-though alternatively, he or she might definitionally *approve* the *partner* as "good" or "worthy" while still assessing some of his or her *behaviors* as "bad" or "wrong."

Let me illustrate with one of my (AE's) recent cases. Jack and Jill had a fairly good marriage for five years until Jack not only continued his regular 9 to 5 job but began to spend most evenings and weekends writing what he hoped would be the Great American Novel. Jill began to be very angry at him for "deserting" her and self-deprecatory and depressed for not being more interesting and attractive so that Jack really wanted to be with her more. I at first helped her see, in our joint couple sessions, that Jack was not deliberately slighting her and that even if he were doing so and was somewhat bored with her that never made her a *lowly*, *bad* person. At worst, it proved that she had some "bad" traits and might think about improving them. In short, I helped her to give up *disapproving* of herself and helped her to start *accepting* herself.

Jill did very well after only four therapy sessions, plus reading the books, *A New Guide to Rational Living* (Ellis & Harper, 1975) and *How to Stubbornly Refuse to Make Yourself Miserable About Anything—Yes, Anything!* (Ellis, 1988a). But Jack, though agreeing to spend a minimum amount of time with her each day—that is, at least a half hour—did exactly that: talked with her for no more than that amount of time and kept spending the bulk of his "spare" time writing.

Jill was quite discontent with this "solution" and used RET to make herself *un*angry at Jack. She seriously thought of leaving him for a "better" partner but for a number of economic, sexual, safety, and other reasons clearly decided not to do so. I then worked with her for five more sessions, mainly by herself, to help her accept Jack in several main ways.

First, Jill was able to accept *Jack* while still disliking his somewhat obsessive writing behavior. She worked on several different kinds of acceptance and finally, with my collaboration, often came to these conclusions.

   a) "I accept the fact, the reality, that Jack will not change that much and that for an indefinite period of time, perhaps forever, he will devote much more time to his writing than to me."

   b) "I accept the fact. the reality, that I probably will never like Jack's neglecting me but that he will also not like neglecting his writing and spending more time with me. I also can accept his right to do what he really wants, just as I accept my right to want him to do what I really want, and therefore not blame him for putting his wants and his right to have those wants ahead of his pleasing me."

   c) "I love Jack for several reasons, but not some of the things he *does*, especially his constant writing and neglect of me while writing. His writing is, for me, bad but he is still not a *rotten person* for depriving me in that respect. So I still accept *him*."

   d) "Because I love Jack, I really *want* him to do and enjoy his writing. I also want him to enjoy being with me. But I can accept and love him with *his* wants, even though they at times seriously conflict with mine."

   e) "I could tell myself that if he *really* loved me he would give me what I want—more contact with him. But I could also say that if I really loved him I would gladly let him do what he wants. No, we can both love each other and still mainly do what we want and that doesn't make either of us a *rotten person*."

These conclusions show how Jill was able to accept rather than approve Jack's personhood despite his disapproved behaviors. Next we will see how she, and anyone else, can accept human behaviors and traits or general life conditions despite disapproving of them.

Acceptance of Frustration

When marital and other partners don't get along together they not only put the other person down (as well as abhorring some of her or his traits) but often they also have low frustration tolerance (LFT) or what I (AE) have called "discomfort disturbance," which is different from their self-downing or "ego disturbance" (Ellis, 1979a, 1980, 1990a, 1990c, l991a, 1991b, 1997, 1992c; Ellis & Dryden, 1987). Because of this tendency they make hassles into "horrors," insist that their mate's annoying behavior *absolutely must not* exist, that it's *awful*, and that they *can't stand* it. These demandings and awfulizings are the causes of their not accepting the human behaviors and traits as well as general life conditions of which they disapprove. RET shows people that they can gracefully lump that which they do not like instead of agreeing with the notion that people cannot accept those things of which they don't approve.

When they use RET to work at *accepting* without *liking* the difficulties presented by their mates, they strongly convince themselves (many times) that their mate's obnoxious behavior predictably *should* exist (because, alas, it does), that it is *uncomfortable* but not *awful* (because however bad it is, it most probably is not worse than totally and completely bad and certainly not worse than bad), and that they definitely can *stand* it (because they are, as *a matter of fact*, standing it. They then often learn to tolerate *it* as well as to tolerate their *partners* for having it. By acquiring this kind of high frustration tolerance (HFT), along with other tolerance they usually feel much happier about their hassle-ridden relationships.

Following Hauck (1984), I (HR) show people there is an "A" solution and a "B" solution to any of life's problems. "A" solutions are: (1) do nothing, (2) work for change, or (3) leave. "B" solutions are: (1) do nothing *and get disturbed*, (2) work for change *and get disturbed*, or (3) leave *and get disturbed*. Acceptance is the key to sticking with an A rather than a B solution. Notice how this differs from the admonition to *change* what we can and *accept* what we cannot. Both solution two and three are change solutions. But if they are to be done nondisturbedly, they most probably had better be done with acceptance of that which we do not approve and wish to change. From the perspective of RET, acceptance is not what we do when we can't make changes, it is what we do to avoid disturbance whether we can make changes or not. We *accept* what has existed, what currently exists, or might possible exist, not because we *approve* of it but because it, *as a matter of fact*, has existed, is existing or might exist. Even that which can only be imagined and could never exist can still be accepted with this approach because, *as a matter of fact*, we have imagined its existence. RET'ers have frequently pointed out that even if you adopt solution three and leave, you are usually wise to stay in the situation long enough to fully accept it and no longer be emotionally disturbed by it (Ellis, 1960, 1962, Ellis & Harper, 1961a; Ellis, Sichel, Yeager, DiMattia & DiGiuseppe, 1989). Only then will you get over your disturbance and be relatively free to choose your course of action instead of being compulsively driven to it. Clients are not simply achieving *resignation* to horrors which must not happen and turn people into nogoodnicks when they do. Instead, they are achieving *acceptance* by cognitively, emotionally and behaviorally renouncing these various forms of nonsense.

This is what my client, Jill, did during therapy and with RET reading and audio cassette material:

1. She began to see Jack's constant writing as *unfortunate* and *inconvenient* but not *awful* and *horrible*.
2. She saw some of its advantages—e.g., Jack's giving her the freedom to see her friends and relatives more—as well as its disadvantages and deprivations.
3. She convinced herself that Jack *preferably should not* write as much as he did but that he *predictably should* do so because, right now, that was his compulsive nature.
4. She told herself many times, and strongly, until she started to consistently believe, "I *can* stand Jack's obsession with his writing, though I'll never *like* it. Even if he persists in neglecting me I *can* be a happy woman, though not *as* happy as if he paid more attention to me."

5. She kept showing herself that her frustration about Jack's writing was appropriate but that her low frustration tolerance—her whining about it—was only self-defeating and helped to turn Jack off and to encourage him to become more involved with his writing. She therefore was motivated to change her thoughts and feelings and to accept some of the grim realities of Jack's behavior.

Secondary Symptoms of Non-Acceptance

When people don't accept themselves, others, and frustrating conditions, regardless of their ability or inability, not to mention their willingness or unwillingness to change them, they very frequently bring on neurotic symptoms-especially anxiety and depression-and then they neurotically refuse to accept themselves with these symptoms and deprecate themselves for having them. Thus, they think, "Because I put myself down and feel depressed, I'm no good for having no confidence in myself and for making myself depressed. 'Because I hate my partner, I'm a rotten person for hating her." "Because I can't accept and live reasonably well with life's hassles, I'm a weak, ineffective person." They thereby create secondary symptoms (self-downing) or nonacceptance of nonacceptance!

Again, when people are non-accepting of themselves, of others, and of frustrating conditions they frequently have low frustration tolerance about their nonacceptance—and once more produce a secondary form of nonacceptance. For example, "I *must* accept myself, others, and frustrating conditions because otherwise I will make myself anxious and depressed, and I *can't stand* the pain of these symptoms. It's so *awful* to suffer this way that my life isn't worth living!" They thereby, once again, create the secondary symptoms of low frustration tolerance about their primary symptoms of nonacceptance.

Thus, before she came to therapy Jill hated her *self* for her angry and depressed *behaviors* about Jack's neglect; and she also had low frustration tolerance (or discomfort depression) about her feelings of anger and depression, because she experienced them as "too hard" to bear and consequently as "horrible."

System-Oriented Symptoms of Non-Acceptance

Humans almost always live in the social system and couples certainly do. Each person's acceptance or nonacceptance of his or her self, of the other person, and of non-changeable hassles in the system therefore affects others and if one partner acts disturbedly she or he encourages the other partner to act disturbedly, too. A vicious circle of non-acceptance and disturbance easily ensues (Ellis, 1991a; Ellis, Sichel, Yeager, DiMattia & DiGiuseppe, 1989).

Let us put Jack and Jill's nonacceptance and later greater acceptance into the ABC format of RET. Jill's original A or Activating Event (A) was Jack's neglecting her for his obsessive writing. At B, her Belief system, she thought, "He *shouldn't* do this to me! He's *no good*. I can't stand it! Maybe I'm doing something wrong and am unlovable. If so, I'm an inadequate person." Jill then made herself feel angry and depressed at C, her emotional Consequence.

Jack then experienced Jill's anger (her C1) as an Activating Event (his A1) and thought at his B (Belief System), "Jill's angry at me and that's unfair. She *shouldn't* condemn me for my trying to write my novel!" So he felt, at his C, angry at Jill for being "unfairly" angry at him.

Then Jill made Jack's anger at her—his C—into a new Activating Event (A2) and told herself (at B2), "Jack's very angry at me and loves me even less. How awful! My anger at him is stupid and is doing me no good! I *shouldn't* be so angry. I deserve to lose his love." She then felt (at her C2) even more self-hating and depressed.

Jack then noticed (at his Activating Event, A2) Jill's depression and thought to himself (at his B2), "It looks like I'm making her depressed—as I must not do! I'm a nasty person!" So he felt (at his C2) quite guilty or non-accepting of himself. But then he also noticed his anger at Jill and his guilt about her depression (his A3) and told himself (at his B3) "I'm a weak person for feeling so angry and guilty; and my feelings are interfering with my writing, and that's terrible!" So at his C3 he felt more nonaccepting of himself, as well as low frustration tolerance about his "bad" feelings, and therefore. he threw himself more compulsively into his writing.

Jill then noticed (at her A3) that Jack was becoming more compulsively addicted to his writing, told herself (at her B3), "Now I *really can't stand it.* What a terrible marriage I have!" and felt (at her C3) more hopeless and depressed.

So Jack and Jill's nonacceptance of themselves, of the other, and of the grimly realistic conditions kept actively interacting with each other, thus helping to bring about more nonacceptance and more accompanying disturbed feelings (Ellis, 1991a).

When Jill finally used RET to accept herself, Jack, and the obnoxious conditions of her life, she thereby significantly changed Jack's Activating Events (A, and A,), helped him feel unangry and unguilty (at his C,, C2, and C3), and their relationship considerably improved. His giving up his anger and guilt then helped her feel much better at her C1, C2, and C3. So considerably more interactive acceptance of themselves, of the other, and of the hassles of their lives, ensued.

Acceptance-Enhancing Therapy

A number of behavioral therapist-arranged techniques of enhancing individuals and couple's ideas and feelings of acceptance can be effective, as Jacobson (1992) has shown. RET uses these, as well as a number of emotive and behavioral methods (Ellis, 1971, 1973, 1982, 1985a, 1985b, 1988a, 9190; Ellis & Dryden, 1987, 1990a, 1990c, 1991b, 1992; Ellis & Becker, 1982; Ellis & Harper, 1975; Ellis & Velten, 1992; Ellis, Abrams & Dengelegi, 1992).

Most uniquely, however, RET stresses the *philosophy* of people' s unconditionally accepting themselves, others, and obnoxious conditions that they can't change. It therefore, as noted above, models and gives acceptance to clients, no matter how poorly they behave in and out of therapy. At the same time it actively-directively teaches them its importance and value and shows them how to forcefully dispute both their nonacceptance and their nonacceptance of their nonacceptance. It encourages them to make a profound philosophic change that will include and embrace unconditional self-, other-, and world-acceptance.

Does RET succeed in these respects? Not always! Because most people seem to be both born and reared to damn themselves, others, and the world, and because they endlessly practice doing so during their lifetimes, they have one hell of a time achieving unconditional acceptance; and when they do achieve it they often fall back again to anger, rage, vindictiveness, damning, and other forms of nonacceptance. RET can help them in this respect (Ellis, 1977; Haaga & Davison, 1989; Lyons & Woods, 1991), but not perfectly!

RET, however, does help many clients (and readers) to be partially and sometimes more accepting than they would otherwise be. Great. Let us hope that it and other kinds of behavioral and nonbehavioral therapy, continue to investigate methods of helping individuals, couples, and groups to become more accepting and less damning of themselves, of others, and of unchangeable, obnoxious conditions. In this direction much is to be gained in intrapersonal and interpersonal relations.

Conclusion

Actively and strongly disliking some of one's own or other people's behavior and hating many world conditions seems to be very healthy and life-preserving. But hating and damning oneself and others for their poor behaviors, and life damning conditions for their very existence does little good and much harm. Thus, whether one can or cannot change behaviors or conditions, one had better have the courage to accept—that is, dislike but stop horrifying oneself about—them. When, therefore, it seems almost impossible to change behaviors or conditions, one had better have the courage to accept—that is, dislike but stop horrifying oneself about—what one cannot presently change. And, for the nonce, to accept oneself even with one's nonacceptance. This won't necessarily lead to individual, marital, or social bliss. But it most probably will help!

References

Alcoholics Anonymous (1976). *The big book.* Rev. ed. New York: Alcoholics Anonymous World Services.

Bandura, A. (1986). *Social foundations of thought and action: A social cognitive theory.* Englewood Cliffs, NJ: Prentice-Hall.

Branden, N. (1970). *The psychology of self-esteem.* New York: Bantam.

De Bono, E (1991). *I am right-You are wrong: From rock logic to water logic.* New York: Viking.

Ellis, A. (1949a). Some significant correlations of love and family behavior. *Journal of Social Psychology, 15,* 61-76.

Ellis, A. (1949b). A study of the love emotions of American college girls. *International Journal of Sexology, 3,* 15-21.

Ellis, A. (1953). Marriage counseling with couple's indicating sexual incompatibility. *Marriage and Family Living, 13,* 53-59.

Ellis, A. (1954). *The American sexual tragedy*. New York: Twayne. Rev. ed., New York: Lyle Stuart and Grove Press.

Ellis, A. (1957). *How to live with a neurotic: At home and at work*. New York: Crown. Rev. ed., Hollywood, CA: Wilshire Books, 1975.

Ellis, A. (1960). *The art and science of love*. Secaucus, NJ: Lyle Stuart.

Ellis, A. (1962). *Reason and emotion in psychotherapy*. Secaucus, NJ: Citadel.

Ellis, A. (1963). *The intelligent woman's guide to manhunting*. New York: Lyle Stuart. Rev. ed.: *The intelligent woman's guide to dating and mating*. Secaucus, NJ: Lyle Stuart, 1979.

Ellis, A. (1971). *Growth through reason*. North Hollywood, CA: Wilshire Books.

Ellis, A. (1972a). *Psychotherapy and the value of a human being*. New York: Institute for Rational-Emotive Therapy. Reprinted in A. Ellis & W. Dryden, *The essential Albert Ellis*. New York: Springer, 1990.

Ellis, A. (1972b). Psychotherapy without tears. In A. Burton (Ed.), *Twelve therapists* (pp. 103). San Francisco: Jossey-Bass.

Ellis, A. (1973). *Humanistic psychotherapy: The rational-emotive approach*. New York: McGraw-Hill.

Ellis, A. (1976). RET abolishes most of the human ego. *Psychotherapy, 13*, 343-348. Reprinted: New York: Institute for Rational-Emotive Therapy.

Ellis, A. (1977). *Anger-How to live with and without it*. Secaucus, NJ: Citadel Press.

Ellis, A. (1979a). Discomfort anxiety: A new cognitive behavioral construct. Part 1. *Rational Living, 14(2)*, 3-8.

Ellis, A. (1979b). *The intelligent woman's guide to dating and mating*. Secaucus, NJ: Lyle Stuart.

Ellis, A. (1980). Discomfort anxiety: A new cognitive behavioral construct. Part 2. *Rational Living, 15(1)*, 25-30.

Ellis, A. (1982). Intimacy in rational-emotive therapy. In M. Fisher & G. Striker (Eds.), *Intimacy* (pp. 203-217). New York: Plenum.

Ellis, A. (1985a). Intellectual fascism. *Journal of Rational-Emotive Therapy, 3(1)*, 3-12. Reprinted: New York: Institute for Rational-Emotive Therapy.

Ellis, A. (1985b). *Overcoming resistance: Rational-emotive therapy with difficult clients*. New York: Springer.

Ellis, A. (1985c). A rational-emotive approach to acceptance and its relationship to EAPs. In S. H. Klarreich, J. L. Francek, & C. E. Moore (Eds.), *The human resources management handbook* (pp. 325-333). New York: Praeger.

Ellis, A. (1988a). *How to stubbornly refuse to make yourself miserable about anything—Yes, anything!* Secaucus, NJ: Lyle Stuart.

Ellis, A. (Speaker). (1988b). *Unconditionally accepting yourself and others*. Cassette recording. New York: Institute for Rational-Emotive Therapy.

Ellis, A. (Speaker). (1990a). *Albert Ellis live at the learning annex*. 2 cassettes. New York: Institute for Rational-Emotive Therapy.

Ellis, A. (1990b). My life in clinical psychology. In C. E. Walker (Ed.), *History of clinical psychology in autobiography*. Homewood, IL: Dorsey.

Ellis, A. (1990c). Special features of rational-emotive therapy. In W. Dryden & R. DiGiuseppe, *A primer on rational-emotive therapy* (pp. 79-93). Champaign, IL: Research Press.

Ellis, A. (1991a). The revised ABCs of rational-emotive therapy. In J. Zeig (Ed.) *Evolution of psychotherapy: 11.* New York: Brunner/Mazel. Expanded version: *Journal of Rational-Emotive and Cognitive Behavior Therapy, 9,* 139-172.

Ellis, A. (1991b). Using RET effectively: Reflections and interview. In M. E. Bernard (Ed.), *Using rational-emotive therapy effectively* (pp. 1-33). New York: Plenum.

Ellis, A. (1992a). Foreword to Paul Hauck, *Overcoming the rating game* (pp. 1-4). Louisville, KY: Westminster/John Knox.

Ellis, A. (1992b). My early experiences in developing the practice of psychology. *Professional Psychology, 23,* 7-10.

Ellis, A. (1992c). Rational-emotive approaches to peace. *Journal of Cognitive Psychotherapy, 6,* 79-104.

Ellis, A., Abrams, M., & Dengelegi, L. (1992). *The art and science of rational eating.* New York: Barricade Books.

Ellis, A., & Becker, I. (1982). *A guide to personal happiness.* North Hollywood, CA: Wilshire Books.

Ellis, A., & Dryden, W. (1987). *The practice of rational-emotive therapy.* New York: Springer.

Ellis, A., & Dryden, W. (1990). *The essential Albert Ellis.* New York: Springer.

Ellis, A., & Dryden, W. (1991). *A dialogue with Albert Ellis: Against dogma.* Milton Keynes, England and Philadelphia: Open University Press.

Ellis, A., & Harper, R. A. (1961a). *A guide to rational living.* Englewood Cliffs, NJ: Prentice Hall.

Ellis, A., & Harper, R. A. (1961b). *A guide to successful marriage.* North Hollywood, CA: Wilshire Books.

Ellis, A., & Harper, R. A. (1975). *A new guide to rational living.* North Hollywood, CA: Wilshire Books.

Ellis, A., Sichel, J., Yeager, R., DiMattia, D., & DiGiuseppe, R. (1989). *Rational-emotive couples therapy.* New York: Pergamon.

Ellis, A., & Velten, E. (1992). *When AA doesn't work for you: Rational steps to quitting alcohol.* New York: Barricade Books.

Epictetus. (1890). *The collected works of Epictetus.* Boston: Little, Brown.

Erickson, M. H. (1981). *A teaching seminar with Milton H. Erickson.* Edited with commentary with J. K. Zeig. New York: Brunner/Mazel.

Haaga, D. A., & Davison, G. C. (1989). Outcome studies of rational-emotive therapy. In M. E. Bernard & R. DiGiuseppe, Eds., *Inside rational-emotive therapy* (pp. 155-197). San Diego, CA: Academic Press.

Haley, J. (1990). *Problem solving therapy.* San Francisco, CA: Jossey-Bass.

Hauck, P. (1984). *The three faces of love.* Philadelphia, Pennsylvania: The Westminster Press.

Jacobson, N. S. (1992). Behavioral couple therapy: A new beginning. *Behavior Therapy, 23*, 493-506.

Kohut, H. (1977). *The restoration of the self.* New York: International Universities Press.

Korzybski, A. (1933). *Science and sanity.* San Francisco, CA: International Society of General Semantics.

Lazarus, A. A. (1977). Toward an egoless state of being. In A. Ellis & R. Grieger (Eds.). *Handbook of rational-emotive therapy, Vol. 1* (pp. 113-116). New York: Springer.

Lecky, P. (1943). *Self-consistency.* New York: Doubleday/Anchor.

Lyons, L. C., & Woods., P. J. (1991). The efficacy of rational-emotive therapy: A quantitative review of the outcome research. *Clinical Psychology Review, 11*, 357-369.

Marcus Aurelius. (1890). *Meditations.* Boston: Little, Brown.

Maslow, A. H. (1954). *Motivation and personality.* New York: Harper & Row.

Rogers, C. R. (1961). *On becoming a person.* Boston. Houghton-Mifflin.

Russell, B. (1965). *The basic writing of Bertrand Russell.* New York: Simon & Schuster.

Satir, V. (1967). *Conjoint family therapy.* Palo Alto: Science and Behavior Books.

Discussion of Ellis and Robb

The Nature of Acceptance in Rational-Emotive Therapy

Niloofar Afari
University of Nevada

In their paper, Ellis and Robb (1994) assert that self-acceptance is a central tenet of rational emotive therapy (RET). They go on to make a distinction between self-acceptance and self-approval and provide their "philosophically elegant" definition of unconditional self-acceptance. In the remainder of the papers the authors discuss acceptance of environmental factors such as others in an intimate relationships acceptance of frustration, and acceptance of the fallout of nonacceptance.

While the notion of self-acceptance in RET is consistent with other humanistic and acceptance oriented therapies, the issues of environmental acceptance and the acceptance of frustration are not as clear. It appears that RET endorses acceptance on one level. However, the various emphases and language of RET may undermine acceptance at another level. Thus, RET may be internally inconsistent with regards to the issue of acceptance. In this brief paper, some of those areas which may hinder the goal of acceptance in RET will be discussed.

Self-Acceptance

RET proposes that it has an existential-humanistic outlook (Ellis, 1962). From this perspective, individuals are viewed as holistic, goal-directed persons who are important in the world just because they are human and alive. It apparently unconditionally accepts them as they are with their limitations and it focuses on their experiences and values. It distinguishes between the "self" or one's personhood and the content of self, such as thoughts, feelings, and overt behavior. This suggests that the person can accept his/her personhood and evaluate and attempt to change thoughts and feelings. If the client is successful at not evaluating his/her self and focusing on cognitive change, that individual will probably be healthier and happier than otherwise (Ellis, 1990a).

This position is very clear philosophically and quite admirable. With a distinction between the self and its contents, the individual is left free to evaluate the merit of various thoughts, feelings, and behaviors. However, aside from the acceptance of one's personhood or essence, RET seems to be utilize many control-based strategies. The proponents of RET insist on cognitive change, often as a prerequisite to behavioral change. RET, along with other cognitive therapies, proposes that private phenomena, such as thoughts and feelings, are not behaviors but internal states that have a mediating function between environmental events and overt behavior (Ellis, 1962; Beck, 1976). Thus, control of these events is viewed as a change in the causal factors of maladaptive behavior .

From this standpoint, there are several issues, one of which may undermine the theoretical guideline of self-acceptance. First, empirical support for behavioral change with RET via a change in irrational beliefs is weak (Oei, Hansen, & Miller, 1993). Second, it does not seem behaviorally pragmatic to place the causes of behavior within the individual. As therapists, we have little direct control over clients' internal states, except through environmental manipulation. Thus, it seems parsimonious not to assign causal status to these events, especially in light of lacking empirical support.

Thirdly, RET makes no effort to distinguish between the content of thoughts and feelings, and the process of thinking and emoting. While it may be useful to reject the content of specific thoughts, a rejection of thinking and emoting as organic and natural human behavior does not seem adequate. After all, thinking, emoting, breathing, and a host of other activities are inherent in human existence. They are the essence of aliveness and personhood. Without a distinction between the form and process of private events, there is a great risk in the rejection of the process as well as the content of these events. That in turn undermines the goal of self-acceptance.

Environmental Reality

Ellis and Robb (1994) have successfully added to the list of acceptance in different domains. They advocate the explicit acceptance of the conditions of the world, in other words, the external physical environment. RET implies that irrational thoughts are an avoidance of reality and advocates for the acceptance of reality no matter how grim it is. To change these thoughts would bring the person in contact with environmental reality and force the person to accept it. Thus, it is believed that reality exists out there in the world.

This position, however, leads to two interrelated problems. First, placing reality out in the world denies the interaction between the person and his/her environment. It is possible that a person's thoughts and feelings are the result of an interaction between the person's history and the events of the outside environment. This interactionist viewpoint would suggest that while there are objective conditions to the world, these conditions are not absolute reality.

A second related problem, is the denial of an individual's experiential reality. The distressed individual is not fabricating the feelings of frustration and depression. At each moment of experience, these feelings bring with them an experiential reality or truth. However, clients are told that they are factually wrong because their internal experiences do not correspond with an external absolute reality. By making a demand for experiential change, clients are led to believe that thoughts and feelings are the enemy. In effect, they may leave therapy believing that their own experiences are not to be trusted.

Acceptance versus Tolerance

RET seems to be rooted in Stoicism. This becomes apparent in its language. Clients are often told to learn to tolerate an event because it exists. It suggests that there is no point in "awfulizing" an already existing experience. The verbal distortion or irrational thought is believed to be a post hoc view of events that are not liked or wanted. This analysis is obvious in the statement, "RET shows people that they can *gracefully lump* that which they do not like instead of agreeing with the notion that people cannot accept those things of which they don't approve (Ellis & Robb, this volume). Thus, the healthy alternative, from an RET perspectives is to tolerate discomfort in the service of long-range hedonism (Ellis, 1990b).

It is questionable, however, if this resignation or tolerance of environmental factors is truly a sign of acceptance. Is acceptance a "putting up with" or a full experience of events as what they are and not what they say they are? I would suggest, as others in this volume have proposed (e.g., chapters by Greenberg, Hayes, or Linehan), that genuine acceptance is a present-centered openness to emotional experiences. This notion is different from tolerance of emotional discomfort and/or physical conditions of the world. Resignation and tolerance, however, may be on the same continuum with genuine acceptance.

There is also a distinction to be made between emotional and environmental toleration. Whereas emotional tolerance could be in the service of behavior change, the acceptance of some environmental conditions may function to keep a person trapped in dysfunctional situations. This issue is especially important in marital or family systems where power differentials exist. For instance, in the Jack and Jill examples the responsibility for situational and emotional tolerance was placed on Jill, the one with less power in the relationship.

The Language of RET

The terms used in RET are irreverent and evocative of change. Clients are hit over the head with the irrationality of their self-talk. In practice, there seems to be a certain amount of forcefulness or therapist's nonacceptance of the individual's present conditions, as exemplified by Ellis' popular comment, "They damn better do it."

In addition, RET therapists don't seem to believe that a deep or warm relationship between the therapist and client is necessary or sufficient for therapeutic change. The therapists' role is in accepting rather than giving warmth or approval to clients and stresses teaching them the philosophy of self-acceptance (Ellis, 1980). RET therapists can give their clients empathy, sympathy, warmth, etc. But they tend to do so with caution as they believe that this may lead to conditional instead of unconditional self-acceptance. In light of the tone of the therapeutic relationship and the forceful and rigid language used, RET clients may become entirely confused about the goal of self-acceptance. On the one hand, clients are encouraged to accept their personhood, and on the other hand, some aspects of their personhood are forcefully attacked.

Aside from the demandingness of RET talk and its inconsistencies with self-acceptance, the absolutistic nature of its language may pose some problems for functional and flexible behavior. In a recent article, Ellis himself has come to note that there is no absolute criterion for rationality (Ellis, 1993). The same principle may hold for the workability of a thought. The persuasive nature of RET suggests that the therapist has knowledge of the correct way of thinking and behaving. However, as Ellis seems to suggest above, workability is relative to context. It appears that RET therapists propose a second set of rigid, albeit, workable rules regarding rational/irrational thinking. This set of rules may again hinder the individual's behavioral and emotional progress when put in effect in differing circumstances As in the Jack and Jill story, for example, at times it may be beneficial for a woman to learn to tolerate a busy and neglectful husband. However, the forcefulness and rigidity of RET's language may serve to facilitate rigid rule-formulation. Subsequently, rigid tolerance will be physically and emotionally dangerous in an abusive relationship.

This explicit rule-giving does not correspond with the existential/humanistic sense of acceptance, in which the client's behavior is shaped through acceptance. Nor does this process in RET lend itself to flexible behaving. Experimental evidence suggests that behavior under the control of explicit instructions is not as flexible or amenable to environmental conditions as behavior that is shaped through direct control of such conditions (cf., Hayes, Zettle, & Rosenfarb, 1989). Furthermore, several conditions under which following a rule may not allow for workable actions has been described elsewhere (Afari & Hayes, 1991). Suffice it to say that the process of therapy in RET may not be conducive to flexible behaving. On the other hand, an accepting therapeutic relationship without many "oughts," "shoulds," and "damn well betters," may shape adaptive and flexible behavior that is not thoroughly rule-governed.

Summary

In summary, it is indeed the case that Ellis has advocated the acceptance of one's personhood throughout the history of RET (Ellis, 1962; Ellis, 1990a, Ellis & Robb, 1994). This emphasis sets RET apart form other cognitive therapies that may only focus on cognitive change. However, there are several domains within RET that undermine self-acceptance, and may not be consistent with the notion of genuine acceptance or openness to emotional experiences.

In the above discussion, I have made an attempt to delineate some of these areas. This is with the hope that the diversity and utility of acceptance in psychotherapy can be further explored. To this end, it seems important to have a treatment approach that is theoretically and technically consistent with its acceptance goals.

References

Afari, N., & Hayes, S. C. (November, 1991). *Acceptance in psychotherapy: A review and behavioral analysis.* Paper presented at the convention of the Association for the Advancement of Behavior Therapy, New York.

Beck, A. T. (1976). *Cognitive therapy and the emotional disorders.* New York: International Universities Press.

Ellis, A. (1962). *Reason and emotion in psychotherapy.* Secaucus, NJ: Citadel.

Ellis, A. (1980). Rational-emotive therapy and cognitive-behavior therapy: Similarities and differences. *Cognitive Therapy and Research, 4,* 325-340.

Ellis, A. (1990a). Value of a human being. In W. Dryden (Ed.), *The essential Albert Ellis: Seminal writings on psychotherapy.* New York: Springer Publishing.

Ellis, A. (1990b). Chapter one. In W. Dryden (Ed.), *The essential Albert Ellis: Seminal writings on psychotherapy.* New York: Springer Publishing.

Ellis, A. (1993). Changing Rational-Emotive Therapy (RET) to Rational Emotive Behavior Therapy (REBT). *The Behavior Therapist, 16,* 257-258.

Hayes, S. C., Zettle, R. D., & Rosenfarb, I. (1989). Rule-following. In S. C. Hayes (Ed.). *Rule-governed behavior: Cognition, contingencies, and instructional control* (pp. 191-220). New York: Plenum Press.

Oei, T. P. S., Hansen, J., & Miller, S. (1993). The empirical status of irrational beliefs in Rational Emotive Therapy. *Australian Psychologist, 28,* 195-200.

Chapter 6

Emotional Acceptance in Integrative Behavioral Couple Therapy

Kelly Koerner
Neil S. Jacobson
University of Washington

Andrew Christensen
University of California - Los Angeles

Traditional behavioral couple therapy focuses on change through accommodation, compromise, and collaboration. However the nature of some couples' problems limits the extent that change is possible. Consequently, therapy consisting solely of change oriented strategies will not fully address these problems. Andrew Christensen and Neil Jacobson have developed integrative behavioral couple therapy (IBCT) which combines interventions that foster emotional acceptance (EA) with change-oriented behavioral couple therapy (Christensen & Jacobson, 1991; Christensen, Jacobson, & Babcock, in press; Jacobson, 1992; Jacobson & Christensen in preparation). In this chapter we discuss the ways change oriented strategies are limited, explain why promoting emotional acceptance might be more effective, and then briefly describe the emotional acceptance interventions of IBCT.

Fostering Emotional Acceptance

During the natural development of romantic relationships couples inevitably find that what they want and need differs, at least at times. For example, couples often differ regarding their ability to give and receive emotional support, the priority each assigns work, family, and individual pursuits, preferences about planning versus spontaneity which play out in how money and time are spent, styles of decision making or parenting, and so on. Compromise on some issues will be reached easily, but other issues will generate intense, painful conflict. While all couples develop ways to resolve conflict, couples who seek therapy frequently have developed a coercive pattern of responding to their differences. In these couples, one or both partners try to resolve conflict by inducing the other to change. Using means that become increasingly aversive (e.g., withdrawing, complaining, crying, ignoring, saying things that make the other feel guilty or put down, threatening to leave, etc.), one or both partners attempt to get what they want and need from the other. To the extent that the partner being coerced resists before giving in, he or she increases the probability that the other will have to "turn up the volume" in order to induce change; to the extent that the coerced partner gives in intermittently, he or she inadvertently strengthens the pattern. Usually partners assume both the role of coercer and coerced. This use of reciprocal coercion generates a cycle that becomes increasing aversive and painful for both partners.

An Example: Patricia and LeRoy

Patricia and LeRoy have lived together for six years and sought therapy because they "argue constantly." Patricia is gregarious, funny, and excels at her hectic, high pressure work as an account executive. LeRoy, a successful freelance photographer, has much less social interaction during his day, and, unlike Patricia whose schedule changes unpredictably to accommodate clients, he structures his time on projects with freedom. LeRoy was attracted to Patricia's sharp wit, ambition, and sociability, but he has become increasingly jealous of the time she spends at work and with friends. Because she is frequently too busy or preoccupied to do the small thoughtful things that make him feel loved, he feels unimportant. When he asks for reassurance, Patricia feels criticized. Patricia was initially attracted to LeRoy when they met in art school because he was thoughtful and kind, his slight possessiveness made her feel special, and he had a creative knack for making anything fun. Over time LeRoy has become responsible for initiating all of their joint activities, setting him up for perpetual rejection and changed plans given Patricia's work schedule.

The argument that led them to enter therapy was typical of the issues that divide them. Feeling guilty about the time she devoted to a new account, Patricia decided to make it up to LeRoy, turned down the usual happy hour at work, and rearranged work commitments to take time off for a weekend away, a frequent request of LeRoy's. She arrived home late. LeRoy, who after their last fight vowed to be less jealous of her work and more understanding of her unpredictable late hours, managed to greet her in a less peevish but still noticeably stilted way. Slightly resentful that he expected her to apologize for being late but trying to avoid a fight that might spoil the surprise of plans for the weekend, she explained how she passed up happy hour in order to see him. LeRoy took her slightly defensive tone personally. He felt guilty about restricting her and hurt that she never seemed comparably disappointed about missing time with him, and inadvertently mini-mized the importance of her concession by saying, "You should have gone; I know that sort of thing is important." Irritated and feeling like there is no way to please him, Patricia bit back the sharp retort that came to mind, changed the topic by asking about his day, and started dinner in an effort to smooth things over and keep herself from feeling further anger. Under other circumstances, these are the exact things he has been asking for more of and could enhance intimacy. However, in that context, her efforts to make time for him, be attentive, and make dinner drove him further away because it was clear she was irritated- he saw her attempts to make him feel better as insincere and he felt she was humoring him. The argument escalated and eventually LeRoy left and stayed the night at a friend's.

Differences in themselves need not be problematic—Patricia's ambition and LeRoy's possessiveness were part of their initial attraction. The problem comes from the couple's efforts to resolve the conflict generated by these differences. The couple in this example has a history of conflict about the priority of time together: LeRoy alternates between feeling guilty for "needing Patricia too much" and complaining that she is not more available; Patricia appeases him insincerely or sarcastically, criticizes herself for not giving more, and develops activities outside the relationship to escape their constant fighting. Even when they attempt to avoid being angry and blaming, the things each does to try to resolve the conflict actually promote distance. Each partner's well intentioned efforts to solve the problem often elicit problematic behavior in the other which in turn elicits problematic behavior in themselves. LeRoy's ambivalent effort to acknowledge the importance of Patricia's time spent informally with co-workers ended up minimizing her concession; Patricia's effort to avoid conflict by curbing her sharp humor made LeRoy feel patronized and punished with silence.

Limitations of a Change-Oriented Approach

A traditional change-oriented approach to behavioral couple therapy helps couples resolve conflicts with a short term boost in satisfaction from interventions that increase positive interactions (behavior exchange) plus teaching communication and problem solving skills to increase long term satisfaction. Such interventions remedy skill deficits in order to facilitate accommodation to the partner's requests for change. Research shows that behavioral couple therapy helps some couples, but about one third of couples continue to be distressed at the end of therapy and about half of couples relapse at follow-up (Baucom & Hoffman, 1986). These results are comparable to other types of couple therapy (Jacobson & Addis, 1993).

We suspect that traditional change strategies are limited for several reasons. The most pragmatic reason they fail is that the couple can't do what the therapist asks them to do to change. By the time therapy is sought, they are locked into adversarial positions, doubtful or cynical that the partner will change, and unwilling to risk change themselves unless the other makes the first move. Collaboration is prerequisite for even the earliest interventions in the traditional approach. Prefacing therapy on collaboration between a rigidly polarized couple is a formula for failure. Further, learning the skills often does not help the couple avoid or de-escalate arguments; regardless of a person's competent communication or problem-solving, once the argument is underway they are unable to get themselves to stop it (Jacobson & Holzworth-Munroe, 1986). At the same time, the therapist's effort to help the couple use positive reinforcement to induce change is thwarted because the habituation that naturally occurs over the course of a relationship has decreased the salience and power of reinforcers that in the past increased intimacy and pleasure.

A second problem with change oriented interventions is that they can conflict with important therapeutic goals. While structured communication training and problem solving help resolve conflict about discrete instrumental activities such as housework, requests for increased trust, greater interest in sex, or greater respect are not as amenable to negotiation and quid pro quo agreements. For example, LeRoy's complaint was that Patricia gives work higher priority than their relationship and he wants to feel more important to her. The couple could identify specific solutions to the conflict (e.g., Pat will turn down the new contract, they'll have dinner together at least three times a week, etc.). However, there are infinite ways for LeRoy to feel unimportant to her now and in the future. He asks her opinion on his work, she seldom discusses her work with him; he arranges something special for her birthday or work milestones, she scurries at the last minute on his big occasions. Because there are so many different behaviors that could serve the same function, problem solving each specific instance is inefficient.

Further, change oriented interventions draw even skillful therapists into using arbitrary rather than natural reinforcement. Arbitrary reinforcement is a term that describes consequences provided by the therapist that are not available in the person's natural environment or that do not arise naturally from the transaction of the individual and environment (Ferster, 1967). Arbitrary reinforcement comes across as false, manipulative, or gimmicky, and can generate resistance. The main problem with using arbitrary reinforcement is that it creates conditions that are exactly opposite of those that lead to intimacy. Being thoughtful or being a better listener only because one is following the therapist's directive not only interferes with the recipient experiencing it as genuine, but behavior under instructional control is less sensitive to change, therefore, it interferes with the giver's ability to be sensitive to subtle changes in the relationship, a defining characteristic of intimacy.

Particularly with couples who are highly distressed and have extreme difficulty collaborating, therapists often feel pressured to work for change and resort to inducing collaboration solely through directives. However, adopting a change oriented stance with difficult couples predisposes the therapist to make errors. The therapist's change oriented interventions imply that he or she agrees with the view that getting rid of differences is feasible and, inadvertently, may support efforts to coerce oneself and the partner into feeling and acting differently.

The final and most important reason that traditional change-oriented strategies alone are likely to be ineffective is that the differences that spur the conflict may not be amenable to change. Limited potential for change is due in part to choice of partner. Assortative mating and other factors that influence choice of partner are not the same as those that influence the relationship's longevity: differences that originally attract two people may or may not wear well. Then, too, differences can be exacerbated as each partner naturally grows and changes in response to events inside and outside their relationship. Easy accommodation to one's pursuit of individual interests becomes difficult after the birth of the first child; insecurity about one's competence becomes a problem only after the other is promoted; differences in spending versus saving generate conflict when retirement decreases income.

For these reasons we think it is unlikely that change oriented techniques alone will resolve all important couple problems. Traditional change strategies are; difficult to use with very distressed couples and hard to adapt to complex or subtle problems; tend to over-rely on therapist instructional control to induce change which has effects counter to therapeutic goals; and don't take into account differences that generate conflict but are relatively unchangeable.

Advantages of Acceptance-Oriented Approaches

Emotional acceptance interventions are intended to help remedy these limitations. IBCT proposes that the resolution of numerous couples' problems is better approached by changing the context that makes the behavior problematic, rather than by changing the problematic behavior. The term "emotional acceptance" means a shift in the interpersonal context that influences the emotional response of the partner who makes the complaint, in addition to, and sometimes instead of, changing the other's problematic behavior. The therapist structures the couple's interaction during therapy so that each partner stops struggling to change the other and comes to experience the other's previously aversive behavior in a new way that allows for intimacy enhancing dialogue about problems and differences. What was offensive or blameworthy is seen as an understandable, tolerable, or even a valuable, though at times unpleasant, difference. For example, a successful emotional acceptance intervention regarding LeRoy and Patricia's different priority of time together might result with the issue creating mild irritation rather than full blown conflict. In therapy LeRoy might learn that Pat works so hard, in part, to compensate for disappointment that she never made it as an artist herself. He remains dissatisfied that they don't have more time, but now understands why Pat has difficulty turning down opportunities at work.

The guiding principle of emotional acceptance work is to identify the contingencies of the couple's interaction pattern that are associated with pain, accusation, and blame across the content of their disagreements. Then, rather than trying to teach new behaviors that must come to strength under adverse circumstances (for example, teaching the clients to use communication skills in the midst of an argument), EA interventions alter the salient aspects of the situation to make the most of the couple's capabilities to respond compassionately to each other's pain. EA interventions create a context that naturally draws out each partner's existing positive repertoire in order to increase intimacy and decrease distress.

The advantage of interventions that promote emotional acceptance is that contingencies that evoke emotion not only produce broad shifts in all the behaviors that covary with mood, but also change the stimulus functions that obtain. For example, Patricia's interest in LeRoy's day and taking time from work to be with him usually would make LeRoy feel he was important to her. However, in the context of an argument when he feels hurt and angry, the same behaviors make him feel patronized and create distance. As a consequence of evolution and individual adaptation, a complex covariation of physiological/somatic, cognitive, and overt behavioral responses occur when an event interrupts an individual's typical chain of behavior in a particular situation (Kelley, Berscheid, Christensen, Harvey, Huston, Levinger, McClintock, Peplau, & Peterson, 1983). This sort of rapid reorganization characteristic of emotional responding allows for more advantageous reactions to a changed social or physical environment.

EA interventions make use of the nature of emotional responding. For example, one EA intervention, empathic joining around the problem, increases emotional acceptance because it amplifies emotions such as sadness and disappointment that encourage empathic approach and that compete or interfere with simultaneous blame, anger, defensiveness, and distancing. Most people have long histories of approaching, comforting, commiserating with, and working to help relieve the distress of a loved one. Thus, in the context of a fight, therapist comments that highlight or change certain aspects of the situation (e.g., make emotions that tend to evoke empathy more salient) increase the probability that these aspects will come to exert control over behavior. They may also rapidly alter how the person experiences and responds to what had been troubling by radically changing its meaning, well beyond any immediate in-session effect. When the therapist successfully fosters emotional acceptance, the resulting reorganization of behavior brings forth an already potential repertoire that blocks or interferes with problematic behavior.

Emotional Acceptance Interventions

IBCT uses four interventions designed to foster emotional acceptance: 1) empathic joining around the problem; 2) turning the problem into an "it"; 3) building tolerance; and 4) enhancing self-care. In each, the therapist identifies and makes maximum use of naturally occurring contingencies in the couple's relationship. The therapist attempts to alter stimulus control just enough to generate competing responses. Simultaneously the therapist blocks the couple's usual responses to the problem in order to promote the positive reinforcement of alternative behaviors. By drawing attention to and making salient certain aspects of the situation the therapist helps the couple experience intimacy despite their differences.

Empathic joining around the problem is similar to reframing in Emotion Focused Therapy (Greenberg & Johnson, 1988). The therapist guides the couple's in-session interaction to help the partners experience the other's pain without the blame and accusation that usually obfuscate it. The therapist asks the couple to discuss or recreate a recent conflict. Then he or she reflects and summarizes as each partner explains what happened until each partner feels that the therapist understands. While talking with one and then the other partner, the therapist is aware of the listening partner as an audience. Therapist comments selectively draw out and amplify disclosure of feelings and thoughts that are likely to make the listening partner better understand or feel more compassion toward the speaker. The therapist's comments separate the blame and accusation from the vulnerability that the speaker experienced, particularly early in the conflict. For example, as Patricia and LeRoy each recount the argument that led them to therapy, the therapist asks more about the vulnerability each felt in the opening moves of the fight. As the therapist pursues why LeRoy feels so upset when she is late from work, Leroy is able to express how intensely he misses Pat and he describes several tender memories of their times together. He gets teary eyed and says he is terrified he will lose her. As Pat hears this, she remembers with him how special these times felt, she understands more clearly why he is upset about working overtime, and lets him know that, despite the way she's felt lately, she has no intention of leaving him. The couple feel closer and experience an intimate conversation as they discuss what separates them.

The therapist's interventions enable the person to be able to attend and be affected by many aspects of the situation rather than only those congruent with angry mood. The therapist guides discussion of conflict so that the couple have an intimate conversation in the session that in turn may alter the meaning of the problem. Even if Pat continues to be late from work and LeRoy doesn't like it, after this conversation his first comment is more likely to be "I missed you today" and Pat is less likely to react defensively.

One caveat regarding empathic joining is that expression of emotions such as sadness, fear, or disappointment do not necessarily lead to more compassion or understanding of the partner's behavior. In the worst case, expressions of vulnerability may invite attack. Expressions of tender feelings or requests for reassurance may be unwise if the other is likely to defend his or her position in ways that punish openness and vulnerability. Some people have had extensive experience and modeling that make another person's expression of tender feelings the conditions for asserting one's superiority (or insecurity), for example, by expressing disgust at vulnerability. Therefore, the therapist must carefully determine the contingencies that actually lead to compassion and intimacy on an individual basis.

As the therapist attempts to promote empathic joining around the problem, he or she develops an idea of a theme that cuts across the couple's conflicts. In a collaborative manner, the therapist develops a verbal description, or formulation, of the couple's interaction pattern. The therapist phrases the formulation in terms of differences between the partners that are inevitable, understandable, complementary, etc., and illustrates the understandable but problematic reactions to those differences that lead the couple to conflict. The therapist's comments clarify how it is the couple's response to their differences rather than the differences themselves that generate conflict. He or she points out the partners struggle to induce change through coercion of oneself or the other. It includes a clear description of the mutual contribution that each makes to maintain the conflict. It points to the self-defeating and unavoidable trap created by their attempts to resolve the conflict. While the therapist acknowledges the negative aspects of each partner's behavior, he or she also points out its positive features that the couple is ignoring or that were valued by them in the past.

The therapist comments phrase the entire interaction pattern as an "it", a common enemy or obstacle that the couple share and must cope with together rather than something one does to other. To encourage emotional distance the therapist uses humor and techniques like the empty chair. The therapist introduces as little arbitrary format as possible during discussions of the theme, but actively blocks and resists any shift into blaming each other for the problem or discussing solutions until the couple clearly have adopted some shared view of their problems. Turning the problem into an "it" draws on the couple's pre-existing repertoire of rallying together to face a common obstacle.

Acceptance through tolerance building seeks to desensitize the partner to the other's negative behavior. The first way this is done is to ritualize the conflictual interaction pattern. The therapist asks the couple to role play their problem behaviors both in and outside of the session, but through directives, changes the context and, therefore, the function of these negative behaviors. The therapist may prescribe the symptom, that is, ask one partner to do what upsets the other when they don't feel like it. For example, Patricia might be asked to be either withholding or sarcastic the next time LeRoy asks for any form of reassurance even though in truth she felt like being reassuring. The instructions to fake the problem are given in front of the partner, and the assignment is explained as an opportunity to observe the effect of their behavior on the other when they themselves are not upset. After a short time, the partner is to let the other know that it was a fake and the can discuss what they learned.

This sort of intervention may work in two ways. First it makes it difficult to know when the person is "just doing the assignment", thus disrupting immediate escalation into their conflictual pattern. Also, by "faking" the behavior when they don't really feel it, the partners have a chance to observe the effect of their actions on the other and thereby understand the other person's reactions more clearly.

The therapist also helps the couple anticipate slipups, recurrences of the problem, as a natural part of their relationship and helps them discover ways to recover from slip-ups more quickly. The therapist may ask the couple to rehearse the slip-up in the session to expose the couple to potential scenarios, so that when they inevitably fall into their old ways, they might be less reactive and have some ideas of how to minimize the damage and recover as quickly as possible.

The therapist enhances self-care by helping each partner become more resourceful at meeting his or her needs both within and outside the relationship. Within the relationship, for example, one partner may make minimal requests of the partner in order to avoid conflict, resulting in non-engagement on important issues that interferes with both the avoider's individual needs and the potential for intimacy. The therapist might enhance self-care by helping the person make more direct and persistent demands of the partner. At the same time the therapist encourages the partners to consider how they could meet their needs through other relationships. Deprivation fuels the intensity of the struggle to get the partner to change. To the extent that interaction with the partner is the sole source for feelings of well-being and purpose, then even subtle unavailability becomes significant. Developing other significant relationships or individual pursuits may reduce the pressure on the partner to be the main source of reinforcement.

Conclusion

Emotional acceptance interventions are designed to augment the traditional change oriented strategies of behavioral couple therapy. EA work changes the interpersonal context so that differences that were aversive and produced alienation and conflict become the occasion for observing one's own and the other's behavior with compassion and tolerance. EA interventions alter the meaning of the problematic behavior (change stimulus control) by: 1) amplifying affect that encourages engagement; 2) turning the problem into an it by providing non-blaming alternative descriptions of the interaction pattern, and by blocking any understandable but problematic "solutions" to differences so that the couple gain emotional distance and unite in efforts to cope with a shared burden; 3) increasing tolerance through ritualizing the problematic and planning for inevitable slip-ups; and 4) increasing self care. Successful emotional acceptance interventions not only help the couple be more influenced by the more beneficial contingencies available in the situation, but also transform the meaning of the differences that led to pain and conflict. We believe this transformation of the meaning of the differences represents a powerful and efficient means of reducing couple distress.

References

Baucom, D. H., & Hoffman, J. A. (1986). The effectiveness of marital therapy: Current status and application to the clinical setting. In N. S. Jacobson, & A. S. Gurman (Eds.), *Clinical handbook of marital therapy* (pp. 597-620). New York: Guilford.

Christensen, A., Jacobson, N. S., & Babcock, J. (In press). Integrative behavioral couple therapy. In N. S. Jacobson, & A. S. Gurman (Eds.), *Clinical handbook of marital therapy*, Second edition. New York: Guilford.

Ferster, C. B. (1967). Arbitrary and natural reinforcement. *Psychological Record, 22,* 1-16

Greenberg, L. S., & Johnson, S. M. (1988). *Emotionally focused therapy for couples.* New York: Guilford.

Jacobson, N. S. (1992). Behavioral couple therapy: A new beginning. *Behavior Therapy, 23,* 493-506.

Jacobson, N. S., & Addis, M. E. (1993). Research on couples and couple therapy: What do we know and where are we going? *Journal of Consulting and Clinical Psychology, 61,* 85-93.

Jacobson, N. S., & Holtzworth-Munroe, A. (1986). *Marital therapy: A social learning-cognitive perspective.* In N. S. Jacobson, & A. S. Gurman (Eds.), Clinical handbook of marital therapy (pp. 29-70). New York: Guilford.

Jacobson, N. S., & Margolin, G. (1979). *Marital therapy: Strategies based on social learning and behavior exchange principles.* New York: Brunner/Mazel.

Kelley, H. H., Berscheid, E., Christensen, A., Harvey, J. H., Huston, T. L., Levinger, G., McClintock, E., Peplau, L. A., & Peterson, D. R. (1983). *Close relationships.* New York: W. H. Freeman.

Discussion of Koerner, Jacobson, & Christensen

Acceptance in Couples Therapy

William C. Follette
Melissa A. Polusny
University of Nevada

*...grant me the serenity to accept the things I cannot change,
the courage to change the things I can,
and the wisdom to know the difference.*
The Serenity Prayer

This little homily seen hanging on kitchen walls, and heard in AA meetings comes to mind whenever the issue of acceptance is raised in clinical psychology. The issues addressed in the previous chapter are important extensions to the traditional behavior change strategies used for years by those who studied behavioral approaches described in seminal works by these and other authors (e.g. Jacobson & Margolin, 1979; Stuart, 1980). Koerner, Jacobson, and Christensen are making a bold move to acknowledge that not only can't some marital problems be changed, but perhaps they even shouldn't be. Integrative behavioral couple therapy (IBCT) still makes use of change strategies, but now allows for the possibility that topographical change goals are not always possible or desirable. For people who are identified with formally teaching marital change strategies, this is seemly quite significant.

It is clear how acceptance strategies are appropriate and necessary for issues such as conducting therapy with clients who have experienced trauma or who have to accept the consequences of other actions as they currently impinge on their lives. To some extent this is obviously true for any responding person. A behavior analytic understanding of behavior implies that all behavior results from a complex set of factors coalescing in the moment behavior occurs.

What and When to Accept

The presentation of IBCT is vague about what and when to accept unsatisfying conditions in an ongoing relationship. Traditionally, regardless of intervention strategy, marital therapy has been time–limited because couples are not infinitely patient in tolerating distressed relationships once they have decided to seek therapy. If the therapist doesn't help, couples have the solution of divorce readily available to them. Initially some evidence of change is required to have couples recognize the potential for important improvement in satisfaction to occur. It would be useful for the therapist to be able to have some guidance in determining which client identified problems should be the focus of actual change strategies and which should be accepted.

Clearly, physically or emotionally abusive behavior emitted by either member of the dyad should be changed. One could come to accept the history of a person that gives rise to abusive behavior, and perhaps one could even accept the person who might be abusive, but the abusive behavior itself should never be tolerated in spite of the fact that the prevalence of domestic violence is higher than previously suspected (Straus & Gelles, 1986). Given the authors' public statements on this subject (Jacobson, 1993), we presume that they believe this is implicit, though we prefer it explicit.

Who Does the Accepting

Past research has identified negative predictors of treatment response that include differences in the desired closeness preferred by each member of the dyad (Jacobson, Follette, & Pagel, 1986). In the case of LeRoy and Patricia it was the male who preferred a more affiliative style, though many times the woman finds herself in this situation. Koerner, Jacobson, and Christensen would try to promote an understanding of the preference of the other to be more independent and suggest that the more affiliative person get their needs met elsewhere. Couples who are mismatched on the affiliation/independence dimension and distressed do not, on average, do as well in marital therapy. The authors' attempts to address this problem may be a step forward in helping heretofore difficult cases. We will be interested to see if sending the more affiliative person outside the relationship to get those needs met will be helpful or make more clear how unfulfilling the marriage is if they meet someone more affiliative.

Power differences are understood to be important variables in relationships (Gray-Little & Burks, 1983), though the construct is not as well understood as might be useful. IBCT attempts to reduce coercive elements in relationships, but at some level the therapy accepts, as it must, the fact that one person in the dyad will have more accepting to do than the other. We hope the therapy does not too easily present a framework for women to accept more than their fair share.

Equivalence Classes and the Lack of Theory to Support Therapy Development

Much of what Koerner, Jacobson, and Christensen describe is the existence of dysfunctional equivalence classes in relationships. For the purposes of this discussion, equivalence classes are expressed relations between stimuli such that different stimuli can have the same stimulus functions without a person ever having had all relationships between elements explicitly trained. In classical conditioning stimulus generalization is a well known phenomenon. Stimuli similar to the conditioned stimulus can develop eliciting properties without ever having been paired with the unconditioned stimulus. Generalization takes place because of the similarity of formal (physical) stimulus properties. In verbal behavior, equivalent functions can be seen in the absence of physical similarity, but equivalence classes can form on the basis of historical relationships between stimuli (Hayes, 1991; Hayes & Hayes, 1992). It is this phenomenon that we see when LeRoy responds to Patricia's coming home late as being functionally equivalent to rejection. The problem is that research on equivalence and relational frame theory is still in its infancy. How stimulus relations emerge, and if and how they can be eliminated are unknown. The challenge of understanding how Patricia changed from initially seeing possessiveness, for example, as being treated as special, to later seeing LeRoy as being too needy is a long way from being met. That does not obviate the need to address the clinical problems that arise from the formation of dysfunctional equivalence classes, but it makes knowing how to do so a matter of guesswork that cannot yet be based on an application of principles, because the principles explaining the formation and changing of equivalence classes are presently unknown. The authors recognize the problem and are admirably bootstrapping a solution, but they are doing so with little theoretical guidance.

At the level of practice, we would have some concern about the strategy Koerner, Jacobson, and Christensen use when they describe talking about the couple's problem as an "'it', a common enemy or obstacle." Talking about the problem as "it" makes good sense from a relational frame theory perspective. One is trying to establish the problem as a problem and not invoke other elements of a negative equivalence class which might include such things as bad, failure, divorce, etc. This useful move of having the problem be a problem and nothing more, is immediately undermined when the therapist then calls the "it" an "enemy" because "it" and "enemy" could form an equivalence class where "it" takes on the functions of enemy, bad, evil, adversarial, and so on. Since it is inevitable that "it" (the clinical issue) will occur during the course of therapy, it could be seen as more distressing than need be than if "it" and "enemy" were not presented together. If one were to be consistent with what we think the theoretical underpinnings of IBCT are, we would applaud construing the problem as "it" but reject calling it an "enemy." This may seem picky, but if one believes in relational frame theory, it is no trivial matter.

Assessment

As we said earlier, one ominous task the IBCT therapist faces is identifying which distressing aspects of a relationship can and should be changed, which are unchangeable, and which should be treated by increasing the emotional acceptance of the spouse and his or her behavior. It cannot be the case that everything the spouse does that is troubling should be accepted and tolerated. Relatedly, there may be behaviors or response classes that can be changed, but the less well-trained therapist may opt for promoting acceptance of the problem. Two areas that need to be studied are how to assess how amenable to change a problem is, and how to assess the appropriateness of therapist choices about what to change.

Other Comments about Therapy and Therapists

It is clear that Koerner, Jacobson, and Christensen are offering a significant advance in couples therapy. In extending IBCT we hope that some of the thoughtful aspects of more traditional behavioral marital therapy (BMT) (Jacobson & Margolin, 1979) are not abandoned. For example, there is a wonderful procedure for developing collaboration between partners that involves having couples talk about the time they began dating and the formation of their romance. Couples are asked to describe what they liked about each other and what they enjoyed. A skillful therapist can sometimes recreate positive feelings, albeit often short-lived, and a useful collaborative set. This is not always possible and IBCT addresses some of those difficulties. Neither BMT nor IBCT can address the occasional comments from one or both partners saying "I never did really like him, and I don't know why we ever got married in the first place." However, we did notice the similarity between the empathetic joining strategies of IBCT and building a collaborative set or perspective taking exercises that described in BMT.

The authors point out the difference between natural and arbitrary reinforcement (Ferster, 1967) which is indeed important. However, one of the distinctions between couples and individual therapy is that natural contingencies can readily occur when couples are behaving in a session. The therapist can have difficulty setting up the situation where positive behaviors are not discounted as being done to please the therapist. BMT had several methods for minimizing those occasions, and it taught clients to become empirically sensitive to how what each of them does affects his or her spouse.

One last issue that could be addressed by IBCT is the acceptance of discomfort in the context of a happy, satisfying committed relationship. Some couples present for therapy believing the relationship is in trouble merely because one or both of them occasionally gets angry, hurt, or disappointed. Couples therapy that can make occasional negative affect consistent with a well-functioning relationship rather than one that is flawed, would go a long way toward establishing a safe and secure relationship.

Overall IBCT begins an interesting processes during which couples and therapists face the challenge of knowing what to change, what to accept, and how to know the difference. Time will tell if meeting these treatment goals produces serenity.

References

Ferster, C. B. (1967). Arbitrary and natural reinforcement. *The Psychological Record*, *22*, 1-16.

Gray-Little, B., & Burks, N. (1983). Power and satisfaction in marriage: A review and critique. *Psychological Bulletin*, *93*, 513-538.

Hayes, S. C. (1991). A relational control theory of stimulus equivalence. In L. J. Hayes & P. N. Chase (Eds.), *Dialogues on verbal behavior* (pp. 19-40). Reno, NV: Context Press.

Hayes, S. C., & Hayes, L. J. (1992). Some clinical implications of contextualistic behaviorism: The example of cognition. *Behavior Therapy, 23*, 225-250.

Jacobson, N. S. (1993, October). Domestic violence: What are the marriages like? Plenary I address at the annual meeting of the American Association of Marriage and Family Therapy, Anaheim, CA.

Jacobson, N. S., Follette, W. C., & Pagel, M. (1986). Predicting who will benefit from behavioral marital therapy. *Journal of Consulting and Clinical Psychology, 54*, 518-522.

Jacobson, N. S., & Margolin, G. (1979). *Marital therapy: Strategies based on social learning and behavior exchange principles.* New York: Brunner/Mazel.

Straus, M. A. & Gelles, R. J. (1986). Societal change and change in family violence from 1975 to 1985 as revealed by two national surveys. *Journal of Marriage and the Family, 48*, 465-479.

Stuart, R. B. (1980). *Helping couples change: A social learning approach to marital therapy.* New York: Guilford Press.

Chapter 7

Acceptance and the Therapeutic Relationship

James V. Cordova
Robert J. Kohlenberg
University of Washington

Promoting acceptance is one of the key ingredients in any successful psychotherapy. Many psychotherapists believe strongly in the importance of acceptance and have several techniques which they use to promote it. In addition, there is growing interest in the issue of acceptance among clinical researchers. Despite this widening belief in the importance of acceptance, several issues remain to be grappled with. First, what exactly do we mean when we talk about promoting acceptance in our clients? To what behaviors are we referring and how can we tell when acceptance is taking place? Second, how does promoting acceptance help our clients? Exactly what benefits are gained by learning to accept? Third, what are the most effective ways of promoting acceptance? What can we as clinicians do to help our clients learn to accept?

In this chapter we will present what we believe to be a very useful approach to answering these important questions. The approach we will take is rooted in the behaviorally based approach to interpersonal psychotherapy called Functional Analytic Psychotherapy (FAP; Kohlenberg & Tsai, 1991). Our goals for this chapter are to (1) offer a definition of acceptance, (2) discuss the clinical benefits achieved through promoting acceptance, (3) discuss how interpersonal therapy achieves these benefits, and (4) discuss how other approaches to promoting acceptance can benefit from considering some of the basic tenets of FAP.

What is Acceptance?

First we'll provide our definition of acceptance and then we'll attempt to explain it. We define acceptance as the toleration of the emotions evoked by aversive stimuli. Allow us to elaborate. In the presence of aversive stimulation a person often 1) feels emotions and 2) avoids (escapes, attacks, etc.). When both the feeling and the avoidance occur, the person is very likely to say that the reason they avoid is because of the feeling, e.g., they feel threatened, sad, vulnerable, invaded, fearful, etc. Our position is that the emotions as well as the avoidance are most likely evoked by the same aversive stimulus (see Kohlenberg & Tsai, 1991, for a more complete discussion). Since the emotion usually comes first, there is an inclination to attribute an illusory causal relationship to the emotion. In any event, the feeling of the emotions and the avoidance of the stimuli that evoke them are usually two sides of the same coin. We feel it is useful to speak of the emotional toleration side of the coin when doing acceptance work because the client is usually more aware of his/her feelings than of environmental determinants.

Avoidance is often appropriate and results in the removal of the aversive stimulus and the emotional states that it evokes. For example, escaping from the path of an oncoming car both eliminates the fear and the danger. Because of this, we all have long histories of being reinforced for avoiding, escaping, or attacking in the presence of aversive stimuli. Although these behaviors are often functional in removing aversive stimulation, in certain circumstances such aversively motivated (negatively reinforced) behaviors also create more problems than they solve. In other words, although aggression or escape might rescue us from an aversive situation, sometimes the cure is worse than the disease. For example, we often see clients who because of painful experiences with intimate relationships in the past currently do many things to avoid intimacy in the present. The form of the avoidance is quite variable but often is described by the partner as "being emotionally distant." We view being "emotionally distant" as a result of the client's avoidance of the aversive stimuli (and hence its evoked emotions) inherent to intimate relating. If the person was less avoiding, they would be feeling the evoked emotions and perhaps expressing or showing emotions (for a more complete discussion see Kohlenberg & Tsai, 1991). Technically speaking therefore, the "distance" in being "emotionally distant" is not from emotions but from lack of contact with the stimuli that evoke them (i.e., intimacy). Nevertheless, these intimacy avoiding behaviors are effective in limiting contact with the threat inherent in interpersonal relationships. Although effective at avoiding the potential aversiveness of intimate relationships, these behaviors also lead to a decreased quality of the relationship and can eventually produce painful isolation and loneliness, as well as perpetuating fear and mistrust. Therefore, although these clients are rescued from the pain of certain aspects of intimacy, they are also denied its joys.

It is within just such situations that therapists often work to promote acceptance. Since the client, in general, has better access to the feeling side of the coin than to the aversive stimuli that evoke them, promoting acceptance means helping him/her to tolerate those feelings (e.g., fear, vulnerability, threat, etc). The toleration of feelings is defined as staying in contact with the stimuli that evoke them. Toleration is accomplished by learning to do something besides avoiding, escaping, or attacking in the presence of aversive stimuli. In our example, successful acceptance promotion would lead to a client who could tolerate the fear (or other avoided emotion) evoked by interpersonal relationships by not running away or attacking the other person. Once again, we would define acceptance as tolerating the emotions associated with an aversive situation by not avoiding, escaping, or attacking.

It's important to note that the aversive stimulation we are referring to is always ultimately public. Although clients may be aware of how they are feeling, they may not focus on, or be aware of the public origins of those feelings. A client is usually aware of such public stimuli as stressful interactions with other people like spouses or employers, places (e.g., the mall for an agoraphobic), or things (e.g., spiders, planes, etc). On the other hand, the client may not be able to easily access the public stimuli responsible for the behaviors involved in remembering painful events, thinking unwanted thoughts, or feeling unwelcome emotions such as some anxieties and depressions. Behaviors such as avoidance, escape, or attack take different forms when directed against public aversive stimuli or their private sequelae. Escape from public aversive stimuli is often relatively straightforward. If you don't get along with your neighbor or you're afraid of snakes, avoiding these things is fairly easy. It is more difficult to apply these same methods to the private world. For example, it is easier to stop looking at a traumatic accident scene than to stop imagining that scene (as in PTSD flashbacks). Attacking the private aspects of aversive stimulation sometimes involves attacking the self. These self attacks can take the form of self-criticism, self-loathing, self-injury, or even suicide. On the other hand, escaping from private aversive stimuli can take the form of drug or alcohol abuse, excessive distracting (e.g., watching too much TV), or obsessive-compulsive behaviors.

What are the Benefits of Promoting Acceptance?

What are the benefits to the client of promoting this kind of emotional toleration? We believe the benefits are many, including (1) increased contact with previously missed reinforcers, (2) increased potential for productive action, and (3) decreased negative arousal. We will discuss each of these benefits in turn.

In the above example of the intimacy avoiding client, it is easy to see that although such a client might be successful in avoiding being hurt by others, he/she suffers because he/she also avoids all the positive and healthy benefits only available through intimate relationships. In other words, the client suffers because of the decreased contact with potentially necessary reinforcers. Part of the benefit of helping such a client tolerate the fear of intimacy comes from the increased likelihood that the client will make contact with the positive and healthy aspects of interpersonal relationships despite his/her fear. If the client's only available responses to the fear associated with intimacy are avoidance, escape, or aggression, then he/she will never experience a healthy relationship. Promoting acceptance teaches the client to stay with someone they are growing close to *despite* their fear. Or as Hayes (1987) puts it in the case of an agoraphobic "the next question is, 'are you willing to go to the mall *and* be afraid?'"

Another benefit of promoting acceptance is that emotional toleration increases the possibility of productive action. Again let's use the example of an intimacy avoiding client. For a client who is successfully avoiding the intimacy of interpersonal relationships, one of the unintended side effects of that avoidance is that he/she never learns how to nurture a healthy relationship, or how to handle the aversive aspects of a relationship without destroying it. Lacking these skills and the opportunity to learn them increases the chances that such a client will suffer again and again from ill-formed relationships. Promoting emotional toleration encourages the person to stay with a relationship despite their fears and frustrations. Through this increased contact with relationship situations, the odds are increased that the person will learn more productive ways of handling those situations and their own reactions to them. If they do not run away despite their fear, then they place themselves in a situation where they must try some other productive way of being. Oftentimes the situation itself will shape more constructive behavior. However, even in cases where constructive relationship behaviors must be actively taught, this education cannot possibly take place until the person first learns to tolerate the situation and his/her own reaction to it without running away or attacking.

Another, paradoxical, benefit provided by promoting acceptance is that it decreases negative arousal. If a person can learn to stay with a situation despite its aversiveness, the negative feelings associated with that situation often begin to extinguish. An example of this phenomena is illustrated in the case history presented later in this chapter. Helping a person to notice their negative arousal without responding to it creates a condition in which over time that negative arousal will become less and less powerful. For example, if someone who experiences a great deal of anxiety in intimate situations can be helped to tolerate that anxiety without running away, then over time intimate relationships will evoke less and less anxiety. Paradoxically, the person must be willing to have the anxiety without struggling against it in order for extinction to take place (cf., Hayes, 1987). It is because of this paradox that acceptance therapists do not present decreasing negative arousal as a goal.

FAP and Acceptance?

Clients often come to therapy wanting to get rid of their painful feelings (anxiety, depression, fear, loneliness, etc). They often complain of not being able to tolerate these feelings and hope their therapist can provide a bona fide cure. However, acceptance therapies focus not on getting rid of the painful feelings, but on changing the client's intolerance. In the next section we will discuss how FAP pursues this goal. It is our belief that FAP illustrates how most, if not all, forms of interpersonal therapy promote acceptance.

What is FAP?

FAP is an approach to psychotherapy rooted in the philosophy of radical behaviorism (Skinner, 1953; 1957; 1974). This approach to the study of behavior is much too broad to discuss in detail here. Therefore, rather than spend a great deal of time discussing the radical behavioral roots of FAP, we will provide a brief functional outline of FAP and refer the interested reader to other sources (Kohlenberg & Tsai, 1991).

The most basic principle underlying FAP is that the effects of psychotherapy treatment are stronger if the client's problem behaviors and improvements occur during the session. This principle derives from two basic tenets of radical behaviorism. The first is the assumption that all behavior is contingency shaped. The second is that the closer in time and place a behavior is to its consequents, the more effective those consequents will be in shaping that behavior. The first principle basically states that what we do affects our environment, and that effect in turn affects our subsequent behavior. If that effect increases the likelihood that we will engage in that behavior again, then we call it reinforcement. If that effect decreases the likelihood that we will engage in that behavior again, then we call it punishment. The second principle basically states that if our behavior has a close and immediate effect on the environment, that effect will in turn have a more powerful effect on our subsequent behavior than if it were further away and delayed. These two principles imply that psychotherapists are more helpful to their clients when they focus on and respond to what occurs within the session than when they simply talk about things that have occurred outside the session. Thus FAP as an approach to psychotherapy advocates attending to and working with those aspects of the client's problems that manifest themselves within the relationship between therapist and client.

Clinically Relevant Behaviors

Within FAP, clients in-session behaviors are classified into three categories. The first category of clinically relevant behaviors (CRB1) are those behaviors occurring in-session that are actual instances of the client's problem. For example, for a client who complains about having a hard time making friends, CRB1 might include poor eye contact, tangential and unfocused speech, and frequently interrupting the therapist. For a client who avoids intimate relationships, CRB1 might include changing the subject when it becomes too personal or talking exclusively about other people.

The second category of clinically relevant behaviors (CRB2) are those behaviors whose absence or infrequency are directly related to the presenting problem. In other words, these are things that the client needs to do more frequently or consistently in order to alleviate their problem. They might include being more assertive, more self-disclosive, or more accepting.

The third category of clinically relevant behaviors (CRB3) are those things the client says about his/her problems and what he/she believes to be their cause. FAP stresses the importance of discriminating between CRB3 and CRB1. This is because there is a fundamental difference between a client saying he/she feels frightened by and withdraws from intimate relationships (CRB3) and that client actually feeling frightened and withdrawing from the therapist during the session (CRB1). Many therapies focus on what the client says to the exclusion of what the client actually does in session. Making the distinction between CRB1's and CRB3's lessens the likelihood of making this mistake. However, CRB3's remain vitally important within FAP, particularly in the promotion of acceptance. We will return to this point later.

Five Rules for Therapists

In addition to advocating the advantage of classifying client's in-session behavior into the above categories, FAP also specifies five therapeutic rules believed to help therapists become more helpful to their clients. We will briefly outline these five rules.

Rule 1 states that the therapist should attempt to develop a repertoire for observing possible instances of CRB's within the therapy session. In other words, therapists should practice identifying those aspects of the client's problems that occur within the therapy hour. This skill is essential to FAP because interventions based on the client-therapist relationship are most effective when the therapist is able to discriminate in-session occurrences of the client's problem.

Rule 2 states that the therapist should strive to construct a therapeutic environment that is evocative of CRB's. Basically this means that therapists should attend to those aspects of the therapeutic environment or relationship that are likely to set the stage for the client's problem. If these evocative situations are available to the therapist, he/she should make use of those situations to evoke the relevant client problem in-session. For example, if the client has a hard time talking about relationships, the therapist can initiate a discussion with the client about their relationship. Again, this is based on the assumption that therapy has its most powerful effect on clients when their problems occur in session.

Rule 3 states that the therapist should arrange for the positive reinforcement of CRB2. In other words, the therapist should be prepared to respond to healthy client behaviors in such a way that those behaviors will become more likely in the future. In order for a client's healthy behavior to become more likely in the future and to generalize outside of therapy, it is important that therapists make use of natural as opposed to arbitrary reinforcers. Arbitrary reinforcers would be those responses by the therapist that, although effective, are unlikely to occur outside of therapy. The classic example of an arbitrary reinforcer is the M&M. Although giving M&M's to a client for showing clinical improvement may work in the short term, over the long run improvements will be short-lived and have low generalizability. A more relevant example is the therapist who says "good job" whenever the client risks a self-disclosure. Although this may increase self-disclosure with the therapist, it is unlikely to have an effect outside of therapy because other people in the client's life are unlikely to respond to him/her by saying "good job." Natural reinforcers, on the other hand, would be those responses by the therapist that are more likely to occur outside of therapy. For example, natural responses to self-disclosure are demonstrations of appropriate concern, attention, and interest. These are responses that the client is likely to encounter not only from the therapist but from other people in their lives as well. Client improvements (CRB2's) are more likely to generalize outside of therapy if the therapist uses natural reinforcers (cf., Ferster, 1967).

Rule 4 states that the therapist should strive to observe the potential reinforcing properties of his/her behavior that are contingent upon the client's CRB. Basically this rule is asking the therapist to pay close attention to the things he/she does that are having an impact on the client's in-session manifestations of the problem. The therapist may notice ways in which he/she is helping, or the therapist may notice that he/she has been inadvertently punishing CRB2s. This self-observation can lead to improvements in the therapists technique. If this type of self-observation is also shared with the client, it can in turn help the client learn how to observe and talk about his/her own behavior.

Rule 5 states that therapists should attempt to develop a repertoire for describing the functional relationships between controlling variables and the client's CRB. Basically this means that therapists should practice talking with the client about those things that appear to be setting the stage for both CRB1 and CRB2. For example, if the therapist notices that the client tends to change the subject whenever the therapist expresses caring for the client, describing this for the client increases his/her awareness of his/her own behavior and the effect it has on other people.

How does FAP Promote Acceptance?

How does a FAP approach to psychotherapy promote the emotional toleration of aversive stimuli? The primary assumptions from a FAP perspective are (1) that emotional toleration is best achieved through the client's experiences within the therapeutic session, and (2) that an interpersonal focus naturally leads to the types of experiences necessary for promoting emotional toleration. The interpersonal relationship between client and therapist often evokes difficult emotions thus providing many opportunities to promote emotional toleration. In this section we will discuss three ways that FAP promotes acceptance: (1) through encouraging self-observation, (2) through the reduction of self-blame, and (3) through the experiencing of in-session emotional responses.

Emotional Toleration through Self-Observation

In FAP, self-observation is categorized as CRB3. It is basically the process through which the client comes to identify and talk about his/her problems and their believed causes as they are happening. FAP therapists model self-observation (as noted in Rule 4) by describing for the client the therapist's own thoughts, feelings, hopes, and fears as they occur in session. Often this type of modeling is the simplest way for clients to learn how to make self-observations. We believe that therapist modeling of self-observation is often more effective than simply explaining to the client what self-observation means and asking him/her to try it.

FAP therapists also describe their own observations of the client's behavior and what sets the stage for it (Rule 5). This again provides a model of what to look for and how to talk about it. The types of descriptions FAP therapists provide are always cast in terms of the function the client's behavior serves within a particular context. Functional explanations are based on the client's history and on what certain behaviors have accomplished for the client in the past. It is assumed that the reason clients do what they do in the present is determined by what has worked for them in the past. In other words, the behaviors that led to the client's current problems are not wholly dysfunctional. They do serve some important function for the client such as self-protection. However, in the process of serving that important function these behaviors also create other problems in the client's life. It is also assumed that the client's behavior is *determined* by the function it has served and is not a reflection of the client's morality, stupidity, or ill-will.

Clients are encouraged to observe their own behavior as it occurs and to provide this type of functional explanation for that behavior. In addition to the fact that our own philosophical leanings are toward functional explanations, we believe deterministic functional explanations avoid the self-blame, guilt, and shame that often accompany a client's own explanations for his/her problems. Functional explanations are devoid of moral judgment and determinations of good and bad. In summary, within FAP, clients are helped to tolerate aversive emotions by being taught to step back and observe their own emotions while they are having them. They are also taught to notice what they do in response to those feelings and to provide a nonjudgmental explanation for those reactions. For example, a client afraid of intimacy can be taught to notice that he/she feels anxious and changes the subject whenever it becomes too personal, and that the reason they do that is to protect themselves from being hurt like they have been in the past. Focusing on the relationship between the client and the therapist provides many such opportunities for clients to observe their emotions in session.

We believe self-observation helps clients tolerate the emotions evoked by aversive stimuli by changing the context that was previously deemed intolerable. If a client can be taught to observe his/her reactions while they are occurring, then the context is changed from one in which he/she simply reacts to one in which he/she reacts *and* observes his/her reaction. The addition of the self-observation changes the context and allows for the occurrence of other behaviors besides avoidance, escape, or attack. For example, a client may learn to say certain things to himself in the presence of the aversive stimuli that help him to better tolerate it. Additionally, observing her reaction and having a nonjudgmental explanation for it may help a client make contact with other, less aversive, aspects of that situation. This additional contact may in turn actually make the situation less aversive in the future.

Self-observation and the understanding provided by a non-blaming explanation can have an enormous curative effect. This assumption is common to almost all psychotherapies including psychoanalysis, client-centered therapies, and cognitive-behavioral therapies. The reason such explanations are curative is open to interpretation, but the effect itself is almost universally recognized.

For example, Rational Emotive Therapy (RET; Ellis, 1989) places more emphasis on promoting self-acceptance and discouraging self-criticism than on promoting overt change. Ellis states "RET is not really oriented toward symptom removal, except when it seems that this is the only kind of change likely to be accomplished with clients. It is primarily designed to induce people to examine and change some of their most basic values -- particularly those values that keep them disturbance-prone" (p. 198). Basically Ellis' approach to changing people's values is to provide for them interpretations of their behavior free of moral judgment and self-blame. "...Both RET and client-centered therapy have basically the same goal: helping people to refuse to condemn themselves even though they may be utterly unenthusiastic about some of their behavior" (p. 201).

Another example of promoting emotional toleration through self-observation is provided by Integrative Behavioral Couples Therapy (IBCT; Jacobson & Christensen, in press) they discuss promoting acceptance between the partners in a marriage by "making the problem an `it'". Essentially, this means providing a couple with a common perspective from which they can view an irreconcilable problem as external to the relationship. Rather than simply engaging in the problem, the couple is taught to see "it" as it happens. "Through reformulating the problem as an `it,' each partner is expected to become increasingly able to tolerate this difference between them without feeling either personally guilty or blaming of his/her partner" (Cordova & Jacobson, 1993).

Another example is provided by Hayes (1987). Hayes trains clients directly in the skill of self-observation by describing for them the process of self-observation. After asking a client to close his eyes and notice his thoughts, Hayes says, "I want you to notice that when I asked these questions, you were there noticing the reactions... the observer you" (Hayes, 1987, p. 361). By the "observer you" Hayes refers to that aspect of the person that notices what is happening from a neutral perspective.

Emotional tolerance through self-observation is also a primary characteristic of what psychoanalysts call the therapeutic alliance. For example, Sterba (1934) viewed the therapeutic alliance as involving one of the two aspects of the ego. Sterba (1934) stated that the defensive part of the ego was driven by instinctual and repressive forces that interfered with the progress of therapy. The therapeutically allied part of the ego, on the other hand, was regarded by Sterba as realistic and seeking understanding, psychic change, and psychic growth. Similarly, Paolino (1981) described the therapeutic alliance as "the therapist and patient agree to observe the patient's psychic functioning and behavior in an attempt to achieve a deterministic understanding of such behavior" (p. 100). These notions have as a theme the client not only acting but also standing back from and observing these actions. Furthermore, once this self-observation occurs, the client can describe what happened from a historical perspective. For example, the client might have an angry outburst at the therapist for not answering a question, but also can observe and describe the outburst as an irrational act based on how his father never answered his questions because they were considered stupid.

Blame Reduction

As noted above, in FAP when attempting to help a client learn to accept the feelings associated with aversive stimuli, it is vitally important to offer nonblaming and nonjudgmental interpretations of the client's reactions. Often clients believe that the feelings they are having are wrong, stupid, weird, or evil. These beliefs necessarily lead the client to want to change or get rid of the feelings they experience. If a client believes he is wrong to experience particular feelings, then he also believes there must be something wrong with him as a person. Self-blame makes it difficult for a client to accept the feelings evoked by aversive situations, because if he/she is to blame, then somehow changes or amends must be made. Hayes (1987) explains to his clients that "fault and blame are established when we add in social condemnation to try and motivate someone to change." Emphasizing nonjudgmental interpretations, on the other hand, creates a therapeutic environment in which the client is less likely to blame his/herself or to feel guilty or shameful. As these threats are removed, clients begin to be in a better position to acquire more personally effective ways of dealing with previously feared or frustrating situations (CRB2). The more a client can stay in touch with situations that used to be unbearable, the more opportunity the client has to learn from those situations how to behave more effectively. Through their own experience, and perhaps with the help of the therapist, new approaches to the situation can be tried. If these new approaches are effective for the client, then they will become more likely in the future.

Note that in promoting acceptance of the emotions evoked by aversive stimuli we are not necessarily promoting acceptance of the status quo. Certainly in many cases the client's world simply will not bend and he/she will have to learn to come to terms with that. But in other cases, both the client's world and the client are open to change if only the client can learn to tolerate the situation long enough to learn from it and develop new behavior. Acceptance in this respect does not mean the absence of change. Quite the contrary, it denotes the profound personal change necessary to not run away when you're scared and to not attack when you're angry.

Other acceptance-oriented therapies also emphasize the importance of creating a nonblaming therapeutic environment when promoting client acceptance. For example, Linehan in her work with borderline clients advises them to experience the world "without adding judgment of good or bad." Further, she states that acceptance "is seeing what *is* clearly, without the haze of what we want it to be or what we don't want it to be. Without screaming YES or screaming NO the moment we experience what *is*" (M. M. Linehan, personal communication, 1993).

IBCT (Jacobson & Christensen, in press) also strives to create a nonblaming therapeutic environment. In couples therapy the issue is not so often self-blame as it is blaming the other partner. Partners in a distressed relationship often find it easier to blame each other than to accept their mutual roles in perpetuating their pain. "The job of the IBCT therapist in the context of this kind of cross-blaming is to help the couple reformulate their problems as arising out of the common and understandable reactions they are having to equally common and understandable differences between them" (Cordova & Jacobson, 1993). Here, as in FAP (Kohlenberg & Tsai, 1991) and DBT (Linehan, 1993), in promoting acceptance the emphasis is on nonblaming and nonjudgmental interpretations of aversive situations.

B. F. Skinner also recognized the importance of moving beyond the punishment of blame and moral punishment. He believed, as do we, that many of the problems people experience in their day-to-day lives are the result of the great effort they necessarily expend avoiding unnecessarily punitive situations. He believed that as behavior analysts and therapists "our task is not to encourage moral struggle or to build or demonstrate inner virtues. It is to make life less punishing and in doing so to release for more reinforcing activities the time and energy consumed in the avoidance of punishment" (Skinner, 1971, p. 76).

Evoking Emotional Responses

Once again one of the main tenets of FAP states that an interpersonal focus naturally leads to the types of experiences necessary for promoting emotional toleration. Therefore we believe that both self-observation and blame reduction are most effectively learned through focusing on the client-therapist relationship. In order for emotional toleration to be promoted most effectively, emotions evoked by aversive stimuli must be evoked during the therapy session. Within the therapy session, emotions evoked by situations the client finds aversive (e.g., self-disclosure) can be observed by both the client and the therapist and interpreted nonjudgmentally without avoidance. FAP therapists, recognizing the importance of evoking emotional reactions within the session, encourage and reinforce such emotional responses. In FAP, as in most interpersonal therapies, clients are assured that within therapy all of their feelings are acceptable and they are encouraged to talk about those feelings. Developing a close client-therapist relationship is an essential aspect of FAP particularly because such a relationship is highly evocative of problems the client may be experiencing with intimacy. A close client-therapist relationship often evokes feelings of fear, mistrust, or even hostility depending on the client's personal history with similar relationships. Strong emotional reactions on the part of the client can also be evoked by therapist self-disclosure and by bringing up the client-therapist relationship as a topic to discuss. In fact discussing the client-therapist relationship as it stands within the therapy hour is often one of the most evocative therapy topics.

The success of promoting emotional toleration is measured by the degree to which the client can learn to experience and observe these feelings without running away from therapy or attacking against either themselves or the therapist. In fact, the absence of emotional responses within the session would indicate to the FAP therapist that therapy is not working as effectively as it could. Usually in such circumstances either the client is successfully avoiding evocative topics or evocative conditions are simply not present in therapy. Because FAP emphasizes encouraging client emotional expression in-session, building emotional tolerance is a natural outcome of FAP therapy. As noted earlier, simply making contact with what may have seemed unbearable emotions can lead to several beneficial outcomes including contact with previously missed reinforcers, the increased possibility of more productive action, and the actual reduction of aversive arousal.

An Example of Acceptance Promotion in FAP

The following transcript demonstrates the utility of the client-therapist relationship in promoting acceptance. The client, a 42-year-old technician, was diagnosed with schizoid personality disorder and major depression. The client had no sexual relationship or satisfying communication in what he described as "a barren relationship" with his wife of six years. When previously in marital therapy he was unable to do even the simplest of activities requested and his wife had filed for divorce. At the time he began treatment he was unable to hold a job because whenever there was a conflict at work he "came down" with a variety of physical symptoms and simply didn't show up. He was unable to talk about his feelings and lacked any insight into his problems. From a behavioral standpoint, most of his presenting problems could be seen as the result of his inability to deal with interpersonal conflict. Specifically, he avoided and escaped from interpersonal conflict involving disapproval or demands that he couldn't meet. At the beginning of treatment this avoidance often took the form of dissociation in which he spaced out and withdrew into a near "catatonic state." A major component of treatment was using within-session conflicts with the therapist as opportunities for evoking and reinforcing improved repertoires for dealing with interpersonal conflict. At first this mainly focused on limiting or finding less extreme methods of escape than complete dissociation. Later, as illustrated in the transcript below, more sophisticated repertoires involving tolerance and self-observation were developed. After 10 years of FAP treatment, the client was responsibly employed and was actively involved in marital counseling. A major marital milestone was reached when he began to argue with his wife.

The transcript concerns an interaction regarding a substance abuse problem which was largely under control except for relapses involving one last refillable prescription. Every couple of months, when it was refillable, he would go on a 2-3 day binge. In the first part of the session the therapist had asked for permission to call the client's doctor and end the prescription. The discussion mainly centered on the pros and cons of this. The client was resistant and the therapist became more insistent. Thus there was an ongoing conflict between therapist and client involving a therapist request which the client was resisting. Although the client's response to this conflict was much improved compared to the earlier dissociations, it was obviously very distressing and he became more depressed during the session as a result of it. A resolution of the conflict would have involved some problem solving and perhaps either the client saying "yes" or "no" or the therapist withdrawing or modifying the request. Rather than attempting to achieve any of these resolutions and thereby reduce the distress and depression, the therapeutic strategy was to encourage acceptance through emotional toleration and self-observation. The therapist's response in line 1 represents a shift in focus from "the client either giving or not giving permission" to the "observing of the conflict without necessarily resolving it." Throughout the interaction the therapist encourages toleration by blocking avoidance and making the unresolved conflict (without attempting to resolve it) the main topic of discussion.

1. T: So, just kind of this struggle between the two of us.
2. C: I wouldn't call it a struggle but...
     (Avoidance-tries to end discussion, non-acceptance, no toleration.)
3. T: Why not?
(blocks avoidance)
4. C: I guess it is, ah...

5. T: A struggle, it's an issue. I mean I want permission to cancel this prescription and you don't want to give me permission and that's a struggle. It's a conflict. Now how big, that aspect of it, how important is that in terms of making you depressed?

   (The therapist continues to present the aversive stimulus thereby encouraging contact. The therapist acknowledges the struggle and the negative emotions without efforts to ameliorate them. In effect the therapist is saying "the problem is here, let's stay with it, let's not necessarily resolve it, let's discuss its functions, let's discuss your having negative emotions without having to get rid of them").

6. C: Well I mean, I know it makes me depressed, but I don't know what effect it has on the overall depression.

7. T: Does it get you depressed in here as we are talking about it?

8. C: Yeah.

9. T: And is that feeling of depression like your usual feeling of depression?

   (This is a standard FAP question aimed at assessing CRB. That is, is the within session depression you are experiencing the same as the daily life problem for which you are seeking treatment?)

10. C: I would say so yeah. I mean, as best I can describe it, depression is always a little hard to put a finger on.

11. T: To pinpoint. But at least there is a similarity of some type. Well, now I'm calling this a conflict, is that fair to call it that?

12. C: Uh huh.

13. T: Are there any other conflicts that you are experiencing right now with other people that remind you of this in some way?

    (Again, this is an attempt to assess the relationship between the within-session behavior and daily life.)

14. C: Well I had a conflict with Bill a few weeks ago. (Client goes on to describe the incident and how it bothered him.)

    (a few minutes later)

19. T: And in some way it resembles you not doing what I want you to do for your own good?

    (The conflict is brought up and the relationship between daily life and within session is acknowledged, keeping the aversive stimulus present without implying that the situation has to change.)

20. C: Yeah I think that's part of the disapproval essentially, that I can get depressed if I sense disapproval in others. I'm seeming to see it at work and I'm seeming to see it here, and I don't know how to deal with it very well. Other than, as of late, I can intellectually look at it and say "pull your other self along, there could be other reasons."

    (this is client self-observation and evidence of acceptance.)

    (a few minutes later after more experience with staying with the conflict, observing it, having the emotions, and not resolving it)

43. T: Right, and I'm basically saying this prescription stuff is pretty important. But I think this other thing (staying with and not avoiding) is even more important. The fact that my disappointment or disapproval of your refusal produces depression in you. That whole interaction and being able to figure out what's going on there is even more important, from a psychological standpoint, than the details of the prescription. Although I still think that's pretty important too. Okay, so you're smiling a little bit what's that?
44. C: I'm just feeling better.
45. T: Feeling better.
    (The client is reinforced for tolerating the conflict and not avoiding it. It has become a workable problem.)

How can FAP Contribute to Other Acceptance Therapies?

We believe an emphasis on the in-session relationship between client and therapist is beneficial within any acceptance-oriented approach to psychotherapy. In-session approaches to promoting acceptance emphasize more of an experiential rather than didactic method. Didactic methods rely heavily on cognitive and instructional interventions and place less emphasis on the client-therapist relationship. Although didactic methods for promoting acceptance are often effective and necessary, we are concerned about the possible implications of overlooking in-session variables. The client-therapist relationship provides an invaluable arena in which to positively impact a client's capacity to tolerate his/her emotional experience. Indeed the most powerful interventions available to us may exist solely within this context.

In this section, we would like to emphasize that, in attempting to promote emotional toleration, it is vitally important that the therapist pay close attention to the things he/she does that are having an impact on the client's in-session manifestations of the problem (Rule 4). We want to emphasize this point here because we believe that by failing to assess the in-session impact of the therapist on the client, didactic approaches to promoting acceptance are made vulnerable to inadvertently punishing CRB2s or strengthening CRB1s. As examples, we have chosen some previously presented work done by experts we have referred to earlier in this chapter. We have chosen these authors for their expertise in the area of acceptance promotion. Each example we present represents a highly effective and innovative approach to promoting acceptance which we believe benefits from consideration of factors advocated by FAP.

As our first example let us consider an intervention from Hayes' (1987) presentation of Acceptance and Comittment Therapy (see Comprehensive Distancing). Hayes (1987) offers as Goal 1 of therapy the creation of a state of creative hopelessness. Essentially the goal is to help the client give up the way he/she is currently seeing and trying to deal with the problem so that other, more effective means can be tried. One of the interventions in the service of this goal is to delay giving the client easy answers to their problems while at the same time discussing the fruitlessness of continuing to approach those problems as they have in the past. For example, in response to the client's wanting to be told how to get better, Hayes responds by saying "see, the reason I can't answer that now is that it wouldn't do any good until you really let go of this determination to dig your way out" (Hayes, 1987, p. 347). The therapist goal of creating a state of creative hopelessness guides a therapist to induce an emotional state that is difficult for the client and thus offers the opportunity to encourage and reinforce emotional toleration in the session. The therapist communicates that if the client is patient and tolerates the anxiety evoked by the therapists refusal to provide simple answers, then he/she will benefit in the long run. This intervention is very powerful and provides an excellent opportunity for the client to learn emotional toleration in-vivo.

If proper attention were not given to the effects of the therapist on the client, however, the therapist could inadvertantly reinforce a client CRB1 through the use of the same intervention. For example, if the client has the type of personal history where giving in to authority and discounting his/her own feelings has been reinforced by avoiding punishment, then refusing to provide some kind of answer may inadvertently strengthen this CRB1. We believe that attending to the in-vivo experience of the client mitigates against the potential for this type of unintended effect. For example, since one would expect a refusal of this type to be somewhat difficult for a client, noticing that the client complies with little struggle may indicate that a CRB1 has inadvertantly been strengthened.

A similar example stems from the acceptance concept of surrender. Surrender in the context of promoting acceptance refers to giving up the struggle to change something that cannot be changed. In instances where struggling against the unchangeable does the client more harm than good, helping the client to surrender that struggle is often the goal of acceptance work. For example, in reference to a client giving up such a struggle, M. M. Linehan (personal communication, 1993) states "it was surrender, even though that is not currently viewed as a good word." Ellis' RET also promotes the concept of surrender as a strategy for promoting acceptance. He states "RET especially holds that minimal disturbance is correlated with people's surrendering all pretensions to superhumanness and with fully accepting their own and the world's intrinsic limitations" (Ellis, 1989, p. 210). Surrender as an aspect of acceptance can be considered a CRB2 for most of us, particularly in cases where struggling with a problem leads to avoidance or aggression. However, this is not universally true. Surrender for some people may be a strategy which they have adopted for dealing with aversive situations in which assertiveness, honesty, and emotional expression would be more productive. In such cases surrender would be a CRB1 and the therapist would want to reinforce the client for not surrendering. Again, in-session responses by the client can cue the therapist that he/she has inadvertantly reinforced such a CRB1. If a client embraces surrender unquestion- ingly and with little difficulty, this may be a sign that he/she is facile with this strategy as a means of avoidance.

As our final example, let us consider the concept of making the problem an "it" from IBCT (Jacobson & Christensen, in press). As noted earlier, this strategy provides a couple with a common perspective from which they can join together in viewing an irreconcilable problem as external to both partners. The partners are encouraged to see the problem as something that "just happens" in their relationship and for which neither of them is to blame. This strategy increases acceptance on the part of both partners by decreasing cross-blaming. As in the above examples, however, there are circumstances in which such an intervention might inadvertantly reinforce a client problem or punish a client improvement. For example, consider a couple in which one partner has only recently begun to express his/her feelings and concerns to the other partner. This new behavior is obviously important for the future health of the relationship and should be encouraged by the therapist. Attempting at this point to teach the couple to see their problem as an "it" could supress this emerging CRB2. That partner's emerging capacity to talk about his/her concerns may initially be too fragile for such an intervention. Attending to the client's in-session experience mitigates against the potential for introducing this intervention prematurely.

Our main point here is that even powerful and effective strategies such as those presented are made vulnerable to unintentionally contributing to a client's problems if insufficient attention is given to what exactly the therapist is reinforcing through his/her interventions in session. In other words, the application of acceptance strategies must be guided by continual in-vivo monitoring of the effects of such interventions on the particular client (Rule 4), as well as by a thorough understanding of that client's personal history. The effectiveness of any acceptance strategy in promoting actual acceptance is wholly dependent on the unique reinforcement history of the particular client. Acceptance therapists must thoroughly consider not only the strategy itself, but also the client context into which it is to be introduced. If this type of in-vivo observation is not done, acceptance therapists risk inadvertently contributing to the very problems they are attempting to solve.

Conclusion

In conclusion we will summarize the various points made throughout this brief chapter. First, we have defined acceptance as toleration of the emotions evoked by aversive stimuli. More technically, acceptance is the absence of escape, avoidance, or attack behaviors in response to the various private events evoked by aversive stimuli. Second, we believe the primary clinical benefit that clients derive from the various acceptance techniques is this capacity to tolerate the emotions evoked by aversive stimuli without attacking or running away. We believe the promotion of emotional toleration provides several benefits for the psychotherapy client. First, through increased contact with avoided situations, the client is provided an opportunity to contact reinforcers present within that situation that were previously missed. Second, increasing contact with avoided situations increases the possibility that the client will learn new and more constructive ways of dealing with the problem besides attacking or running away. Third, and paradoxically, increased contact with the emotions evoked by aversive stimuli results in decreased aversive arousal over time (extinction).

In this chapter we have also provided a brief overview of the approach to interpersonal psychotherapy known as Functional Analytic Psychotherapy (FAP; Kohlenberg & Tsai, 1991). We believe FAP and other interpersonal psychotherapies promote acceptance through three different processes. The first process is the shaping of self-observation. Self-observation is the capacity to observe and describe your own behavior as it is happening. The addition of self-observation to an aversive situation changes the context enough to make tolerance more attainable. Second, FAP promotes emotional toleration by offering nonblaming and nonjudgmental interpretations of the client's responses. This leads to reduction in self-blame and thus necessarily increases the tolerability of aversive emotions. Thirdly, because of its focus on the in-session relationship between the client and the therapist, FAP promotes emotional acceptance by evoking emotional responses within the session where the client can be reinforced for tolerating them. Experiencing aversive emotions within the session is the most effective way for clients to learn to tolerate those emotions without attacking or running away. Finally, in this chapter, we caution against paying too little attention to the interpersonal context within which acceptance techniques occur. We believe that inattention to the reinforcement history of the client and his/her in-vivo reaction to certain techniques could inadvertently lead the therapist to contribute to the very client problems they are attempting to alleviate.

We are very pleased to see the upsurge of interest in acceptance work characterized by this book. We have been both impressed and influenced by the exceptional acceptance work done by Steve Hayes, Neil Jacobson, and Marsha Linehan. Promoting acceptance promises to provide many, many benefits to psychotherapy clients suffering from a range of clinical problems. We believe that the relationship between client and therapist provides an invaluable opportunity to do in-vivo acceptance training, and we advocate adding this type of relationship focus to any therapy designed to promote acceptance.

References

Cordova, J. V., & Jacobson, N. S. (1993). Couple distress. In D. H. Barlow (Ed.), *Clinical handbook of psychological disorders* (2nd ed., pp. 481-512). New York: Guilford.

Ellis, A. (1989). Rational-emotive therapy. In R. J. Corsini & D. Wedding (Eds.), *Current Psychotherapies* (pp. 197-238). Itasca: F. E. Peacock Publishers, Inc.

Ferster, C. B. (1967). Arbitrary and natural reinforcement. *Psychological Record, 22*, 1-16.

Hayes, S. C. (1987). A contextual approach to therapeutic change. In N. S. Jacobson (Ed.), *Psychotherapist in clinical practice: Cognitive and behavioral perspectives* (327-387). New York: Guilford.

Jacobson, N. S., & Christensen, A. (in press). *Couple therapy: An integrative approach.* New York: Norton.

Kohlenberg, R. J., & Tsai, M. (1991). *Functional Analytic Psychotherapy.* New York: Plenum Press.

Linehan, M. M. (1993). *Cognitive-behavioral treatment of borderline personality disorder.* New York: Guilford.

Paolino, T. J., Jr. (1981). *Psychoanalytic psychotherapy.* New York: Brunner/Mazel.

Skinner, B. F. (1953). *Science and human behavior.* New York: The Free Press.

Skinner, B. F. (1957). *Verbal behavior.* New Jersey: Prentice-Hall Inc.

Skinner, B. F. (1971). *Beyond freedom and dignity.* New York: Bantam.

Skinner, B. F. (1974). *About behaviorism.* New York: Vintage Books.

Sterba, R. F. (1934). The fate of the ego in psychoanalysis. *International Journal of Psycho-Analysis, 15,* 117-126.

Discussion of Kohlenberg

Acceptance and the Therapeutic Relationship

Christopher McCurry
University of Nevada

In the various chapters of this volume, there is, as expected, disagreements over the definition of acceptance. Two positions on the nature of acceptance, as I understand them, are notable. A definition put forward by the adherents of the Gestalt and related psychological perspectives suggests that acceptance is unfettered experience of what is, unclouded by judgements and without appeal to consequences. A second group, primarily the Radical Behaviorists, define acceptance as willingness to have certain experiences in the service of certain goals. Differences in definition appear to stem from the units of analysis employed by the Gestalt and Radical Behavioral theorists: the private experience and the act in context, respectively.

Cordova and Kohlenberg define acceptance within Functional Analytic Psychotherapy (FAP) as an "emotional tolerance" based on the client's learning to "take one step back in the situation and observe." This definition would have benefitted from elaboration. In the context of promoting acceptance, I find the term *tolerance* problematic because it connotes for me "enduring" or "gritting one's teeth" to "get through" an experience. This quality is suggested by several of the word's formal definitions, e.g., "the capacity to endure hardship or pain" or "to put up with" (American Heritage Dictionary, 1991). This quality of tolerance seems to fit neither the Gestalt nor the Radical Behavioral (e.g., Steve Hayes' Acceptance and Commitment Therapy) definitions of acceptance as I understand them. In the Gestalt view, the implied adversarial relationship to the stimulus being "put up with" would suggest that one was not truly experiencing acceptance but was in some way still struggling with one's experience. In Acceptance and Commitment Therapy, the verbal behavior of applying valuative labels ("hardship and pain") to one's experience would in turn become grist for the mill of acceptance, ad infinitum.

Still, an examination of the processes (units of analysis) within FAP suggests that Cordova and Kohlenberg have presented an approach to acceptance and change that is fundamentally contextual. We may even continue to use the term *tolerance* if we employ a different definition of the word, one from engineering-- "the permissible deviation from a specified value of a structural dimension" (American Heritage Dictionary, 1991). For example, there is a certain tolerance, or optimal working space, between the surfaces of machine parts. Too little tolerance and high levels of friction and wear and tear occur. Too much tolerance and the parts will not operate smoothly, if at all. This would suggest that successful working (at least within machines) stems, not from aspects of the parts themselves, but from the relationship of parts to one another. It is the client's relationships with, or stances toward, the world that are changed in the course of FAP. The metaphor of taking "one step back in the situation" suggests creating an optimal "working space" between oneself and a historically problematic stimulus. This concept is found in the work of Beck and of Hayes as the act of "distancing."

Two mechanisms or processes within FAP may permit new self-stimulus relationships to be experienced and integrated into the client's history. One process corresponds to reorienting the client to his or her history. A second process in FAP involves the client establishing relationships which are "tolerant," beginning with the relationship between therapist and client. I will suggest that this latter mechanism necessarily replicates important developmental processes from the client's history.

Functional Analysis and Client History

In pursuit of FAP's stated therapeutic objectives of increasing experience and decreasing negative emotions, Cordova and Kohlenberg attempt to create a new framework for the client's experiences. The client's behaviors are framed in terms of a functional analysis, reorienting the client toward the antecedents and consequences of his or her behavior and away from mentalistic explanations. These functional analytic interpretations provide the client with "deterministic and blameless" reasons or rules for behavior based on acts in context. Generalization occurs through the application of these verbal rules to comparable situations outside of therapy (Kohlenberg & Tsai, 1987).

Our discussion of Cordova and Kohlenberg's paper included interesting questions about the process by which the client comes to embrace this new functional analytic paradigm. For example, would a client more readily and effectively adopt new interpretations of behavior that she had developed on her own (presumably with the guidance of the therapist) compared to the adoption of rules given to the client by the therapist? Kohlenberg responded that any interpretation of behavior that oriented the client toward external events and away from mentalistic processes was compatible with FAP, regardless of the means by which the interpretation is developed. A second question concerned the verbal nature of the FAP process; might some part of this process be "nonverbal", especially when working with children? To this question Kohlenberg stated that there are certainly nonverbal aspects of the FAP process comparable to the contingent shaping that occurs in play therapy. However, he took the view that therapist-client talk speeds up the therapeutic process through the creation of verbal rules or statements of functional relations.

The Therapeutic Relationship in FAP

In FAP the means for eliciting, examining, and shaping client behaviors is the interaction of the therapist and client in the therapeutic context. Kohlenberg emphasized this point when he stated that he is most interested in "what transpires in the therapeutic interaction;" and "The most important characteristic of a problem that makes it suitable for FAP is that it can occur during the therapy session." In order for the behaviors that constitute client improvement to generalize to important contexts outside of therapy something must change in the way the client perceives and organizes stimuli. How might the therapist-client relationship bring about this change?

Developmental theorists have long appreciated the role of relationships in establishing the direction of psychological growth. In children, assessments that describe the quality of early relationships (e.g., aversive parent-child interactions, attachment behaviors) have greater power to predict future psychopathology than do measures based on the individual child's characteristics (e.g., I.Q., temperament; Sroufe, 1989). Developmentalists suggest that early relationships, primarily the transactions between mothers and their young children, create "cognitive-emotional schema" (Behrends & Blatt, 1985). These schema (also described variously as models, rules, object-relations, or psychological structures) will be brought to bear on future relationships, with implications for psychological growth throughout the lifecycle. To the extent that these schema are responsive to contingencies and to the changing demands of the environment, the person will respond adaptively.

The functional analytic interpretations derived through FAP may be thought of as replacing older, less adaptive schema. The process by which these new schema are formed should be, and quite possibly must be, similar to processes which formed the original structures. A client's current difficulties may be considered recurring echoes of earlier, salient relationships. The therapeutic transactions between client and therapist in FAP add to the client's history and thereby alter its trajectory.

Cordova and Kohlenberg describe some of the therapy and therapist-related situations that evoke clinically significant client behaviors. These situations include extra-therapeutic events brought into session, negotiations around aspects of therapy such as scheduling, fees, termination, and so on. Additionally, therapist mistakes and expressions of positive and negative emotions are particularly powerful means for eliciting emotional experiences in the client. Speaking in terms of parent-child interactions, Behrends & Blatt (1985) stated, "Disruptions in the relationship are not only inevitable, they are required... for psychological development" (p.16). As long as the magnitude of the disruption does not exceed the adaptive capacities of the individuals involved, psychologically healthy change is probable. In the context of the therapeutic relationship, the therapist exercises some control over the timing and dosage of disruptors and is alert to naturally occurring perturbations in the relationship and how these might be used to occasion psychological growth.

Conclusion

The processes in FAP described above represent a contextual approach to therapy. Through functional analysis the client comes to see his or her behavior as acts in context, with implications for choice and responsibility. The client-therapist relationship creates a model field comprised of the client, the therapist, and the "space" between them in which the work of experiencing and the experience of successful working can occur. Through these processes the client continues to recognize other functional relationships in the world and adjusts the tolerances within these fields to bring about acceptance and change.

References

American Heritage Dictionary, 2nd College Edition. (1991). Boston: Houghton Mifflin.

Behrends, R. S., & Blatt, S. J. (1985). Internalization and psychological development throughout the lifecycle. *Psychoanalytic study of the child: Vol. 40* (pp. 11-39). New Haven: Yale University Press.

Kohlenberg, R. J., & Tsai, M. (1987). Functional analytic psychotherapy. In N. S. Jacobson (Ed.) *Psychotherapists in clinical practice: Cognitive and behavioral perspectives* (pp. 388-443). New York: Guilford Press.

Sroufe, L. A. (1989). Relationships and relationship disturbances. In A. J. Sameroff & R. N. Emde (Eds.) *Relationship disturbances in early childhood* (pp. 97-124). New York: Basic Books.

Section 3

Acceptance and Approaches
to Specific Problems
and Populations

Chapter 8

Acceptance and Broad Spectrum Treatment of Paraphilias

Joseph LoPiccolo
University of Missouri

This paper will discuss the possible application of acceptance based therapeutic procedures to the treatment of sexual deviations or paraphilias. This discussion will be restricted to non-violent paraphilias such as exhibitionism, voyeurism, frotteurism, and most cases of pedophilia. More coercive and violent sexual deviations, particularly rape, will not be included in this paper. In many cases rape is at least partially aggressively motivated, rather than being exclusively sexually motivated. Furthermore, there is very little research evidence that supports the effectiveness of psychological treatment for violent rapists (Marshall, Laws, & Barbaree, 1990).

There is a long tradition of acceptance based procedures being part of sex therapy techniques used to treat sexual dysfunctions. For example, one element of the treatment program for male erectile failure involves helping the man to accept that he may not always get an erection, and that failure to accept this possibility leads to the performance anxiety that creates and maintains erectile failure (LoPiccolo, 1990).

Treatment procedures for sexual deviation or paraphilias, however, have typically not included any acceptance based procedures. Currently, the mainstream approaches to paraphilias are primarily cognitive and behavioral (Marshall, Laws, & Barbaree, 1990). These cognitive-behavioral procedures typically operate on the assumption that deviant thoughts are precursors to deviant actions. Following on this assumption, current procedures generally try to suppress deviant thoughts in a variety of ways that appear to be antithetical to an acceptance based approach.

Acceptance based therapy was developed primarily in the context of anxiety disorders, depressive states, and obsessive-compulsive disorders. In this class of disorders, the patient is troubled by an unpleasant emotional state, and would like to be free of these negative emotions. Additionally, the behavior resulting from these negative emotions is also unpleasant and unrewarding. For example, agoraphobic patients experience anxiety at the thought of leaving the house, and this anxiety leads to avoiding pleasant events such as shopping trips and social gatherings, leaving the patient bored or depressed at home. Patients with anxiety or depressive disorders often experience a great deal of conflict, struggling with their wishes to be able to participate in events and behaviors which are purely pleasurable to most people, but which cause them anxiety and distress.

For anxiety and similar dysphoric disorders, the acceptance approach has an immediate logical appeal. If agoraphobic patients can accept their anxiety, and not make it a reason to stay home, they may find themselves able to enjoy a shopping trip, while merely noticing that they also do experience some anxiety during the trip. Similarly, obsessive patients who accept their obsessive thoughts may not feel compelled to engage in compulsive behavior, thus freeing themselves from hours of unrewarding rituals (Hayes, 1987; Hayes & Melancon, 1989).

Paraphilias, at first glance, might seem to be so dissimilar to anxiety and dysphoric disorders as to bring into question the utility of acceptance based procedures.

In the case of anxiety and depressive disorders, we are dealing with aversively motivated behaviors, with the patient experiencing negative emotions that block their ability to engage in normally pleasurable behaviors. Instead of being able to engage in reinforcing behaviors, the negative emotional state leads the patient to engage in intrinsically unrewarding avoidance behaviors.

The emotional valence of the emotions and behaviors involved in a paraphilia is quite the opposite of what the patient experiences in an anxiety or depressive disorder. Sexual desire is a pleasurable emotion, and the approach behaviors motivated by it result in sexual arousal and orgasm, which are intrinsically rewarding. Many paraphiliac patients are not troubled by their deviant arousal, and they enjoy their deviant sexual behavior. For many paraphiliac patients, their deviation is ego syntonic, and it is only the societal consequences of their behavior which cause them distress.

If the patient already accepts his paraphiliac thoughts and emotions, an acceptance based procedure would appear to have little to offer. However, this is not necessarily the case. While paraphiliac patients do not often come spontaneously to treatment, when they have been arrested and are facing prison, loss of job, familial sanctions, or negative community reactions, their motivation to rid themselves of their deviance may be genuine and intense. At this point, acceptance based procedures, in a seeming paradox, may add considerably to the effectiveness of existing treatment techniques, as will be discussed below.

There is another type of paraphiliac patient for whom acceptance based procedures may also be very useful. Some patients repeatedly go through cycles of trying to suppress all their deviant thoughts and urges, eventually losing this struggle, engaging in their deviant behavior, and then being consumed with guilt and remorse about their sexual behavior. For example, heterosexual transvestites often engage in a type of "binging and purging" cycle. A transvestite may struggle for days or weeks, trying not to think about how much he is aroused by cross dressing. After some period of struggle with these thoughts, he eventually cross dresses and has an orgy of masturbation lasting hours or even days. When he is finally sexually satiated, he is overcome with guilt and disgust, and he throws away all his female clothing, body padding, makeup, and wigs. For a while, he does not feel an urge to cross dress, but as his sexual appetite returns, he begins to struggle with the transvestic urges and thoughts, and the cycle begins again. Acceptance theory argues that it is the very struggle not to have transvestic thoughts that insures that these thoughts will eventually overpower the patient's resolution never to cross dress again (Hayes & Melancon, 1989).

Another difference between anxiety type disorders and paraphilias might argue against the utility of acceptance based approaches. There is no hormonally based, evolutionarily ingrained drive to engage in anxiety or depression based behaviors. On the other hand, there is a innate biological drive to engage in sexual behavior, and as noted above, this behavior is intrinsically rewarding. Therefore, it might appear that acceptance of deviant thoughts would automatically lead to deviant behavior, unlike what seems to be the case with anxious or depressive thoughts.

A related issue has probably hindered the application of acceptance theory to treatment of paraphilias. If anxious or depressed patients act on their emotions, no one is harmed but themselves. However, if acceptance of deviant thoughts and urges automatically leads to deviant behavior (because of our innate biological sex drive), other people are victimized. Clinicians have thus tended to try to suppress *both* deviant thoughts and deviant behaviors, and are resistant to the notion that acceptance of deviant thoughts may actually *reduce* the chances of the patient engaging in deviant behavior. There seems to be some confusion that acceptance theory would imply acceptance of the actual deviant behavior. Even when no overt victimization is involved (as, for example, in sending an exhibitionist to a nudist colony), acceptance theory does *not* argue that having the patient *act* on deviant urges and accept deviant behavior would be an effective treatment.

It would seem then, that the current lack of application of acceptance based procedures to treating sexual deviance results from several factors. First, paraphilia is a pleasurable disorder, rather than being aversive, as is the case with anxiety or depressive disorders. Second, paraphilia is ego syntonic for many patients. Third, our innate sex drive implies that deviant thoughts come with a biological imperative to action that cannot be ignored, so deviant thoughts must be suppressed, not accepted. Finally, there has probably been some confusion around the issue that "acceptance" implies acceptance of deviant behavior, with attendant harm to innocent victims.

In what follows, it will be argued that despite these reservations, acceptance based procedures have the potential to add to our effectiveness in treating paraphilias. Certainly, it is worthwhile to consider adding acceptance procedures to current techniques, as research indicates that we are not yet optimally effective in treating sexual deviation (Furby, Weinrott, & Blackshaw, 1989).

Definition and Clinical Description

Before discussing treatment techniques, some background information about the nature of paraphilias will be presented.

Paraphilia refers to deviant sexual arousal of a compulsive nature. In one type of paraphilia, fetishism, the patient experiences sexual arousal to objects, persons, or situations that the average person does not find to be intrinsically erotic. Examples of this type of paraphilia include arousal to shoes, leather garments, or, in one of the author's cases, bicycle handlebars. Other fetishes include arousal in response to urination and defecation (urophilia and coprophilia), arousal to corpses (necrophilia), and arousal in situations involving physical restraints, pain or humiliation (bondage and discipline, sadism, and masochism). Heterosexual transvestism, in which a man is aroused by dressing in women's clothing, is also an example of fetishism. Another type of paraphilia involves sexual behavior which the average person might find arousing, but does not engage in because of moral values and the threat of negative social sanctions. Examples of this type of paraphilia include peeping (voyeurism) and exhibitionism. Other paraphilias involve pedophilia (sexual arousal to children), making obscene telephone calls, frotteurism ("accidentally" bumping into or rubbing up against a woman's body in a crowded place), and some types of sexually motivated rape. Some paraphilias do not involve non-consenting victims or fetishistic objects. For example, triolism involves a man who is aroused by watching his wife have intercourse with another man. Similarly, enough men are aroused by listening to descriptions of sexual activity to make the 900 number phone sex business highly profitable, so this activity qualifies as a paraphilia only if it is compulsively engaged in, and preferred to actual sexual activity with a partner.

In all paraphilias, the defining characteristics are the compulsivity and preferential nature of the sexual activity. Exhibitionists, for example, will leave a willing sexual partner at home to go out to exhibit themselves. When the exhibitionist is arrested, the wife cannot believe that he would prefer this activity to sex with her, and, at most, may have only wondered if his absences from home meant he was having an affair with another woman.

Paraphilia is what might be called a "high fidelity, narrow band width, high intensity" phenomenon. That is, paraphiliacs have a driven, focused, and compulsive quality to their deviant arousal. Because the probability of being arrested for paraphilia is very low, most paraphiliacs seen in treatment have been engaging in their deviant behavior for many years, and often have literally hundreds of offenses in their history other than the one which finally got them arrested (Abel, Becker, Cunningham-Rathner, Mittelman, & Rouleau, 1988).

The overwhelming majority of paraphiliacs are men. Examples of fetishistic paraphilia, exhibitionism, or voyeurism in women are so rare as to be worthy of case reports in the professional literature. Over 95% of pedophilia cases involve a male perpetrator (Finklehor & Lewis, 1988). For this reason, male gender pronouns will be used to refer to paraphiliac patients throughout this chapter.

The cause of paraphilia remains an area of theoretical speculation, more than one founded in large amounts of empirical research data. While a full discussion of etiology is beyond the scope of this paper, a few comments can be made. There is certainly no evidence that there are any familial genetic factors involved in paraphilias. Research has not revealed any sex hormone or neurotransmitter abnormalities in paraphiliacs (Hucker & Bain, 1990). However, there is a small but intriguing literature that suggests an elevated rate of temporal lobe abnormalities in paraphiliacs, based on EEG and sophisticated MR, PET, and CAT imaging studies (Langevin, 1990). Sociologists and feminists have stressed that our male dominated, double standard, and sexually repressive culture leads to paraphilia, as does the availability of pornography (Marshall, Laws, & Barbaree, 1990). This reasoning ignores the fact that all men are raised in the same culture, but only a small percentage become paraphiliacs. Learning theorists stress the role of early "accidental conditioning" experiences, such as seeing a careless neighbor undressing without drawing the curtains, which are then reinforced by masturbation involving memories and fantasies about the event (Laws & Marshall, 1990). Again, as such experiences are common in the life histories of men who do not become paraphiliacs, this explanation is, by itself, inadequate. It seems likely that paraphilias are complex, multiply determined conditions, and that any single element theory of etiology is oversimplified and incorrect. Rather, we should realize that paraphilias clearly involve a host of factors, including arousal conditioned to inappropriate objects, lack of internalized moral values, inability to weigh long term negative consequences against short term sexual pleasure, distorted thinking about sexuality, lack of access to gratifying normal sexual outlets, lack of empathy for victim distress, disinhibition by alcohol or drugs, and possibly, temporal lobe pathology. In individual cases, various combinations of these factors may be more or less important.

The ego syntonicity of most paraphilias leads patients to overstate therapeutic gains, and to resist or prematurely terminate treatment. Similarly, paraphilias are highly prone to relapse, even after apparently successful treatment, and need to be reassessed and perhaps retreated periodically following the intensive treatment stage of therapy.

Treatment of Paraphilias

Biologic Treatments

Before considering psychotherapeutic treatment of sexual deviation, a brief summary of biological treatment will be offered.

Paraphilias have been treated with neurosurgery in Eastern European countries, primarily via temporal lobe ablations. Historically, castration was used to treat paraphilias, with some occasional usage continuing into the last decade. There is virtually no scientific evidence of the effectiveness of either of these procedures (Maletzky, 1991).

Neuroleptic agents, because of their effect of reducing sexual arousal (possibly related to elevated prolactin levels seen with these medications), have also been used to treat paraphilias. Thioridazine (Mellaril) has been the agent most commonly prescribed. Effectiveness of this treatment is not established in empirical research, but clinical reports suggest that perhaps 50% to 70% of patients experience a moderate reduction in interest in paraphiliac activities.

More effective, and more commonly used, is treatment with hormones which deplete testosterone levels and, with some agents, also block end organ response to testosterone. Cyproterone acetate is widely used in Europe and Canada, but is not approved for use in the United States, where medroxyprogesterone acetate (Depo-Provera) is the agent of choice. Considerable research evidence indicates that these agents are effective in reducing sexual arousal, sexual fantasies, and nocturnal penile tumescence, but are somewhat less effective in reducing penile erection in response to laboratory presentation of erotic videotapes or slides. Normal sexual functioning with a consenting partner is also typically disrupted, but some patients report that this is an acceptable trade-off for being freed of the problematic deviant sexual urges. Current thinking is that the best use of hormonal treatment is to reduce the risk of re-offending during the early stages of psychotherapeutic treatment, especially in cases where a recurrence would involve harm to a victim. Another valid use of Depo-Provera is in cases of sexual compulsivity at very high levels. A patient who is currently masturbating with paraphiliac fantasies several times per day, or obsessively ruminating with paraphiliac thoughts throughout the day, is extremely unlikely to respond to the psychotherapeutic techniques to be discussed later in this chapter. In such a case, Depo-Provera is useful in reducing sexual compulsivity to a level where other therapeutic interventions become possible.

Recently, there has been considerable interest in the treatment of paraphilias with the new serotonergic anti-anxiety/anti-depressant agents such as Prozac. While double-blind, placebo studies are lacking, initial clinical results are somewhat encouraging, and further study seems warranted.

The author's own clinical experience with a few paraphiliac patients on anti-androgenic or serotonergic agents has been that the patients tend to report that, at least initially, they still have a high level of paraphiliac thoughts, but that these thoughts are no longer accompanied by an imperative to engage in sexual behavior, nor are the thoughts upsetting to them. In a sense, the initial effect of the drug seems to be to facilitate acceptance of the deviant thoughts, and drug therapy may therefore be easily integrated into an acceptance based approach.

Psychological Treatments

A central element in treatment of paraphilia is the reduction or elimination of deviant sexual arousal through behavioral reconditioning procedures. In the early years of behavior therapy, reconditioning was attempted with electric shock aversion therapy, in a variety of classical conditioning, escape, avoidance, or signalled punishment designs. While studies showed that deviant arousal could be suppressed in the laboratory, clinical experience was that generalization to external "real life" situations was poor. Because of our human facility for cognitive mediation of conditioned responses, what the patients actually learned in these paradigms was not to be aroused by a particular set of stimulus slides, while wired up to a shock generator, in the laboratory. Generalization of arousal suppression effects to, for example, actual little girls in the real environment of a pedophile, was basically nonexistent. Similar results were obtained with using emetic drugs or noxious odors as the aversive stimuli, in place of electric shock. As simple aversion techniques were found to be ineffective, they are no longer in widespread use. Indeed, acceptance theory would predict that this sort of non-cognitive aversion therapy would actually raise the risk of recidivism. That is, a patient who has undergone aversive conditioning, who then re-experiences deviant thoughts outside the laboratory, will likely label his treatment as a complete failure, and accordingly feel compelled to *act* on his deviant arousal.

The major techniques currently used to reduce deviant arousal are *masturbatory satiation* and *covert sensitization with olfactory aversion* (Marshall, Laws, & Barbaree, 1990; Maletzky, 1991). In masturbatory satiation, the paraphiliac arousal is reduced by continuing exposure to the deviant stimuli after the patient is sexually satiated. In this procedure, the patient is instructed to go home and masturbate with normal fantasies and erotic stimuli such as Playboy or Penthouse centerfolds, books of erotic fantasies, and so forth. The patient verbalizes normal fantasies and descriptions of what he is looking at or reading, and uses a cassette tape recorder, so the therapist can review his fantasies and make sure that they do not contain any subtle paraphiliac elements. The patient uses the normal stimulus material, and verbalizes normal fantasies, until he ejaculates, and for a minute or so thereafter, until he loses his erection and enters the refractory period, during which further masturbation is unpleasant. At this point, he switches to fantasizing or reading aloud about his paraphiliac behavior, while he continues to masturbate for an additional 45 minutes to one hour, with a flaccid penis. His speech during this phase is also tape recorded for therapeutic review. In a typical case, the patient will ejaculate within 5 or 10 minutes of masturbation with normal stimuli, and then have a very unpleasant, boring, and physically uncomfortable experience while focused on his formerly exciting paraphiliac fantasies and memories. If the patient gets a second erection while verbalizing deviant fantasies, he switches back to normal stimuli and fantasies until he ejaculates again, and then returns to masturbation with deviant fantasies. Married paraphiliac patients who were not masturbating prior to entering therapy may conduct their satiation by having intercourse with their wives, and following ejaculation, immediately going into another room, turning on their tape recorder, and masturbating with deviant fantasies for an additional 45 minutes or so. Masturbatory satiation is typically carried out by the patient 2 to 5 times per week, for one to three months. This procedure is discontinued when the patient has no intrusive paraphiliac thoughts or urges for at least two successive weeks.

What does acceptance theory have to say in regard to masturbatory satiation? On the surface, acceptance theory would seem to be incompatible with the use of masturbatory satiation, as the aim is to suppress, rather than accept, deviant thoughts and deviant arousal. However, if one reconceptualizes satiation therapy as not just an arousal reduction technique, this seeming incompatibility is resolved.

Masturbatory satiation might be reconceptualized as an acceptance procedure known as "deliteralization", in which the patient experiences the deviant thoughts "for what they are, not for what they seem to be" (Hayes & Melancon, 1989). That is, during satiation, the patient experiences the thoughts and images without sexual arousal, so they are *just thoughts*. Deliteralization through satiation dramatically changes the context in which the patient experiences his deviant thoughts, which leads to breaking the link between deviant stimuli and sexual gratification.

Acceptance theory also suggests some possible modifications of satiation therapy. One modification would simply be to allow patients to accept their deviant thoughts, and to masturbate with deviant stimuli. Traditional behavior therapy logic would argue that this procedure would only reinforce deviant arousal, and thus lead to deviant behavior involving not just masturbation but actual sexual behavior with real victims. However, acceptance theory would argue that this giving up of the struggle to control deviant sexual impulses would actually reduce the chance of deviant behavior involving victims, and simply contain the deviance to harmless solitary masturbation.

This line of argument is similar to the rationale offered for the legalization of child pornography. This argument suggests that if child pornography is available, the rate of sexual offenses against children will decrease, as pedophiles will masturbate using these legal stimuli in preference to seeking out child victims, which involves the attendant risk of legal sanctions. Studies of pedophilia in jurisdictions which have liberalized access to child pornography, comparing offense rates pre and post the liberalization, tend to suggest that this reasoning might be valid, but the data are rather weak and subject to a variety of alternative explanations (Murrin & Laws, 1990).

One sexual offender program based at a state mental hospital is currently conducting an experiment in which patients are allowed to masturbate with deviant stimuli and fantasies. This treatment element is part of a larger strategy emphasizing "relapse prevention", an approach that will be discussed later in this paper. There are no outcome data yet available; but as the program involves many other elements, even when such data are available, the results will not constitute a test of satiation versus acceptance in controlling deviant behavior. However, this is an interesting experiment, in that it is rather contrary to accepted practice to include masturbation with deviant fantasies as part of a treatment program for paraphiliac patients.

Another acceptance based modification of satiation therapy would be to instruct the patient simply to spend an hour each day immersed in deviant fantasies, but without masturbating during this immersion. Unlike satiation, the patient would not masturbate with normal fantasies prior to this session. This procedure would bring the deviant thoughts under the patient's control, instead of having him struggle to keep the thoughts out of consciousness throughout the day. In this approach, the patient would accept having the thoughts, but would not act on them. This procedure is functionally equivalent to having an obsessive patient engage in directed overpractice of obsessive thoughts, which seems to both reduce intrusiveness of these thoughts at other times, and to reduce compulsive behavior. The author of this paper has actually used this procedure, with apparent success, with several patients who could not become aroused in masturbation using normal stimuli, and thus were not amenable to standard satiation therapy.

The success of this modification of satiation therapy raises an intriguing possibility—perhaps acceptance is the underlying mechanism in the effectiveness of standard satiation therapy. It may be that it does not really matter whether the patient masturbates, so long as he accepts and experiences his deviant fantasies for prolonged periods of time, rather than trying to control them. A comparative study of standard satiation therapy, satiation of deviant thoughts without masturbation, and allowing the patient to masturbate to orgasm with deviant thoughts would seem to be indicated at this point.

A second procedure used to eliminate deviant arousal is *covert sensitization*, which can be used with or without olfactory aversion. Covert sensitization is not used to reduce actual arousal and orgasmic responses to paraphiliac stimuli (the satiation procedure accomplishes this). The use of covert sensitization is to disrupt and suppress paraphiliac urges, thoughts, and images that precede actual paraphiliac sexual arousal and behavior. In this procedure, the patient generates a list of all the situations in which he would be at risk to commit his paraphiliac behavior. A second list of the possible negative consequences of his behavior is also generated, including items such as loss of job, rejection by family and friends, humiliation, harm to a victim, and so forth. The patient picks one of the risk situations, closes his eyes, visualizes the situation, and briefly elaborates on it aloud, until he begins to feel some slight arousal. At this point, he exhales fully, and then takes a deep breath while inhaling a noxious substance such as ammonia or valeric acid. The patient then immediately visualizes and verbally elaborates on one of the negative consequence scenarios, for some time. This procedure is carried out during therapy sessions and the patient also does sessions at home, daily. In addition, whenever he finds himself spontaneously experiencing a paraphiliac thought or urge, he immediately inhales an ammonia capsule and visualizes and verbalizes an aversive consequence. There is not clear evidence that olfactory aversion adds to the effectiveness of the covert sensitization, so the cognitive elements of visualizing and elaborating upon negative consequences are probably the "active ingredients" of this procedure. To illustrate a typical use of these techniques, the situations that cue off deviant urges and the list of aversive consequences for Mr. A, a patient with the paraphilia of exhibiting himself to children, are shown in Tables 1 and 2. In Table 1, the situations are listed in descending order of likelihood of the patient exhibiting himself.

Acceptance theory would question the effectiveness, or even the need for, covert sensitization procedures.

Most people who do not commit sexually deviant acts do have "deviant" thoughts intrude into their consciousness at some frequency. For example, it seems likely that most men, upon seeing an attractive 13 year old girl in a currently fashionable skimpy bathing suit, will experience some thoughts and arousal that are frankly pedophiliac in nature. Yet most men are not troubled by such thoughts, and the thoughts and arousal have little or no potential for leading to deviant behavior.

Table 1

Mr. A's Situation List: Exhibiting to Children

Situations in the car

Attractive girl with long brown hair, at street corner, about 13 years old wearing a skirt and knee socks. There is no one else around. I am alert and have erection. The girl shows an interest.

Girl with short blonde hair, at corner, not very attractive, about 13 years old. I am hung over - no erection. There is no one else around. The girl shows an interest.

Several girls at the corner. I am alert and have an erection. There is no one else around. The girls show an interest.

Girl with short blonde hair, not very attractive, in middle of block. No one else around. I am alert and have an erection. Girl shows an interest.

Attractive girl with skirt and knee socks, in middle of block. No one else around. I am alert and have erection. Girl turns away from car.

Attractive brown haired girl, at corner, about 13 years old wearing a skirt. There is a car behind me. I am not very alert, no erection.

Mixed boys and girls in middle of block. No one else around. I am alert and have erection.

Situations in a parking lot

Girl about 10-11 years old alone in a car. Space next to her car empty. No one else around. I am alert and have erection. Girl shows an interest.

Girl about 10-11 years old alone in car. Space next to her car empty. No one else around. I am alert and have an erection. Girl runs from her car.

Attractive girl alone by wall. No one else near by. I am hung over, no erection. The girl runs away from the car.

Situations at a party

Attractive young girl about 10 years old near bathroom window (outside). I am alert and have an erection. No one else around. Girl shows an interest.

Attractive girl about 10 years old wearing a skirt and knee socks, near bathroom door. Other adults in the area.

Table 2

Mr. A's Situation List: Aversive Consequences

In My Car / Street

1) Car breaks down, I'm stuck there, girl complains.
2) She takes down my license number, is clearly going to remember it.
3) Girl runs off frantically, crying, hit by car, I see her die.
4) Parent looking from house, sees event, gets car description and license plate number.
5) Neighborhood group stops the car, attacks the car and gets me.
6) Police get me.

In a Parking Lot

1) Parent comes back to car, during event, my car blocked, can't get away, they get my license number.
2) Child runs from my car and gets hit by car--I see her bleeding.
3) Parent returns and confronts me directly.
4) Security patrol or police catch me--arrested, taken to jail.
5) Runs into child again, she points me out as person who exhibited.
6) Car won't go - stuck there.

At a Party

1) Caught by adult - spreads like wildfire to other adults – caught by female adult -- somebody I know - by friend's wife – they stone me - throw me out.
2) They call police.
3) Girl's father punches me out.
4) Wife knows. Very embarrassed -- gets up and leaves me there - breaks down, weeps and cries, goes in kitchen, cuts her wrists.
5) Girl screams, runs away, weeps.
6) Fear of person telling parent -- stomach knots up – but doesn't knot up to the point of me vomiting.

Non-Specifics

1) Final rejection by father/sister/in-laws.
2) Losing job -- losing house, having to move.
3) Learn to live at lower economic level.
4) Marital problems -- wife leaves.
5) Children problems - cut back on vacations, less good things.
6) Daughter - disappointed in me.
7) Six year old son -- favorite child -- he finds out.
8) Wife kills self - cuts wrists.
9) Children teased at school--"Your old man's a wienie wagger"

Covert sensitization seems to assume that paraphiliac patients are somehow different from other men.

The underlying premise in covert sensitization is that if sexually deviant men allow themselves to have deviant thoughts, they will act on them. Acceptance theory would suggest that a better method to prevent deviant behavior would be to teach the patient to accept the occurrence of deviant thoughts, but learn *not* to act on them. Paraphiliac patients do experience their deviant thoughts as behavioral imperatives, and teaching them that this is not the case is certainly a viable treatment approach. Indeed, this approach is part of what occurs in "relapse prevention" therapy, as will be discussed later in this paper.

The real issue in using both satiation and covert sensitization is not just to reduce deviant arousal and deviant thoughts *per se*, but rather to prevent deviant behavior; as these thoughts and arousal are seen as the motivating force for deviant behavior. Acceptance theory argues that internal thoughts, feelings, and emotional arousal need not be seen by the patient as a reason for behaving in a particular way. In the acceptance strategy called "Comprehensive Distancing" (Hayes & Melancon, 1989), the patient learns that anxious or depressive thoughts can be noted, accepted, and not be responded to as if they were behavioral imperatives. However, as noted previously, sexual thoughts may be different than anxious or depressive thoughts because of their intrinsically pleasurable nature and their association with arousal and orgasm.

This conflict between thought suppression procedures and acceptance procedures taps into a larger debate in the sex research literature: What is the relationship between various classes of sexual stimuli and deviant responses? One might conceptualize of an ascending hierarchy of intensity of sexual behavior as follows:

1. Brief flashes of Deviant Fantasy/Imagery/Thoughts (D-FIT)
2. Prolonged D-FIT, with attendant arousal
3. Prolonged D-FIT, with attendant masturbation and orgasm
4. Actual deviant behavior with a victim

If item 4 is seen as the last link in a non-cognitively mediated conditioned stimulus-response chain, the utility of acceptance procedures becomes questionable. However, if there is a discontinuity between items 1-3 and 4, then acceptance procedures become more viable.

Some insight into the nature of stimulus-response links in deviant behavior is provided by the literature on the conditionability of deviant sexual responses. If engaging in deviant thoughts indeed does, through reinforcement mechanisms, lead to conditioned elicitation of deviant behavior, it should be possible to demonstrate that paraphiliac arousal can be classically or operantly conditioned in previously normal subjects. While it appears that something analogous to paraphiliac arousal can be conditioned in Japanese quail (Domjan, 1990), the research evidence for such a possibility in humans is very dubious at best (Laws & Marshall, 1990).

A few studies have purported to demonstrate classical conditioning of deviant sexual arousal. Rachman (1966), in a widely cited study, claimed to have experimentally induced a shoe fetish. Similarly, Quinn, Harbison, and McAllister (1970) reported operant conditioning of deviant arousal. However, these studies all had "methodological problems which reduce the persuasiveness of their findings" (Laws & Marshall, 1990, p.213). More importantly, in the years since these early studies appeared, there have been any number of failures to replicate the conditioned creation of deviant arousal. It is now generally accepted that deviant arousal cannot be created through laboratory conditioning procedures.

While this failure does not prove that naturally occurring deviant arousal is not created or maintained by conditioning processes, it does imply that acceptance of deviant thoughts, reinforced by arousal (and even, perhaps, orgasm), need not automatically lead to deviant behavior via a conditioning mechanism. Apparently, exposure to deviant stimuli with accompanying sexual arousal does not lead to replacing voluntary control over sexual behavior with an automatic conditioned response.

Another line of evidence concerning the link between acceptance of deviant thoughts and occurrence of deviant behavior is provided by the research literature on the relationship between pornography and deviant sexual behavior. While the research literature on this topic is large, few clear conclusions can be reached, partly because much of the research is contaminated by the intrusion of a political agenda, either pro- or anti-pornography, into scientific methodology. However, in general, it appears that the potential for conditioning deviant arousal through exposure to deviant pornography is quite low (Fisher & Barak, 1991).

Rather than citing research on this issue, simply consider the following proposition: A sexually normal person is shown explicit videotape of a very attractive couple, engaged in highly erotic lovemaking. The normal person is aroused by this video, and masturbates while watching it. However, at some point in the videotape, as part of their lovemaking, the couple engages in coprophiliac behavior, smearing each other with feces. Does it seem likely that we can condition coprophilia in previously normal people with this procedure? Research evidence is not really needed on this issue, as simple introspection strongly indicates that conditioning of coprophilia will not occur.

The research on the link between exposure to deviant pornography and behavior, then, at least tangentially suggests that sexually deviant patients could come to accept their deviant thoughts and images, without conditioning mechanisms leading to these thoughts becoming deviant behaviors. Acceptance based therapy might let the patient give up the struggle to keep deviant images out of consciousness, thus freeing him to concentrate on not acting on these thoughts and victimizing others.

However, the possibility remains that allowing deviant patients to accept their paraphiliac thoughts, or accept these thoughts and act on them by masturbation and orgasm, may lead to increased potential for actual deviant behavior. As a clinical example, consider the 900 number telephone sex services. I have seen patients who came to treatment because they had "maxed out" their credit cards with these numbers. These men were not sexually deviant before calling the telephone sex service, and did so for the first time essentially on a lark. However, they masturbated to orgasm while listening to the woman on the telephone, and through the reinforcement of arousal and orgasm, seemed to become conditioned to this form of paraphiliac stimulus. This conditioning can be very powerful, as some of these men have willing sex partners that they enjoy having sex with, yet they will preferentially call the 900 number for phone sex. Of course, most men who initially call the 900 number phone sex services do not develop a compulsion to engage in this behavior, so a simple conditioning explanation for this paraphilia seems inadequate. In addition to the conditioning effect of masturbation while listening on the telephone, there are probably personological variables that account for the vulnerability of some men to this conditioning.

How can one reconcile this apparent conditioning of a paraphilia in a normal person with the previous discussion of the failure to show such conditioning in laboratory studies, and the general lack of conditioning effects for deviant pornography? There are probably two important issues involved.

First, the 900 number situation involves actual masturbation to orgasm, in the caller's private home. This is quite different than the laboratory conditioning experiments, in which arousing normal pictures are simply paired with previously neutral stimuli, such as the shoes in the study by Rachman (1966). Second, there is an issue of "biological readiness," meaning the ease with which a response can be conditioned. It is probably much easier to condition arousal to the stimulus of a woman's voice on the telephone talking about making love than it is to condition arousal to shoes. A woman talking about making love has an intrinsic association with sexual behavior, while shoes do not. These differences probably account for the apparent conditionability of the phone sex paraphilia.

The conditionability of the phone sex paraphilia does suggest that acceptance of deviant thoughts and images might best be confined to allowing the patient to experience the thoughts, but not to masturbate while experiencing them. As noted previously, an experimental test of satiation and covert sensitization versus acceptance of deviant thoughts would be very useful in guiding the content of treatment programs for deviance. Whether acceptance should only encompass experiencing the deviant thoughts, or also include acceptance of masturbation with deviant thoughts, is an empirical question. At this point, prudent concern for future victims in the event of a relapse would suggest that acceptance be limited to thoughts only, and not include masturbation with deviant imagery. As noted previously, one state hospital program is experimenting with allowing paraphiliac patients to masturbate to orgasm with deviant stimuli. While the results of this study will be most interesting, the ethical propriety of such a seemingly risky intervention is open to question.

The other major technology that is used in treating paraphilia is *relapse prevention training* (Laws, 1991). Relapse prevention training has several elements. One element involves having the patient identify "high risk" life situations, emotional states, and stimulus cues that elicit his deviant urges. The patient is then taught avoidance and escape strategies for these high risk situations, and for situations that can not be avoided or immediately escaped from, alternative coping responses to replace the paraphiliac behavior. A second element involves having the patient identify "Seemingly Irrelevant Decisions" (SIDS) that may seem to be unrelated to his paraphilia, but actually are the first steps in a chain of events that leads to acting on the paraphiliac urges. For example, the decision to stop for a drink on the way home from work may seem irrelevant to voyeurism. In one patient's case, however, doing so reliably provokes his wife into an argument with him, leading her to refuse to have sex with him that night. Unable to sleep, he would next make the seemingly irrelevant decision to go out for a late night snack. During this trip, he would then "impulsively" engage in peeping. Relapse prevention teaches the patient that paraphiliac acts are not engaged in impulsively. Rather, when the patient decided to stop for a drink on the way home from work, he knew the result would be feelings of resentment about what he sees as his wife's nagging, which, combined with his sexual frustration, justify his voyeurism in his own mind.

These aspects of relapse prevention training are quite compatible with an acceptance based approach. Relapse prevention teaches the patient to label his behaviors as part of a chain leading to deviance, without him having to take responsibility for the voluntary nature of this chain. Relapse prevention, conceptualized in an acceptance framework, teaches the patient to accept his deviant thoughts, label seemingly irrelevant behaviors correctly, and not act on his urges.

Another element of relapse prevention training involves what is termed the abstinence violation effect (AVE). During and following treatment, patients will, of course, occasionally experience brief urges or fantasies about their paraphilia. This constitutes only a manageable "lapse," but patients typically feel that they have experienced a major "relapse," and thus are no longer abstinent from their paraphilia. They then reason that since they have already relapsed, they might as well actually engage in their paraphiliac behavior. This reasoning constitutes the abstinence violation effect. Relapse prevention training stresses that involuntary intrusions of deviant thoughts are only lapses, and that actual relapse behavior is subject to voluntary control. Patients are taught to view lapses as an opportunity to learn more about themselves, identify new high-risk situations that they were not aware of, find new coping strategies for dealing with whatever cued the lapse, and not to see a lapse as an excuse to act on a deviant urge. All of these procedures, of course, are entirely compatible with an acceptance based treatment program, as they teach the patient to accept deviant thoughts, and not see these thoughts as catastrophic behavioral imperatives.

In relapse prevention therapy, it is usually stressed that the patient not allow himself to dwell on deviant thoughts, with attendant arousal and masturbation, because of what is called the "problem of immediate gratification" (PIG). "Feeding the PIG" refers to the immediate pleasure that occurs when the patient allows himself to have an extended lapse, even if this only involves fantasies and "harmless" masturbation, as opposed to actually going out and offending against others. During an extended lapse, the pleasure is real and immediate, and self-destructive consequences are only future possibilities that may never arrive. According to relapse prevention theory, feeding the PIG both reinforces deviant arousal and exacerbates the AVE. Instead of feeding the PIG, the patient is taught to avoid situations that cue off lapses, to escape from such situations if they arise unexpectedly, and to engage in alternative coping responses to deal with external situations and internal emotional states that previously elicited lapses.

The concept of not "feeding the PIG", but rather avoiding, escaping, and practicing alternative responses in situations that elicit deviant thoughts would appear to be antithetical to an acceptance based approach. At one level, this is clearly the case, as the patient is not allowed to accept deviant thoughts, but rather must engage in behaviors that short circuit their occurrence. However, at a deeper level of analysis, the procedures used to avoid feeding the PIG could be considered to be consistent with acceptance theory.

Sexual deviations are not determined only by deviant arousal. Sexual deviation can be a way of regaining a feeling of power and self-effectance after failing to be appropriately assertive in a situation which called for it. Sexual deviation can be a form of self-medication, to ward off anxious, lonely, or depressed feelings. Sexual deviation can result from heterosocial anxiety and skills deficits which block access to consenting adult sexual partners. Sexual deviation can be a way for the patient to reduce stress he is otherwise unable to deal with. In all such cases, the patient typically is not allowing himself to accept the reality of his life situation and his emotional reaction to it. Instead, he is displacing his emotional distress onto sexually deviant acting out. The procedures involved in identifying situations and emotional states that cue off lapses and lead to feeding the PIG force the patient to accept the reality of his life, and to deal with his problems directly. Thus, if deviant behavior is partially motivated by the patient's being unable to accept anxious or depressed feelings, the relapse prevention procedures can be thought of as acceptance based procedures.

An integration of acceptance procedures with the relapse prevention element of not feeding the PIG would involve having the patient accept both dysphoric emotions which previously elicited deviant behavior, and also accept deviant thoughts and urges, without having to escape or avoid either type of thoughts and feelings. This would be a major modification of traditional relapse prevention therapy. Such a modification would probably not gain clinical adherence until empirical research demonstrated that allowing the patient to accept, rather than avoid, deviant urges during lapses does not lead to increased probability of an actual relapse.

As part of relapse prevention, the patient writes up a relapse prevention manual, listing high risk situations to be avoided, escape responses, alternative coping responses, ways to prevent the abstinence violation effect, and strategies for dealing with the problem of immediate gratification. A very brief selection from the relapse prevention manual of a paraphiliac who makes obscene telephone calls to children is shown in Table 3. In examining this material, the reader may gain some insight into the complexity of integrating acceptance into the relapse prevention program.

As previously noted, paraphilias are complex, multiply determined phenomena. While reducing deviant arousal and relapse prevention constitute the core of current therapy, there are a host of other procedures used to meet individual patient's needs. These procedures are generally consistent with or unrelated to acceptance based procedures, so the difficult integration issues that arise with regard to satiation, covert sensitization, and some aspects of relapse prevention do not occur with most of these adjunctive procedures.

For patients who are too shy, inhibited, and unskilled to be able to make contact with adults for normal sexual relationships, a course of *social skills training* is usually undertaken. This procedure involves modeling and role playing of normal social interactions with the client (Hollon & Trower, 1986).

Most married sex offenders claim they have an adequate sexual relationship with their wives, and that sexual frustration is not an element in their motivation to commit offenses, but this is generally untrue. Sexual activity with the wife is typically stereotyped, infrequent, narrowly focused on penile-vaginal intercourse, and lacking in playful, erotic, unrestrained activity. For most married paraphiliacs, a course of *sex therapy* is indicated, focusing more on sexual enhancement and reducing sexual inhibitions in both the patient and his wife than on the elimination of a specific dysfunction (LoPiccolo, 1990).

Some paraphiliacs feel a profound relief from tension and feelings of inadequacy when they engage in their paraphiliac ritual. Often, these are men who are

Table 3

Mr. B's Relapse Prevention Manual for One High Risk Situation: Staying Alone Too Long in the Apartment

Lapse: Problem of Immediate Gratification-Flash Fantasies

Bringing happiness to young girls
Fantasizing about submissive young girls doing what I tell them to do sexually

Relapse Action

Calling random phone numbers to talk about sex with teenage girls

Alternative Coping Behavior

Just simply leave the dwelling--go play tennis, visit a friend, etc.
Find an AA or NA meeting and go
Get a *healthy* roommate
Read

(continued on next page)

Table 3

Relapse Prevention Manual for One High Risk Situation: Continued

Problem of Immediate Gratification–Dealing with Flash Fantasies

Try to leave immediate location
Call my probation officer if possible
Call up friend for tennis match
Practice hobby immediately
Use ammonia and think of my legal problems and my divorce
See the urge as a wave that crests then resides. I will handle this. Close my eyes
and visualize myself dealing successfully with controlling and not feeding
the PIG. See a wave cresting and then disappearing.

Relapse Actions–What To Do if I Start on a Relapse

Do ammonia and negative consequence cards immediately
Call probation officer or therapist, be honest
Leave environment immediately
Open notebook, read this manual
Unplug phone, lock in trunk of car
Call support network

Patterns of Abuse

Planned my day's activities to be able to use phone in mid-afternoon, when kids
are home from school but parents are not
Planned to be alone always

Coping Responses for Patterns of Abuse

Visualize myself getting through this temporary urge.
If that fails, take ammonia and do negative consequence visualization
Organize other activities for afternoons, such as fishing, tennis, library, practice,
etc.
See the urge as a wave that has already crested, and is now ready to subside.
Do not feed this PIG; control him.
I am 39 years old. Think about the responsibilities I have to myself and others.
Deal with my age. Act it.
Unplug phone or remove myself from room where the phone is.

List of Social Support People To Call

Probation officer, therapist, mother, Alcoholics Anonymous, Narcotics
Anonymous, five different friends

*Note: Mr. B's manual included several other high risk situations, such that his
actual manual was more than 20 pages long.*

lacking in assertive skills, and so feel powerless and abused by others. For example, an exhibitor who feels he is unjustly criticized at work may be especially likely to exhibit later that day. For these patients, a course of *assertiveness training* to increase their self-efficacy, and a course of *relaxation training* for stress and tension reduction are indicated (Marshall, Laws, & Barbaree, 1990).

Most paraphiliacs know very little about the realities of sexual functioning and about emotional and sexual relationships between adult men and women. Therefore, most sexual deviation treatment programs include a *sex education* component. This education occurs through discussion with the therapist, reading of appropriate level sex education books, and viewing of educational films and videos.

There is one adjunctive procedure that does relate directly to acceptance. Most paraphiliacs have a variety of *cognitive distortions* that are intimately related to their deviant behavior. Pedophiles typically endorse ideas such as the belief that sex between an adult and a child is good for the child; that children can consent to have sex with an adult and thus are not being "molested," and so forth. Patients with fetishistic arousal often think of themselves merely as sexually liberated, rather than as deviant. In such cases, the therapist actively attacks these defensive cognitive distortions. While a simple analysis might suggest that attacking cognitive distortions is inconsistent with acceptance, this is not really the case. Attacking cognitive distortions allows the patient to "experience events as they are, and not as they say they are," which is an acceptance procedure. Cognitive distortions are motivated by the patient's lack of acceptance of his deviance, and a need to relabel his offensive behavior as benign. Attacking cognitive distortions helps the patient to see himself and his paraphilia in a realistic way, which is certainly consistent with acceptance based therapy.

The Sexual Addiction Model and Acceptance

The concept of "sexual addiction" is primarily associated with the work of Patrick Carnes (Carnes, 1991), who argues that paraphiliac sexual deviance is a type of addiction. In the addiction model, sexual deviation is a lifelong "disease" afflicting addicts who are powerless to overcome their behavior. The model has led to the formation of groups such as Sex Addicts Anonymous, Sexaholics Anonymous, and Sex and Love Anonymous.

The addiction model has generated much popular support, but has been less well received by mental health professionals. A major concern has been whether it is useful to apply a model based on physical addiction to alcohol or drugs (which includes physical dependence, increased dose tolerance, and physical withdrawal symptoms) to a behavior problem that has no physiological component. Coleman (1990) has offered a carefully reasoned critique of the addiction model, and suggests that paraphilias are better conceptualized as a type of obsessive-compulsive disorder. As previously noted, acceptance based therapy appears to have a good deal to offer in the treatment of obsessive-compulsive disorder, so this conceptualization of paraphilias as a form of OCD is interesting.

One troubling aspect of the addiction model is that it constrains the content of therapy, as illustrated in the concept that "Addiction is a disease that can only be treated by embracing the twelve-step recovery program," The addiction model is suspicious of complex psychological explanations of the behavior disorder ("keep it simple"), which leads to therapy that does not address the complex, multiple determinants of sexually deviant behavior.

Perhaps the major problem with the addiction approach is the emphasis on a "celibacy contract" for the first three months of treatment, followed by a commitment to lifelong "sexual sobriety," The celibacy contract, which allows no sexual activity of any kind, prevents the use of masturbatory satiation and other conditioning procedures to reduce deviant arousal and increase normal arousal during therapy.

Lifelong sexual sobriety means that sex is to be confined to long term, monogamous, loving and committed heterosexual relationships. One might argue that this is an essentially Victorian view, but the more important issue is that this approach is at odds with acceptance procedures. By requiring the patient to control and limit his sexual thoughts and actions to such a narrow range of situations, this sobriety contract may well set up the patient for a relapse to deviant behavior. That is, if the patient, after treatment, is comfortable with masturbation using normal stimuli and fantasies, and can have casual sex with other consenting adults, his sexual needs are being met. On the other hand, if he tries to remain sexually "sober" and is not in a committed relationship, sexual frustration may well lead him to re-offend. Sobriety is a notion that may make sense when applied to alcohol addiction, since there is not an innate, biologically based drive to drink alcohol. However, there is an innate, hormonally based sex drive; and trying to suppress it completely unless one is in a committed relationship is unrealistic. Rather, it would seem more useful to foster acceptance of the patient's normal sexual needs, and encourage normal sexual fantasies, masturbation, and casual sex with other consenting adults.

There is also the problem that the concept of sobriety does not teach the patient to distinguish between appropriate and inappropriate forms of sexual expression. In the addiction model, masturbation or consenting sex with a casual acquaintance is apparently just as wrong as having sex with a child, as all of these activities violate the commitment to sexual sobriety.

Success Rates and Relapse/Recidivism

The success rate for comprehensive treatment programs such as the one described in this paper is unclear at this point. There have been some studies on the effectiveness of various components of the program, but none that have looked at the whole package compared to an appropriately matched untreated control group, with long term follow up. The best studies on multi-faceted programs show a range of failure or relapse rates as low as 10% and as high as 50% (Marshall & Barbaree, 1990). Results seem to be best with child molesters and exhibitors, and worst for violent rapists. Obviously, how patients are selected for such programs, and how diligently and how long one follows up with the patients greatly influences these rates.

It is clear that even with the type of intensive, aggressive, multi-faceted treatment program described in this paper, the risk of relapse is always present for sex offenders (Furby, Weinrott, & Blackshaw, 1989). It may well be that no one is ever "cured" of a sexual deviation, but rather that patients remain at an elevated risk of re-offending for their entire lives. The clinician who works in this area must be prepared, sooner or later, to be in the difficult, guilt-inducing, and embarrassing position of having a current or former patient re-arrested for another offense. While society may hold the clinician responsible for these relapses, if we did not undertake treatment of paraphiliacs, they would *all* commit repeat offenses. There are no spontaneous remissions of sexual deviation, and punishment through jail sentences is ineffective in preventing further offenses once the prisoner is released. After all, during incarceration, patients are denied access to normal sex with women. Instead, prisoners typically masturbate with their favorite deviant fantasies and memories, thus reinforcing and strengthening their sexual deviation during their prison term. Unless we are going to keep sex offenders in prison for life, or use the death penalty, we *must* treat these patients. The alternative is to accept the fact that they will re-offend and harm new victims. Unfortunately, the current level of funding of sex offender programs suggests that as a society, we have not been willing to face up to the high rate of recidivism shown by untreated paraphiliac sexual offenders.

Conclusion

Acceptance based therapy would seem to offer some exciting possibilities to add to the effectiveness of treatment of paraphilias. However, some elements of currently mainstream treatment procedures are based on a very different view of the relationship between conditioned emotional responses and actual behavior than is posited by acceptance theory. In particular, empirical work is needed to guide the possible integration of acceptance techniques with the arousal reconditioning procedures of masturbatory satiation and covert sensitization. Similarly, it is not clear that acceptance therapy is consistent with all elements of relapse prevention therapy. Given that our current treatment techniques leave much to be desired in effectiveness, further exploration of an acceptance based approach certainly is worthwhile.

References

Abel, G. G., Becker, J. V., Cunningham-Rathner, J., Mittelman, J. S., & Rouleau, J. L., (1988). Multiple paraphilic diagnoses among sex offenders. *Bulletin of the American Academy of Psychiatry and the Law*, 16, 153-168.

Carnes, P. (1991). *Don't call it love: Recovering from sexual addiction*. New York: Bantam

Coleman, E. (1990). The obsessive-compulsive model for describing compulsive sexual behavior. *American Journal of Preventive Psychiatry and Neurology*, 2:3, 9-14.

Domjan, M. (1990). The modification of sexual behavior through conditioning: An avian model. In J. R. Feierman (Ed.), *Pedophilia: Biosocial dimensions*. New York: Springer Verlag

Finklehor, D., & Lewis, I. (1988) An epidemiologic approach to the study of child molestation. *The Annals of the New York Academy of Sciences*, 528:64-77.

Fisher, W. A., & Barak, A. (1991). Erotica, pornography, and behavior: More questions than answers. *International Journal of Law and Psychiatry*, 14, 65-83.

Furby, L., Weinrott, M. R., & Blackshaw, L. (1989). Sex offender recidivism: A review. *Psychological Bulletin*, 105, 3-30.

Hayes, S. C. (1987). A contextual approach to therapeutic change. In N. Jacobson (Ed.), *Psychotherapists in clinical practice: Cognitive and behavioral perspectives*, pp.327-387, New York: Guilford Press.

Hayes, S. C., & Melancon, S. M. (1989). Comprehensive distancing, paradox, and the treatment of emotional avoidance. In M. Ascher (Ed.), *Paradoxical procedures in psychotherapy*. New York: Guilford Press.

Hollon, C. R., & Trower, P. (1986). *Handbook of social skills training*. Oxford: Pergamon Press.

Hucker, S. J. & Bain, J. (1990). Androgenic hormones and sexual assault. In W.L. Marshal, D. R. Laws, & H.E. Barbaree, (Eds.), *Handbook of sexual assault*, pp. 93-102. New York: Plenum Press.

Langevin, R. (1991). Sexual anomalies and the brain.. In W. L. Marshal, D. R. Laws, & H. E. Barbaree, (Eds.), *Handbook of sexual assault*, pp.103-113. New York: Plenum Press.

Laws, D. R. (1991). *Relapse prevention with sex offenders*. New York: Guilford Press.

Laws, D. R., & Marshall, W. L. (1990). A conditioning theory of the etiology and maintenance of deviant sexual preference and behavior. In W. L. Marshal, D. R. Laws, & H.E. Barbaree, (Eds.), *Handbook of sexual assault*, pp. 209-231. New York: Plenum Press.

LoPiccolo, J. (1990). Treatment of sexual dysfunction. In A. S. Bellak, M. Hersen, & A. E. Kazdin, (Eds.), *International handbook of behavior modification and therapy (2nd. Edition)*, pp. 547-563. New York: Plenum Press.

Maletzky, B. M. (1991). *Treating the sexual offender*. Newbury Park, California: Sage Publications.

Marshall, W. L., & Barbaree, H. E. (1990). Outcome of comprehensive cognitive-behavioral treatment programs. In W. L. Marshal, D. R. Laws, & H. E. Barbaree, (Eds.), *Handbook of sexual assault*, pp. 363-388. New York: Plenum Press.

Marshal, W. L., Laws, D. R., & Barbaree, H. E. (1990). *Handbook of sexual assault*. New York: Plenum Press, 1990.

Murrin, M. R., & Laws, D. R. (1990). The influence of pornography on sexual crimes. In W. L. Marshal, D. R. Laws, & H. E. Barbaree, (Eds.), *Handbook of sexual assault*, pp. 73-92. New York: Plenum Press.

Quinn, J. T., Harbison, J., & McAllister, H. (1970). An attempt to shape human penile responses. *Behaviour Research and Therapy*, 8, 27-28.

Rachman, S. (1966). Sexual fetishism: An experimental analogue. *Psychological Record*, 16, 293-296.

Discussion of LoPiccolo

The Overt-Covert Link

Kelly Koerner

University of Washington

LoPiccolo contended that adding interventions designed to increase acceptance of covert deviant sexual activity would increase the efficacy of current change-oriented treatments for paraphilias. The premise that there is a one-to-one correspondence between covert sexual activity (e.g., deviant fantasies, arousal, urges to engage in deviant behavior) and overt deviant sexual activity (e.g., masturbation up to involvement of others in deviant sexual activity) underlies typical treatment for sexual deviance. From this view, the more a person is aroused to deviant material, the more likely it becomes that some corresponding deviant sexual act will follow. Engaging in the first steps of the chain inevitably results in the higher probability of reaching the later stages of the chain. Therefore, treatment targets the early part of the chain through attempts to recondition arousal in order to change or stop the occurrence of deviant covert activities. Cure, then, is the same as never having any deviant sexual thoughts.

LoPiccolo questioned this basic premise and instead argued that interventions should foster acceptance of covert and some overt deviant sexual activity (e.g., activity that does not involve non-consenting others such as masturbation to deviant fantasies). Rather than encouraging the client to inhibit and suppress deviant covert activity, acceptance strategies seek to alter the contingencies that maintain the link between covert and overt activity. In this view, the client accepts private events but actively inhibits deviant actions.

The major points during the discussion regarded the nature of the problem, the nature of change brought about by acceptance interventions, and the nature of cultural practices that both foster the problem and might impede the adoption of acceptance strategies. The first point clarified the key question regarding the nature of the problem: To what extent is it accurate to think of arousal to deviant fantasies, urges to perform some sexual act, and masturbation as part of a chain that inevitably leads to more serious deviant acts?

On the one hand, if the covert-overt link is strong enough to warrant the metaphor of one-to-one correspondence, then acceptance of covert deviant sexual activity may strengthen overt deviant action. Acceptance strategies may inadvertently strengthen unwanted behavior and interfere with the inhibiting effect of social sanctions against overt deviant activities. On the other hand, if it is more accurate to think that the link between covert and overt sexual activity is maintained through contingencies, which while strong are not immutable, then acceptance strategies may extinguish harmful overt activity through repeated non-reinforced exposure to arousing deviant fantasies. Certain types of acceptance strategies may refine and augment the extinction procedure of masturbatory satiation, for example, by powerfully altering the verbal contingencies that maintain the link between covert and overt sexual activity. Therefore, depending on which view is more accurate, accepting covert activity may either reinforce or extinguish overt deviant sexual activity. Although no decisive case was made for either position, the ideas presented in LoPiccolo's paper were amenable to empirical tests that might illuminate the merits of acceptance oriented treatment strategies.

The second point raised was how to best understand the nature of change brought about by acceptance strategies. A distinction was drawn between first and second order change through acceptance. In first order change, acceptance is considered to increase contact with "better" contingencies, that is, increasing control of behavior by contingencies already available but for various reasons exerting little influence. In other words, increasing acceptance of deviant covert activity decreases avoidance of and increases contact with alternative aspects of the social environment. For example, the process of accepting one's arousal to deviant fantasies may concurrently increase awareness of issues that deviant sexual activities help one avoid such as feelings of powerlessness, anger, and loneliness in work or in marriage.

Second order change, however, is change that *transforms the context*. That is, one does not come only into contact with aspects of the situation which had been present but had not exerted a controlling influence on behavior. Rather, acceptance interventions actually change the stimulus properties of the context so that prior contingencies are experienced differently. For example, fantasies that are engaged in under conditions that lead to "deliteralization" alter the stimulus properties of one's thoughts and emotions in ways that decrease the strength of covert-overt links. Because various therapeutic interventions aimed at increasing acceptance of deviant covert sexual activity may differentially foster either first or second order changes, a question raised but left unanswered was to what extent should acceptance strategies seek to foster one or the other sort of change? Is first or second order change a more accurate understanding of how acceptance strategies work?

The final point of discussion was the nature of cultural practices that create the problem of paraphilias and that might impede the adoption of acceptance strategies in treatment of paraphilias. In part the occurrence of paraphilias was viewed as a byproduct of our culture's relative repressiveness toward sexuality. Socialization in the United States is such that the one-to-one correspondence of covert and overt sexual activity is ascribed to by most in our culture. Particularly for men, we believe that if one becomes sufficiently aroused, ability to control sexual actions is not possible. Similarly, this view influences the extent to which funding agencies might be willing to fund research using acceptance strategies in treatment of sexual deviance because within our culture it is hard to conceive of the possibility that one can have deviant sexual thoughts and not act on them were it not for strong aversive consequences. Many cultural practices seem to promote paraphilias and impede development of what may result in more effective treatment interventions based on the acceptance of deviant covert sexual activities. However, community interventions that increase openness and comfort regarding sexuality paradoxically may reduce the occurrence of paraphilias.

Chapter 9

Addiction, Mindfulness, and Acceptance

G. Alan Marlatt

University of Washington

The purpose of this paper is to illustrate how the concept of acceptance applies to the problem of addiction. Definitions and theoretical models of addiction are first described. In this analysis, the psychology of addiction or the addicted state of mind is contrasted with mindfulness, an aware, non-attached state of mental acceptance, as described in Eastern meditation practices. Treatment strategies based on mindfulness are then reviewed, drawing upon relapse prevention approaches to addictive behavior change. The paper concludes with an overview of harm reduction principles, a "kinder, gentler" alternative than the current American "War on Drugs" mentality.

Definitions and Models of Addiction

The root of the verb addict stems from the Latin verb "addicere," meaning "to devote," to "give oneself up or over to as a constant practice; to devote; habituate" (Webster, 1961). Addicts are devoted to the experience that drugs or other addictive behaviors provide; they "give themselves up or over to" the drug experience, much as religious seekers develop a devotion to their experience of God or a Higher Power. For the devoted addict, drugs provide the Power to get High. Implicit in this definition is the notion that an addict's experience in the non-drug state is somehow deficient, a "lower" state of consciousness that can only be "fixed" by a "higher" drug experience.

Addicts speak of a drug fix as a solution or remedy to their lows, particularly those associated with drug withdrawal or intense craving. Devotion to obtaining the next fix illustrates the compulsive nature of many addictive behaviors. Alcohol is the fix for the alcoholic in the same way that nicotine is the fix for the addicted smoker. Heroin provides a fix for the opiate addict's cravings in the same way that cocaine is the fix of choice for crack addicts. For some, the fix derives from the high of sexual excitement whereas others seek the thrill of gambling as a fix for boredom or depression. In each of these cases, there is a devotion to the fix as a desirable experience that the addict would like to prolong as long as possible, to maintain the "high" (or the relief that the fix provides) indefinitely. Because ordinary (non-drug) experience is less desirable to the addict than the high produced by the fix, preoccupation with the "next fix" takes precedence over acceptance of the present moment. Between fixes, the addict experiences ongoing present experiences as less favorable, as "broken" in some way that only the next fix can fix. Ordinary reality pales in contrast with the allure of the "rush" that the fix provides. As a result, the addicted mind is fixed on the future, unable to accept the here and now.

A cartoon once published in the New Yorker illustrates the opposite of the addicted mind. The cartoon depicts two monks sitting on their meditation cushions, one an experienced, older meditator and the other a young novice with a perplexed look on his face. In the caption, the older monk says: "Nothing happens next. This is it!"

In the practice of meditation, the mind is trained to focus on the present experience (as compared to dwelling on either the past or future). Meditators focus on an ongoing, repetitive "here and now" experience, such as the rhythm of the breath, the repetition of a mantra, or the constantly changing patterns of thought, images, emotions, and physical sensations that characterize the flow of our immediate experience. Buddhist teachers describe this open, present-oriented, nonjudgmental state of awareness as mindfulness. Consider the following definitions of mindfulness drawn from the Buddhist literature:

> Mindfulness is that quality of attention which notices without choosing, without preference; it is a choiceless awareness that, like the sun, shines on all things equally (p. 19). Mindfulness is where we start; it is the first ingredient in the Buddha's recipe for awakening. Mindfulness means seeing how things are, directly and immediately seeing for oneself that which is present and true. It has a quality of fullness and impeccability to it, a bringing of our whole heart and mind, our full attention, to each moment (Goldstein & Kornfield, 1987, p. 62).

> Meditation is bringing the mind back home, and this is first achieved through the practice of mindfulness ... the practice of mindfulness defuses our negativity, aggression, and turbulent emotions... Rather than suppressing emotions or indulging in them, here it is important to view them, and your thoughts, and whatever arises with an acceptance and generosity that are as open and spacious as possible. Tibetan masters say that this wise generosity has the flavor of boundless space, so warm and cozy that you feel enveloped and protected by it, as if by a blanket of sunlight (Sogyal, 1992, p. 123).

> The practice of mindfulness is not reserved for the meditation cushion. It should be brought to bear on what is happening at any and every moment. Needless to say, our usual condition is a kind of waking dream... If we are able to wake up, if only occasionally and for a few moments at first, stand back from the ongoing drama of our lives and take an objective look at the habit patterns in which we are caught, then their compulsive hold over us begins to loosen. We dis-identify from them; that is, we begin to see that those thoughts and feelings are not us. They come along accidentally. They are neither an organic part of us nor are we obliged to follow them (Snelling, 1991, p. 55).

Over time, practitioners of mindfulness meditation directly perceive the nature of present experience as one of constant change or flux. Thoughts come and go and physical sensations rise and fall much like the pattern of one's breath (inbreath, outbreath). This ever-changing flow of present experience illustrates the doctrine of impermanence in the Buddhist teachings. Nothing remains the same. All experiences arise and pass away like waves on the sea. Mindfulness meditation trains the mind to become aware and accept the constantly changing nature of life itself on a moment-to-moment basis. There is no attempt to control the process or "fix" what happens next. "Nothing happens next. This is it!"

We see from the above discussion that the addicted mind, with its constant devotion to the "next fix" and its inability to accept the present moment (the non-drug state), is quite the opposite of mindfulness. If mindfulness is the state of mind that is trained to accept the constantly changing nature of ongoing experience, then addiction is a mindless state characterized by an inability to accept impermanence. The addict desires to "fix impermanence" by clinging or grasping on to the "high" associated with a particular drug or habit. There is a devotion to controlling the nature of reality by maintaining the highs and avoiding the lows. Mindfulness, in contrast, is marked by an acceptance of the vicissitudes of moment-to-moment experience. Essentially it is a nonjudging, relaxed state of awareness open to the basic nature of the impermanence of the process of living.

An analysis of addiction based on a mindful/mindless perspective has also been advanced by Western theorists. Harvard psychologist Ellen Langer has described a cognitive model of mindfulness (Langer, 1989). In a recent article applying this model to addiction, Margolis and Langer (1990) make the following distinction between mindlessness and mindfulness:

Mindlessness can be defined as a cognitive state in which an individual relies rigidly on categories and distinctions created in the past. Mindlessness involves acting on the basis of a formalized set of rules and attitudes. Each new event or situation is classified into a preexisting category. On the basis of that category, behavioral and attitudinal responses are prescribed. Mindfulness, on the other hand, can be defined as a state of continuous category formation. A mindful individual creates new approaches to events and situations. He or she is not bound by previously formed rigid attitudes; rather, the mindful person, situated in the present, explores a situation from several perspectives (p. 107).

The authors go on to apply this model to the addict who is attempting to quit his or her addictive behavior. A mindless approach to quitting focuses on only one cognitive category: the negative aspects of the addiction itself. Mindless addicts may be more vulnerable to relapse to the extent that they attribute a failure to change (e.g., to lapse despite a commitment to abstinence) to personal failure and weakness (i.e., the Abstinence Violation Effect). A mindful approach would include an appraisal of both negative and positive aspects of the addictive behavior from the addict's perspective:

Marlatt (1978) noted that... the Abstinence Violation Effect results from acceptance of the (observer's) prevailing perception of the need for total abstinence. The observer demands abstinence of the alcoholic because from the observer's point of view, a drink leads to only negative results; there is no consideration of the possible benefits (p. 109)... a mindful addict would be more likely to consider both negative and positive aspects of the addiction. The mindless addict would be more likely to see only one valence. We believe that when an addict tries to kick an addiction and fails, he or she focuses solely on the negative aspects of the addiction (Margolis & Langer, 1990, p. 110).

In one study by this group of investigators (Langer, Perlmuter, Chanowitz, & Rubin, 1988), recovering alcoholics were divided into two groups–mindful (exposure to alcoholism from several different perspectives) or mindless (exposure to only a single perspective). In this retrospective study, the mindful group was much more successful in maintaining abstinence (of those alcoholics who had successfully given up drinking, 100% had had mindful exposure to alcoholism; none of those in the mindless group achieved a successful outcome).

Langer's theory, in summary, defines mindfulness as a cognitive style characterized by a freedom from rigid attitudes or cognitive categories. Situated in the present moment, the mindful individual shows a flexibility of cognitive processing, one that views the situation from several perspectives. Although Langer espouses an essentially Western theory based on cognitive psychology, there are some obvious parallels with Eastern (Buddhist) definitions of mindfulness. Both approaches describe mindfulness as rooted in the present moment, an awareness of the here-and-now process of ongoing experience. Whereas Langer describes a cognitive style marked by flexibility and freedom from rigid attitudes, Eastern authorities point to mindfulness as a relaxed, non-judging awareness of the continuously changing (impermanent) nature of existence.

In studies with elderly patients, Langer and colleagues reported that mindfulness training can have positive effects on health. Patients were trained to be mindful by encouraging them to consider the novel aspects of their environment and to exercise greater choice and control over daily routines and activities. Results showed that elderly individuals who received such training became healthier and had significantly longer life expectancies than those not trained to be mindful (Alexander, Langer, Newman, Chandler, & Davies, 1989).

Although no controlled treatment outcome study has directly evaluated the effects of meditation or mindfulness training in the treatment of addiction (with abstinence as the goal), our group at the University of Washington Addictive Behaviors Research Center has conducted research on the effects of meditation on alcohol consumption in heavy social drinkers (cf., Marlatt & Marques, 1977). In one study (Marlatt, Pagano, Rose, & Marques, 1984), college students identified as heavy social drinkers (not in treatment) were randomly assigned to either meditation, progressive muscle relaxation, bibliotherapy, or a no-treatment control group.

Subjects in all four groups were asked to keep daily self-monitoring records of their drinking during a six-week training period and a subsequent follow-up assessment period. Results showed that meditation, progressive relaxation, and bibliotherapy groups all showed significant reductions in alcohol consumption during the training period compared to no-treatment control subjects. A second study compared meditation training with aerobic exercise in a similar population of heavy drinkers (Murphy, Pagano, & Marlatt, 1986). The results of this study showed that both training in meditation and aerobic exercise were associated with significant reductions in daily alcohol use, compared to no-treatment controls.

The results from these two studies show that meditation, relaxation, and exercise are all capable of leading to reduced alcohol intake in heavy drinkers. It seems unlikely that this decrement in consumption is mediated by mindfulness per se, since the effect appears to be common to both several types of relaxation training and aerobic exercise. Another explanation for the effect is that both relaxation and exercise can be considered "positive addictions" as defined by Glasser (1976):

(1) It is something noncompetitive that you choose to do and you can devote an hour (approximately) a day to it. (2) It is possible for you to do it easily and it doesn't take a great deal of mental effort to do it well. (3) You can do it alone or rarely with others but it does not depend upon others to do it. (4) You believe that it has some value (physical, mental, or spiritual) for you. (5) You believe that if you persist at it you will improve, but this is completely subjective—you need to be the only one who measures the improvement. (6) The activity *must* have the quality that you can do it *without criticizing yourself. If you can't accept yourself during this time, the activity will not be addicting.* This is why it is so important that the activity can be done alone. Any time you introduce other people you chance introducing competition or criticsm, often both (p. 93).

To put it another way, a "negative addiction" is something that feels good right away but is bad for you in the long run, whereas a "positive addiction" often feels negative in the short-run (the pain of starting to jog on a cold winter morning or the initial boredom that often characterizes sitting meditation), but is considered beneficial for health and well-being in the long run. From this perspective, activities such as meditation and exercise can be considered "addictive" to the extent that they both provide rewarding consequences such as deep relaxation and tension reduction. To the extent that exercise, relaxation, and drinking all have the same effect on tension reduction, they can be considered functionally equivalent behaviors. As such, the substitution of positive addictions such as meditation for the "negative addiction" of excessive drinking represents a healthy exchange of habits. Various types of meditation (e.g., transcendental, vipassana, concentrative meditation, etc.) have also been described as functionally equivalent by Benson (1975) in that they all seem to elicit a common physiological "relaxation response" despite their procedural differences.

In our meditation and drinking research, subjects were asked to practice a mantra meditation for two 20-minute periods a day, once in the morning and again in the late afternoon. While this method generates a total of 40 minutes of relaxation with some degree of mindfulness, it does not necessarily promote mindfulness as an "on the spot" response to addictive craving or urges. If an urge triggers a mindless act of indulgence or consumption, mindfulness can be elicited contingently as a response to the urge itself. Addicts often respond in a conditioned, automatic manner to urges, giving themselves over mindlessly to the consummatory response.

Acceptance and Coping with Urges

In contingent mindfulness training, clients are taught to first recognize the stimulus or cue that triggers the urge (e.g., the sight of someone smoking triggers an urge to smoke). The craving (desire for the effects of nicotine) and the urge (intention to smoke) are both described as classically conditioned responses. Clients are taught that they can accept cravings and urges without automatically engaging in the consummate addictive behavior.

In contingent mindfulness, the client is taught to be mindfully aware of the conditioned response to the cue (craving) and/or the urge to indulge. Craving and urges are recognized and observed, labeled or designated ("I am experiencing an urge to drink"), and accepted without judgment. Mindful awareness of the urge occurs without the necessity of mindlessly giving in to the urge. Craving and urges are themselves impermanent; they arise and pass away like conditioned responses. The goal of mindfulness training is to become aware of the conditioning process itself—to "rise above" the automaticity of stimulus-response linkage by the practice of detached awareness. Mindfulness in this sense is learning to let go of the desired outcome, to practice "non-doing" as an alternative to the addictive fix.

Consider the story of how natives in Southeast Asia sometimes catch wild monkeys to sell or keep as pets. A trap is built consisting of a wooden box shaped something like a birdhouse. The trap is fastened to an iron or cement foundation and cannot be moved or pulled away. The circular opening to this wooden trap is just big enough for a monkey to insert (or withdraw) one empty paw. Inside the trap is a fresh banana. A hungry monkey approaches the trap, smelling the banana inside. Reaching in with its paw, the monkey grasps the banana but cannot remove it to eat because it will not fit through the opening. In order to free itself from the trap, the monkey must first let go of the banana in order to remove its paw and escape. But most monkeys do not let go and are then easily captured. Addiction is a similar trap: in order to escape, one must first learn to let go of the object of desire.

As in the above anecdote, stories and metaphors can be used to great advantage in teaching clients to accept urges and to "let go" of the desired outcome. Metaphors provide a framework of imagery to guide clients through the difficult process of habit change in both general psychotherapy (McCurry & Hayes, 1992) and in therapy for addiction problems (Marlatt & Fromme, 1987). Here are two metaphors that we have used with clients as an imagery technique in coping with urges.

The first metaphor is called "urge surfing" (Marlatt & Gordon, 1985). In this example, the urge is portrayed as an ocean wave. Like a wave, an urge begins slowly and gradually grows in size until it crests and then gently subsides. Since urges are conditioned responses, they too start slowly and gradually get stronger as they reach a peak intensity. It is at the peak of the urge (crest of the wave) that the tendency to give in is at maximum strength. Clients often believe, however, that the urge will continue to grow in size or strength unless they give in to it. However, by learning to maintain their balance and mindfully riding the urge through its course, they can experience the urge waning and passing away. The client becomes a skilled "urge surfer" who can experience the rising and passing of urges without getting "wiped out" by them.

Another metaphor we have developed to cope with urges is the "PIG"—an animal acronym standing for the Problem of Immediate Gratification. Here clients are taught to externalize their inner craving by visualizing it in the form of a pig:

The first task in coping with the PIG is to become familiar with its behavior: how it manifests itself in craving and urges, what makes it hungry, and how it is gratified. In presenting these ideas to clients, it is helpful to objectify the PIG. Imagining the problem of immediate gratification as a PIG may help clients grapple with this otherwise vague motivational construct. Most people have a stereotyped image of pigs. They see them as greedy animals, fat and dirty swine rutting around in the mud (a stereotype that is probably unfair to the pig as an animal but that seems to fit the concept of PIG as we have discussed it in this context). The PIG craves (food, sex, drugs, etc.) and gives in to its urges with abandon. Each indulgence in gratification makes the PIG grow fatter. Never fully satisfied, the PIG is hungry again soon after each meal or sexual act; the more it has, the more it wants. Its appetite is insatiable; its cravings can never be fully gratified (Marlatt, 1989, p. 228).

Implicit in the above examples is the assumption that urges and cravings cannot be directly controlled or modified. Rather, the client is encouraged to recognize and accept the urge as "normal"– a conditioned response to an appetitive cue. Mindfulness of the urge is the first step in breaking the otherwise automatic tendency to give in to it by indulging in the addictive behavior. Rather than "giving in" the client is instructed to "let go" and allow the urge to rise and fall on its own. The urge can serve as a discriminative stimulus to let go and to engage in an alternative coping response. In this sense, the urge signals a choice, a fork in the road, rather than a one-way road to indulgence.

Traditional behavior therapy has taken a different tack in working with urges. Rather than encouraging acceptance, behavior therapists have tried to modify the urge by behavioral intervention strategies. In chemical aversion therapy for alcoholism, for example, an attempt is made to condition an aversive response by a classical conditioning paradigm in which alcohol cues are paired with administration of an emetic drug that produces intense nausea. Despite the intuitive appeal of this procedure, the goal of which is to substitute an aversive reaction for an appetitive urge, outcome research studies have failed to show a significant treatment effect for aversion therapy (Wilson, 1987).

Another behavioral approach to urge modification is cue exposure, originally conceptualized as an operant extinction procedure. In this technique, the addict is exposed repeatedly to drug cues (e.g., the sight and smell of alcohol) but is instructed to refrain from any drug use (response prevention):

> Conditioning theories suggest that alcoholics are likely to have classically conditioned reactions to stimuli associated with heavy drinking, and that these reactions may be extinguished by extended exposure to these stimuli while preventing the drinking response (Monti et al., 1993, p. 235).

Although research supports the hypothesis that cue reactivity can be reduced or attenuated through repeated exposure to drug cues in the laboratory or treatment setting (e.g. Monti et al., 1987), the literature fails to show that cue exposure has a significant impact on outcome in follow-up trials (Laberg, 1990; Powell et al., 1990). The lack of generalization of cue exposure effects outside the laboratory is probably due to the fact that the addict is exposed to a wide variety of drug-related stimuli in the post-treatment environment that cannot possibly all be included in the initial exposure trials. In one inpatient cue exposure study, an addict who had shown a consistent extinction effect over repeated trials suddenly showed a complete reversal with pronounced physiological reactivity to drug cues on a particular treatment day. The patient reported an angry altercation with a hospital official just prior to his cue exposure session; the negative emotional experience fully reactivated his craving for drugs (McLellan, Childress, Ehrman, O'Brien, & Pashko, 1986).

Addicts receiving passive cue exposure treatment may be at greater risk of relapse when they experience negative emotions or are exposed to novel drug cues in their natural environment. They may be more vulnerable because they believe that the cue exposure treatment works by protecting them from strong craving or urges; when an unexpected urge occurs, they are ill-equipped to cope with it and may give up and give in (Marlatt, 1990). In recognition of this risk, some investigators have combined cue exposure with training in urge coping skills (Cooney, Baker, & Pomerleau, 1983; Cooney, Gillespie, Baker, & Kaplan, 1987).

Acceptance and Coping with Lapses

What if the abstinent addict yields to the urge and experiences a lapse? Considerable controversy exists in the addiction treatment field about the causes of relapse and how best to deal with the problem. Two paradigms clash with regard to this topic: the disease model and the behavioral model strongly disagree on definitions of relapse and the role of acceptance.

Proponents of the disease model insist the addiction (e.g., alcoholism) is caused by genetic/biological factors beyond the control of the individual. The disease is progressive and cannot be cured; the progressive course can only be "arrested" by a life-long commitment to total abstinence (Jellinek, 1960; Milam, 1971; Milam & Ketcham, 1981; Royce, 1981). The disease model promotes a dichotomous, all-or-none view of both addiction ("Once an alcoholic, always an alcoholic") and relapse ("You are only one drink away from a drunk"). Any drug use, even a single instance, is tantamount to afull relapse, a return to the disease state. Relapse is thus determined by the same biological factors that cause the disease (e.g., physiologically-based craving and loss of control).

The disease model is ardently embraced by self-help groups based on the "Twelve-step" model (Alcoholics Anonymous, Narcotics Anonymous, etc.). AA devotees insist that an inability on the part of a problem drinker to accept the disease paradigm constitutes denial. Denial is, in fact, often included as a symptom of the disease itself. Consider the following definition of alcoholism proposed in 1992 by the Joint Committee of the National Council on Alcoholism and Drug Dependence and the American Society of Addiction Medicine and published in the Journal of the American Medical Association:

> Alcoholism is a primary, chronic disease with genetic, psychosocial, and environmental factors influencing its development and manifestations. The disease is often progressive and fatal. It is characterized by impaired control over drinking, preoccupation with the drug alcohol, use of alcohol despite adverse consequences, and distortions in thinking, most notably denial (Morse & Flavin, 1992, pp. 1012-1014).

An alcoholic cannot be helped unless he or she is able to "break through" the denial and accept the diagnosis of alcoholism as described in this definition. A refusal to accept the disease diagnosis with its emphasis on impaired control ("loss of control") constitutes denial. Anyone who therefore disputes or disagrees with this definition (including academics and researchers) is also considered to be in denial. Taking the "first step" in AA is necessary to break through denial–to accept that one is an alcoholic and personally powerless to exert control over one's drinking. In accepting powerlessness, the alcoholic is encouraged to turn over control to a Higher Power: "We admitted that we were powerless over alcohol and that our lives had become unmanageable" (Brown, 1993, p. 141.).

In essence, the problem drinker in AA must accept two basic tenets: (a) personal acceptance that one is an alcoholic and that alcoholism is a disease marked by a loss of personal control; (b) turning one's control over to a Higher Power such as God is the only way to maintain abstinence. There are no exceptions to this blanket requirement of acceptance–alcoholism is considered a uniform disease that renders all victims equally powerless. Personal identity, including one's full name, is stripped away in the insistence upon Anonymity for all members of the group. The success of this approach may, in fact, rely upon a paradoxical attribution process, as argued recently by Davies:

> AA and other similar agencies encourage their clients to believe they are powerless to control their own behavior, and that they must therefore recruit the power of some higher being to assist them; that is, God in some form. Paradoxically, by believing that the power of a higher being is the only thing that can help them in their helplessness, they cease to be helpless,

because belief in an *external* higher power changes internal motivation. *By invoking an all-powerful external locus for the control of their behavior, they increase their internal desire to behave differently.* A paradoxical external locus in fact has the most profound internal implications (Davies, 1992, p. 125).

To the extent that the addict accepts or buys in to the Twelve-Step philosophy and successfully maintains abstinence, all is well. Even though the evidence is mixed concerning the validity of the disease paradigm or the existence of God, if it works, so what? The problem is that the evidence of the superiority of AA or other Twelve-Step programs for addiction as compared to other treatment approaches does not exist (Institute of Medicine, 1990). Are those who refuse to accept this paradigm all in denial? More people drop out of AA than stay with it, despite the insistence on daily meetings in the early stages ("90 meetings in 90 days") and lifelong attendance.

A critical problem with the Twelve-Step approach is relapse. Given the emphasis on genetic causation of the disease and personal powerlessness, how is it possible to cope with the problem of relapse? Is relapse an inevitable consequence of losing touch with the Higher Power? Does even a single lapse render the individual a helpless victim of a biological disease?

Just as the disease itself is considered to be all-or-none (one either has the disease or not), relapse is viewed as a dichotomous state: Either one is abstinent or has relapsed. Disease model advocates refuse to recognize relapse as a continuous variable with degrees of intensity or levels of improvement. When asked if the alcohol and substance abuse fields should follow the lead of smoking researchers such as Mermelstein, Karnatz, and Reichmann (1992), who reported several different relapse patterns among smokers who had tried to quit, Stephanie Brown replied, "When it comes to substance abuse, you are either using or not using" (Brown, 1993). In the dichotomous black/white conceptualization of relapse/ abstinence, there is no gray area, no distinction between a lapse and a relapse. Until recently, treatment outcome studies in substance abuse and alcoholism reported outcomes in terms of either using/not using (e.g., Hunt, Barnett & Branch, 1971).

The behavioral paradigm, in contrast to the disease model, views relapse as a continuous variable instead of a dichotomous category. Behavioral theorists see addiction as having multiple determinants and embrace a biopsychosocial model of etiology (Marlatt, 1992). By the same token, relapse is thought to be determined by a multitude of factors. Although biological factors such as physical withdrawal symptoms play a role, behavioral and psychosocial processes are major determinants of relapse. Such factors as motivation, efficacy, outcome expectancies, coping skills, and situational factors have all been found to influence relapse (Marlatt & Gordon, 1985). These determinants are more modifiable (e.g., training clients in more adaptive coping skills) than genetic or other biological factors.

Based on a continuum model of relapse, attention can be paid to relative changes that may indicate improvement even though total abstinence is not achieved. Meaningful distinctions can thus be made in assessing treatment outcome, ranging from a single lapse or slip to a full return to pretreatment baseline levels of drug use. In addition, the direction of change is important: over a one-year follow-up period, does the client's drug use show a pattern of increase or decrease in terms of the frequency and intensity of occurrence? In place of the black/white absolutism of the disease model, the behavioral approach focuses on shades of gray between these two extremes.

Buddhist psychology is parallel to the behavioral paradigm in its acceptance of a "middle way" between the extremes of total indulgence and absolute restraint. It is said that the Buddha became enlightened only after moving beyond the extremes of his early life of either indulgence (as a young man, Siddharta was a prince who lived a rich and protected life) or strict asceticism (abstinence from all indulgences). Buddhism teaches that a balanced life is based on a mindful awareness and practice of the middle way as an alternative to the duality of extremes (Tulku, 1977). An unbalanced life, on the other hand, is characterized by suffering rooted in attachment (an inability to "let go" or accept impermanence; attachment to ego or a central unchanging self). Buddhists teach that the way out of suffering and attachment is to practice the "Noble Eightfold Path"–the path to mindfulness and enlightenment consisting of the following steps: Right view, right intention, right speech, right action, right livelihood, right effort on the path, right awareness, and right meditative concentration (Hanh, 1990). Note that each of these eight paths emphasizes personal responsibility and empowerment (e.g., "right action," also known as "skillful means," is equivalent to the acquisition of coping skills). There is no mention of the need for God or a "Higher Power" as a necessary condition for change. In this sense there is a basic difference between the Christian deistic philosophy of the Twelve-Step approach and the Buddhist non-deistic nature of the Eightfold Path.

In his book, *Zen Mind, Beginner's Mind*, the Buddhist scholar Shunryu Suzuki (1970) writes: "To give your sheep or cow a large spacious meadow is the way to control him." We cited this quotation in the preface to our book, *Relapse Prevention* (Marlatt & Gordon, 1985), because it embraces the underlying philosophy of our approach to dealing with relapse in addiction treatment. In our work with clients, we attempt to provide a "large spacious meadow" to allow for the possibility of lapses and to work with them as a natural part of the habit change process. The majority of clients experience temporary setbacks or "slips" in their attempts to change behavior. Although some are able to quit smoking or drinking on their first attempt without any backsliding, such cases are relatively rare; in our study of self-initiated smoking cessation, for example, we found that only one out of five smokers (20% of our sample) were able to quit without experiencing any lapses (Marlatt, Curry, & Gordon, 1988). As Schachter (1990) has noted, people who report eventual, long-term success in giving up smoking or coping with a significant weight problem typically report that their rate of progress was uneven, marked by many setbacks on the path. These eventually successful cases seem to prove the old adage: "If at first you don't succeed, try, try again!"

For the vast majority of individuals who are not 100% successful in achieving their habit change goals on any one attempt, the therapist's major challenge is to prevent them from giving up and dropping out of treatment. Once clients drop out, there is no way to reach them. Many drop-outs experience a motivational break-down, sliding down the slippery path from lapse to relapse to potential collapse. The critical juncture for potential drop-out is the client's reactions to his or her first lapse. In the RP model (Marlatt, 1985), one reaction that often undermines the client's motivation to persist and to "try again" following a lapse is the Abstinence Violation Effect (AVE). Clients who experience a strong AVE report feelings of guilt and shame for violating their goal of absolute abstinence (in cases in which abstinence is not the goal, e.g., dietary restrictions, we refer to this reaction as a Rule Violation Effect). Based on attribution theory, the AVE is characterized by the client's internal, stable, and global attributions as to the cause of the lapse. The client believes that he or she is to blame for the lapse because of internal failures (e.g., lack of willpower or inability to resist the strength of the addictive disease). Often this cause is viewed as stable across time ("This proves that I'll never be able to quit") and global across situations ("No matter what I try or where I go, nothing works").

To combat the motivational deficit associated with the AVE and to prevent treatment drop-out, RP therapists make every attempt to create a context of acceptance for clients who experience lapses. The AVE is a reaction marked by non-acceptance ("It's my fault—I shouldn't have let this happen"). Cognitive dissonance may also motivate giving in to relapse or dropping out (Festinger, 1964). In this case, the behavior of the lapse is in conflict or dissonant with one's self-image of abstinence. In order to reduce or eliminate this conflict, the client may redefine the self-image ("This just goes to prove that I'm an addict") and abandon all change efforts. Once the client gives up restorative coping following a lapse, the previously taboo behavior may rebound in the form of a binge or total relapse ("Since I have already smoked one cigarette, I might as well finish the whole pack"). Lapses can then be used as an excuse for further backsliding, particularly if the client embraces an all-or-none belief about abstinence/relapse.

In working with lapses, the therapist is faced with the following challenge: How to encourage the client to accept lapses as a normal challenge in recovery without at the same time "giving permission" for future lapses to occur. A lapse is both a danger sign and an opportunity for new learning. Lapses can be reframed as errors, mistakes that can be learned from, rather than seeing them only as indicators of failure.

Clients are encouraged to draw upon other examples from their lives in which mistakes or errors are considered a normal part of learning a new skill or habit. For many, learning to ride a bicycle is a good example: a few painful spills are to be expected as one gradually acquires balance and mastery ("Next time, I'll use the hand brakes when I'm coming into a sharp turn"). People do not expect to play a musical instrument without first making many errors as they practice. The same principles apply to giving up old habits. One must learn new coping skills to replace the maladaptive addictive behavior. Mistakes are common to any new learning process.

How should therapists respond when clients report lapses? To facilitate acceptance (and to prevent relapse or dropping-out), RP therapists attempt to recreate the pattern of events that preceded and followed the lapse itself. In this "relapse debriefing" method (Shiffman, Read, Maltese, Rapkin, & Jarvik, 1985), clients are encouraged to give their personal account of what happened prior to, during, and after the lapse occurred. What was the situation when the lapse occurred—when did it happen, where were you, with whom, and how were you feeling? Were there any "warning signals" that preceded the lapse? Did you make a decision (change your mind) about your goals before the lapse occurred? How did you feel after the lapse? Did you think or do anything to get back on track or did you just "give in" after the first lapse? The aim of this line of questioning is to reframe attributions associated with the AVE—to point out situational or external high-risk situations that may have triggered the lapse, to focus on alternative coping responses, and to highlight the fact that a lapse is a single discrete episode in space and time.

Acceptance of a lapse as a "single discrete episode in space and time" is illustrated in the following Buddhist story. Two monks were walking along a forest path somewhere in southeast Asia. Both were silent in keeping with their precept of not talking to preserve the mindfulness of "Noble Silence." As they proceeded around a bend in the trail, they spotted an attractive young woman dressed in white robes, hesitating at the brink of a muddy creek that rushed across the trail in front of her. Clearly there was no way for her to cross the creek alone without soiling her robes in the muddy waters. Both monks knew that they had taken vows not to touch or even look at any woman, as part of their religious tradition. As they approached the woman, however, one of the monks quickly lifted the woman in his arms and carried her across the creek, setting her down safely on the other side, without saying a word. The other monk became increasingly incredulous as they continued walking along the path for the next few hours. Finally he could stand it no longer and he broke his vow of silence, crying out "How could you do that? Not only did you look at the woman—you also held her in your arms as you carried her to the other side!! How could you break our sacred vows like that??" The other monk looked at his accusing comrade calmly, replying "I put her down hours ago. It seems as though you are still carrying her."

Relapse Prevention and Harm Reduction

Preventing lapses is the primary goal of relapse prevention. If lapses occur, however, the goal is to work with clients to prevent further relapse and/or dropping out of treatment. If clients continue in the relapse process, tertiary prevention becomes necessary to reduce the frequency and magnitude of relapse episodes. Training clients in restorative coping skills becomes the focus. Learning how to interrupt or check the course of ongoing relapse episodes is central to this phase of RP. Further practice in implementing cognitive and behavioral skills in high-risk situations is also encouraged. In one study, chronic male alcoholics who received skill training to cope with a series of relapse trigger situations showed significantly less drinking and shorter relapse episodes during a one-year follow-up compared to alcoholics who had not received RP (Chaney, O'Leary, & Marlatt, 1978).

Harm reduction refers to any procedure or method designed to reduce the harm of ongoing addictive behaviors (Marlatt & Tapert, 1993). The tertiary prevention methods described above represent one application of the harm reduction approach: here the goal is to reduce the harm of relapse in clients in treatment who are pursuing a goal of either abstinence or moderation. But what about addicts who are not in treatment or who reject abstinence-based treatment goals? Harm reduction programs encourage such people to take steps toward minimizing the risk or harm of their addictive behavior even though abstinence may not be achieved. As described by Parry (1989), a leader of harm reduction approaches in Liverpool, UK:

Harm reduction takes small steps to reduce, even to a small degree, the harm caused by the use of drugs. If a person is injecting street heroin of unknown potency, harm reduction would consider it an advance if the addict were prescribed safe, legal heroin. A further advantage if he stopped sharing needles. A further advance if he enrolled in a needle-exchange scheme. A much further advance if he moved on to oral drugs or to smoked drugs. A further advance in harm reduction if he started using condoms and practicing safe sex practices. A further advance if he took advantage of the general health services available to addicts. A wonderful victory if he kicked drugs, although total victory is not a requirement as it is in the United States (p. 13).

In an article reviewing this approach (Marlatt & Tapert, 1993), we included the following as examples of harm reduction: needle exchange programs for injection drug users, methadone maintenance for opiate addicts, nicotine replacement methods for smokers, weight management programs for the obese, controlled drinking for problem drinkers, and safe-sex programs to reduce the risk of HIV infection and AIDS. In each of these cases, the goal is to reduce the ongoing or potential damage associated with an ongoing risky behavior. In some examples (eating or sexual behaviors), abstinence is not the goal; changing behavior is (reduced consumption of food or using condoms during sexual activity). For substance abuse problems, abstinence is viewed as an ideal, distal goal, which may not be attainable by all addicts. Harm reduction promotes a series of proximal (attainable) goals to reduce risk.

Harm reduction programs were first introduced by drug policy makers in Europe, particularly in the Netherlands and part of the U.K. The "Dutch model" of harm reduction is particularly well known:

In the eighties a new treatment philosophy emerged... Increased encouragement by the government has been given to forms of aid which are not primarily intended to end addiction as such, but to improve addicts' physical and social well-being and to help them function in society. At this stage the addicts' (temporal) inability to give up drug use was accepted as a fact. This kind of assistance may be defined as harm reduction or more traditionally: secondary and tertiary prevention. Its effectiveness can only be ensured by low-threshold facilities and accessible help, which are the key concepts in Dutch drug policy (Engelsman, 1989, p. 216).

Clearly the Dutch policy is characterized by acceptance, a "kinder, gentler" approach than the contemporary American "War on Drugs" (read: War on Addicts). Addicts are treated neither as criminals to be locked up nor victims of a genetic disease, as they so often are in the USA. As Engelsman (1989) states, "The drug abuse problem should not be primarily seen as a problem of police and justice. It is essentially a matter of health and social well-being" (p. 212). The Dutch reach out to the addict population by making harm reduction programs easily available, a "low threshold" approach that contrasts sharply with the barriers to treatment access often associated with American "high threshold" programs (e.g., the requirement of abstinence as a precondition for treatment). Amsterdam sponsors mobile vans that provide the addict populations with needle exchange, condoms, medical first-aid and other social services. In contrast, current American drug policy is based on a "zero tolerance" philosophy: there is no acceptance or tolerance of even the smallest amount of illegal drug use. Unlike the Dutch who distinguish between soft drugs (cannabis) and hard drugs (heroin), American policy treats all illegal drugs with the same harsh zero tolerance mentality.

American drug policy shaped under the direction of Drug Czars appointed by the Republican administration (e.g., William Bennett) has been sharply critical of the harm reduction approach. In their view, anything short of imprisonment or enforced abstinence for the intravenous drug user is unacceptable. Despite evidence supporting the effectiveness of needle-exchange programs in Europe (Marlatt & Tapert, 1993), American policy in the Reagan-Bush years has remained firmly opposed to this method of reducing the risk of HIV infection. At the time of this writing (April, 1993), needle exchange is still illegal in most states, despite the best efforts of supporters, including the mayors of several major American cities (e.g., New York and San Francisco). Research designed to evaluate the effectiveness of needle-exchange programs has not been funded by government agencies such as the National Institute on Drug Abuse (NIDA) because it conflicts with national drug policies. As recently as 1990, the White House Office of National Drug Control Policy issued a "white paper" condemning needle exchange. The language in the report is clearly moralistic and condescending in tone with respect to the IV drug user:

> What Doesn't Work: Needle Exchange. Although it is not touted as treatment, the high rate of HIV transmission among intravenous drug users has prompted some to call for the free distribution of hypodermic needles. The rationale most frequently given is that these addicts won't share needles if clean ones are provided for them, and informal studies done in Holland are often cited as evidence....No matter what addicts promise when they aren't on drugs, they may still share needles when they shoot up heroin or cocaine... More often, drug-induced stupefaction overwhelms rational

thinking. Many addicts know that they can get AIDS from dirty needles. Yet hazards to their health—even deadly ones—do not weigh heavily on their minds, especially when they are strung out. We have to remind ourselves that drug addicts are primarily concerned with the instant gratification of drugs; their time limits are extremely limited... (Office of National Drug Control Policy, 1990, p. 29).

It is unfortunate that polemical statements such as this are made on the basis of conservative political theorizing (e.g., that providing needle exchange programs will increase the overall rate of addiction) rather than on data from public health studies of HIV infection rates. Any discussion of other policies that contradict the zero tolerance mentality of American drug policy, including the possibility of drug decriminalization or legalization are similarly dismissed—decisions that are made on the basis of dogma instead of data (Friedman & Szasz, 1992; Trebach & Zeese, 1990).

Although alcohol is a legal drug, drinking under the age of 21 is illegal in the U.S. Despite the fact that alcohol-related accidents represent the leading cause of death in late adolescence, coupled with the fact that the vast majority of underage youth drink, the official government policy is one of zero tolerance: no one shall drink until he or she reaches the age of 21. Educational programs in our schools have the same message for our children from kindergarten to high school graduation: "Just say no!" By the time students reach high school, most of them have already said "Yes" to alcohol. Yet schools offer no instruction in responsible alcohol use, leaving this experience to the "school of hard knocks," often with tragic consequences. Schools offer instruction in other high-risk activities such as driving, but when it comes to alcohol, there is no such thing as "Drinker's Ed" programs.

College students represent a high-risk group for alcohol-related problems, including drunk driving, accidents, unsafe sex and date rape, vandalism and impairment of academic performance (Berkowitz, & Perkins, 1986). Most of the harm associated with drinking in this population stems from "binge-drinking" episodes in which alcohol is consumed rapidly for its intoxicating effects (Wechsler & Issac, 1992).

In our research at the University of Washington, we are applying a harm-reduction approach to alcohol abuse problems in the college student population (Baer, Kivlahan, Fromme, & Marlatt, 1992; Marlatt, Larimer, Baer, & Quigley, 1993). Traditional prevention programs for alcohol problems with young adults have adopted an information and values-clarification model, stressing the dangers of alcohol and promoting abstinence as the ideal outcome (Miller & Nirenberg, 1984). While such programs lead to changes in knowledge and attitudes about alcohol, they rarely eventuate in significant changes in actual drinking behavior (Moskowitz, 1989).

Adopting harm-reduction as our guiding philosophy, we acknowledge that most students drink during their college years and that heavy drinking can cause harm. We also acknowledge that most youthful drinkers show a "maturing out" effect in that they drink more moderately as they grow older and assume major life experiences (Fillmore, 1988). The purpose of our secondary prevention programs is to teach students responsible drinking skills so as to facilitate their own maturational development *vis a vis* alcohol use. Our training programs are based on a skills-acquisition, cognitive-behavioral model of moderate drinking. Information and discussion of blood-alcohol levels, limit-setting, biphasic effects of alcohol, home-work assignments to experiment with moderate drinking, and placebo beverage consumption trials are all included in our "Drinker's Ed" program.

In our preliminary study evaluating the effectiveness of this approach (Kivlahan, Marlatt, Fromme, Coppel, & Williams, 1990), we compared our cognitive-behavioral group program (groups met for eight weekly sessions) with an information-only group and an assessment-only control group. The results were encouraging, with students reporting drinking rate reductions of 40%-50% at one-year follow-up. The results of our first study were replicated in a two-year follow-up study (Baer, Marlatt, Kivlahan, Fromme, Larimer, & Williams, 1992).

In our current research project, we are evaluating a stepped-care model of harm reduction for alcohol abuse (Baer, 1993; Marlatt & Tapert, 1993). In a five-year longitudinal design, students were screened for alcohol problems and other risk factors (e.g., history of conduct disorder and alcoholism in the family) while in their final year of high-school, during the spring preceding their freshman year in college. Subjects in our high-risk sample of approximately 400 students were randomly assigned to either receive the stepped-care prevention program or to a "natural history" (no-treatment) control group.

The rationale for the stepped-care program is based on the assumption that many students will respond to a brief intervention designed to modify high-risk drinking behavior. In our second study (Baer et al., 1992) for example, we found that significant reductions in excessive drinking were maintained over a two-year follow-up period, after students were exposed to a single session of professional feedback and advice. Other research has indicated that brief interventions can have a significant impact on heavy drinkers (Larimer & Marlatt, 1994). In the stepped-care approach, students who do not respond favorably to the initial brief intervention are offered additional "steps" to choose from, including group training sessions, self-help manuals, outpatient counseling, and even (as a last resort) inpatient treatment. Students with more serious drinking problems can of course be quickly "bumped up" to an appropriate level of intervention.

We patterned our brief intervention sessions after the motivational interviewing procedure described by Miller and Rollnick (1991). The goal of motivational interviewing is to minimize resistance by adopting a more accepting stance while interviewing students about their drinking and associated risks. Rather than adopt-ing a direct confrontative style as advocated by the disease model approach, our interviewers made every attempt to accept the perspective of the student while at the same time encouraging steps to reduce harmful drinking. Since most college student drinkers are in the "precontemplation stage" according to the Prochaska and DiClemente (1986) model of addictive behavior change, our goal was to gently "nudge" them forward into the contemplation and action stages. Direct advice is blended with the student's reports of his or her own efforts in recognizing risks and taking preventive action. Initial results of our motivational interviews are encouraging: two-year follow-up results show a significant reduction in both alcohol consumption and drinking-related problems for students in the stepped-care group compared to control subjects.

Final Thoughts

In this paper I have reviewed some examples of how acceptance theory has direct applications in the understanding and treatment of addiction problems. After analyzing the concept of addiction in terms of the mindful/mindless distinction, research employing meditation as an alternative "positive addiction" for problem drinkers was described. Acceptance strategies were then discussed as part of a comprehensive relapse prevention approach. Skills and imagery related to coping with urges and lapses were selected as clinical examples. Harm reduction methods were introduced which are based on the acceptance of non-abstinent goals in working with ongoing addiction problems.

Buddhist psychology provides a cognitive framework to understand the subjective phenomenology of addiction. In its barest essentials, Buddhism views attachment as the root cause of addiction. Addiction problems represent a mindless attachment to the "high" and an inability to accept the impermanence of this or any other experience. Does acceptance of this view imply that addiction is entirely a matter of mind? Many people would strongly disagree, stating that addiction is regarded as a disease of the body, a physiological mechanism rooted deep within the chemistry of the brain and the body. To view addiction as primarily a psychological problem is a radical view indeed.

During one ten-day meditation retreat based on the Buddhist Vippassana tradition, I had the opportunity to raise this question with an Indian meditation teacher, S. N. Goenka (see Hart, 1987 for a description of his teaching methods). In a private interview session, I asked Goenka the following question: "Here in the West, addiction is viewed as a physical disease, caused primarily by genetic and biological factors. Based on your own experiences as a Dharma teacher, do you agree?" Goenka paused for a moment before giving his reply: "Disease? Yes! Addiction is a disease of the mind."

Does acceptance of this Buddhist view of addiction promote an artificial duality between mind and body? Buddhists do not make a distinction between the two; indeed, the goal of the teachings is to achieve enlightenment, based partly on the realization that the subjective sense of a separate, individual ego or self is an illusion. The whole notion of a separate "I", an independent controlling force, is at the base of all suffering, including addiction. As Hart (1987) interprets Goenka's teaching on this point:

"Any effort to hold on to something, saying "This is I, this is me, this is mine" is bound to make one unhappy, because sooner or later this something to which one clings passes away, or else this "I" passes away. Attachment to what is impermanent, transitory, illusory, and beyond one's control is suffering, dukkha. We understand all this not because someone tells us it is so, but because we experience it within, by observing sensations within the body (p. 95)."

Addiction is viewed by Buddhism as a problem of ego attachment. The ego's voice is manifested in thoughts such as, "I know how to control my feelings. By taking this drug, I can eliminate pain and unpleasant moods. I can control the way my body feels simply by ingesting this substance. After a short time, I will experience the rush of the drug high. If I feel unpleasant physical feelings when the drug wears off, I will be able to control this too by taking more. I can exert control over how much I take whenever I want to. I'm in control!" The stronger the belief in the ego's ability to control bodily states and subjective physical sensations, the stronger the addictive attachment. What appears to the addict as an ability to control his or her emotional and physical well-being by taking drugs appears to the observer as an addiction in which the drug has taken control of the user. It is not overly difficult for the "body" to overcome a drug dependency: the most intense physical drug withdrawal experiences rarely last more than a few hours or days. Psychological dependence, on the other hand, often lingers on indefinitely. Goenka was right.

References

Alexander, C., Langer, E., Newman, R., Chandler, H., & Davies, J. (1989). Transcendental meditation, mindfulness, and longevity: An experimental study with the elderly. *Journal of Personality and Social Psychology, 57,* 950-964.

Baer, J. S. (1993). Etiology and secondary prevention of alcohol problems with young adults. In J. S. Baer, G. A. Marlatt & R. J. McMahon (Eds.), *Addictive behaviors across the life span* (pp. 111-137). Newbury Park: Sage Publications.

Baer, J. S., Kivlahan, D., Fromme, K., & Marlatt, G. A. (1992). Secondary prevention of alcohol abuse with college students: A skills training approach. In N. Heather, W. R. Miller & J. Greeley (Eds.), *Self-control and the addictive behaviours* (pp. 339-356). Botany Bay, Australia: Maxwell Macmillan.

Baer, J. S., Marlatt, G. A., Kivlahan, D. R., Fromme, K., Larimer, M., & Williams, E. (1992). An experimental test of three methods of alcohol risk-reduction with young adults. *Journal of Consulting and Clinical Psychology, 60,* 974-979.

Benson, H. (1975). *The relaxation response.* New York: William Morrow.

Berkowitz, A. D., & Perkins, H. W. (1986). Problem drinking among college students: A review of recent research. *Journal of American College Health, 35,* 1-28.

Brown, S. D. (1993). Therapeutic processes in Alcoholics Anonymous. In B. S. McCrady & W. R. Miller (Eds.), *Research on Alcoholics Anonymous: Opportunities and alternatives* (pp. 137-152). New Brunswick, NJ: Rutgers Center of Alcohol Studies.

Chaney, E. F., O'Leary, M. R., & Marlatt, G. A. (1978). Skill training with alcoholics. *Journal of Consulting and Clinical Psychology, 46,* 1092-1104.

Cooney, N. L., Baker, L., & Pomerleau, O. F. (1983). Cue exposure for relapse prevention in alcohol treatment. In R. J. McMahon & K. D. Craig (Eds.), *Advances in clinical therapy* (pp.174-210). New York: Brunner/Mazel.

Cooney, N. L., Gillespie, R. A., Baker, L. H., & Kaplan, R. F. (1987). Cognitive changes after alcohol cue exposure. *Journal of Consulting and Clinical Psychology, 55,* 150-155.

Davies, J. B. (1992). *The myth of addiction: An application of the psychological theory of attribution to illicit drug use.* Reading, UK: Harwood Academic Publishers.

Engelsman, E. E. (1989). Dutch policy on the management of drug-related problems. *British Journal of Addiction, 84,* 211-218.

Festinger, L. (1964). *Conflict, decision, and dissonance.* Stanford: Stanford University Press.

Fillmore, K. M. (1988). *Alcohol use across the life course.* Toronto: Addiction Research Foundation.

Friedman, M., & Szasz, T. S. (1992). *On liberty and drugs: Essays on the free market and prohibition.* Washington, DC: Drug Policy Foundation Press.

Glasser, W. (1976). *Positive addictions.* New York: Harper & Row.

Goldstein, J., & Kornfield, J. (1987). *Seeking the heart of wisdom: The path of insight meditation.* Boston: Shambhala.

Hanh, T. N. (1990). *Transformation and healing: Sutra on the four establishments of mindfulness.* Berkeley: Parallax Press.

Hart, W. (1987). *The art of living: Vipassana meditation as taught by S. N. Goenka.* San Francisco: Harper & Row.

Hunt, W. A., Barnett, L. W., & Branch, L. G. (1971). Relapse rates in addiction programs. *Journal of Clinical Psychology, 27,* 455-456.

Institute of Medicine (1990). *Broadening the base of treatment for alcohol problems.* Washington, DC: National Academy Press.

Jellinek, E. M. (1960). *The disease concept of alcoholism.* New Haven, CT: Hillhouse Press.

Kivlahan, D. R., Marlatt, G. A., Fromme, K., Coppel, D. B., & Williams, E. (1990). Secondary prevention with college drinkers: Evaluation of an alcohol skills training program. *Journal of Clinical and Consulting Psychology, 58,* 805-810.

Laberg, J. C. (1990). What is presented, and what prevented, in cue exposure and response prevention with alcohol dependent subjects? *Addictive Behaviors, 15,* 367-386.

Langer, E. (1989). *Mindfulness.* Reading, MA: Addison-Wesley.

Langer, E., Perlmuter, L., Chanowitz, B., & Rubin, R. (1988). Two new applications of mindlessness theory: Aging and alcoholism. *Journal of Aging Studies, 2,* 289-299.

Larimer, M. E., & Marlatt, G. A. (1994). Addictive behaviors. In L. W. Craighead, W. E. Craighead, A. E. Kazdin, & M. J. Mahoney (Eds.), *Cognitive Behavioral Interventions*. Needham Heights, MA: Allyn & Bacon.

Margolis, J., & Langer, E. (1990). An analysis of addictions from a mindful/mindless perspective. *Psychology of Addictive Behaviors, 4*, 107-115.

Marlatt, G. A. (1978). Craving for alcohol, loss of control, and relapse: A cognitive-behavioral analysis. In P. Nathan, G. A. Marlatt, & T. Loberg (Eds.), *Alcoholism: New directions in behavioral research and treatment* (pp. 119-242). New York: Plenum Press.

Marlatt, G. A. (1985). Cognitive factors in the relapse process. In G. A. Marlatt & J. R. Gordon (Eds.), *Relapse prevention: Maintenance strategies in the treatment of addictive behaviors* (pp. 128-200). New York: Guilford Press.

Marlatt, G. A. (1989). How to handle the PIG. In D. R. Laws (Ed.), *Relapse prevention with sex offenders* (pp. 228). New York: Guilford Press.

Marlatt, G. A. (1990). Cue exposure and relapse prevention in the treatment of addictive behaviors. *Addictive Behaviors, 15*, 395-399.

Marlatt, G. A. (1992). Substance abuse: Implications of a biopsychosocial model for prevention, treatment, and relapse prevention. In J. Grabowski & G. R. VandenBos (Eds.), *Psychopharmacology: Basic mechanisms and applied intervention* (pp. 127-162). Washington, DC: American Psychological Association.

Marlatt, G. A., & Fromme, K. (1987). Metaphors for addiction. *Journal of Drug Issues, 17*, 9-28.

Marlatt, G. A., & Gordon, J. R. (1985). *Relapse prevention: Maintenance strategies in the treatment of addictive behaviors*. New York: Guilford Press.

Marlatt, G. A., & Marques, J. K. (1977). Meditation, self-control, and alcohol use. In R. B. Stuart (Ed.), *Behavioral self-management* (pp. 117-153). New York: Brunner/Mazel.

Marlatt, G. A., & Tapert, S. F. (1993). Harm reduction: Reducing the risks of addictive behaviors. In J. S. Baer, G. A. Marlatt, & R. J McMahon (Eds.), *Addictive behaviors across the life span* (pp. 243-273). Newbury Park, CA: Sage Publications.

Marlatt, G. A., Curry, S., & Gordon, J. R. (1988). A longitudinal analysis of unaided smoking cessation. *Journal of Consulting and Clinical Psychology, 56*, 715-720.

Marlatt, G. A., Larimer, M. E., Baer, J. S., & Quigley, L. A. (1993). Harm reduction for alcohol problems: Moving beyond the controlled drinking controversy. *Behavior Therapy, 24*, 461-504.

Marlatt, G. A., Pagano, R. R., Rose, R. M., & Marques, J. K. (1984). Effects of meditation and relaxation training upon alcohol use in male social drinkers. In D. H. Shapiro & R. N. Walsh (Eds.), *Meditation: Classic and contemporary perspectives* (pp. 229-244). New York: Aldine.

McCurry, S. M., & Hayes, S. C. (1992). Clinical and experimental perspectives on metaphorical talk. *Clinical Psychology Review, 12*, 763-785.

McLellan, A. T., Childress, A. R., Ehrman, R., O'Brien, C. P., & Pashko, S. (1986). Extinguishing conditioned responses during opiate dependence treatment: Turning laboratory findings into clinical procedures. *Journal of Substance Abuse Treatment, 3*, 33-40.

Mermelstein, R. J., Karnatz, T., & Reichmann, S. (1992). Smoking. In P. H. Wilson (Ed.), *Principles and practice of relapse prevention* (pp. 43-68). New York: Guilford Press.

Milam, J. R. (1971). *The emergent comprehensive concept of alcoholism.* Kirkland, WA: ACA Press.

Milam, J. R., & Ketcham, K. (1981). *Under the influence: A guide to the myths and realities of alcoholism.* Seattle: Madrona Publishers.

Miller, P. M., & Nirenberg, T. D. (Eds.) (1984). *Prevention of alcohol abuse.* New York: Plenum Press.

Miller, W. R., & Rollnick, S. (1991). *Motivational interviewing.* New York: Guilford Press.

Monti, P. M., Binkoff, J. A., Abrams, D. B., Zwick, W. R., Nirenberg, T. D., & Liepman, M. R. (1987). Reactivity of alcoholics and nonalcoholics to drinking cues. *Journal of Abnormal Psychology, 96*, 122-126.

Monti, P. M., Rohsenow, D. J., Rubonis, A. V., Niaura, R. S., Sirota, A., Colby, S. M., & Abrams, D. B. (1993). Alcohol cue reactivity: Effects of detoxification and extended exposure. *Journal of Studies on Alcohol, 54*, 235-245.

Morse, R. M., & Flavin, D. K. (1992). The definition of alcoholism. *Journal of the American Medical Association, 268*, 1012-1014.

Moskowitz, J. (1989). The primary prevention of alcohol problems: A critical review of the research literature. *Journal of Studies on Alcohol, 50*, 54-88.

Murphy, T. J., Pagano, R. R., & Marlatt, G. A. (1986). Lifestyle modification with heavy alcohol drinkers: Effects of aerobic exercise and meditation. *Addictive Behaviors, 11*, 175-186.

Office of National Drug Control Policy. (1990, June). *White paper: Understanding drug treatment.* Washington, DC: Author.

Parry, A. (1989). Harm reduction [Interview]. *Drug Policy Letter, 1*(4), 13.

Powell, J., Gray, J. A., Bradley, B. P., Kasvikis, Y., Strang, J., Barratt, L., & Marks, I. (1990). The effects of exposure to drug-related cues in detoxified opiate addicts: A theoretical review and some new data. *Addictive Behaviors, 15*, 339-354.

Prochaska, J. O., & DiClemente, C. C. (1986). Toward a comprehensive model of change. In W. R. Miller & N. Heather (Eds.), *Treating addictive behaviors: Processes of change* (pp. 3-27). New York: Plenum Press.

Royce, J. E. (1981). *Alcohol problems and alcoholism: A comprehensive survey.* New York: Free Press.

Schachter, S. (1990). Debunking myths about self-quitting: Evidence from 10 prospective studies of persons who attempt to quit smoking by themselves: Reply. *American Psychologist, 45*, 1389-1390.

Shiffman, S., Read, L., Maltese, J., Rapkin, D., & Jarvik, M. E. (1985). Preventing relapse in ex-smokers: A self-management approach. In G. A. Marlatt & J. R. Gordon (Eds.), *Relapse prevention: Maintenance strategies in the treatment of addictive behaviors* (pp. 472-520). New York: Guilford Press.

Snelling, J. (1991). *The Buddhist handbook.* Rochester, VT: Inner Traditions.

Sogyal, S. (1992). *The Tibetan book of living and dying.* San Francisco: Harper.

Suziki, S. (1970). *Zen mind, beginner's mind.* New York: Weatherhill

Tulku, T. (1977). *Gesture of balance: A guide to awareness, self-healing, and meditation.* Emeryville, CA: Dharma Publications.

Trebach, A. S., & Zeese, K. B. (1990). *The great issues of drug policy.* Washington, DC: Drug Policy Foundation Press.

Webster, N. (1961). *Webster's third new international dictionary of the English language unabridged.* Springfield, MA: G & C Merriam Co.

Wechsler, H., & Issac, N. (1992). 'Binge' drinkers at Massachusetts Colleges. *Journal of the American Medical Association, 267,* 2929-2931.

Wilson, G. T. (1987). Chemical aversion conditioning as a treatment for alcoholism: A re-analysis. *Behaviour Research and Therapy, 25,* 503-516

Discussion of Marlatt

Mindfulness and Recovery from Substance Dependence

Kelly G. Wilson
University of Nevada

When an addict says that they "need a fix," the most obvious meaning is that they are experiencing a condition that is some how "broken," which the drug can repair. Marlatt suggests another meaning of the term "fix" that is relevant to addiction: addicts are intolerant of the normal ups and downs of experience. They seek to hold fast to some particular preferred state. Some may seek to fix a state absent of painful thoughts, emotions, or memories. For some, these painful states are what initiates the abuse. For others, these states may result from problems created by using. Still others may begin abusing substances for more innocuous social reasons (e.g., peer pressure). In the end though, a number of substances leave aversive states in their aftermath. Then the addict may seek to fix their experience in some state absent of the direct effects of abstinence. It may be that not all addicts begin as avoiders of negatively evaluated private experience, but it seems almost certain that if substance abuse continues for a long enough period, they will end up as avoiders.

Fixing by Addicts

The Shorter Oxford English Dictionary defines "fix" in various ways. Among them are to "make rigid, as in death," or to "deprive of volatility or fluidity" (Brown, 1993, p. 961). The addict may attempt to fix their experience in a variety of ways. As mentioned, they use their substance of choice. In addition, drug seeking and use may become highly ritualized. Intravenous heroin users sometimes inject part of a dose, then draw blood back into the syringe, then reinject part of the dose, repeating this process several times before completing the injection (sometimes called rebooting). Users of intranasal and smoked cocaine may engage in elaborate drug preparation and use rituals. Marijuana users may have favorite pipes or papers. The alcoholic has drink preferences and favorite bars. All of the rituals, settings, and trappings of addictive use of substances serve as a context which funnels experience into a fixed and venerated state–the high.

Paradoxically, attempting to fix life at some preselected "ideal" state, means that one must give up the one ingredient that is essential to life–change. When the botanist dries and presses foliage and bloom, they are trying to fix color and shape. If well executed, the end product gives the impression of a living thing. Close examination, though, reveal desiccation and two-dimensionality.

Fixing by the Treatment Community

Interestingly, this appetite for fixedness is not restricted to the addict. One may also find it within the substance abuse treatment community. Across the country, in hundreds of treatment facilities, clients are indoctrinated into a startlingly uniform view of substance abuse. Aspects of the dogma typically include the following: addiction is a unitary disease process. Its course, if untreated, is an inevitable downhill slide ending in physical, mental, and spiritual bankruptcy. The only appropriate treatment goal is total and permanent abstinence from all mood altering substances. Denial, deceptiveness, and rationalization are signs of the disease of addiction. Confrontation is the remedy for these aspects of the disease. Any client who rejects, or even questions, any of these articles of faith is in denial. (Which, of course, should be treated by confrontation.) Any treatment professional who rejects, or even questions, any of these articles of faith is either unethical or in denial. (Which, of course, should be treated by confrontation.)

Although disappointing, it is not particularly surprising that this is the case. Prior to the expansion of third party payment for substance abuse treatment, there were few incentives for treating addicts. The fact that addiction left clients less likely to be able to pay for treatment, coupled with dismal recovery rates, left few traditional treatment disciplines (e.g., medicine, psychology, & psychiatry) interested in this population. What emerged was a lay treatment community which consisted predominantly of persons who themselves had recovered from addictions. Early on, the addiction was alcoholism, and the treatment providers came largely from the ranks of those who recovered using Alcoholics Anonymous.

Narrowness of treatment strategy and view of the "disease" result from a self-selection process which may not benefit all persons presenting for treatment. The providers of treatment are persons who benefited from treatment-as-usual. Their friends and co-workers are likely to be persons who have also benefited from treatment-as-usual. It is bad science, but predictable human psychology, that such persons would embrace a treatment dogma which upheld as valuable their own experience, and which denigrated as diseased any contrary view.

Addiction is a difficulty with often tragic results. It is only natural that persons treating afflicted individuals would seek ways to bind their anxiety about the limits of their treatment technologies. Thus, another aspect of dogma comes into play when individuals fail in treatment. It usually sounds like "They just haven't hit their bottom yet," or "They just couldn't get honest about their disease." A rigid categorization of disorder and response to disorder may help the treatment provider fix their own experience in a place absent the pain and uncertainty of treating a poorly understood and treatment resistant problem.

Fixing in the Research Community

Nor is the research community exempt from a certain fixedness of view. AA and treatment centers are often lumped together and rigidly categorized as dogmatic and monolithic. While it is almost certainly true that many members of AA are dogmatic, and while it is also true that AA-promoting treatment facilities are often dogmatic, it does not necessarily follow that AA is itself dogmatic. Close examination of AA's official literature reveals some decidedly libertarian themes.

An example of the research community's fixedness of view is their insistence that AA does not recognize as important any outcome other than total and permanent abstinence. However, in the forward to the second edition of the book *Alcoholics Anonymous* (Alcoholics Anonymous World Services, 1976), one may find the following quotation: "Of alcoholics who came to AA and really tried, 50% got sober at once and remained that way; 25% sobered up after some relapses, and *among the remainder, those who stayed on with AA showed improvement*" (emphasis added). Similar remarks may be found in the basic text of Narcotics Anonymous:

> Many consider continuous abstinence and recovery as noteworthy and therefore synonymous, while relapsers are sort of pushed aside, or worse yet, used as statistics that in no way give a true picture of the entire addiction pattern. We in the recovery program of Narcotics Anonymous have noted with some satisfaction that many of the relapsers when again active in the prime or substitute addiction have dropped many of the parallel behaviors that characterized them in the past. This change alone is significant to us. (World Service Office, 1984, p. 71)

These quotations suggest a recognition of nonabstinence outcomes as important (if not ideal).

AA's work, in a nutshell, has been to describe the experiences of persons who have recovered in AA, and to invite, at no charge, and under no coercion, others troubled by alcohol to join them. It is certainly true that many advocates of AA are more strident and coercive than this. However, close examination of the differences between official 12-step organization literature and its alleged advocates' positions (e.g., Brown, 1993) should cause researchers to be cautious in viewing these positions as monolithic.

Mindfulness as the Fix

Addiction as a rigid concept seems intrinsically problematic. Its outcome is a fixedness of view that may obscure important alternatives. Treatment centers adopting (and interpreting) AA's perspective too often ignore research findings. Researchers, with a few exceptions, find themselves blind to what does work in AA, and for whom. Any certitude within the discipline of substance abuse treatment or research seems premature. Even among promising interventions, none have been demonstrated to be promising for all addicted persons. It seems especially imperative that we within clinical science ought not narrow the search too soon, lest we miss important aspects of existing views. Whatever differences there are among treatment personnel, members of self-help groups, and researchers, persons of good intent labor toward a common goal: minimizing the suffering imposed by addictive processes. The last thing we need is a fix (in the making rigid sense). Perhaps we ought to take Mao's admonition and "let a hundred flowers blossom and a hundred schools of thought contend." A mindfulness perspective suggests that it is within such an environment that we are likely to find innovations and solutions.

References

Alcoholics Anonymous World Services (1976). *Alcoholics Anonymous* (3rd ed.). New York: Author.

Brown, L. (Ed.) (1993). *The new shorter Oxford English dictionary*. Oxford: Clarendon Press.

Brown, S. D. (1993). Therapeutic processes in Alcoholics Anonymous. In B. S. McCrady & W. R. Miller (Eds.), *Research on Alcoholics Anonymous: Opportunities and alternatives* (pp. 137-152). New Brunswick, NJ: Rutgers Center for Alcohol Studies.

World Service Office (1984). *Narcotics Anonymous* (2nd ed.). Van Nuys, CA: Author.

Footnote

Preparation of this discussion was supported in part by a grant from the National Institute on Drug Abuse, #DA08634.

Chapter 10

Acceptance in the Treatment of Alcoholism: A Comparison of Alcoholics Anonymous and Social Learning Theory

Edelgard Wulfert
The University at Albany, State University of New York

Somewhere between 15 and 20 million people, or roughly 6 to 8 percent of the United States population, suffer from a serious alcohol problem. Some people daily imbibe large amounts of alcohol; others drink heavily every weekend; and still others alternate periods of sobriety and heavy binges. Alcohol is involved in almost half of all criminal offenses (NIAAA, 1987) and fatal traffic accidents (National Highway Traffic Safety Administration, 1988), and costs the tax payer $137 billion per year in terms of health care and employment-related consequences (NIAAA, 1990).

As alarming as these data are, the actual problem is still worse because alcoholic drinking does not occur in isolation. It permeates many aspects of the drinker's existence and leads to impairments in physical and emotional well-being, relations with family and friends, occupational functioning, finances, and leisure activities (Fingarette, 1988). A change in drinking habits therefore requires concomitant changes in many other routines, attitudes, and behaviors. This may be one of the reasons for the high recidivism rate because changes in lifestyle are not easy to effect. Only about 10 percent of all alcohol-dependent persons seek and receive treatment per year (NIAAA, 1987). Of those who initiate treatment, over half drop out prematurely; and of those who remain in treatment, less than one-third are still abstinent one year later (Miller & Hester, 1986; Nathan & Skinstad, 1987). Judged by these numbers, our ability to treat individuals with alcohol problems is very modest indeed.

If we are to improve the effectiveness of alcoholism treatment, it is important to understand the diverse manifestations of alcohol dependence and the processes underlying change. Reviews of the treatment literature (e.g., Miller & Hester, 1986; Institute of Medicine, 1989) have concluded that no single treatment approach is effective with all alcohol-dependent individuals and that different methods lead to successful outcomes with different clients. Numerous treatment components and process factors associated with an extended reduction or elimination of alcohol consumption have been identified, but as in the treatment of other human problems, outcomes have been varied and no one factor has proved to be superior in all cases (Institute of Medicine, 1990).

One process variable that to date has received little attention in the substance abuse treatment literature is acceptance. Overlapping with the humanistic concept of "openness to experience," acceptance means to cease struggling with and come to terms with the inevitable events in one's life. In alcohol-dependent persons, the need for acceptance arises from two sources. First, these individuals experience a conflict surrounding the immediate versus the delayed consequences of their drinking. Imbibing alcohol momentarily satisfies cravings and enhances their mood, but these effects are attained at a high cost considering the devastating long-term consequences of chronic alcohol abuse. Second, alcoholics struggle with a conflict involving emotions they consider undesirable and therefore seek to avoid. Emotional avoidance is effective in the short run but over time leads to a restricted range of experiences and impaired interpersonal relations. To resolve either of these two conflicts through acceptance, alcoholics must be willing to experience and tolerate feelings they have normally numbed with alcohol, whether these feelings be urges and cravings for alcohol, or emotions such as anxiety, depression, anger and resentment. Without a fundamental change in their willingness to embrace such feelings, recovery from alcoholism is difficult at best. Because many of those who work in the clinical trenches with substance abusers have an intuitive understanding of the importance of acceptance (e.g., Cusack, 1992), implicitly or explicitly they work towards enhancing their clients' level of acceptance over the course of treatment. Except for AA and similar twelve-step programs, however, the importance of acceptance has generally not been explicitly acknowledged or discussed in the substance abuse literature.

This chapter will present two approaches to alcoholism that in many ways seem diametrically opposed. One of these approaches is Alcoholics Anonymous (AA), and the other one is a view based on social learning theory (SLT). I will compare and contrast how these approaches conceptualize the etiology and treatment of alcohol-related problems, and I will examine the role that acceptance plays within each conceptual framework. Finally, I will attempt to show that AA and SLT, despite many surface differences, are not incompatible when viewed from a functional perspective. These two approaches seem to emphasize different aspects of acceptance that in the final analysis may both be important in the recovery process. Let us begin this endeavor with a review of the main concepts of AA and the steps it considers necessary for recovery.

AA and the Disease Concept of Alcoholism

In 1935, two reformed alcoholics, a surgeon by the name of Bob and a stockbroker named Bill, founded a self-help movement that came to be known as Alcoholics Anonymous. The AA founders' view of alcoholism and its treatment consisted of a body of ideas imported from religion and medicine and was later formalized in a number of publications (e.g., AA World Services, 1978; Alcoholics Anonymous,

1976). With this, the classic American disease model was born, and to this day it constitutes the dogma espoused by AA.

A basic tenet of the AA view is the belief that alcoholics have a biological vulnerability to alcohol that makes them different from normal individuals. In predisposed persons, even a small amount of alcohol is thought to trigger an allergy-like reaction with uncontrollable urges to drink. Thus, central to this model is the idea that the disease takes away people's ability to control their drinking. This is captured in the AA slogan "One drink, one drunk." As the vulnerability to alcohol is assumed to be genetically based and incurable, the only way predisposed individuals can prevent becoming addicted is through permanent abstinence. If they start using alcohol, their drinking will progress through a series of stages until they are completely powerless over alcohol and "hit rock bottom." Joining the AA fellowship, adopting its principles as a way of life, and asking a Higher Power for spiritual guidance in their recovery allows them to conquer their obsession with alcohol and to return to a normal life.

It is important to understand that AA views alcoholism primarily as a "spiritual disease." Therefore it places emphasis not on the alcoholic's physiological dependency or poor marital and social functioning but on his or her internal loss of faith, hope, and spirituality. Healing can only be achieved through a spiritual solution (McCrady & Irvine, 1989).

Let us now briefly review the twelve steps comprising the AA program of recovery (Alcoholics Anonymous, 1976). These steps, summarized in Table 1, consist of a group of spiritual principles which AA proposes as guidelines for the recovery process. The alcoholic's admission of complete defeat over alcohol (Step 1) is considered the foundation for all other steps because without it recovery cannot even begin. Next, the alcoholic must be willing to acknowledge the existence of a Higher Power (Step 2), which is synonymous with accepting that he or she is not the center of the universe. AA views alcoholics as self-centered, dishonest, and self-absorbed individuals. "The Big Book" puts it as follows: "Like an actor who wants to run the whole show, alcoholics try to arrange the stage of their lives. They manipulate the scenery, the light, and the other players, and when the show does not come off well they get indignant, self-pitying and blame others. Then they are surprised and angry at retaliation, but fail to see that they themselves caused most of their problems through their extreme self-centeredness" (Alcoholics Anonymous, 1976, p.60 ff.).

To overcome these defects, the alcoholic must relinquish control and turn his or her life over to a Higher Power (Step 3). For most individuals, this is a difficult task. In fact, AA assumes that few people sincerely give up control unless their obsession with alcohol has led them to hit rock bottom. Only at that time may they come to accept the futility of trying to control their drinking and be motivated to adopt a new course of action. This course begins with a process of intense introspection and self-evaluation and culminates in the launching of a lifelong quest for spiritual growth. In the course of this process, the underlying "causes and conditions" of the

---

Table 1: The Twelve Steps of Alcoholics Anonymous

---

1. We admitted we were powerless over alcohol; that our lives had become unmanageable.

2. Came to believe that a power greater than ourselves could restore us to sanity.

3. Made a decision to turn our will and our lives over to the care of God as we understood Him.

4. Made a searching and fearless moral inventory of ourselves.

5. Admitted to God, to ourselves, and to another human being, the exact nature of our wrongs.

6. Were entirely ready to have God remove all these defects of character.

7. Humbly asked Him to remove our shortcomings.

8. Made a list of all the persons we had harmed and became willing to make amends to them all.

9. Made direct amends to such people wherever possible, except when to do so would injure them or others.

10. Continued to take personal inventory and when we were wrong, promptly admitted it.

11. Sought through prayer and meditation to improve our conscious contact with God as we understood Him, praying only for knowledge of His will for us and the power to carry that out.

12. Having had a spiritual awakening as the result of these steps, we tried to carry this message to alcoholics and to practice these principles in all our affairs.

---

alcoholic's compulsion to drink must be eliminated through a course of "personal housecleaning." AA members must identify people, institutions and principles they feel have wronged them (AA World Services, 1978) and, instead of blaming those for their drinking, they are encouraged to focus on their own shortcomings and to take responsibility for their behavior (Step 4). Further, they must honestly discuss their personal defects and rationalizations with another person (Step 5). This can be a humbling experience, but it also creates a sense of intimacy and connectedness with that person and teaches the alcoholic the importance of forgiving and being forgiven. Finally, AA members must open themselves up to the intervention of a

Higher Power to overcome their personal defects (Step 6) and to receive guidance in all aspects of their lives (Step 7).

In Steps 8 and 9, AA members examine and amend their interpersonal relations. As alcohol-dependent individuals often wreak havoc in other people's lives, they must be willing to face up to past wrong-doings (Step 8) and, if possible, repair the damage done to others (Step 9). Admitting wrong-doings and offering amends is not synonymous with "unloading" and getting rid of guilt over past actions at the expense of another person. Instead, the intention is to make honest restitutions and to live in peace with oneself and others.

Steps 10 and 11 are considered safeguards to prevent AA members from slipping back into destructive thoughts and habits. Continued stock-taking, problem-solving (Step 10), and reliance on a Higher Power (Step 11) ensure continued spiritual growth and self-awareness. Developing self-control and a deeper self-understanding are not goals that can be achieved all at once. They require a life-long effort because growth is process, not outcome.

As a last step, AA members are encouraged to live by the twelve principles and to assist other alcoholics in need. Step 12 rests on the assumption that "you can't keep it unless you give it away" (AA World Services, 1978, p.107). Being actively involved as a role model and sponsor in the healing of newcomers to AA has the added advantage that the recovering alcoholic is constantly reminded of his or her own past and progress. This may be the best way to become inoculated against relapse because "(h)elping others is the foundation stone of ... recovery" (Alcoholics Anonymous, 1976, p.97).

The Role of Acceptance in AA

The need for acceptance arises within a context of conflict or ambivalence when competing goals "pull the person in different directions." With alcoholism, part of the ambivalence comes from the immediate mood-enhancing and the delayed self-defeating consequences of chronic alcohol abuse. Another part stems from the alcoholic's unwillingness, and sometimes inability, to deal with life's problems and to accept frustration, anger, and sadness as part of the human condition instead of numbing these feelings with alcohol. Achieving sobriety requires a fundamental change in the drinker's attitude toward conflict and unpleasant emotions. Acceptance therefore plays a pivotal role in the recovery process.

According to AA teachings, alcoholics cannot be blamed for their genetic endowment, but they are fully responsible for their behavior. If they truly want to overcome their problem, the *only* solution to their plight is to admit and accept their powerlessness over alcohol. Embracing their disease frees them from further struggles with alcohol because they *know* they are fighting a losing battle. In a sense, their condition is not unlike that of individuals who suffer from an allergy. The most sensible action for a person allergic to strawberries is not to eat them. Analogously, the most sensible action of a person suffering from the "disease of alcoholism," as viewed by AA, is not to drink. Yet while people usually refrain from eating food that triggers an allergic reaction, many alcoholics reject the disease concept and struggle for years to control their drinking. When they first come to AA, they may be willing to acknowledge a drinking problem and have an honest desire to receive help; but true acceptance usually comes much later. According to Cusack (1992), acceptance is the process of learning to live with chemical dependency. Most people achieve sobriety only after repeated episodes of relapse because they deceive themselves into thinking that they are not truly powerless over alcohol: "I am not really an alcoholic; I can have a couple of drinks" (p.125). Paradoxically, once they accept their powerlessness, they cease to struggle and simply decide not to drink anymore. This occurs because identifying with the belief that one suffers from an incurable disease leads to a shift in context that permanently changes the alcoholic's perspective and attitude toward alcohol.

AA also promotes acceptance in the form of greater openness to experience. In the process of "personal housecleaning," AA members must own up to having blamed their drinking on external factors when they were actually using alcohol to control undesirable emotions arising from internal and external conflict situations. All people occasionally have to face adverse circumstances that are beyond their control, but the alcoholic often uses them as excuses for his or her drinking. If, for example, an alcoholic has lost his wife because of his drinking, he may feel he cannot recover without her. Yet recovery does not depend on other people. Many alcoholics achieve sobriety although they have lost everything dear to them; and others relapse despite the support of their families (Alcoholics Anonymous, 1976). Thus, recovery largely depends on the alcoholic's willingness to experience and accept emotions he or she has grown accustomed to numbing with alcohol.

In summary, from the vantage point of AA, acceptance means to admit being powerless over alcohol. Acceptance is achieved by practicing the twelve steps that are the tools for attaining a healthy level of spiritual, emotional, and physical adjustment. Progressing through these steps helps recovering alcoholics to stop blaming external circumstances for their drinking and to accept responsibility for their behavior. Moreover, the AA fellowship serves an important function in the recovery process. It provides a social context that reinforces an alcohol-free lifestyle and allows the recovering alcoholic to develop a sense of self-esteem and self-acceptance because other AA members validate and accept him or her as a person.

Alcoholism as a Lifestyle: A Social Learning View

The just-described classic disease model of alcoholism is widely accepted among the public and among professionals engaged in the treatment of substance abuse. In contrast, the scientific community advocates a biopsychosocial model by viewing alcoholism as the product of physiological, behavioral, and socio-cultural factors (e.g., Institute of Medicine, 1990; Zucker & Gomberg, 1986). The etiology and course of a drinking problem is thought to be strongly influenced by social learning factors (e.g., Peele, 1985) and may be best understood from a developmental perspective. Zucker and Gomberg (1986), for example, summarized several longitudinal studies. They found that alcoholics tended to come from less supportive childhood environments than their normal peers. Although they did not differ in IQ level from their normal peers, they showed a pattern of early social maladjustment, including more conduct problems in school and more truancy. Their maladjustment persisted into adulthood where they tended to engage in antisocial activities, spent more time unemployed, and showed poorer mental health than their non-alcoholic peers. Zucker and Gomberg hypothesized that many of these children may suffer from a genetically based vulnerability which manifests itself in some type of early neural dysfunction and is associated with hyperactivity. If children so predisposed are reared in an inconsistent environment, conduct and academic problems will ensue and eventually provide the basis for other socially deviant behaviors including substance abuse.

There is consensus in the scientific community that the origins of alcoholism are complex and possibly as varied as the individuals who develop substance abuse. Ample evidence shows that some individuals are genetically at higher risk for alcoholism (Cloninger, Bohman, & Sigvardsson, 1981; Goodwin, 1985). But it is important to note that most children of alcoholics drink moderately and without problems (Cotton, 1979), and that the majority of alcoholics do not have an alcoholic parent (Merikangas, 1990). Hence, a genetic predisposition may be neither necessary nor sufficient for alcoholism to develop. To comprehend the complexities of alcoholic behavior, a better understanding is required not only of genetic risk factors and their modus operandi, but also of people's learning histories, the typical behavioral and emotional characteristics associated with alcohol abuse, and the social-environmental context in which drinking occurs.

An interesting perspective on alcoholism, compatible with social learning theory (SLT), has been proposed by Fingarette (1988). He sees alcoholics as people for whom drinking has developed into a "central activity." A central activity occupies a significant portion of a person's life and largely defines his or her identity, values and choices. Most people reserve this place for their spouse and children, their job, or perhaps a hobby; but for some individuals life begins to revolve around alcohol. This tendency develops gradually as the outcome of numerous choices and decisions. Individual differences in ability and interests may play a role in initial choices, but they may also be shaped by reinforcement from family and friends and by chance factors. Over time, decisions narrow the range of future choices until certain activities gradually emerge as dominant.

The following example illustrates how the development of alcoholism can be understood within an SLT framework. Imagine a boy with an alcoholic father growing up in an unstable family environment. The boy lacks discipline, is hyperactive and aggressive. As his behavior makes him unpopular with many of his well-adjusted peers, he gravitates toward children who are similar to him and reinforce his socially deviant behaviors. In adolescence he begins to experiment with alcohol and drugs and spends increasing amounts of time with friends who drink heavily or abuse other substances. His alcohol abuse begins to shape his daily routines: He has hangovers, misses class, his grades suffer, and he faces numerous conflicts with his teachers, parents, and his girlfriend. Due to the many failure experiences and conflict areas in his life, his drinking gradually emerges as the major source of satisfaction for him. Over time, his alcohol abuse may develop into a full-blown alcohol dependence.

Viewing alcohol dependence as a gradually shaped lifestyle, albeit self-destructive, obviates the search for a defect in some unidentified self-control mechanism. The physiological effects of alcohol and the circumstances associated with drinking serve as powerful reinforcers that shape the quantity and frequency of alcohol consumption and by themselves suffice to explain how alcohol dependence may develop. The conditions leading to alcoholism may therefore *qualitatively* not differ from the processes that shape other self-destructive behaviors, such as overeating, smoking, impulsive sexual behaviors, and compulsive gambling (Fingarette, 1988).

SLT also provides a parsimonious explanation of several other behaviors typically associated with alcoholism that are often ascribed to a not yet identified disease process. Denial, for example, can be viewed as a natural defensive reaction of a person who realizes that his or her behavior deviates from accepted social norms. Alcoholics who hide their drinking act no differently from other people who feel guilty or are afraid of censure. When criticized, most people justify and rationalize their behavior, and alcoholics are no exception (Fingarette, 1988). In a similar vain, drunk individuals often become violent, sexually suggestive, or behave in other inappropriate ways. Most people believe that such behaviors are directly attributable to the pharmacological effects of alcohol. However, research (e.g., Marlatt & Rohsenow, 1980) has shown that the effects of alcohol cannot be understood without taking into account the concurrent reinforcement contingencies that operate in the person's environment. In other words, reprehensible behavior is blamed on alcohol when in fact it is more likely that the drinker has learned to use intoxication as a convenient excuse for acting out and evading responsibility for his or her actions (cf. Critchlow, 1986).

In summary, SLT views alcoholic drinking as an acquired habit pattern that develops over time through multiple influences, including biological, psychological, and socio-cultural factors. Alcoholism is not a problem with self-control in an isolated area but the manifestation of a generalized self-defeating lifestyle that has been shaped by the consequences of many decisions and choices the alcoholic has made along the way.

The Role of Acceptance in Lifestyle Changes

Once drinking has become a way of life, it permeates many aspects of the alcoholic's existence and is difficult to reverse. Therefore, like AA, SLT also views recovery from alcoholism not simply as a change in drinking habits but as a reorganization of the alcoholic's entire lifestyle. Acceptance enters into several aspects of this process.

At the most basic level, the alcoholic must learn to tolerate cravings. From an SLT perspective, the drinker has learned associations between the effects of alcohol and a seemingly endless array of concomitant stimuli, including the sight and smell of alcohol, environments and interpersonal situations associated with drinking, and internal states that precede or accompany drinking. These cues are ubiquitous and can elicit unpredictable cravings in a wide variety of contexts that the alcoholic must be willing to experience and tolerate.

Acceptance also means willingness to experience emotions the alcoholic has habitually avoided. Research has shown that alcoholics tend not to cope well with stressful events. In fact, over two thirds of relapses occur in situations involving negative emotional states, interpersonal conflict, and social pressure to drink (Annis and Davis, 1984; Marlatt and Gordon, 1980). These findings suggest that situations inducing negative emotions serve as powerful motivators for drinking. Technically speaking, using alcohol to numb aversive inner states is maintained by negative reinforcement, and negatively reinforced behavior is notoriously difficult to change. Alcoholics who are serious about recovery must be willing to experience feelings such as tension, anger, rage, anxiety, guilt, shame, and depression. If they confront these feelings, they may eventually be motivated to generate more adaptive solutions; rather than numbing their feelings with alcohol, they might begin to change the circumstances that elicit them.

A different aspect of acceptance, related to the willingness to experience negative emotions, is the alcoholic's readiness to assume responsibility for his or her actions. For many substance abusers, intoxication has come to serve as a cue for acting out without having to face negative consequences because our culture tends to excuse drunken individuals as not fully responsible for their actions. Despite its popular appeal, this assumption seems largely a myth since research has shown that behavior is guided more by what a person believes about the effects of alcohol than by the physiological effects of alcohol per se (e.g., Critchlow, 1986; Marlatt & Rohsenow, 1980). SLT therefore emphasizes the importance of social skills and assertiveness training so that alcoholics learn to express their impulses in socially acceptable ways (e.g., Monti, Abrams, Kadden, & Cooney, 1989). The person who behaves assertively when sober is less likely to accumulate anger and frustration. This, in turn, eliminates the motivation for using alcohol as a face-saving device and acting out built-up hostilities when intoxicated.

Last but not least, acceptance means being open to new experiences and willing to risk failure. The recovering alcoholic needs to develop new friendships and social activities that do not involve the use of alcohol. As any exposure to new people and situations brings with it anxiety and the possibility of frustration and rejection, the recovering person must be willing to tolerate this risk and make the required changes in spite of it.

In summary, when viewed within an SLT framework, recovery hinges upon a change in lifestyle. The recovering person must be willing to tolerate urges and cravings for alcohol, get in touch with aversive emotions instead of blocking them out with alcohol, and try out new ways of interacting with the world. Without a fundamental willingness to accept whatever experiences are associated with change, lasting recovery is improbable. As treatment within an SLT framework is active and directive, alcoholics who seek help are not expected simply to "endure" these stressful events. Rather than encouraging them to turn to a Higher Power, SLT provides them with a number of tools to confront stressors and to build a repertoire of new skills and activities. Helping recovering persons through cognitive restructuring, direct training, and exposure to models to develop effective coping skills is thought to be the best protection against relapse.

Evaluation

At the level of theory, SLT and the classic disease model proposed by AA disagree in substantive ways about the nature and etiology of alcoholism. At the clinical level, however, SLT and AA share many goals, although they may be attained in different ways. Therefore, the two approaches are not necessarily incompatible as long as treatment is oriented toward abstinence (McCrady & Irvine, 1989).

AA and SLT both view alcoholic drinking as part of a generalized cluster of self-defeating attitudes and behaviors, embedded in a social context that supports them. Both stress the need for changes not only in drinking but in various life areas. Most importantly, these changes need to occur in the emotional arena where the recovering person must learn to accept negative feelings as a normal part of the human experience. Thus, acceptance plays a central role within both frameworks, but it is important not to gloss over differences in meaning.

From the vantage point of SLT, acceptance means tolerance. Recovering individuals must be temporarily willing to tolerate aversive feelings while practicing new coping responses. Developing more adaptive coping skills allows them to confront stress more effectively and to acquire a sense of accomplishment. SLT does not consider alcoholics to be powerless over their drinking but views them as individuals who are capable of making rational decisions and of exercising personal control (e.g., Trimpey, 1992a). Some clinicians therefore view moderation as a viable goal for the less severely impaired problem drinker. However, most clinicians advocate total abstinence for more seriously impaired alcohol-dependent individuals (Nathan & McCrady, 1986; H. A. Skinner, 1985).

Within an AA framework, acceptance means that alcohol-dependent individuals admit their powerlessness over alcohol and give up the struggle to control their drinking. Acceptance is therefore synonymous with capitulation and admission of total defeat. Alcoholics drink to cope with stress and to medicate emotional pain. If they give up drinking they need to fill the remaining void with something significant enough to replace the purpose previously served by alcohol. The solution is to fill this void with the belief in a benevolent and caring entity that provides strength and comfort in times when the alcoholic feels troubled, abandoned, and powerless. By believing in a Higher Power, the alcoholic need no longer dull these painful feelings but can experience them and turn to a supreme being for comfort (Bisogna, 1992).

Zealous claims that AA is "by far the best (alcoholism treatment) program we know of" (Bisogna, 1992, p.138) and AA's emphasis on a spiritual dimension in recovery have generated a great deal of impassioned debate (e.g., Chappel, 1990; Ellis & Schoenfeld, 1990; McCrady, 1990; Miller, 1992; Rotgers, 1992; Talbott, 1990; Trimpey, 1992b). AA partisans (e.g., Bisogna, 1992) have charged therapists with being "enablers" and even "committing malpractice" if they view interventions other than AA "as anything more than a helpful adjunct" to the treatment of addiction (p.139). In contrast, AA adversaries (e.g., Ellis and Schoenfeld, 1992; Ellis & Velten, 1992) have accused AA partisans of promoting religious beliefs and inappropriately mixing religious philosophy with the treatment of addiction. They object that mandating people into twelve-step programs and using AA principles in publicly funded treatment facilities violates the principle of separating church and state. In their opinion, large numbers of people not only cannot relate to but are repelled by spiritualism (sic), and even religious people are offended at the idea that God is needed to undo what they have done to themselves (Velten, 1992).

Like many feuds about matters of belief, AA's emphasis on spirituality evokes strong emotions on both sides of the fence. As nonbelievers usually equate spirituality with religion, they reject AA for this reason. Others (among them many scientifically minded psychologists) deny a matter/spirit distinction on philosophical grounds and reject AA because of the dualism implied by its teachings.

It is possible, however, to look at spirituality from a dispassionate perspective that does not hinge upon a literal acceptance of the term and therefore permits an objective analysis of its value in the treatment of substance abuse. This perspective is behaviorism. For the behaviorist, words are not "literally true" but are part of the behaviors of speaking and listening. Understanding a word means determining under what conditions it is emitted and what consequences result from its use. According to Hayes (1984), the notion of spirituality may well be a linguistic by-product of the process by which the verbal community establishes self-awareness in its members. Through language, people learn to distinguish between themselves as persons and their behavior: the "I" (psychoanalysts have called it the "observing self", e.g., Deikman, 1982) serves as the context (the unchanging perspective) from which people observe the content (the ever-changing experiences) of their lives. Experientially, the "observing self" is not a thing; it is limit- and timeless because no one can know the beginning or end of their own experience, nor can they *consciously* be anywhere without their "observing self" (Hayes, 1984). The matter/spirit distinction may well have originated as a "metaphorical extension" (cf. Skinner, 1957, p.95) from this experiential content/context distinction.

Sometimes problems arise when people take their thoughts to be literally true. Thoughts such as, "I am worthless" are then taken as an accurate indication of one's value as a human being and come to control behavior. Helping people to identify with their "observing self" weakens the control exerted by thoughts and allows people to behave more effectively (Hayes, 1984). Several cognitive (e.g., Beck, 1976) and behavioral (e.g., Hayes & Melancon, 1989) therapies recognize this and help clients to disengage or distance themselves from their automatic thoughts and put them in perspective. An analogous disidentification with thoughts occurs when a person believes in a benevolent Higher Power. Self-defeating or self-deprecating thoughts lose their grip on people when they believe that God accepts them in spite of their shortcomings and defects. Thus, spirituality and identification with the "observing self" serve similar functions: both can disrupt the control by automatic thoughts and allow the person to behave more effectively.

For alcoholics, then, a belief in spirituality may have significant benefits because it helps them to put their obsessive preoccupations with alcohol in perspective: The belief in a Higher Power releases them from their compulsion to act on their cravings and comforts them when they feel dejected and worthless. The emphasis on spiritual healing is therefore potentially of great value in the treatment of alcoholism, at least for those who are disposed to accept the belief in a Higher Power.

However, many alcoholics are not good candidates for AA's spiritual approach because they cannot relate to ideas of spirituality or a supreme being (Trimpey, 1992a). These individuals never join AA or, if mandated into AA, show no better outcomes than individuals who receive other types of treatment (e.g., Brandsma, Maultsby, & Welsh, 1980) or no treatment at all (e.g., Ditman, Crawford, Forgy, Moskowitz, & MacAndrew, 1967). The approach advocated by AA and other twelve-step programs is undoubtedly effective with many alcohol-dependent persons (e.g., Institute of Medicine, 1989), and probably most so for those who are attracted by this approach and *voluntarily* seek affiliation with AA (Miller, 1992). But AA's superiority over other treatment approaches, which AA members and twelve-step treatment professionals so frequently profess, has yet to be demonstrated (McCrady & Irvine, 1989). Interestingly, the original founders of AA were much less dogmatic than many of their current followers because they never claimed "exclusive rights" to recovery. In their writings, they advise that alcoholics follow their own conscience if they believe they can achieve sobriety without AA or if they prefer some other spiritual approach: "We have no monopoly ...; we merely have an approach that worked with us" (Alcoholics Anonymous, 1976, p.95).

Unfortunately, the greatest fallacy is that many professionals, regardless of their theoretical affiliation, insist they have the "one true answer" to a very complex problem. Too many people fall in the trap of viewing alcoholism as a unidimensional problem for which there is one universal treatment to which all alcoholics respond. But alcoholism manifests itself in multiple forms, and evidence shows that different people benefit from different approaches (McCrady & Irvine, 1989). This is illustrated in Miller and Hester's (1986) review of a large body of outcome literature which led them to conclude that (1) there is no single superior approach to treatment that works with all alcoholics; (2) different types of individuals respond best to different treatment approaches; and (3) matching treatment to individual clients' needs leads to better outcomes.

How do the present findings tie into acceptance? The answer to this question is complicated by the fact that there is no universally agreed upon definition of acceptance. For AA, acceptance seems to be synonymous with acknowledging powerlessness and defeat over alcohol. From an SLT perspective, it means being willing to face difficult situations and to tolerate whatever feelings come up. These views are not mutually exclusive but simply address two different aspects of alcoholism. AA focuses mainly on the topography of the problem, i.e., alcoholic drinking itself; whereas SLT focuses on the function of drinking, i.e., emotional avoidance. On the surface, AA seems to endorse a more passive form of acceptance by advocating complete reliance on a Higher Power. But spiritual healing is only the beginning of the long road to recovery, which requires many active steps and changes along the way besides relying on a Higher Power. SLT seems to promote a more active form of acceptance. It emphasizes the importance of openness to experiences and emotions the alcoholic has avoided, but it also stresses the active use of coping skills to master difficult situations. In the final outcome, AA and SLT both seem to advocate a balanced approach of acceptance and change.

The present chapter has attempted to show that different treatment approaches to alcoholism, while using different strategies and techniques, may be effective because of a common underlying mechanism; that is, they increase the alcoholic's level of acceptance and his or her motivation for change. This idea is certainly not foreign to those familiar with the addictions, as it has long been aptly expressed in the "Serenity Prayer:"

> God grant me the serenity
> To accept what I cannot change,
> The courage to change what I can,
> And wisdom to know the difference.

References

AA World Services (1978). *Twelve steps and twelve traditions.* New York: Author.

Alcoholics Anonymous (1976). Alcoholics Anonymous: *The story of how many thousands of men and women have recovered from alcoholism* (3rd ed.). New York: Author.

Annis, H.M., & Davis, C. (1984, November). Relapse prevention treatment for alcoholics: Initial findings. Paper presented at the Third International Conference on the Treatment of Addictive Behaviours, North Berwick, Scotland.

Beck, A.T. (1976). *Cognitive therapy and the emotional disorders.* New York: Meridian.

Bisogna, G. (1992). Recovering from chemical dependency: Spirituality, abstinence, & alternatives. *The Behavior Therapist, 15* (6), 138-139.

Brandsma, J. M., Maultsby, M. C., & Welsh, R. J. (1980). *Outpatient treatment of alcoholism: A review and comparative study.* Baltimore, MD: University Park Press.

Chappel, J. N. (1990). Spirituality is not necessarily religion: A commentary on "Divine intervention and the treatment of chemical dependency." *Journal of Substance Abuse, 2,* 481-483.

Cloninger, C. R., Bohman, M., & Sigvardsson, S. (1981). Inheritance of alcohol abuse: Cross-fostering analysis of adopted men. *Archives of General Psychiatry, 38*, 861-858.

Cotton, N. (1979). The familial incidence of alcoholism. A review. *Journal of Studies on Alcohol, 49*, 89-116.

Critchlow, B. (1986). The powers of John Barleycorn: Beliefs about the effects of alcohol on social behavior. *American Psychologist, 41*, 751-764.

Cusack, J.S. (1992). *Let's get back to basics: Chemical dependency and its treatment.* New York: Carlton Press.

Deikman, A. J. (1982). *The observing self: Mysticism and psychotherapy.* Boston: Beacon Press.

Ditman, K. S., Crawford, G. C., Forgy, E. W., Moskowitz, H., & MacAndrew, C. (1967). A controlled experiment on the use of court probation for drunk arrests. *American Journal of Psychiatry, 124*, 160-163.

Ellis, A., & Schoenfeld, E. (1992). Divine intervention and the treatment of chemical dependency. *Journal of Substance Abuse, 2*, 459-468.

Ellis, A., & Velten, E. (1992). *When AA doesn't work for you: Rational steps to quitting alcohol.* New York: Barricade.

Fingarette, H. (1988). *Heavy drinking: The myth of alcoholism as a disease.* Berkeley: University of California Press.

Goodwin, D. W. (1985). Genetic determinants of alcoholism. In J. H. Mendelson and N. K. Mello (Eds.), *The diagnosis and treatment of alcoholism* (pp.65-87). New York: McGraw-Hill.

Hayes, S. C. (1984). Making sense of spirituality. *Behaviorism, 12*, 99-110.

Hayes, S. C., & Melancon, S. M. (1989). Comprehensive distancing, paradox, and the treatment of emotional avoidance. In M. Ascher (Ed.), *Paradoxical procedures in psychotherapy* (pp. 184-218). New York: Guilford.

Institute of Medicine (1989). *Prevention and treatment of alcohol problems: Research opportunities.* Washington, D.C.: National Academy Press.

Institute of Medicine (1990a). *Research on children and adolescents with mental, behavioral, and developmental disorders.* Rockville, MD: National Institute of Mental Health.

Institute of Medicine (1990b). *Broadening the base of treatment for alcohol problems.* Washington, DC: National Academy Press.

Marlatt, G. A., & Gordon, J. R. (1985). *Relapse prevention.* New York: Guilford Press.

Marlatt, G. A., & Rohsenow, D. J. (1980). Cognitive processes in alcohol use: Expectancy and the balanced placebo design. In N. K. Mello (Ed.), *Advances in substance abuse* (Vol.1, pp.159-199). Greenwich, CT: JAI Press.

McCrady, B. S. (1990). The divine, the saturnine and the internecine: Comments on Ellis and Schoenfeld. *Journal of Substance Abuse, 2*, 477- 480.

McCrady, B. S., & Irvine, S. (1989). Self-help groups. In R. K. Hester & W. R. Miller (Eds)., *Handbook of alcoholism treatment approaches. Effective alternatives* (pp. 153-169). New York: Pergamon Press.

Merikangas, K. R. (1990). Comorbidity for anxiety and depression: Review of family and genetic studies. In J. D. Maser and C. R. Cloninger (Eds.), *Comorbidity of mood and anxiety disorders*. Washington, DC: American Psychiatric Press.

Miller, W. R. (1992). Spirituality, abstinence, and alternatives in addictions treatment: Taking exception to "no exceptions." *The Behavior Therapist, 15*, 214-215.

Miller, W. R., & Hester, R. K. (1986). The effectiveness of alcoholism treatment: What research reveals. In W. R. Miller & N. Heather (Eds.), *Treating addictive behaviors: Processes of change* (pp.121-174). New York: Plenum Press.

Monti, P. M., Abrams, D. B., Kadden, R. M., & Cooney, N. L. (1989). *Treating alcohol dependence*. New York: Guilford Press.

Nathan, P. E., & Skinstad, A.-H. (1987). Outcomes of treatment for alcohol problems: Current methods, problems, and results. *Journal of Consulting and Clinical Psychology, 55*, 332-340.

Nathan, P. E., & McCrady, B. S. (1986). Bases for the use of abstinence as a goal in the treatment of alcohol abusers. *Drugs and Society, 1* (2/3), 109-131.

National Highway Traffic Safety Administration, National Center for Statistics and Analysis (1988). *Drunk driving facts*. Washington, DC: NHTSA.

NIAAA (National Institute on Alcohol Abuse and Alcoholism) (1987). *Sixth special report to the U.S. Congress on alcohol and health*. Washington, D.C.

NIAAA (National Institute on Alcohol Abuse and Alcoholism) (1990). *Seventh special report to the U.S. Congress on alcohol and health from the secretary of health and human services*. U.S. Department of Health and Human Services.

Peele, S. (1985). *The meaning of addiction*. Lexington, MA: Lexington Books.

Rotgers, F. (1992). Is Bisogna's view rigid? *The Behavior Therapist, 15*, 215.

Skinner, B.F. (1957). *Verbal behavior*. Englewood Cliffs, N.J.: Prentice-Hall.

Skinner, H.A. (1985). Early detection and basic management of alcohol and drug problems. *Australian Alcohol/Drug Review, 4*, 243-249.

Talbott, G.D. (1990). Commentary on "Divine Intervention and the Treatment of chemical dependency." *Journal of Substance Abuse, 2*, 469-471.

Trimpey, J. (1992a). *The small book: A revolutionary alternative for overcoming alcohol and drug dependence*. New York: Delacorte.

Trimpey, J. (1992b). Rational Recovery: A wall between religion and recovery? *The Behavior Therapist, 15*, 178-179.

Velten, E. (1992). More on 12-step programs. *The Behavior Therapist, 15*, 247-248.

Zucker, R. A., & Gomberg, E. S. L. (1986). Etiology of alcoholism reconsidered: The case for a biopsychosocial process. *American Psychologist, 41*, 783-793.

Discussion of Wulfert

Setting a Course for Behavior Change: The Verbal Context of Acceptance

Elizabeth V. Gifford
University of Nevada

Wulfert has provided a thoughtful description of acceptance in Alcoholics Anonymous and Social Learning Theory. Offering a dialogue between the two systems' interpretations of acceptance is useful because it both encourages a closer empirical look at acceptance as a clinical process, and illuminates valuable directions for such research.

As psychologists we are concerned with behavior change; as scientists we are concerned with methods for the development of systematic knowledge. How we conceptualize science will dictate the means by which we accumulate knowledge about behavior change as it relates to acceptance.

Setting a Course
(Or, Where do we want to go from here?)

Wulfert discusses two different theoretical approaches which share a mutual emphasis on acceptance. Were we to adopt a traditional hypothetico-deductive model of science our analysis would likely take the shape of a dispute between these theories: does theory A (spiritual disease) represent reality, or does theory B (social learning)? In deductively-oriented systems a hierarchy exists between theory, method and data. The process of scientific justification assumes a "top down" direction (Laudan, 1984), and the emphasis is on constructing explanations rather than looking at the actual phenomena in question. Theoretical constructs are represented by indicators which battle like gladiators on the field of empirical evidence (Pedhauzer & Schmelkin, 1991). Theory then becomes verbal behavior which is largely cordoned off from actual observation.

A functional contextualistic approach offers a different option (Hayes, 1993). Instead of wrangling over theoretical systems, we may use Wulfert's analysis to begin a journey directly toward the goal of behavior change. This does not mean divesting ourselves of theory; however, it does mean capturing theory and forcing it to serve our purposes. Theory thus constrained becomes "verbal descriptions of an act-in-context that may assist the analyst in reaching some goal" (Biglan & Hayes, under submission, p. 14). Where theory has been relieved of the burden of etiological ontology, it is free to serve in a reciprocal relation with the goals or aims of investigation (Hayes, 1993; Laudan, 1984). Induction provides the power and thrust of the analysis, and we can focus directly on the event of interest.

Mapping the Terrain
(Or, How do we get to where we want to go?)

Wulfert's analysis emphasizes the ubiquity of acceptance in alcoholism treatment. This pervasiveness is clearly a signal for attention. How then might we approach this phenomenon from a functional contextual position? Biglan and Hayes (in press) suggest the following:

1. *Examining the applied phenomenon*

The present discussion regards the use of acceptance in the treatment of alcoholism. As Wulfert describes, acceptance is pervasive in the treatment literature, and appears to operate fairly consistently in spite of the differing theoretical approaches in which it is embedded.

2. *Attempting a conceptual analysis*

What is acceptance? From a functional contextual perspective this question must translate into a theoretical analysis which will both provide a definition of the activity of accepting, and clarify the conditions under which this activity occurs. We are interested not in acceptance as a reification, but acceptance as an action.

3. *Testing this analysis with theoretically derived intervention techniques*

Can we use our analysis to increase acceptance? Does this analysis aid in establishing necessary and sufficient conditions for the development of acceptance in therapeutic contexts? In other words, does our analysis enable us to accomplish our goals in a parsimonious manner consistent with our theory?

Acceptance and Self-as-Context
(Or, One possible route)

Wulfert's discussion indicates that the different aspects of acceptance in both AA and SLT largely represent different facets or points of emphasis rather than divergent phenomena. As she says "different treatment approaches to alcoholism, while using different strategies and techniques, may be effective because of a common underlying mechanism; that is, they increase the alcoholic's level of acceptance and his or her motivation for change" (p. 13). Wulfert has accomplished the first step in our outline above—examining the applied phenomenon. We can then move on to the second step—attempting a conceptual analysis. Acceptance and Commitment Therapy is an example of a functional contextual approach that offers a conceptual analysis of acceptance, and a technology based directly upon this analysis (Hayes, 1987; Hayes & Wilson, 1993; Hayes & Wilson, in press). Our goal in the development of a conceptual analysis is the identification of critical variables which allow for more effective behavior change in therapeutic interventions for alcoholism. The discussion which follows is an ACT-based approach.

What is the underlying mechanism of acceptance? Psychologically useful facets of acceptance which Wulfert describes (e.g., accepting the negative feelings which drinking obscures, accepting the long-term life consequences of self-destructive behavior, etc.) all ultimately entail acceptance of private experience. If acceptance for our purposes is described as the act of being open to one's inner experience, then self-acceptance implies the most fundamental level of this action: to accept the self is to allow contact with one's own experience without condition. Self acceptance, or being fully present to one's inner experience, may function as a critical therapeutic process.

What is the self? Skinner argues, as have others before him, (Dewey, 1929) that the self is culturally created, a product of language (Skinner, 1957, 1974, 1988). One by-product of the culture instilling a sense of self-awareness is that this locused sense of self operates as a kind of context for the content of verbal experience (Hayes, 1984). Wulfert refers to this in her discussion of spirituality; however, the analysis may have usefulness beyond understanding the function of theistic talk. James (1967) identified this direction when he said:

> To deny plumply that 'consciousness' exists seems so absurd on the face of it—for undeniably 'thoughts' do exist—that I fear some readers will follow me no farther. Let me then immediately explain that I mean only to deny that the word stands for an entity, but to insist most emphatically that it does stand for a function....That function is *knowing*....a given undivided portion of experience, taken in one context of associates, plays the part of a knower, of a state of mind, of 'consciousness'; while in a different context the same undivided bit of experience plays the part of a thing known, of an objective 'content'. (pp. 3-10)

We would argue that "knowing" is a context created by the verbal community, and that the self as knower is distinguished from the self as content of a literally held thought (Hayes, 1984). The functional experience of the literally held thought "I am X" is different than the functional experience of the thinker as an active locus. Self as context is inherently conscious. Contact with all aspects of experience is unlimited by definition, because it is the perspective which we experience *from*. Content, on the other hand, is inherently limited—objectified or thinglike—and therefore can, and does, include properties of evaluation. We can evaluate or literalize the self, e.g., "I am a worthless person", but then the self in this instance is functioning as content not context. We can reject consciousness only if we have objectified or literalized it, in which case it is no longer functioning as context.

If the self as context is accepted, the control exerted over the individuals' behavior by literally held private events is undermined. Accepting the "unacceptable" emotion/thought requires some identification with self as context—otherwise it would be unendurable. For example, where a client has learned a rule that expressing anger is bad, and the functions of this rule transfer to an event in which they experience anger, then the emotion and the thought "I am bad because I am angry" may occur. If this is responded to as literal truth, then the avoidance of anger and of thoughts identifying the self as angry is a necessary move for psychological survival–avoidance functions as a learned, negatively reinforced behavior. In this case, avoidance (including, most likely, avoidance of knowing that one is avoiding) is operantly conditioned. On the other hand, contacting the experience of self-as-context allows other contingencies to come into play. If "I am bad because I am angry" is observed from the perspective of self-as-context, then it is identified as a thought/feeling instead of as literal truth. When the thought/feeling has been discriminated as such, it is not necessary to incorporate the literal evaluative assumption. The anger and the thoughts about anger now have additional functions (i.e., the properties of observed thoughts and feelings–"this is a thought/feeling I'm having that I am bad because I am angry"), and therefore no longer serve as stimuli tightly controlling avoidance responding (Hayes & Wilson, 1993; Hayes & Wilson, in press). Accepting the experience of the self-anger and criticism- and accepting the self as the perspective from which this occurs, is the basic mechanism which allows for behavior change.

Although the instrument of self-knowledge is language, language may restrict as well as expand the range of effective behaviors available to the individual. As psychotherapists we often see the underside of this verbal demesne. Accepting literally the negative valences attached to private events, as well as assuming that these private events are the source of behavior–both activities which are created by the training for language and the development of a language of self-knowledge–establishes conditions which support avoidance or rejection of aspects of the individual's experience. This avoidance may develop into anticipatory cycles that function in such a way that they magnify the experiences they are supposed to avoid. Most importantly, these cycles support the development and maintenance of maladaptive repertoires such as addiction and alcoholism. Without intervention–specifically, without acceptance-oriented intervention–avoidance limits the range of stimulus and response functions available to the individual, restricting the probability of more adaptive patterns of behavior.

Conclusion

Wulfert's analysis clearly indicates that acceptance in the treatment of alcoholism is an important applied phenomenon that merits further attention. A functional contextual analysis allows us to deal directly with the nature of acceptance and the conditions under which we can support its occurrence. One such approach is Acceptance and Commitment Therapy, which posits that self-acceptance consists of allowing contact with one's own experience beyond the conditions imposed by the literal use of language.

Asking alcoholic clients to fully face their inner experience is a potent demand. Often what awaits them is exactly what they previously considered unendurable: rage, grief, despair, fear. In essence, we are asking them to face directly into the sorrows at the heart of the human condition, self-acceptance is an act of hope even in the face of despair: it entails accepting hopelessness as a necessary condition of hope. In this context it is important to remember that the act of self-acceptance is, at bottom, an act of profound courage.

References

Biglan, A., & Hayes, S.C. (in press). Should the behavioral sciences be more pragmatic? The case for functional contextualism in research on human behavior. *Applied and Preventive Psychology: Current Scientific Perspectives.*

Dewey, J. (1929). *Experience and Nature.* LaSalle, Ill: Open Court.

James, W. (1967). *Essays in radical empiricism: A pluralistic universe.* Gloucester, Mass: Peter Smith.

Hayes, S. C (1984). Making sense of spirituality. *Behaviorism, 12,* 99-110.

Hayes, S. C. (1987). A contextual approach to therapeutic change. In N. Jacobson (Ed.), *Psychotherapists in clinical practice: Cognitive and behavioral perspectives* (pp. 327-387). New York: Guilford.

Hayes, S. C., & Hayes, L. J. (1989). The verbal action of the listener as a basis for rule-governance. In S. C. Hayes (Ed.), *Rule-governed behavior: Cognition, contingencies, and instructional control.* (pp. 153-190). New York: Plenum.

Hayes, S. C. (1993). Analytic goals and the varieties of scientific contextualism. In S. C. Hayes, L. J. Hayes, H. W. Reese, & T. R. Sarbin (Eds.), *Varieties of scientific contextualism* (pp. 11-27). Reno, NV; Context Press.

Hayes, S. C., & Wilson, K. G. (1993). Some applied implications of contemporary behavior-analytic account of verbal events. *The Behavior Analyst, 16,* 283-301.

Hayes, S. C., & Wilson, K. G. (in press). Acceptance and Commitment Therapy: Altering the verbal support for experiential avoidance. *The Behavior Analyst.*

Laudan, L. (1984). *Science and values: The aims of science and their role in scientific debate.* Berkeley: University of California Press.

Pedhauzur, E. J., & Schmelkin, L. P. (1991). *Measurement, Design, and analysis: An integrated approach.* Hillsdale, NJ: Lawrence Erlbaum.

Rorty, R. (1982). *Consequences of Pragmatism.* Minneapolis: University of Minnesota Press.

Skinner, B. F. (1957). *Verbal Behavior.* Englewood Cliffs, NJ: Prentice Hall.

Skinner, B. F. (1974). *About behaviorism.* New York: Knopf.

Skinner, B. F. (1988). Behaviorism at fifty. In A.C. Catania and S. Harnad (Eds.), *The operant behaviorism of B.F. Skinner: Comments and consequences* (pp. 278-292. New York: Cambridge University Press.

Footnote

Preparation of this discussion was supported in part by a grant from the National Institute on Drug Abuse, #DA08634.

Chapter 11

Acceptance and the Family Context

Karen Griffee
University of New Mexico

The notion of "acceptance" may seem out of place in a discussion of clinical work with families. Family therapists typically use techniques specifically aimed at behavior change. For example, the use of token programs, problem-solving training, behavior contracts, and communication skills training are all typical of family therapy and are used to facilitate behavior change.

When a family comes in for treatment, their explicit goal also may be one of overt behavior change. Families typically seek to change the behavior of one specific family member, the "identified patient" (Minuchin, 1981). But, many families want more. Even when there is an identified patient, the family may have a broader sense of dissatisfaction with their life together. For example, a family may come in for therapy because one or more members have identified an overall lack of closeness as the primary problem, but they also recognize that the family has problems with frequent and honest communication. They hope that, by improving their communication, they will also come to feel closer to one another. Other families may simply want advice to smooth conflicts in the everyday, practical functioning of the family because they often seem to be sad or angry with one another.

Although these families desire behavior change, they are also seeking to change the broader state that they have gotten into or that they feel the identified patient has thrown them into. They see their family as being or becoming fractioned. In other words, there is a sense that the family is in danger because they are missing the things which make them a whole. They are looking for something they can do to put themselves together again.

This family portrait exemplifies some issues which seem almost always to arise in the course of family therapy. These may be described in different ways, depending on one's theoretical orientation. I will describe these as 1) attempts by family members to understand one another better and 2) a pull by family members towards greater intimacy with one another while retaining a degree of independence within the relationship. It is argued that these family goals can most effectively be addressed by an orientation to clinical work with families which focuses on acceptance. It is the purpose of this chapter to present such an orientation by clarifying the meaning of "acceptance" within a family context and by describing some of the implications of acceptance as a treatment goal. To facilitate this, the implications of acceptance as a goal will be described specifically as related to the two family issues described above. The "families" referred to here will be families with children, and most of the discussion will be oriented towards parent-child relationships. Finally, a presentation of specific treatment methods are beyond the scope of this chapter (and possibly inappropriate as well, as it would be inconsistent with the therapy goals discussed here to conduct family therapy work by using a specific set of "how to" techniques). However, some implications of this approach for the therapy process will be addressed.

General Definition

At the level of the individual, "acceptance" is here defined as a stance towards living which involves a kind of emancipation. This emancipation comes from an openness to nature, to others, and to ourselves. Being open to experience also carries with it the "freedom" to make important, difficult, and healthy choices in the face of adversity and anxiety. Therefore, a somewhat arbitrary distinction can be made between two essential aspects of acceptance as it is conceptualized here.

The first component is being open to experience. This is a willingness to open oneself up to potentially painful realities such as seeing oneself and others as they really are. The second is making important, difficult, and healthy choices in the face of adversity and anxiety or doing what "matters" although the cost may be emotional pain. This second component is commitment. Both components of this general definition are directly borrowed from Prochaska's (1984) discussion of existential psychotherapy, such as is exemplified in the work of Yalom (1975) and Bugental (1965). The existentialist perspective underlying it can be applied to some classic family issues in ways that may be both unexpected and useful.

According to the existentialists, death, chance, meaninglessness, and isolation are some conditions that are inherently involved in existence. These can be viewed as kinds of non-being. If we directly confront "non-being," it is terrifying and immobilizing. This terror and immobilization is the existential anxiety, or "angst." Rather than confront this, the natural response is to flee from it. When we hide the world from ourselves in various ways, existentialists say we are not "authentic," not fully present in our own lives. This has been referred to as "lying" (Prochaska, 1984). One form of "lying" occurs when we are not authentic and honest with ourselves and with others within a relationship. For example, it is inevitable that we will hurt and be hurt by the people we love. If we deny these hurt feelings to ourselves or to them, we are "lying" in the existential sense. We cannot "lie" and at the same time be fully present in the relationship.

What the existentialists would have us do instead, is to be open to experience. This is the first component of acceptance. It was previously noted that being open to experience carries with it the freedom to make difficult, important, and healthy choices in the face of adversity and anxiety. In other words it makes possible the second component of acceptance, which is a commitment to doing what matters although the cost may be emotional pain.

In the existential sense, commitment is choosing to live in an authentic way by doing what is honest and by making the choices which create meaning and value out of our existence. This is almost always difficult. As Prochaska (1984) notes, "...we are continually under the threat of being profoundly guilty. We must make decisions in relative ignorance of their ramifications, knowing we will hurt people regularly without intending to. In critical choices we alone are responsible, and inherent in our responsibility is the anxiety of knowing that we will make serious mistakes but not knowing whether this choice is one of those mistakes" (p. 67). Making these choices in an authentic way in the face of this anxiety is what I mean by the "commitment" component of acceptance. It is courage in action.

Acceptance Within the Family Context

Still to be addressed is how this general notion of acceptance might play itself out in the family context. As previously noted, there are important issues that seem to emerge consistently in family work. These are divided somewhat arbitrarily into two main areas of conflict within the family. One of these is the struggle of the members to understand and feel close to one another despite their individual differences. Another is the classic struggle of intimacy vs. autonomy, similar to Erikson's (1963) stage of "intimacy vs. isolation." Acceptance will be presented as a goal which has important implications for understanding these sources of family conflict in a new way.

Understanding One Another

Family members often struggle to understand one another so that they can feel truly close, yet they are likely to find that they never quite succeed. There are two important reasons for this failure. One is that people often have difficulty understanding themselves. Another is that unique learning histories and current circumstances necessarily limit understanding among individuals.

Knowing Oneself First

People often have difficulty understanding themselves because it is a deceptively difficult task. Although it can be described in many ways, self-knowledge can be seen as understanding the reasons why one acts, thinks, and feels as one does. These reasons include previous life experiences and current circumstances; these have an interactive impact on what one does. The outside influences and learning history that a parent brings into the relationship with his child is at least as important a source of his behavior as is the parent-child relationship itself. For example, a mother may have a history which tells her, "good mothers have children who are successful, obedient, brave, etc..." and "being a good mother is the most important accomplishment." This history may give rise to parenting in such a way that the success, obedience, bravery, etc. of her children is the index by which she judges her own life. A result of this may be that the daily decisions she makes in her role as a mother are driven primarily by the desire to feel good about her own life.

This kind of failure to be open to a true understanding of oneself is at the cost of understanding and intimacy in the parent-child relationship. To return to the above example, the mother who does not acknowledge her own reasons for what she does remains distanced from her children. She is unable to see her children for who they are rather than vehicles through which she might have a meaningful life. Her children are unable to see her for who she really is because she is so busy "lying" about her motivations for her children's success.

Being open to experience with respect to this issue involves being open to who one really is and how this impacts the relationship. Ultimately one will discover who one really is when one stops judging, censoring, and distorting one's own experiences as they unfold, and when one notes the circumstances that give rise to the experiences and their consequences. These consequences include the effects of one's behavior on one's children.

In addition to openness to experience, acceptance was defined in terms of commitment. With respect to the issue of understanding within a family, commitment is in the work of self-discovery and self-disclosure. Failure to commit to understanding one another occurs, for example, when parents and children tell "white lies" to spare one another pain or disappointment. Failure to make this commitment also occurs when parents choose not to examine their responses to their children and where these responses come from. Suppose that a father has a son he once dreamed would be a "chip off the old block." Instead, the son has grown into a person who differs in ways the father feels to be very important—he has different political beliefs, social values, or religious beliefs. If the father is to avoid finding aspects of this parent-child relationship painful, then he will have to ignore or deaden himself to those aspects. For example, the father could avoid the painful aspects of their relationship by avoiding contact with his son or by not discussing the ideas about which they differ. The father could reduce his sensitivity to their differences by explaining away his son's views. The father could deny himself to himself and others by insisting that his own personal values really aren't so important after all. He could even numb his painful feelings through alcohol abuse. However, any of these strategies would carry a tremendous cost. The cost is to miss out on the relationship by deadening himself to the relationship as it really is. He loses the relationship through a failure to be authentically involved in it. The relationship does not "matter."

Commitment instead is opening up oneself to being "understood" by the other by being as authentic as one can be within a relationship. It involves living in ways which matter within a relationship, in more authentic ways.

The Effects of Unique Learning Histories

It was noted that understanding among family members is also necessarily limited by the fact that individuals have different learning histories and different current circumstances. Different learning histories ensure that what is said and done will "mean" different things for different people (Skinner, 1957). That is, one's unique history cannot be separated from what one does, so the meaning of an act is necessarily different for different people. Skinner (1957) noted that when we say we fail to understand another person, "what we mean is that we do not find ourselves responding in the same way...under the same circumstances." Similar circumstances give rise to different actions, speech, thoughts, and feelings between people because they have different learning histories with respect to these circumstances.

A related problem is misunderstanding. Misunderstanding happens, when, although we respond the same as another person, we do so because of the operation of different variables (Skinner, 1957). Different learning histories also make it possible for very different, current circumstances to give rise to topographically similar actions, speech, thoughts, and feelings between people. What they do seems similar, but it serves different functions.

In the family, each member has a unique history. Although parents and their children may share a home environment, significant life events, and some of their genetic history, their total histories remain unique. The contingencies parents provide in shaping the behavior of their children are very important; however, school, friends, babysitters, television, etc., all play a part, so the child has a unique learning history and a unique current environment in which her behavior occurs. Thus, the "meaning" of what a child does or says to his mother can never be entirely "understood" by her. That is, the mother will never be in contact with all the conditions which gave rise to her child's behavior. One's children will think, act, and feel in ways one cannot understand, and this can be frustrating and painful. Even if one's child does exactly what the parent would have them do, it may be an instance of "misunderstanding" in the Skinnerian sense: a child who grows up to be a medical doctor likely does so for reasons other than those of her proud parents. Even important joint decisions will necessarily mean something different to each person in a family. For example, a couple will probably have slightly (if not greatly) different motivations for their halves of an agreement to get married, buy a house, or have a child.

These limits in understanding between people are compounded by the fact that their unique histories are continually evolving so they and the nature of their relationship are constantly changing. Even as family members struggle to understand each other more fully, time passes. At each moment the context in which behavior occurs is in flux. Thus, who we are and the nature of our relationships is changing moment to moment. This is particularly evident when one considers the developmental life of a family. What the members of a family say and do in relation to each other necessarily changes in form and meaning over the life span. Consider a relationship between father and daughter. As the daughter grows through infancy, childhood, puberty, adolescence, young adulthood, and middle age, their ways of interacting with each other change, as does the "meaning" of the individual acts between them. Eventually they may even reverse roles if, for example, the daughter finds herself "parenting" her elderly father. Even as they struggle to maintain a loving, close, and authentic relationship, they and the relationship are changing.

Just when it seems they have learned what to do, it may no longer be appropriate. People in important relationships are likely to discover that just when they understand the other, the other is no longer the person they "understand." Now that I am a parent, I better understand my mother as she was when she was parenting me; I have not come to understand her more as she is now. She has continued to age, develop, and experience events so that I never can quite "catch up."

Awareness of this separateness among people who love one another is painful. There are many ways people avoid the separateness that is part of the human condition. "Lying" about this aloneness, in the existentialists' use of the term, can take many forms. For example, siblings may assume they do understand one another to avoid getting closer. Parents may try to force their children to become understandable to them. People may insist that something is wrong inside of themselves or the members of their family and demand a "cure" when they get a glimpse of their inevitable differences. The cost of "lying" in these ways is high. Because misunderstanding and failing to understand a loved one is hurtful, to avoid feeling bad when it occurs is to be out of touch with reality. It necessarily precludes being open, genuine, "authentic" within the relationship. In other words, it necessarily precludes real intimacy.

Being open to experience with respect to this issue means that, rather than avoid the pain that comes with never entirely being able to know one another, it could instead be acknowledged as inherent in the relationship (and indeed, any relationship), much as the existentialists describe "facing" meaninglessness. To do this is to be "open to experience" by being open to the nature of the relationship. It means allowing oneself to see the relationship as it really is.

Earlier, it was argued that being "open to experience" makes commitment possible. With respect to the issue of understanding, commitment can be described metaphorically as diving headfirst into the relationship. It is not only committing to family relationships in spite of the unavoidable divisions between people but also behaving "as if" an understanding of one another is possible. In other words, it is to embrace the paradox: commitment to the family involves acting on good faith to understand one another despite the limits of understanding. This kind of commitment is in action when a mother struggles to know her daughter as she really is—at her age, in her stage of development, in this environment, at this moment—and does so without deluding herself that she will ever fully "get a handle on it."

Intimacy and Autonomy

Another important issue in family relationships can be conceptualized as a struggle for intimacy vs. autonomy. This is similar to Erikson's "intimacy vs. isolation" adult stage of development (1963). Family relationships always put the members in a sort of bind. The members are necessarily autonomous to the extent that different histories control their behavior; yet, they are necessarily dependent to the extent that they provide contingencies for one another. For example, because one can never "leave behind" one's learning history, one can never escape the influence of those by whom one was raised. In this sense, parent-child relationships are irrevocable; they always "matter." At the same time, children will and must grow to find meaning in their lives outside of the influence of their parents. Thus, the struggle of "intimacy vs. autonomy" can be seen not as a struggle but as a kind of paradox. It is only by retaining a degree of autonomy that the members of a family can really be intimate with one another. An implication of this interpretation is that intimacy and autonomy are not ends of a continuum. Instead, they together comprise what are relationships.

The intimacy/autonomy paradox naturally gives rise to conflict in family relationships. "Lying" about the hurt this brings, in the existentialists' use of the term, is probably what makes intimacy vs. autonomy such a struggle. Probably the most common of these existential "lies" involves attempts to "resolve" the conflict by choosing either intimacy or autonomy while denying the other. For example, a father may abandon his only daughter, literally or emotionally, when she behaves in ways which disappoint him. If he "lies" by denying the pain of losing her, a shallow kind of autonomy emerges but at great cost. Conversely, the daughter could adopt all her father's goals and values as her own. If she "lies" by denying the pain of losing herself, a shallow kind of intimacy emerges but at great cost.

An alternative to these lies is acceptance. Being open to the conflictual paradox of intimacy/autonomy is another form of "acceptance" in the sense of trying to be in contact with the relationship as it really is. It is accepting that intimacy and autonomy both are inherent in relationships; and it is giving up the struggle to have one without the other.

Again, it is also this "openness to experience" which makes commitment possible. Commitment in the "intimacy vs. autonomy" struggle is to embrace this paradox: remaining open to, or authentically responsive to, the (historical and current) influences outside of the family, is needed if family members are to commit to meaningful relationships with one another. Commitment is acting on good faith to be intimate with one another despite the limits of intimacy. This kind of commitment occurs when a mother chooses to be vulnerable in her relationship with her adolescent son by allowing his actions to deeply matter to her. This becomes a commitment to real intimacy when she also chooses to create and acknowledge meaning in her life apart from his accomplishments. Similarly, the son may begin to live in ways he finds rewarding but that differ from what his mother would have him do. Commitment for him would be to bring these differences into the relationship while choosing to be vulnerable as well, by allowing his mother's feelings to deeply matter to him.

In summary, acceptance as a general goal has important implications specific to the family context. In particular, the recurring family issues of understanding, intimacy, and autonomy can be understood in new ways when viewed in terms of openness to experience and commitment. When families present these issues in therapy, an adoption of acceptance as a treatment goal also has important implications for the therapy process.

Implications For Psychotherapy

Symptom Reduction

One implication of the "acceptance" stance is that it is incompatible with simple symptom reduction or elimination of unpleasant feelings as a primary treatment goal. From an existential perspective, to help someone feel better in circumstances which are naturally painful would be to help her become a better "liar." Similarly, a Skinnerian approach (1974) suggests that behaviors and the people who do them are not inherently "pathological," given that all behavior is necessarily a natural response to the conditions which give rise to it. When overt behavior change is the end goal of therapy, the underlying assumption is that the behavior is the problem. If, as is often the case, it is also believed that observable behavior is caused by pathological thoughts and feelings, then it is further assumed that the source of psychopathology is inside the person. This assumption underlies the more general medical model of psychopathology, as exemplified by the use of DSM-IV diagnoses.

Desire for symptom reduction of some form is probably what brings most individual clients into therapy. The individual client usually comes in asking for relief from suffering. They want to stop feeling sad, angry, or anxious; they want to stop thinking about things in "unhealthy" ways. When families seek treatment, usually they want to eliminate symptoms as well. Typically these are the problem behaviors of an identified patient within the family. It may be that this is often adopted as a therapy goal because it is seen as a solution to a larger problem, the emotional pain the identified patient is causing the rest of the family members. Even if the identified patient's problem behavior cannot be eliminated, family members are likely to come to therapy wanting to stop feeling hurt because of it. Alternatively, the identified patient may not be hurting the family members directly, but is in pain him/herself; the family members care about him/her and are willing to use their influence to help that person to feel better.

This is not to argue that symptom reduction is unimportant or that continued suffering matters little. When a client engages in overt behavior which has consequences that are clearly harmful to herself and others, techniques which promote behavior change are needed. For example, it would be a gross disservice to the victim in incest families if elimination of the sexual abuse were not the most immediate therapy goal. Other clients need specific, practical skills training to avoid harming themselves or others. For example, physically abusive parents may need to learn to use disciplinary methods such as sticker programs, special time, etc., to reinforce appropriate behavior and time-outs, loss of privileges, etc., to punish undesired behavior.

In all of these cases, however, an acceptance approach would suggest that this kind of behavior change should be an initial rather than final therapy goal. It is suggested that the therapist be as honest and explicit with the family as possible in explaining that what she offers is not symptom reduction or relief from emotional pain. Minuchin (1981) stresses that it is important that the therapist begin the therapy process by using the family's interpretation of the problem. Certainly a lecture on intimacy and authenticity would not be useful. Perhaps the therapist should say that feeling good all the time is not the primary treatment goal. Destructive behavior will certainly be addressed but not in order to eliminate bad feelings among family members. Rather the goal is to help the family know each other and the nature of their relationships better. This also involves discovering for themselves what their values are, that is, what ways of living, within the relationships, matter.

Psychotherapy Techniques

It seems that no single technique or set of techniques is demanded by an acceptance approach. It may even be the case that using specific techniques would be inconsistent with this goal, because pre-planned treatment methods are inconsistent with being open or authentic to what is happening in the therapy room. The essential work for the therapist is to establish a context which allows the family to become aware of how they avoid acceptance in the therapy room. In this way they may come to understand how they more generally avoid acceptance in their relationships with one another.

In individual therapy, existential psychotherapists will attend to ways clients avoid authenticity, intimacy, and choosing in the client-therapist relationship. The therapy can be viewed as establishing a context which allows the client to be aware of the conditions under which this avoidance occurs. It is suggested that the family therapist take a similar approach in acceptance work. For example, in a discussion of intimacy as a therapy goal, Weingarten (1991) suggested that "it is only in confronting the tensions and ambiguities of intimate and non-intimate interactions that people will be able to give themselves whole-heartedly to intimacy, certain that pleasure is not taken at another's expense" (p. 302). Furthermore, Weingarten suggests that it is not so important to "enshrine" intimacy as to attend to how it is produced. It is perhaps more important to scrutinize the ways that non-intimate interactions occur and the consequences when they do. The process of working out failures to understand one another (i.e., "failed intimacy") may increase intimacy. The role of the therapist would be to assist the family to see the causes and consequences of their own intimate and non-intimate interactions more clearly. This may be a difficult task because the family will have each other (as a sort of mini-culture) to collude with. They will often support each other's avoidance of intimacy at home and in the therapy room. For example, a child will sometimes help her parents to avoid potential conflict with one another by calling attention to herself through unruly behavior. If the therapist is to help the parents explore the causes and consequences of their avoidance of intimacy with one another, the therapist will also have to address the daughter's behavior as a form of collusion with her parents.

Family Systems Methods

The "family systems" literature has much to say about how families tend to support each other's avoidance of acceptance and attempts at acceptance. From this perspective, members do more than support one another's behavior; in many ways the family functions as a unit. General Systems Theory, a theory of wholeness, has its basis in biology. Bertalaffy (1968) described living organisms as systems, composed of mutually dependent parts and processes standing in mutual interaction. Family systems theorists have used the analogy of the family as a living system, and so have given particular attention to the ways each family member influences and is influenced by the others.

A particularly well-known family systems approach is Salvador Minuchin's "Structural Family Theory" model (1974). Minuchin's approach is called "structural" family therapy primarily because the family can be viewed as having a "structure." It is not necessary to view this "structure" literally, but rather as a metaphor which describes the organization of the family according to functional groupings, the style or pattern of family interactions, and the family's responses to outside pressures.

These phenomena can also be interpreted from a more contextual perspective, in that the family provides a context for the behavior of each member. That is, the family provides many of the conditions under which behavior occurs. For example, an incest family with the kind of interpersonal dynamics often seen in clinical practice would be one in which the victim has come to function as mother and wife within the family. Minuchin might describe these families as having father-daughter, rather than father-mother, parental and sexual "subsystems." These "subsystems" can further be described (metaphorically) by the nature of the "boundaries" between family members.

The family context is surely important. It may often provide the most powerful and most immediate contingencies for behavior. Therefore, understanding the family context is particularly important when the goal is to understand the behavior of the children. While family systems theorists will surely recognize that the individual histories and genetic endowment of the members play roles in psychopathology, the family systems approach takes a working assumption that the family context is the most important determinant of behavior (Jacob, 1987). Arguably, this has been a shortcoming of family systems approaches. It was recently noted (Merkel & Searright, 1992) that assuming "most problems are best conceptualized and/or treated in a familial context...leads to a kind of family-based reductionism" (p. 35). Although family therapy carries with it a focus on the family as the critical context for the behavior of each individual, it is important to recognize that the family is not the only influence on behavior. The larger culture, individual learning history, present events, and genetic determinants are all among the conditions which give rise to behavior. In a family, the parents in particular come into the family relationships with unique personal histories. These include early learning histories, which (as previously discussed) may often be more important than the current family in determining how members behave with one another. Current environments outside the family may also determine behavior. For example, a child who has been molested by a neighbor is likely to have behavior changes at home.

Group Process Methods

In contrast to typical family therapy methods, Irvin Yalom's work on group therapy (1975) is a "process" approach which takes both inter- and intra-personal dynamics into account. Because he is an existential psychotherapist, it seems obvious that his treatment methods would also be consistent with the goal of acceptance. This is clearly the case. The critical aspect of group process therapy for the present purpose is the attention to "why, from a relationship aspect," is the client saying or doing what they are "at this time, to this person, in this manner" (Yalom, 1975, p. 123). Process can be observed not only in individual statements or actions but in the broader interactions among members of a group. The focus is on behavior in its context. It is suggested that just such a process approach might be used to promote acceptance within the family because it may help them to develop sensitivity to the contingencies they provide for each other, rather than provide more rules about what they do and why. It is suggested that this approach would be particularly appropriate for families with young children if child therapy methods were incorporated. For example, a family therapist could retain Yalom's emphasis on process but incorporate nonverbal means such as play therapy to bring young children into the work.

However it is achieved in family therapy, acceptance seems to be an appropriate and important therapy goal. It involves developing a stance of openness to oneself, to the other family members, and to the true nature of the family relationships. This openness makes possible a commitment to better understanding oneself and each other. It is essentially a commitment to learn, over and over again, how to best love one another.

References

Bugental, J. (1965). *The search for authenticity*. New York: Holt, Rinehart, & Winston.

Erikson, E. H. (1950). *Childhood and society*. New York: Norton.

Jacob, T. (1987). Family interaction and psychopathology. In T. Jacob (Ed.), *Family interaction and psychopathology: Theories, methods, and findings*. New York: Plenum.

Merkel, W. T., & Searright, H. R. (1992). Why families are not like swamps, solar systems, or thermostats: Some limits of systems theory as applied to family therapy. *Contemporary Family Therapy, 14*, 33-50.

Minuchin, S. (1974). *Families and family therapy*. Cambridge, MA: Harvard University Press.

Minuchin, S., & Fishman, H. C. (1981). *Family therapy techniques*. Cambridge, MA: Harvard University Press.

Prochaska, J. O. (1984). *Systems of psychotherapy*. Chicago: Dorsey.

Skinner, B. F. (1957). *Verbal behavior*. Englewood Cliffs, NJ: Prentice-Hall.

Skinner, B. F. (1974). *About behaviorism*. New York: Vintage.

Weingarten, K. (1991). The discourses of intimacy: Adding a social constructionist and feminist view. *Family Process, 30*, 285-305.

Yalom, I. D. (1975). *The theory of practice of group psychotherapy*. New York: Basic Books.

Discussion of Griffee

The Costs of Non-Acceptance

Carol W. Metzler
Oregon Research Institute

In her chapter, "Acceptance and he Family Context," Karen Griffee describes the relationship of acceptance to two primary issues of the family context— lack of understanding among family members and struggles between intimacy and autonomy— and argues that these issues may be most effectively addressed in clinical work with families by an approach which focuses on acceptance. Griffee then lays out the implications of this approach for family, therapy, and stresses that a focus only on behavior change is incompatible with acceptance in family work. Four issues in particular merit further discussion here: (a) the increase in the level of complexity of acceptance when the family context is considered; (b) the cost to the family system of avoidance of pain; (c) the appropriate goals for family therapy within an acceptance framework and the role of behavior change within this framework; and (d) the limits of acceptance within the family context.

First, attention to the family context adds layers of complexity to the analysis of acceptance beyond the individual level. At this level, one is faced with the acceptance of oneself, of one's thoughts and feelings, and of one's own experiences. In the context of a relationship, however, one is also faced with two additional layers: (a) acceptance of the other person, their thoughts, feelings, and experiences; and (b) acceptance of the nature of the relationship itself, or the holistic system of interaction among family members. As Griffee states in her chapter, acceptance in the family context implies not just being open to one's own experience, but to that of other family members and to the nature of the relationship itself as well. Thus, those attempting to understand and practice acceptance at the family level are presented with additional challenge and complexity beyond the individual level alone.

The second issue raised by Griffee's chapter is the cost of avoiding pain in the family context. Just as the avoidance of emotional pain comes at a great cost for an individual (as described elsewhere in this book), so also the avoidance of pain comes at a great cost to the family. Griffee states that the costs to the family are decreased understanding and intimacy among family members and decreased authenticity in the relationship. Indeed, family members can build formidable barriers within and among themselves to avoid dealing with anxiety or discomfort in their relationship.

In my view, however, avoidance of pain carries an even broader cost to the family that is only subtly implied in Griffee's chapter. Avoidance of unpleasant thoughts and feelings can interfere with pursuing effective family functioning more generally, undermining not only understanding, intimacy, and authenticity among family members, but also effective problem-solving and most importantly, effective parenting. For example, when a mother attempts to set and enforce appropriate limits for her young son's demanding behavior, she may , experience a whole host of unpleasant thoughts (e.g. "Hell get mad at me if I say no," "I don't want him to get upset at me," "I can't stand it when he ys," "I'm a failure—I can't do this' or "It's not worth the ha'ssle to stand my ground", and feelings (e.g. frustration, guilt, or anxiety). Unfortunately, avoidance of these thoughts and feelings can mean avoidance of important parenting— the mother backs down and gives in to her child to avoid "a scene" in the short term, thereby contributing to further escalation of his misbehavior in the long term. Just as true understanding and true intimacy do not always feel good, so also honest attempts at effective parenting don't either. If this mother is to help her child reduce his problematic behavior and encourage more cooperative behaviors, she must be willing to accept her own painful thoughts and feelings that accompany providing new contingencies for her son, to accept her child's confusion and anger, and to accept her own role in the relationship dynamic. Then, she must commit to doing what "matters" for her child and family (setting and enforcing appropriate limits consistently).

This point is highly related to a third issue meriting discussion here. In her chapter, Griffee argues that two types of family goals can most effectively be addressed in family therapy within a framework of acceptance: (a) family members' attempts to understand and feel close despite their differences; and (b) their struggle between intimacy and autonomy. Griffee argues that a therapeutic focus on behavior change is inconsistent with an approach based on acceptance. While the author lays out a compelling case for the appropriateness of a therapeutic orientation based on acceptance for addressing these family issues, it is argued here that acceptance can also be built into family work that is primarily behavioral in orientation. That is, even when behavior change is the primary therapeutic goal, attention to acceptance may make behavior change efforts even more successful.

For example, at the individual level, a therapeutic approach to acceptance and change (e.g. Hayes, McCurry, Afari, & Wilson, 1991) suggests that individuals can make changes in their behavior built on a foundation of acceptance of themselves and all of their experiences, and a commitment to "do what works"— that is, to make important and difficult choices, to live more effectively, and to live in keeping with their larger life goals.

By the same token, at the family level, a therapeutic approach to acceptance and change suggests that the family can make changes in its behavior, built on a foundation of: (a) members' acceptance of themselves and their own experience; (b) acceptance of the other family members and their experiences; and (c) acceptance of the true nature of the family relationship; and then (d) a mutual commitment to do what works for the family or for the child, in keeping with family goals.

Griffee states that behavior change could be an initial therapy goal but warns against making it a final goal of family therapy. She suggests, rather, that the ultimate therapy goal should be "to help the family know each other and the nature of their relationships better." I propose, however, that working toward greater acceptance does not preclude work on changing problematic behavior. When behavior change is pursued in the context of increasing family members' willingness to experience their own and each other's anxiety and discomfort that can accompany change, then family members are more open to real behavior change and more effective functioning, whether their goal is more effective parenting, better communication, or greater intimacy, etc.

Thus, perhaps the over-arching therapy goal might be to help the family to function more effectively in ways that "matter" to the family members. Depending on how a family chooses to define "effective functioning," this goal may be manifested in any number of ways, such as increased intimacy and understanding, better communication, decreased abusive or destructive behavior, and/or more effective parenting. Any of these will involve acceptance and behavior change on some level for all family members. In order to move toward more effective family functioning, family members must be willing to accept their own and each other's experiences, while committing to act– even in the face of anxiety or adversity.

Griffee correctly suggests that the therapist be honest and explicit with the family about what can and cannot be accomplished in family therapy. This is a very important point, Acceptance work with families is likely to be much more effective if done in the context of "informed consent"– a frank and open discussion about what therapy goals are appropriate and achievable. The acknowledgement needs to be made up-front that progress toward better and more effective family relationships will not necessarily be pain-free.

A final point to be discussed here concerns the limits of acceptance within the family context. Family members' acceptance of one another's thoughts, feelings, learning history, and many aspects of their overt behavior appear to be important in order for the family to move toward more effective functioning, Acceptance of all overt behavior, however, can be destructive A young child's aggressive, danger-ous, or unsafe behavior, or behavior that is destructive or abusive on the part of any family member, should not be "accepted" in the name of openness to experience. One can accept one's own and another's thoughts, feelings, learning history, and how all of these relate to the relationship and to the behavior at hand, and still not accept the destructive behavior itself. Indeed, to suggest that family members should "accept" aggressive or unsafe behavior in a child without intervening does the child a grave disservice. Similarly, to suggest that physical or sexual abuse be tolerated in the name of acceptance can cause great harm.

It is important to clarify that acceptance in the family context does not mean "anything goes." It means openness to see the family relationship as it is, openness to see oneself and the other family members as they are, and commitment to do what works to make the family relationship more effective, whether that means increased intimacy, better childrearing, or decreased abusive or destructive behavior.

References

Hayes, S. C., McCurry, S. M., Afari, N., & Wilson, K. (1991). *Acceptance and Commitment Therapy (ACT): A therapy manual for the treatment of emotional avoidance disorders.* Reno, NV: Context Press.

Chapter 12

Acceptance, Serentity, and Resignation in Elderly Caregivers

Susan M. McCurry and Amy Schmidt
University of Washington

In a recent therapy hour, an elderly woman who is caring for her husband with Alzheimer's disease quoted to the senior author the well-known "Serenity Prayer": "God grant me the serenity to accept the things I cannot change, the courage to change the things I can, and the wisdom to know the difference." This woman clearly recognizes that her husband's disease falls within the realm of that which must be accepted. Alzheimer's disease (AD) has no known cause, no known treatment, and an unpredictable, but inevitably fatal, progression and end. She hopes that she can accept her husband's disease, and her caretaking role, with serenity: she loves him, and wants to care for him without rancor or resentment.

Unfortunately, for most caregivers, this is not fully possible. Alzheimer's disease is a dynamic illness which requires a continually changing response from care providers. Serenity achieved one moment can be shattered the next, in an endless variety of exhausting, frightening, or publicly humiliating encounters with the demented patient. Caregivers who say "I must accept this" are sometimes trying to stifle the disappointment, grief, loneliness, and rage which can accompany life with an Alzheimer's patient. For them, "acceptance" is synonymous with helplessness and resignation.

It would seem that serenity, acceptance, and resignation are easily confused. In this paper, we will attempt to show that acceptance functions differently for caregivers than does resignation, and that the emotional experience of serenity may be associated with, but is not essential to, the acceptance experience. We will present an operational definition of acceptance that has clear treatment implications for work with elderly caregivers, and we will suggest some therapeutic strategies that can facilitate the acceptance process in this group. Finally, we will discuss the connection between acceptance and the behavioral interventions commonly used with geriatric caregivers. We have chosen caregivers of Alzheimer's disease patients as our focus because AD is largely a disease of the elderly, and represents a significant proportion of the geriatric caretaking population. However, it is reasonable to assume that other types of caretakers could also benefit from a more broad acceptance-based treatment approach (c.f., Biglan, 1989).

Definition of the Caregiving Problem

In 1986, the American Association of Retired Persons estimated that over 5 million community-dwelling older adults in this country required some form of assistance in order to maintain independent living (AARP, 1986). Currently, there are 4 million older adults in the United States with Alzheimer's disease (approximately 10% of the population over age 65), andthis number is expected to more than triple by the year 2050 (ADRDA, 1991). The cost of care for these patients is $90 billion a year; and as the Alzheimer's population expands, the expense will also expand to staggering proportions. Families provide 70% of the care for all AD patients (ADRDA, 1991); however, only about 2% of these receive community support to ease caretaking responsibilities.

There are two types of services that can help caregivers of AD patients. First, caregivers should be given information and education about Alzheimer's disease, and provided basic assistance with patient care. For example, caregivers need training in basic behavior management strategies, awareness of available community resources (such as adult day centers), and information about patient symptoms that may arise as the disease progresses. In addition, caregivers need access toservices for themselves. Caregivers have become known in the medical community as the "second patient", incurring higher incidences of clinical depression, insomnia, family discord, and physical illness than comparable non-caregiving peers (Cantor, 1983; Gaynor, 1989; Kiecolt-Glaser & Glaser, 1991; Pruchno & Potashnik, 1989; Rabins, Mace, & Lucas, 1982; Schulz & Williamson, 1991). Caregivers visit their physicians more often, use more alcohol and psychotropic medications, and have chronically high levels of anger and anxiety (Bergstone, Cheri, Zarit, & Gatz, 1988; Clipp & George, 1990; Haley, Levine, Brown, Berry, & Hughes, 1987; Kiecolt-Glaser & Glaser, 1991).

Recent reviews by Toseland and Rossiter (1989), and Zarit and Teri (in press) have summarized the research on various psychoeducational, psychotherapeutic, and self-help interventions that have been used with caregivers. Relaxation training, support groups, respite care, and brief cognitive-behavioral interventions are the most common treatments currently offered to caregivers. Research available on these interventions has produced inconsistent results: although some studies found that caregivers who participated in treatment showed improvement in their symptoms, in other studies, the improvements were not maintained over time, or did not reach clinical significance (Toseland & Rossiter, 1989; Zarit & Teri, in press). Thus, although the need for psychotherapy with caregivers has been clearly identified, it remains to be determined what forms of treatment are maximally effective over time with this group. The present paper will discuss the role of acceptance as one process variable which may have relevance to psychotherapy with AD caregivers. It is our hope that future research will begin to study the actual impact of acceptance, as well as other therapy process variables, on treatment outcome with this population.

Definition of Terms

Acceptance as Resignation

The term "acceptance" has a variety of meanings in the medical and psychological literature. One common usage of the term refers to a form of resignation. Resignation is taken from the Latin *re-*, meaning "back" or "backward" (as in withdrawal or backward motion), and *signare* (to mark or sign). Thus, the original root of resignation means to give back, or sign over, as in signing over the control or care of another. Once control is lost, inaction and dependency are likely to result.

Caregivers who are resigned to their task often complain of feeling "stuck" and ineffective. They talk in terms of their "obligations" and "what should be done." They can find nothing good in their caregiving role, and they often overlook new opportunities to improve their own or their patient's situation. For example, one caregiver had been in the process of filing for divorce just prior to her husband's diagnosis of AD. She decided to stay in the marriage, saying "I can't leave him now," and "I guess I just have to accept this and stand by him." Predictably, she reported she felt trapped and paralyzed by her situation. Although she was aware of nearby community services that could help with her husband's care, she refused to contact them for assistance. She prematurely dropped out of a university research project designed to treat her husband's depression. For this woman, her "acceptance" neither enhanced her ability to care for her husband, nor did it allow her to choose to go forward with the divorce in such a way that alternative arrangements for his optimal care could be made.

Acceptance as a Desirable Treatment Outcome

When the term "acceptance" is used synonymously with resignation, it generally has a pejorative connotation. Acceptance-as-resignation is a stage or endpoint that most therapists would try to help their clients escape. However, "acceptance" is also used in the treatment literature to refer to a stage or outcome that many clinicians would consider desirable and therapeutic.

For example, acceptance can mean a kind of **consent** or agreement, as when a patient accepts a psychologist's treatment recommendations. Acceptance often refers to a state of **unconditional positive regard**, as when therapists encourage clients to accept and love themselves despite personal weaknesses and flaws. Acceptance is also used to indicate a kind of client **surrender**; for example, we talk about the cancer patient accepting her terminal diagnosis, or the family of an AD patient accepting that his cognitive decline is irreversible (Kubler-Ross, 1969; Oliver & Bock, 1987; Teusink & Mahler, 1984). As stated earlier, each of these uses of acceptance refers to a particular outcome that most clients and therapists would evaluate positively. Each definition also implies that acceptance makes persons (at least temporarily) compliant, serene, reasonable, and free of distressing negative emotions. When negative emotions or noncompliant, unreasonable actions emerge, adherents of outcome theories of acceptance often label these with terms such as "resistance," "overinvolvement," "denial," or "bargaining"; treatment involves helping clients get rid of the unpleasantries as quickly as possible.

Acceptance as Act-in-Process

A few psychological authors have talked about acceptance as an act-in-process, rather than a final goal or outcome that can be achieved. For example, Erik Erickson (1964)noted that someone who accepts his/her life is "endowed with a total quality which we might term 'animated' or 'spirited'" (p. 112). In the present paper, we wish to examine further the construct of acceptance as an experiential process or action. Our purpose in doing so is that we believe acceptance may be more helpful to caregivers when it is viewed as a way of interacting with a dynamic and changing world, than when it is viewed as a specific cognitive or emotional goal. In particular, it may help caregivers who view themselves as failures or inadequate when they are unable to get rid of their embarrassment, irritation, and disappointment with their demented patient.

In taking this approach, we are aware that we are moving against a verbal tradition which emphasizes acceptance as an outcome or stage rather than an ongoing process. Each of the acceptance definitions presented above (resignation, consent, unconditional positive regard, surrender) could themselves be described as dynamic events in progress, rather than final states. However, by verbal convention and common usage, the underlying action-like quality of acceptance is generally unappreciated in those definitions. For this reason, in the present paper we will offer a new definition of acceptance that makes explicit the continually changing nature of acceptance-based interactions. From this definition, we will then go on to describe techniques that interested therapists may find helpful in their work with acceptance in the caregiving population.

Acceptance: A New Working Definition

We propose the following definition of acceptance: *Acceptance is an interaction with the world that creates a context in which the individual's immediate range of available experiences is expanded.* Several points need to be made about this definition. First, *acceptance is an interactive process* of relating to the world, reminiscent of what Hayes and Hayes (1992) have called "situated action" (p.1390). Its interactive nature means that acceptance is not some psychological event which passively occurs within an individual; acceptance is active relating behavior. Furthermore, because acceptance is a continuous process rather than a static event, it cannot be completed or indefinitely sustained. However, the process can be enhanced with practice so that acceptance-interactions occur more frequently or more quickly in future situations.

Second, *acceptance is inclusive*, rather than exclusive. It is expansive in nature. Acceptance-interactions lead to increased awareness of new, previously neglected, or increased numbers of physical and psychological experiences. This in turn can lead to exploration of new behavioral options. In other words, acceptance is characterized by exposure, rather than avoidance, behaviors. It is as if acceptance creates a shift in perspective, a kind of permeability that enables the individual to experience and respond to events that were outside awareness before. For caregivers, this expansive shift in perspective is what makes it possible for them to respond flexibly to the patient, while at the same time pursuing personal and care-related goals.

Third, *acceptance is independent of any specific thought, emotion, memory, or behavior.* The presence of positive emotions (such as serenity), or the absence of negative ones, does not in itself indicate acceptance. Furthermore, nothing has to happen first - the caregiver doesn't have to get rid of denial or resentment - before acceptance-interactions can occur. Acceptance is more readily identified by what *follows* it (such as increased awareness or more effective life choices), than by what immediately accompanies its occurrence. Unfortunately, what follows acceptance-interactions will also vary across situations. It may be this ephemeral quality of acceptance that has led Hayes to refer to it as "No-Thing," an "action of no-action" (Hayes, McCurry, Afari, & Wilson, 1991, p.39).

Fourth, *acceptance creates and occurs in a context,* and this context includes the individual's making choices and observing the consequences of these choices. Since acceptance is "no-thing", that is, independent of any specific experience or outcomes, it can only be evaluated in terms of a goal. For example, for the resigned caregiver described earlier, acceptance could occur whether the caregiver was working towards obtaining a divorce or staying in the marriage but taking steps to become more responsive to her caregiving role. Either choice would offer opportunities to experience a number of new actions, thoughts, and emotions. Either choice would also offer many opportunities to avoid or restrict experiences that were uncomfortable or unpleasant. We hypothesize that acceptance-based responses would allow greater behavioral responsivity and effectiveness than avoidance, but ultimately, each caregiver would need to experience and evaluate that for themselves.

Specific Implications for Treatment

We have defined acceptance to be a process of interacting with the world that leads to increased awareness of experiences which arise while pursuing life choices. We elaborated this definition to emphasize that acceptance-interactions are ongoing and active, and that they are associated with exposure to experiences rather than avoidance. We further stated that since acceptance is not associated with any specific experience or outcome, it can only be recognized and evaluated in the context of making choices and evaluating their consequences. We can now consider whether this operational definition of acceptance has applied utility for clinicians and researchers who are interested in psychotherapy with AD caregivers.

We theorize that caregivers who are able to make choices in the context of an openness to experiences (even unpleasant ones), will be more effective and satisfied with their roles than those whose actions are based in an effort to avoid discomfort or pain. However, to test this hypothesis, it would be necessary for caregivers to learn to distinguish between acceptance- and avoidance-interactions, and to then evaluate the impact of each on their daily functioning. From our operational definition of acceptance, there appear to be at least two areas where clinicians might intervene to facilitate the process of acceptance in the caregiving population. First, caregivers canbe taught techniques to increase *awareness,* which may in turn enhance their capacity for active, expansive relating to the world. Second, caregivers can be helped to identify realistic *goals and choices* within their caretaking role, and to practice evaluating the consequences of these choices from a broader context or perspective.

The Art of Awareness

Awareness is basic to the acceptance process. Simply put, for the individual to be engaging in acceptance he or she must be paying attention. Acceptance requires that the caregiver be aware of the range of external or internal sensations or stimuli which are a part of any particular context, despite the fact that some of these may be psychologically distressing. This level of mindfulness requires practice, and in some cases, training for persons who have never developed the skills of careful attending. It also requires courage and support for the caregiver, who is being asked to face difficulties which may have been habitually avoided in the past. Therapists can provide this support, and can help caregivers improve their observational skills in a number of domains. These include: 1) increasing awareness of external events, particularly involving the patient, 2) improving self-observations of emotional, cognitive, and physical states, and 3) enhancing caregivers' recognition when old patterns of responding are interfering with immediate caretaking needs.

Awareness and External Events. One way to help caregivers become aware of the external world is by giving them information about the physical causes and typical progression of Alzheimer's disease. It is much easier for caregivers to do their job well when they have a better understanding of dementing illnesses and what to expect in the future. This education process can also include helping the caregiver become informed regarding available community resources (such as day activity centers or respite services), experimental treatment options, and long-term care facilities, as well as helping them learn to communicate effectively with medical and social service professionals.

Teaching awareness of external events is at the core of behavioral management strategies that help caregivers identify the antecedents associated with behavior problems in their patients, and their consequent responses to the patient which may inadvertently be shaping and maintaining the problematic behaviors. The act of careful observing can be strengthened with practice and also by teaching caregivers to monitor and describe what they observe with greater detail and accuracy. The recognition of contingencies which surround patient behaviors that previously seemed random and unpredictable helps many caregivers feel a sense of greater control over the situation, and paradoxically, increases their tolerance for ambiguity and unpredictability in the future.

Finally, teaching caregivers to be aware of external events includes time management for themselves and problem-solving strategies to help compensate for the disruption in roles and lifestyles that accompany caring for the AD patient.

Caregivers can easily become overwhelmed with competing responsibilities, often leading them to neglect their own needs in their efforts to provide for the demented patient. For example, one caregiver insisted on being the sole support for her husband with late stage Alzheimer's disease, despite the fact that she herself suffered from severe heart disease. When she began missing the walks and quiet time necessary for her recovery, and had to have a third heart bypass operation, she finally saw that she was painfully stuck in her refusal of help. This awareness led her to begin to reach out and ask for the assistance she needed.

Awareness and Internal Events. Acceptance can be fostered by teaching caregivers to become more aware of their inner experiences (such as thoughts and emotions), some of which may have been ignored or rejected in the past. Too often in a zest to be all and do all, caregivers squelch their feelings, especially "negative" feelings such as resentment and anxiety. Many experiential exercises (such as used in gestalt therapy) can help guide the caregiver to experience these neglected emotions in the safety of the therapy hour.

However, some caregivers believe that increasing their awareness of painful emotions while they are in the midst of the stresses of caregiving is countertherapeutic. As one woman commented, "sure I resent caring for my mother, but what good does it do me to feel those feelings? I still have to care for her night and day." Such caregivers can be helped to see that their patients can sense when they are unhappy or upset, and that suppressing these feelings can negatively impact their quality of their care and level of intimacy with the patient. In her book "Counting on Kindness," Lustbader (1991) relates a story from one of her patients:

"My son says he likes fixing me dinner every night, but he looks so tense when he's here. He comes over right from work, and his wife holds dinner at their house until he gets home. He smiles, makes chitchat, but I know he's racing against time. Sometimes he looks like he's going to explode, his face is so tight, but he keeps on smiling. I wish he could just say it's too much for him. I'd be disappointed, don't get me wrong, but TV dinners wouldn't kill me (p.25)."

It is important for the therapist to know that some caregivers are more willing to discuss their painful inner experiences with other caregivers than family, friends, or professionals. Support groups or other forms of contact between caregivers help them to see that their many reactions to caregiving are not only acceptable, but normal and healthy. For example, caregivers are often surprised that others have also "wished the patient would die" or are ashamed to be seen with their partner in public settings. For these reasons, participation in support groups should be encouraged. However, it is also important to remember that isolation, which is common in caregiving, can be a form of independence as well as a sign of withdrawal. Caregivers who have never been "joiners" in the past may dislike attending group meetings, or may find that listening to others' troubles is more effortful than dealing with their own. For such caregivers, even gentle nudging to visit support groups may be met with a refusal that should be respected by the therapist. In these cases, caregivers may be more receptive to efforts directed at helping them identify alternative sources of support and information.

Finally, it is useful for therapists to themselves practice the art of self-awareness when working with elderly caregivers. There is a tendency for younger therapists to patronize senior clients, or at best, to try to protect their feelings in a way that may be countertherapeutic. In some cases, focusing on advice-giving and offering encouragement during session does more to help the therapist avoid contact with his or her own feelings of helplessness and discomfort, than it serves the needs of the caregiver. As one caregiver noted after the fact:

"The truth is, I was a terrible caregiver. I just barely got through it. I didn't have a clue about what I was doing and I had to do things I was never trained for. But when I told my friends I was doing a terrible job, they didn't want to hear it. Everyone kept offering advice or telling me about what services to try, or saying that they thought I was doing a good job. But I wasn't doing a good job and I just wanted someone to hear this. I just wanted someone to listen to how totally crazy and exhausted I felt."

Awareness of the Past. Increasing awareness includes facilitating caregivers' recall of old family patterns, and helping them recognize when these old patterns are being inappropriately reenacted in the present. For example, the caregiver who yells at his demented wife about her mismanagement of the checkbook may be responding in the same way as he did when his wife incorrectly balanced the checkbook in the past. Since dementia symptoms can accentuate difficult aspects of the patient's preexisting personality, it is very common for caregivers to interpret patients' symptoms as deliberate attempts to manipulate the home situation or "get their own way." As one woman noted about her mother:

"They tell me that her behavior is part of the disease but I can't help but think that sometimes she's being this way on purpose. I can't forget all the years she was irritable, depressed and only concerned with herself. I don't think Alzheimer's has changed that, it's just made it worse."

Studies have shown that caregivers who had a poor relationship with the patient before his or her illness are at increased risk to become depressed or experience health problems (Schulz & Williamson, 1991). By helping caregivers become aware of their historical patterns of interacting with the patient, the therapist can facilitate acceptance of the demented person's symptoms. From there, alternative behavioral responses may emerge, including improvements in caregiver mood. Therapists can promote this awareness of the past by gathering a good history or self-narrative from the caregiver. The narrative should include information about the patient's and caregiver's previous roles, past crises that were either successfully or unsuccessfully resolved, and hopes or expectations each may have had which have been altered by the onset of the dementing illness. This examination of past events can help identify idiosyncratic interaction patterns that the caretaker and patient have developed over time, including how flexible both were when faced with novel circumstances. It will also identify historical factors that may be influencing caregivers' perceptions of current events and their selective responding to them.

Old promises and pacts with the patient or oneself are common deterrents to caregivers' acceptance of their situation, which can include making difficult placement decisions. Oftentimes, caregivers have very negative opinions about long-term care facilities, and have vowed they would never place a family member there. In other cases, it is the demented parent or spouse who has made their loved ones promise they will never send them to "one of those homes." One woman observed: "Ever since I was a teenager my parents made me promise I would take care of them. It was expected of me and I wasn't about to disappoint them." Similarly, caregivers may be influenced by the cultural traditions and social mores in which they were raised. Many elderly caregivers were brought up with the Judeo-Christian messages of "honor thy father and thy mother" and to love and cherish "till death do us part." Caregivers need to become aware of what these cultural messages and old pacts are, when they are operating, what led to their adoption in the first place, and whether they are helpful or appropriate in the current situation.

Finally, caretakers may hold unrealistic expectations about what caretaking involves and how the patient should act that interfere with their providing quality care. When the patient fails to meet these expectations, caregivers can be at a loss for how to respond. For example, many caregivers expect their responsibilities will take less time, or be less disruptive, than is actually the case. Few realize that caring for the AD patient can last as long as 20 years, with an average of 8 to 10 years of progressive decline that may include highly disturbing symptoms such as paranoia, aggression, or delusions (Mendez, Martin, Smyth, & Whitehouse, 1990). Almost all caregivers also secretly expect their patient to appreciate their efforts, even though some dementia symptoms such as agitation or inability to recognize the caregiver may interfere with the patient's capacity for gratitude. When caregivers become aware of these or other hidden expectations, it makes it easier to respond proactively when their patient disappoints them. Therapists can encourage caregivers to create for themselves a new set of expectations that are more realistic. For example, it may not be realistic now to keep the house as clean as before, to keep the patient bathed daily, or to keep up with correspondence during the holidays.

Identifying and Pursuing Goals

A second area of intervention raised by our operational definition of acceptance relates to caregivers' choices or goals. Every AD patient is unique and their caregiving needs highly individualized. However, almost every AD caretaker faces the difficulty of organizing daily life and planning for the future, while at the same time living with a continually changing and unpredictable demented patient. Old hopes and dreams are abandoned, and frequently caregivers' immediate desires and preferences are set aside as well. For the therapist, facilitating acceptance includes helping caregivers to 1) learn to set goals within the context of continually changing conditions of patient care, and 2) grieve for old goals and dreams while making way for new choices and commitments. In the process, caregivers can be taught to examine the consequences of their choices with the help of the awareness skills they are also developing.

Choices in the Context of Continual Change. Identifying goals and making personal choices can seem a burdensome task to caregivers who are overwhelmed with daily responsibilities. This is particularly true for AD caregivers, since so much of their experience is unpredictable and continually changing. One Alzheimer patient writes about his own experience of constant change saying:

> "With Alzheimer's people, there's no such thing as having a day which is like another day—every day is separate—and you don't know what's going to happen in any one day...it's as if every day you have never seen anything before like what you're seeing right now... you have to live it one day at a time (Henderson, 1992, p. 6)."

Similarly, a caregiver who visits her mother in a nursing home comments:

> "When I visit mom, I never know what state she's going to be in. One day she's irritable, the next she's happy. I just have to meet her with an open mind. What matters now is only the moment. The past and future are irrelevant to her."

Caregivers must be prepared to sometimes abandon even the most carefully laid plans on those occasions when their patient is particularly confused, agitated, or sensitive to stimulation and change in the environment. Paradoxically, as caregivers become aware of their lack of absolute control, and learn both to set goals and to modify these goals as needed, it becomes easier to be responsive to changing circumstances, and "just take things a day at a time."

The progressive nature of AD complicates caregivers' long-term attempts to accept and plan for the patient's care. Alzheimer's patients decline regardless of what caregivers do or how well they do it. Caregivers sometimes take this decline personally, feeling that they are to blame if the patient fails to improve or even gets worse despite their continual loving efforts. Therapists can help caregivers remain aware of the inevitable deterioration with AD, and to work with it, instead of against it, by setting realistic goals for themselves. For example, in the early stages, caregivers' goals may revolve around adjusting to the diagnosis and coping with subtle changes in the patient's behavior. In later stages, choices and goals are more likely to reflect the caregiver's physical exhaustion and need for respite, including making future plans for more intensive levels of physical care (either at home or in an institution).

Therapists can encourage caregivers to experiment with alternative strategies for coping with continual change. Caregivers who cultivate a sense of humor are often particularly good at dealing with the sudden shifts in plans or unexpected surprises and problems that arise in daily life with the AD patient. Other caregivers find that it helps them to focus on the aspects of caring that bring them satisfaction. For example, some caregivers receive enjoyment from doing small things, like keeping the patient "frustrated as little as possible." Other caregivers simply enjoy "just being together." Still others see their role as a way of fulfilling larger life "goals," that is, deeply held values or lifelong commitments. For example, one man stated,

"[I feel] a sense of gratitude and payment...for the love and affection and companionship she has given me for 50 years. It is my privilege to serve her."

Therapy can enhance caregivers' recognition of the small joys of caregiving; one research project (Teri, 1992, personal communication), has found that 87% of caregivers who participated in brief therapy to treat their patient's depression were able to identify at least one positive aspect of caregiving at the end of treatment (compared to 66% before treatment began). It is possible that caregivers who look for the positive aspects of caregiving, or who are able to recognize the humor in many interactions with their patient, may be able to view their situation with objectivity, and thus better able to respond in accepting ways.

Conflicts between Old and New Goals. Caregivers often have difficulty learning to set appropriate goals when they have been forced to abandon previous dreams and hopes because their patient became demented. For example, many couples planned to have a happy retirement together and now are disappointed and resentful over previously lost opportunities for quality time with their spouse when he or she was healthy. One woman lamented,

"My husband's work was always so important. He promised me that we'd spend time together when he retired...it was always "later." Well, now he can't do anything and there is no "later." I have to take care of him...that's my retirement."

New goals can also be problematic when they require the caregiver to assume responsibilities that have in the past fallen to the demented partner or parent. Such role reversals are common in AD: adult children become a parent to their parent, and aging spouses take on unfamiliar financial and domestic responsibilities in addition to maintaining their previous commitments to the relationship. One man commented,

"I was the recipient of caregiving most my life - first from my mother, and then my wife. When my wife was diagnosed with Alzheimer's disease, not only was it essential that I learn how to maintain a household, but I was required to learn how to cope with the loss of my friend and companion (Perspectives, 1992)."

These changes in roles and responsibilities have been called "one of the most difficult adjustments that a family member must make" (Teusink & Mahler, 1984, p. 154). This is especially true for adult child caregivers whose demented parents have been powerful, authoritative figures who now refuse to relinquish control over management of their daily affairs, or for caregivers who have been unwillingly thrust into the job simply because there is no one else to do it. Therapists who work with caregivers can help them identify the difficulties inherent in major role reversals, and assist them in making the changes necessary to provide good care.

Some caregivers have particular difficulty establishing new goals for themselves after their caretaking responsibilities have ended. For example, when one caretaker's wife died he felt "massive guilt" that during the entire course of the disease he did not do enough (Billings, 1991). Another husband agonized over his decision to put his wife in a nursing home with, "Surely I could have carried on a bit longer? What has my partner done to deserve this?" (Gent, 1992). Such caregivers can ruminate for years about choices they made in the past, not recognizing that new choices are being neglected in the present. The therapist can help such caregivers explore their guilt and past regrets, while at the same time become aware of present daily needs and opportunities for life to move ahead. Here again, contact with other caregivers in support group settings can be very helpful to the caregiver who has become stuck in rumination about the past.

Acceptance and Behavior Therapy with Caregivers

There is a small treatment outcome literature that describes changes in depression, feelings of caregiver burden, and utilization of medical services following brief therapy with elderly caregivers. Most of the interventions described in these studies have included substantial behavioral components. For example, Lovett and Gallagher (1988) found that caregivers who attended 10 weeks of either a behaviorally-based group focusing on increasing pleasant events, or a cognitive, problem-solving group, experienced decreases in depression and increases in morale that were not observed in wait-list control subjects. Greene and Monahan (1987, 1989) reported significant reductions in caregiver anxiety, depression, and burden levels following eight weeks of group counseling which contained supportive, educational, and relaxation components. Teri and her colleagues (Teri, Logsdon, Wagner, & Uomoto, in press; Teri & Uomoto, 1991) have successfully used principles of social learning theory and behavior therapy to teach caregivers how to manage depression in AD patients by increasing levels of pleasant activity and decreasing aversive person-environment interactions. Although recent authors have noted that the clinical caregiver intervention research suffers from a variety of methodological problems (Toseland and Rossiter, 1989; Zarit & Teri, in press), it is evident that interventions grounded in behavioral theory have potential for helping caregivers manage both patient behaviors and the stresses of the caregiving role.

There is, however, no information to date regarding particular process components of these behavioral interventions that may enhance or detract from their effectiveness. In this paper we have suggested that the process of acceptance is one aspect of psychotherapy that might be systematically manipulated in intervention research with elderly caregivers. We have described a number of ways to help caregivers increase their awareness of past and immediate contingencies, and to enhance their ability to set and pursue realistic caretaking goals. Each of these are compatible with behavioral approaches that view caretaking as a person-environment interaction which develops through and is maintained by one's learning history. Where the proposed acceptance-based approach differs from existing behavioral treatment studies is in its emphasis on process and context, as opposed to intervention and outcome.

From a process perspective, acceptance is a way of relating to one's life that does not have a predictable topography or a predictable outcome, except in the context of particular client goals. Nevertheless, we predict that the process of acceptance can occur more readily under certain conditions, and that these conditions can be identified and, if shown to be useful to caregivers, made more readily accessible through practice. We further predict that caregivers trained in acceptance-based strategies would be less likely to get "stuck" in long periods of resignation or ineffectual action. However, it remains to be seen whether these predictions are empirically validated. Unfortunately, research on changing experiential process is difficult to conduct in controlled, group-design, treatment outcome studies. Therapists interested in evaluating the clinical impact of an acceptance-based orientation may need to rely more on single-case designs (such as multiple-baseline studies), or intensive descriptions of therapy interactions such as are found in discourse analysis or behavioral phenomenology (e.g., Leigland, 1989).

Therapists pursuing such research, however, should be aware of how easy it is to turn a dynamic process construct into a stagnant outcome goal. This danger is evident when examining how acceptance has come to be used in various stage theories of coping with chronic illness or emotional distress (Emery, 1982; Oliver & Bock, 1987; Teusink & Mahler, 1984). Such theories are often implicitly critical of caregivers who fail to achieve a specific outcome. For example, Teusink and Mahler (1984) note that acceptance "comes only *after* relatives...have worked through their anger and guilt, and have recognized that their loved one is no longer the person they once knew" (p.154, italics ours). Although well-intentioned, such approaches to acceptance can lead caregivers to feel that their inability to get rid of disbelief about the diagnosis, anger, guilt, resentment, or other negative thoughts and emotions are a weakness or failure on their part. In contrast, a contextually-based, process approach to acceptance can help caregivers focus instead on whether they are doing what will work best, at this time and in this circumstance, for both themselves and their patient, regardless of what thoughts, emotions, memories, or behavioral predispositions show up while they are doing it. Such an approach may also reduce the risk of therapists' falling into the role of expert judge, since ultimately, there is "no-thing" in particular the AD caregiver needs to experience, solve, or achieve. All that is needed is that caregivers be helped to identify opportunities to improve their current situation, and that these opportunities contain within them a sense of dignity, balance, and purpose. Beyond that, caregivers who are interacting with these opportunities will themselves discover how to be equal to the caretaking role they have been given.

References

Alzheimer's Disease and Related Disorders Association, Inc. *(ADRDA)*. (1991). Alzheimer's disease statistics. Brochure #ED 230Z. Chicago, IL: ADRDA.

American Association of Retired Persons *(AARP)*. (1986). A Profile of Older Persons: 1986. Washington, DC: American Association of Retired Persons.

Bergstone, A., Cheri, R., Zarit, S. H., & Gatz, M. (1988). Symptoms of psychological distress among caregivers of dementia patients. *Psychology and Aging, 3,* 245-248.

Biglan, A. (1989). A contextual approach to the clinical treatment of parental distress. In G. A. Singer & L. K. Irvin (Eds.), *Support for caregiving families enabling positive adaptation to disability* (pp. 299-311). Baltimore, MD: Paul H. Brookes Publishing Co.

Billings, G. (1992). A husband's retrospective. *The Caregiver: Duke Family Support Program Newsletter, 12,* 15.

Cantor, M. (1983). Strain among caregivers: A study of experience in the U.S. *Gerontologist, 23,* 597-604.

Clipp, E. C., & George, L. K. (1990). Psychotropic drug use among caregivers of patients with dementia. *Journal of the American Geriatrics Society, 38,* 227-235.

Emery, G. (1984). *Own your own life: How the new cognitive therapy can make you feel wonderful.* New York: Signet Books.

Erickson, E. (1964). *Insight and responsibility.* New York: Norton Books.

Gaynor, S. (1989). When the caregiver becomes the patient. *Geriatric Nursing, 10,* 121-123.

Gent, G. (1992). Carer's dementia. *The Caregiver: Duke Family Support Program Newsletter, 12,* 14.

Greene, V. L., Monahan, D. J. (1987). The effect of a professionally guided caregiver support and education group on institutionalization of care receivers. *Gerontologist, 27,* 716-721.

Greene, V.L., Monahan, D.J. (1989). The effect of a support and education program on stress and burden among family caregivers to frail elderly persons. *Gerontologist, 29,* 472-477.

Haley, W. E., Levine, E. G., Brown, S. L., Berry, J. W., & Hughes, G. H. (1987). Psychological, social, and health consequences of caring for a relative with senile dementia. *Journal of the American Geriatrics Society, 35,* 405-411.

Hayes, S.C., & Hayes, L. J. (1992) Verbal relations and the evolution of behavior analysis. *American Psychologist, 47,* 1383-1395.

Hayes, S. C., McCurry, S. M., Afari, N., & Wilson, K. (1991). *Acceptance and Commitment Therapy (ACT).* Reno, NV: Context Press.

Henderson, C. (1992). Musings. *The Caregiver: Duke Family Support Program Newsletter, 12,* 6.

Kiecolt-Glaser, J. K., & Glaser, R. (1991). Spousal caregivers of dementia victims: Longitudinal changes in immunity and health. *Psychosomatic Medicine, 53,* 345-362.

Kubler-Ross, E. (1969). *On death and dying.* New York: Macmillan Publishing Company, Inc.

Leigland, S. (1989). On the relation between radical behaviorism and the science of verbal behavior. *The Analysis of Verbal Behavior, 7,* 25-41.

Lovett, S., & Gallagher, D. (1988). Psychoeducational interventions for family caregivers: Preliminary efficacy data. *Behavior Therapy, 19,* 321-330.

Lustbader, W. (1991). *Counting on kindness.* New York: The Free Press.

Mendez, M. F., Martin, R., Smyth, K., & Whitehouse, P. (1990). Psychiatric symptoms associated with Alzheimer's disease. *Journal of Neuropsychiatry and Clinical Neurosciences, 2,* 28-33.

Oliver, R., & Bock, F. A. (1987). *Coping with Alzheimer's: A caregiver's emotional survival guide.* North Hollywood, CA: Wilshire Book Company.

Perspectives. (Winter, 1992). Alzheimer's Disease and Related Disorders Society of Puget Sound.

Pruchno, R., & Potashnik, S. (1989). Caregiving spouses: Physical and mental health in perspective. *Journal of the American Geriatrics Society, 37,* 697-705.

Rabins, P. V., Mace, N. L., & Lucas, M. J. (1982). The impact of dementia on the family. *Journal of the American Medical Association, 248 (July 16),* 333-335.

Schulz, R., & Williamson, G. (1991). A 2-year longitudinal study of depression among Alzheimer's caregivers. *Psychology and Aging, 6,* 569-578.

Teri, L. (1992). Personal communication. Department of Psychiatry and Behavioral Sciences, University of Washington.

Teri, L., Logsdon, R., Wagner, A., & Uomoto, J. (1994). The caregiver role in behavioral treatment of depression in dementia patients. In E. Light, G. Niederehe, & B. D. Lebowtiz, (Eds.), *Stress effects on family caregivings of Alzheimers patients.* (pp. 185-204). New York: Springer Publishing Co.

Teri, L., & Uomoto, J. (1991). Reducing excess disability in dementia patients: Training caregivers to manage patient depression. *Clinical Gerontologist, 10,* 49-63.

Teusink, J. P., & Mahler, S. (1984). Helping families cope with Alzheimer's disease. *Hospital and Community Psychiatry, 35,* 152-156.

Toseland, R. W., & Rossiter, C. M. (1989). Group interventions to support family caregivers: A review and analysis. *Gerontologist, 29,* 438-448.

Zarit, S. H., & Teri, L. (in press). Interventions and services for family caregivers. *Annual Review of Gerontology and Geriatrics, 11.*

Authors' Notes

This paper was supported in part by NIMH Grants #MH43266 and #MH19332. The authors gratefully acknowledge the comments and contributions of early reviewers of this paper, including Allan Fitz, Rebecca Logsdon, Christopher McCurry, Linda Teri, and Amy Wagner.

Discussion of McCurry and Schmidt

Caregiving in Context

Amy E. Naugle
University of Nevada

In their paper "Acceptance, Serenity, and Resignation in Elderly Caregivers," McCurry and Schmidt provide a thoughtful application of acceptance for a population whose clinical issues are complicated by the changing nature of their presenting problems. They offer a worthwhile integration of traditional behavior therapy and a contemporary understanding of acceptance, a traditionally nonbehavioral concept. The authors provoke one to respond to both their theoretical analysis of acceptance, as well as the implications the analysis has for applied clinical work. In my discussion of their chapter I will attempt to address issues they raise at each level of analysis.

Acceptance and Behavior Analysis

An appealing strength of the approach proposed by McCurry and Schmidt as well as the work of Hayes and his colleagues (e.g., Hayes & Wilson, in press; Kohlenberg, Hayes, & Tsai, 1993; Hayes, 1987) is the application of behavioral principles to adult outpatient psychotherapy. Although acceptance has been a familiar concept in other schools of psychotherapy, it has long been excluded from behavioral systems. One plausible reason may be due to the apparent complexity in subjecting such a term to a behavioral analysis. Kohlenberg and Tsai (1991) note that misunderstandings and distortions of what radical behaviorism is have hindered clinicians from applying its tenets to other complex human actions as well. For example, therapists unfamiliar with radical behavioral principles do not perceive thinking and feeling to be legitimate subject matter in a behavioral analysis. Although the authors do not explicitly provide a detailed analysis in this chapter, they allude to radical behavioral tenets in their attempt to define acceptance. It may be the lack of a technical analysis, however, that lends to the reader's confusion in understanding an exact definition of "acceptance".

McCurry and Schmidt offer a definition, which for all practical purposes, is derived through exclusion. They clearly state many of the things acceptance is not. In doing so, the analysis they provide of what acceptance is lacks precision. One criticism the authors offer of traditional definitions of acceptance is that they refer to an outcome or stage. What is not clear is how their alternative definition improves upon this criticism. Rather than focusing on acceptance as an outcome, acceptance is broadly defined in this chapter as an experiential process or action. McCurry and Schmidt further refine this definition, and appropriately, best identify the interactive nature of acceptance by what follows it, that is its function. This is consistent with the tradition of radical behaviorism where units of analysis are functionally defined rather than constructed based on form (e.g., Skinner, 1945). Acceptance, like any other response, should be defined in terms of its relationship to antecedents and consequences. However, in this case a functional analysis that specifies antecedents and consequences of the "situated action" (Hayes & Hayes, 1992) of acceptance appears to be missing. What is not clear is how acceptance is distinguishable from any other and all other actions. Is acceptance best understood as "action of no-action" or as "action of all action"?

Acceptance as a Dialectic

Although there is apparent confusion in the definition of acceptance proposed by the authors, there is also utility in the distinction they make between acceptance and resignation. If caregivers view resignation as a necessary component of their caregiving role, the opportunity for them to expand or improve their situation becomes limited. Resignation suggests that one deny their own feelings or needs in order to function effectively. In contrast, McCurry and Schmidt's premise of acceptance-interactions shifts the action of avoiding events to experiencing them. Taking this perspective not only acknowledges the caregiver's experiences at the moment, it grants permission for their experience to change. Acceptance allows a caregiver to simultaneously feel both love for the patient and resentment about their role. It is this type of dialectic that frequently characterizes the caregiver's role. Linehan (1993) uses the image of a teeter-totter to illustrate the concept of dialectics. In her treatment of Borderline Personality Disorder (BPD), she views the therapist and client on opposite ends of the teeter-totter. The process of therapy, in her illustration, involves "synthesizing" or balancing these opposites and moving ahead in the therapy process. Although the specific dialectics caregivers face are different than those of BPD clients, the need for balance or synthesis is not. A caregiver may experience feelings of love and serenity as well as feelings of annoyance and anger. The process of acceptance makes room for both of these experiences, not as discrete elements, but as a whole. Neither has to be changed or controlled for the caregiver to function effectively in their role. This concept of "wholeness" is elaborated in McCurry and Schmidt's reference to context. Their point that acceptance both creates and is created by the context is significant. McCurry and Schmidt offer insightful and important suggestions for clinical work with caregivers that exemplify this concept.

Facilitating the Process of Acceptance

The view of acceptance as a process implies that it is not sequential but continuous. If this is the case, the strategies McCurry and Schmidt offer for facilitating acceptance can also be understood as continuous. That is, awareness and making choices do not occur sequentially, but within the context of the caregiver's whole experience. Furthermore, neither of these treatment strategies needs to occur before the other, and both are essential to the process of acceptance and therapeutic change.

The art of awareness, the authors argue, involves being mindful of both external events and internal experiences. Although the specific techniques for increasing awareness of external events are different than for internal events, both are important in facilitating acceptance. It may be the case that increasing awareness in one area may lead to increased awareness in the other. For example, educating caregivers about the nature of the patient's illness may foster awareness of the multitude of existential issues that face the caregiver, including issues about their own death. Awareness in either sense shifts one away from the focus on specific caretaking responsibilities and provides the caregiver with an entirely different perspective.

In addition to increasing awareness, the authors also advocate the identification and pursuit of realistic goals for the caregiver. Therapy can be a useful resource to allow caregivers to set goals and make choices for themselves, rather than for the patient. This process can provide an important way for caregivers to discover or establish alternative sources of meaning in their lives distinct from their role as caretaker. Again, increasing awareness and pursuing goals do not occur in isolation from one another. Rather, goals and choices are created by increased awareness and in turn create additional awareness.

The intervention strategies offered by McCurry and Schmidt are both appealing and challenging. The clinical concerns caregivers report in therapy are not only different across clients, but also continually change within an individual caregiver's situation. No specific set of circumstances suitably characterize the caregiver role. The challenge for therapists is to refrain from adopting *a priori* a particular goal or outcome for their caregiver clients. The appeal of their approach is that it does not force us as therapists to provide clients with a specific set of rules or instructions in order to enhace their lives. Rather, the process of acceptance offers possibility and opportunity for novel alternatives and experiences to emerge, both within the context of therapy and in the caregivers life.

References

Hayes, S. C. (1987). A contextual approach to therapeutic change. In N. S. Jacobson (Ed.), *Psychotherapists in clinical practice: Cognitive and behavioral perspectives* (pp. 327-387). New York: Guilford Press.

Hayes, S. C., & Hayes, L. J. (1992). Verbal relations and the evolution of behavior analysis. *American Psychologist, 47,* 1383-1395.

Hayes, S. C., & Wilson, K. G. (in press). Acceptance and commitment therapy: Altering the verbal support for experiential avoidance. *Behavior Analyst*

Kohlenberg, R. J., Hayes, S. C., & Tsai, M. (1993). Radical behavior psychotherapy: Two contemporary examples. *Clinical Psychology Review, 13,* 579-592.

Kohlenberg, R. J., & Tsai, M. (1992). *Functional analytic psychotherapy: Creating intense and curative therapeutic relationships.* New York: Plenum Press.

Linehan, M. M. (1993). *Cognitive-behavioral treatment of borderline personality disorder.* New York: Guilford.

Skinner, B. F. (1945). The operational analysis of psychological terms. *Psychological Review, 52,* 270-277.

Chapter 13

Survivors of Child Sexual Abuse: Treatment using a Contextual Analysis

Victoria M. Follette
University of Nevada

The greatest good you can do for another is not just to share with her your own riches, but to reveal to her her own. Disraeli

In recent years there has been a dramatic increase in the literature focusing on the long term correlates of childhood sexual abuse (CSA; Browne & Finkelhor, 1986; Polusny & Follette, in press). Despite this increase in the empirical literature, frequently there has not been a concomitant elaboration of the theoretical model that would provide a basis for understanding the interrelationship of the many symptoms associated with abuse. This chapter will use the paradigm of emotional avoidance in conceptualizing the long term correlates of CSA. General treatment issues in working with CSA survivors that arise from this conceptualization will be presented, followed by a discussion of the therapist factors that are relevant to treatment. Finally, cultural issues relevant to the abuse of women will be considered.

The prevalence of CSA has been documented repeatedly in both community and clinical samples, with estimates ranging from 15 to 33% (Briere & Runtz, 1989; Finkelhor, Hotaling, Lewis, & Smith, 1990; Saunders, Villeponteaux, Lipovsky, & Veronen, 1992; Wyatt, 1985). While there is some debate over the actual frequency of abuse, related in part to sampling procedures and definitions of abuse, it is generally accepted that about one-third of women in the United States will experience some form of sexual victimization before reaching the age of 18 (Briere, 1992). Moreover, when one examines some clinical populations, approximately 50% of female clients report some abuse history, whether or not that is the presenting complaint (Briere & Zaidi, 1989). Recently, clinicians and researchers have begun to realize that sexual abuse in males is more common than had previously been thought, with prevalence estimates at about 10% in a national sample (Finkelhor et al., 1990). While this is obviously an important issue, the conceptualization presented here has been based almost entirely on work with females. The pandemic nature of child sexual abuse in women warrants an in-depth examination of not only the impact of that abuse on adult functioning, but also factors (including treatment) that may serve to alleviate problems that the survivor encounters.

Psychological Functioning and Emotional Avoidance

Long term correlates of CSA tend to run the gamut of clinical syndromes. Depression, anxiety, couple problems, and general difficulties with interpersonal relationships are just a few of the issues that have been associated with being an abuse survivor (Browne & Finkelhor, 1986). In past reviews of the CSA literature, researchers have frequently used the term "effects" to describe the symptoms associated with sexual abuse. However, the correlational nature of almost all of the literature to date does not allow the inference of a direct causal relationship between sexual abuse and long term psychological problems. Thus, it seems more useful to consider child sexual abuse as a distal risk factor that can lead to the development of a number of painful and serious adult difficulties.

When one considers the pervasiveness of the problems faced by CSA survivors, it is not surprising that they are found in a variety of clinical contexts and are not only presenting for therapy related to abuse experiences. In addition to assessing other distal variables, such as characteristics of the family of origin, it is essential to examine more proximal variables that influence the development and maintenance of current symptoms. Obviously, current intimate relationships, work stressors, and economic difficulties also have an impact on adult functioning. Adult trauma experiences may be particularly important in reactivating symptoms associated with child sexual abuse.

Because of its nature, child sexual abuse involves both physical and psychological danger to the victim. As noted by Herman, "Traumatic events are extraordinary, not because they occur rarely, but rather because they overwhelm the ordinary human adaptations to life" (1992, p. 33). The child is overwhelmed by sexual aspects of the abuse that she is not physically or psychologically prepared to accommodate. Additionally, the sexual abuse is frequently accompanied by physical and verbal abuse. The violation of interpersonal trust and safety issues, particularly when the abuse is perpetrated by a family member, are important factors in understanding the sequelae of abuse that can include significant problems in relating to others (Briere, 1992). Therefore, it is clear that the abuse cannot be considered in isolation and that a contextual analysis of the experience is warranted.

A behavioral analysis of the long term correlates of sexual abuse is particularly appealing because it is inherently respectful of the client. All of the behaviors discussed in this chapter make sense when considered in conjunction with their historical context. Thus, it is not the case that the survivor is "broken" or somehow defective, but rather that her behavioral repertoire, established during childhood, no longer functions in a way that is life enhancing to her. Some of these repertoires can increase vulnerability to further punishing experiences (such as revictimization) and may also preclude access to new reinforcers. An awareness of these issues is critical not only to understanding the symptoms associated with CSA but also to a comprehension of aspects of the client's in session behavior, which will be discussed later.

Trauma researchers have suggested that many of the sequelae associated with abuse represent attempts to avoid the memories and affects that are related to the abuse experience (Briere, 1992; Herman, 1992; Polusny & Follette, in press). Herman (1992) notes that the child who suffers recurrent abuse experiences will experience disproportionately high frequencies of dysphoric emotions, most generally anxiety and depression. Specifically, the anxiety symptoms observed are frequently characteristic of the diagnosis of Post Traumatic Stress Disorder (PTSD; Briere & Runtz, 1991) or the more recently proposed syndrome, Complex Post-Traumatic Stress Disorder (Herman, 1992). A great many studies have documented that a CSA history is significantly correlated with major depression as an adult (Bifulco, Brown, & Adler, 1991; Burnam et al., 1988; Pribor & Dinwiddie, 1992). Sexual abuse often occurs in an environment that is generally invalidating to the child. As noted by Linehan (1993), there are two important features to the invalidation that a child may experience. The child is told repeatedly that "she is wrong in both her description and her analyses of her own experiences," and that she is basically unacceptable as she is (Linehan, 1993, p. 49-50). Thus, this chronic invalidation and victimization can establish an affective state that will continue to be typically dysphoric, even after the abuse stops.

Emotional avoidance can be characterized as an unwillingness to experience unpleasant internal events such as thoughts and feelings associated with the abuse (Hayes, 1987). This unwillingness results in attempts to avoid those stimuli which have been negatively evaluated through a variety of mechanisms, including substance abuse, dissociation, bulimia and other tension reducing behaviors. The avoidance of emotional experiencing is then negatively reinforced by the removal of the acute dysphoric feelings. Returning to traditional descriptions of abuse sequelae, many survivors report re-experiencing of the sexual abuse through dreams, flashbacks, or intrusive images. In some sense the survivor is in a paradoxical state that involves both avoidance of the abuse related memories and an obsessive remembering of those experiences. This aspect of remembering in relation to the abuse is critical in that by remaining under the control of the historical event of the abuse, the survivor is prevented from coming under the control of events in the current context. This may have important implications for later revictimization, a point to be addressed later in the chapter.

Again, somewhat paradoxically to the survivor's lack of sensitivity to environmental cues, she is at times hypervigilant, particularly in relationship to the behaviors of significant others in the environment. This phenomena is familiar to trauma researchers and has been described by Herman (1992) as the dialectic of trauma. Specifically, the survivor vacillates between these two extreme patterns of over, and under-sensitivity to environmental stimuli. In the therapy session, this can result in the acute sensitivity of the survivor that is often observed by clinicians. Kohlenberg and Tsai (1991) note that exquisitely small changes in the behavior of the therapist can serve as a discriminative stimulus for large changes in the survivor's thoughts and feelings about herself. This acute awareness, which often can be a misinterpretation of the therapist's behavior, can result in the marked mood shifts and changes in observable behavior that is seen in some survivors. These sudden and dramatic changes can be confusing or distressing to others, including the therapist, and can lead to an interaction that deteriorates in utility for both participants.

Dissociation is seen by many trauma researchers as a common and expected symptom associated with surviving any long term abuse experience (Briere, 1992; Herman, 1992). Dissociation is described in the DSM IV as "a disruption in the usually integrated functions of consciousness, memory, identity, or perception of the environment" (American Psychiatric Association, 1994, p. 477). While the construct of dissociation is frequently associated with a psychodynamic conceptualization, it is not inconsistent with a behavioral paradigm. Dissociation may be conceptualized as motivated escape or avoidance of thoughts, memories, and feelings associated with the highly aversive experience of the abuse. In that, a behavioral view of memory does not incorporate traditional storage metaphors, but rather is seen as an action. Remembering is an activity not unlike other behaviors (Kohlenberg & Tsai, 1991).

When one considers that a child has limited means of coping with the overwhelming feelings associated with the aversive events surrounding the abuse, the child is motivated to escape or avoid those feelings. Thus, dissociation, or not remembering, makes sense as a strategy employed by the child, as she rarely has any other reasonable choice as an avoidance mechanism. That is, families in which incest occurs are often rather closed systems, with the child having restricted access to outside sources of support. The child, being dependent on the adult, and often mortally afraid of the perpetrator, does not have a sense that safety through exposure of the abuse is possible. This remains partially true even today, despite the increased visibility of child protective services and education regarding abuse. Therefore, the child who must remain in the situation and endure the abuse is best served by a psychological avoidance of the experience. The repeated exposure to the aversive events of the abuse (as well as a number of other stressors that may occur in the family of origin) and the use of a repertoire involving dissociation to reduce the aversive properties of the abuse, results in an overlearned strategy that impairs later adult functioning. The range of the dissociation repertoires varies and in its most elaborated form results in what is known as multiple personality. Kohlenberg and Tsai (1991) have provided an interesting behavioral description of this phenomena which is beyond the scope of this chapter to review. However, what is critical to note here is that all of this behaving, that is dissociation in all of its forms, is in the service of avoidance, of not having one's history. That history is often associated with such painful affects and memories that to experience those behaviors would be terrifying and may even seem life threatening to the survivor.

Once again, there is a paradox involving dissociation and hypervigilance. The survivor may be acutely fearful of danger in the environment and yet inadequately in contact with stimuli that would allow her to avoid that danger. This fluctuation in processes is one probable factor in the increased risk of revictimization that is observed in survivors. Moreover, it does not appear that once abused, women are invulnerable to the effects of additional abusive incidents. In a recent survey of women presenting for services at community agencies, we found evidence for cumulative negative effects related to multiple victimization experiences that included CSA, rape, and domestic violence (Follette, Polusny, Bechtle, & Naugle, in press).

Self destructive behaviors are also frequently observed in CSA survivors. Increased rates of both suicidal ideation and suicide attempts have been documented in this population (Briere & Zaidi; 1989, Saunders, et al. 1992). Of course, suicide can be viewed as the most extreme form of avoidance. Hayes (1992) notes that verbal behavior allows the construction of rules equating death with relief–the end of suffering. In a related manner, Linehan (1993) describes suicide as a form of problem solving behavior. For the survivor whose other attempts at avoidance are insufficient to deal with the trauma, suicide may seem to be the only solution.

Self-mutilation is a behavior that has been related to suicide and has also been labeled as parasuicide (Linehan, 1993). These behaviors are varied in their topography, including for example, cutting, burning, and ingestion of injurious substances. Despite differences in form, these behaviors share a similar function in that they serve to distract the survivor from negatively evaluated internal states such as anxiety and thoughts about the abuse experience. These behaviors tend to be non-life threatening, and because clients are often secretive about self-mutilation, its prevalence may be underestimated (Courtois, 1988). The client may not experience pain while inflicting the injury on herself and at times some individuals have reported feeling relieved after engaging in the behavior (van der Kolk, Perry, & Herman, 1991). Conversely, some survivors report using self mutilation to terminate dissociative states. Thus, a contextual analysis of the behavior is needed in order to determine its function for the client.

The relationship between CSA and somatic complaints, including somatization disorder, has also been documented in the literature (Fry, 1993). A number of medical problems have been studied in this regard. Gynecological problems, gastrointestinal complaints, and other unexplained chronic physical problems have been reported to be higher in frequency for CSA survivors. This somatization may function in two ways. First, it may function to distract the survivor from negative internal experiences that are more generally interpreted in psychological terms. Second, in that emotions are generally accompanied by bodily sensations, the tendency to somaticize may occur as a result of mislabeling of those physical sensations that accompany emotion, with the focus being solely on the somatic aspect of the experience. This medical labeling of internal experiences may receive more support in the survivor's social environment, both as a child and an adult, in that it serves to support the emotional avoidance of other individuals in the environment. The expression of negative affective states may have been punished because acknowledgment of them may have led to an investigation of the sources of those negative emotions. However, it is important to be aware that the individual with somatization disorder may have undiagnosed physical problems, problems that may even be related to the physical trauma associated with the abuse (Polusny & Follette, in press).

Researchers have also identified a link between substance abuse and a history of CSA. Both in community and treatment seeking samples, there is an increased prevalence of alcohol and drug abuse when women with an abuse history are compared to nonabused women (Briere & Runtz, 1987; Briere & Zaidi, 1989; Burnam et al., 1988; Pribor & Dinwiddie, 1992). Addictive behaviors in trauma survivors probably also serve as emotional avoidance mechanisms, functioning as a form of "chemically induced dissociation" (Briere & Runtz, 1987). Survivors report that substance use helps them to cope with, and at times avoid, the memories and affects associated with the abuse. Some survivors report substance use prior to therapy sessions, again to alleviate the distress that is experienced when doing trauma related work.

Interpersonal Issues

Given that sexual abuse frequently occurs within the context of an important interpersonal relationship (particularly in the case of incest), it is hardly surprising that many survivors have impaired relational repertoires. Survivors' adult couple relationships have been described as "stormy and troubled" by Herman (1981). The survivor may describe herself as having problems with trust, communication and intimacy in relationships. In that intimate relationships have proved very dangerous for the survivor of abuse, she may avoid these situations all together. However, many survivors will enter into couple relationships and the relationship itself becomes a cue for the avoidance of the feelings and thoughts associated with closeness to another person. While avoiding these experiences, which the survivor labels as negative, she simultaneously loses access to the directly positive benefits, or consequences, of being in a close supportive relationship. This can lead to an increased sense of loneliness and alienation, even in the context of a relationship. It should be made clear that much of the literature that describes the difficulties experienced by CSA survivors in relationships is anecdotal and little empirical literature exists to document these impressions.

Research has examined the adult sexual functioning of this population. The dialectic of trauma is again evident in this domain. The survivor may be either highly avoidant of sexual activity or may engage in sexual activity in a compulsive way. While some survivors will remain primarily at one end of this continuum, others will vacillate between the two poles. The data suggests that survivors have a number of sexual disorders (Saunders et al., 1992) and report less sexual satisfaction (Jackson, Calhoun, Amick, Maddever, & Habif, 1990). The survivor may demonstrate a great deal of restraint in sexual matters, seeking to control her desires (Wyatt, Newcomb, & Riederle, 1993) or may engage in indiscriminate and high risk sexuality, including commercial sex or prostitution (Briere & Runtz, 1993; Zierler, Feingold, Laufer, Velentgas, Kantrowitz-Gordon, & Mayer, 1991). Regardless of the form of expression taken, these extremely polarized positions in relation to sexuality both seem to represent forms of intimacy avoidance. Moreover, the survivor may find that she is only able to engage in sexual behavior when using drugs or alcohol, thus chemically dissociating herself from the experience (Briere, 1992). Unfortunately, this use of substances has the additional negative consequence of decreasing the probability that she will successfully be able to engage in behavior, such as requesting condom use, that would decrease her risk of exposure to HIV (Clapper & Lipsitt, 1991).

The survivor of CSA is apparently at risk for a number of other interpersonal difficulties. Survivors experience more social isolation (Harter, Alexander, & Neimeyer, 1988) and parenting difficulties (Browne & Finkelhor, 1986). It is well documented that survivors experience increased rates of revictimization, including rape (Wyatt, Guthrie, & Notgrass, 1992), and domestic violence (Briere & Runtz, 1987). More research is needed in order to determine the specific variables that are associated with this increased risk. However, it is clear that this revictimization will lead to an increase in trauma symptoms, including avoidance strategies (Follette, et al., in press).

Acceptance Based Therapy

Acceptance and Commitment Therapy (ACT), developed by Hayes and his colleagues, is a contextual, behaviorally based therapeutic approach which emphasizes the role of emotional avoidance as an underlying theme in a great many clinical problems (Hayes, 1987). In ACT, the avoidance of emotions and other private events is viewed as the primary problem that must be addressed in treatment. Many CSA survivors come for treatment with the agenda of learning how to be in better control of their historically grounded reactions to abuse experiences. As noted above, most of the long term correlates associated with CSA , such as dissociation, substance abuse, and suicide attempts, can be conceptualized as the avoidance of abuse specific affects and memories. Therefore, in evaluating these long term correlates, it seems that ACT therapy is particularly well suited to this population.

The actual details of implementing ACT have been described in other places (Hayes, McCurry, Afari, & Wilson, 1993). Therefore the specifics of therapy will not be elaborated here. Rather, issues critical to the implementation of ACT with survivors will be presented. The essence of ACT has been characterized by its developers as describable in two words: hold and move (Hayes et al., 1993). That is, the therapy centers around giving the survivor a history such that she can hold (accept) what she has in terms of emotions, thoughts, and bodily states and move, making commitments to engage in behaviors that will enhance the quality of her life.

Thus, the ultimate goal in ACT, as in most therapies, is to assist the client in making changes in her life. The approach in facilitating these changes relies on the introduction of language conventions and the use of metaphors that break away from the support that the verbal community gives to emotional avoidance. As noted by Hayes (1987), all of us face the problems that arise from verbal behavior. Verbal behavior is generally seen as defining the self and exerting control over our overt responses. Survivors, who are particularly prone to negative self evaluation, at times describing themselves as bad, evil, or sick, are extremely vulnerable to the pitfalls of using verbal behavior to define the self. Coupled with this negative self evaluation is often times an inability to consider the possibility of positive life changes. Once again, the survivor finds herself in a paradoxical situation in which she is preoccupied with attempts to control verbal behavior, while feeling out of control of overt behavioral responding.

In that light, a great deal of the ACT work involves attacking the agenda of the control of thoughts and feelings. In the early phase of treatment, the therapist works to establish a context from which the client is willing to consider alternatives to prior strategies she has used. The therapist reviews with the client all of the methods that she has tried in the past to exert control over her internal experiences. For the survivor this may include dissociating, avoiding close relationships, substance abuse, and other symptoms discussed earlier in the chapter. The therapist and client examine the utility of these behaviors and the fact that the client is in treatment suggests that these strategies are not optimally effective. Further, we explain to the client that there is no way that we or anyone else can help her to forget or get away from her abuse history.

Control is an enormous issue for CSA survivors and it is important to be clear about this point. Women who were sexually abused had no control over their own lives, nor their own bodies. Because of this inability to have external behavioral control, such as stopping the sexual abuse, most survivors learned to numb themselves and avoid psychological and even physical contact with the abuse experience. Therefore, emotional avoidance made perfect sense at that point in their lives: it was useful in helping the survivor to cope with the abuse as a child. So when the client is told that control is the problem, the therapist must be careful to validate what the client did to survive. At the same time, the therapist and client can work together to examine how well those strategies are currently functioning.

Once the client has experienced that the control of private events is not only not fully possible but also no longer useful, the therapist begins work on the self. This aspect of the treatment focuses on identifying the self as the context for action. The idea of the self as context is that people are not their thoughts or feelings but rather the context in which they occur.

Many survivors, particularly those who come from extremely dysfunctional families or those whose abuse was very early in its onset, have severe disturbances of the self. Linehan (1993) has described how the invalidating parental environment that is combined with punishing a wide range of behaviors in the child can lead to the development of Borderline Personality Disorder (BPD). A review of the empirical literature suggests some overlap in this disorder and the occurrence of CSA (Polusny & Follette, in press). Characteristics of the abuse, and the families in which such abuse occurs, map well on to the conditions that lead to difficulties in experiencing a contextual sense of the self. When the individual experiences control as coming from outside the self, as is the case when the child's behavior is under the control of aversive stimuli such as abuse, an unstable self will develop (Kohlenberg & Tsai, 1991).

In fact, for clients with an abuse history, there is continued reinforcement of the avoidance of the self as context. The awareness of the self has been paired with thoughts and feelings that seem too threatening to be experienced and thus are avoided at all costs. The client, in essence, hides from her own history, living from moment to moment. She experiences the self as content; that is, she thinks that she is the thoughts and feelings that she experiences and has a rather discontinuous sense of self. This explains why she may at times feel as mystified by her own actions as outside observers do.

This difficulty in experiencing the self as context, coupled with the serious deficits in relational repertoires, contraindicate the immediate implementation of ACT as it has traditionally been defined. For example, because of the threat involved in close interpersonal relating, early in the therapy the client may experience difficulty in attending to the therapist's verbal behavior and in making discriminations that are appropriate to the situation. In some instances the client may be extremely frightened of the therapist, including fears of being struck or berated in session. Therefore, many CSA survivors will benefit from therapy early on that is aimed particularly at those problems in relating.

The use of Functional Analytic Psychotherapy (FAP; Kohlenberg & Tsai, 1991) is one mode of treatment that can serve to remediate the problems in basic relating. Extensive amounts of time, often months, is spent building an intense therapeutic relationship with the client. This relationship creates a new history for the client, a history in which it is safe to trust, to be cared about and to care about another individual. Identifying clinically relevant behaviors is critical in strengthening or shaping new and more adaptive repertoires in relating. Moreover, it is within the context of this intense therapeutic relationship that the client can begin the process of identifying a sense of self. (See chapter 7, Cordova & Kohlenberg, for a detailed description of this therapy).

I do not mean to imply that these therapy components (ACT and FAP) are used sequentially in the treatment of the survivor or that they represent distinct entities as they are used in this work. Rather, the treatments are intertwined, with varying emphasis on one or the other depending on the client's needs at that time. This form of therapy should not be seen as an eclectic mix of treatments. Both ACT and FAP share roots in radical behaviorism with its contextual understanding of reality. Additionally, FAP has as a specific goal the task of producing the intense relationship that is generally required to do ACT work with CSA survivors. In my experience, many clients would not have tolerated some of what the treatment requires of them until the essential ground work of the relationship had been well established.

A standard part of almost all therapies for CSA survivors is having the client tell the story of her abuse. Generally, the client tells her story many times, with the first telling often involving very little affect on the client's part. As the therapy progresses, the client is able to tell more details and to fully come into contact with the thoughts and feelings associated with the abuse that she had avoided for so long. The safety of the therapy setting, with the structure of the setting providing a holding environment for the overwhelming feelings of the client, allows the client to explore the abuse issues. The therapist's task then is to provide a safe therapy environment, a place where the client can give up the agenda of control. This process can be a precarious one for the client. The therapist should be aware that there is some risk of decompensation. Particularly, there is a risk for increased suicidal ideation and even suicide attempts. Thus, the therapist should work at the client's pace, doing what is necessary to ensure the client's safety.

As the client gradually experiences the hopeless nature of the agenda of experiential control, the therapist moves into a phase of treatment in which the self becomes the context for action. At this point, willingness to change becomes possible as the client gives up the tug of war with her own abuse history. Thoughts and feelings are labeled as private events that may come and go but that do not serve to define the person. Assisting the client to attain an observer perspective, where the self is the context for these internal experiences, is a critical part of the treatment. The extensive use of metaphors and experiential exercises are part of the method for the work in this phase of treatment.

At this point in the therapy, more traditional modes of behavioral treatments are often employed. The client, having given up the war of not having her own history, can set the direction for her life, identifying changes that will lead to richer opportunities for reinforcement. The setting of goals with the client is a collaborative task, with efforts made by the therapist to minimize power hierarchies that may exist. Consequently, it is the task of the therapist to implement ACT in a manner that is empowering to the client, assisting her to set the agenda for goals and values for her life.

Therapist Factors

It is not only the client's avoidance that is at issue here. Many difficulties may also arise for the therapist in this process. As noted above, a standard part of the therapy is frequently allowing the client to tell the story of her abuse. She may need to tell the story many times, elaborating the details and coming into contact with the affects associated with the abuse. Clients' abuse experiences can cover a wide range of circumstances. While some clients may report relatively circumscribed episodes of fondling, many others have more extensive abuse histories involving penetration, physical abuse, threats and multiple perpetrators. When one considers that this telling of the clients' history occurs in the context of a close interpersonal relationship, it is impossible to imagine that the therapist will not also feel some of the pain that the client is experiencing. It is essential that the therapist is herself willing to hear all of the details that the client wants to discuss and willing to be in the presence of intense affect. The sadness, rage, and other emotions that the client may experience is often beyond what the therapist has previously even been able to imagine as possible. While it may seem obvious that this exposure is a part of the therapist's task, one cannot be too glib about the ability of individuals to be willing and able to engage in this process.

Moreover, the therapist must not simply be a witness to this work on the part of the client. She must also be able to respond empathically to the client. The therapist must have it in her repertoire to do what she is asking of her client, to experience and respond to intense feelings (Kohlenberg & Tsai, 1991). One must also remember that the CSA client is often quite vigilant with respect to cues from others. If the client detects any unwillingness on the part of the therapist to fully engage the task, the client may subtly pull away from the treatment goals, protecting not only herself but also the therapist. Simply put, the therapist is as much a part of acceptance and commitment therapy as the client.

How is the therapist to deal with these difficult issues? First, I believe that it is essential for the therapist to be a part of a supervision or consultation group. This group can provide a safe place for the therapist to process her own thoughts and feelings associated with the work. The right environment can free her to experience her own feelings without regard to the client's reactions, as must happen in session. As Linehan (1993) has noted, the supervision group can treat the therapist so that she is able to do the work necessary to treat the client. Second, the therapist must be aware of her own needs and limits and may need to limit her caseload, recognizing that in order to be effective she will not be able to treat all clients that are referred to her. Finally, it is important that the therapist structure her life such that she is in contact not only with the pain that is part of existence, but also so that she is in contact with the joy that is part of the fully lived life. For this is what the therapist also brings to the therapy. By her nature, she can share with the client what is possible—that there is something beyond the blackness and pain that has characterized much of the clients life to this time.

Cultural Factors

We live in a culture where a simple fact of biology, being a woman, puts her in danger. That danger can be physical, sexual, or emotional. This is not to deny that everyone is at risk, especially in our increasingly violent culture. Although it seems clear that there is some indisputable danger related simply to being female, there has been some recent controversy regarding the issues of child sexual abuse. The debate regarding the validity of memories of sexual abuse may be partly related to a cultural denial regarding the issue of abuse. Of course, there may be some therapists who engage in inappropriate and dangerous practices regarding sexual abuse memory and trauma work. Because of the damage to actual and "constructed" survivors of abuse, we would be the first to decry such therapy practices. However, in our experience this phenomenon is rare, and it seems that the intensity of the response of some proponents of the "false memory" movement is fueled by a backlash against the acceptance of the occurrence of child sexual abuse. Despite this controversy, statistics regarding the prevalence of child sexual abuse, domestic violence, and rape remain fairly constant. Moreover, this violence is not limited solely to events occurring within the family. Recently there have been well substantiated reports that women have been raped in a programmatic way as a part of the war in Bosnia.

Therefore, I believe that we must work to change the culture in which these acts of violence occur. Skinner said, "A society will be cured if it can be changed in such a way that a person is generously and consistently reinforced and therefore fulfills him/herself by acquiring and exhibiting the most successful behavior of which s/he is capable" (1974, p. 204). I would argue that this is not possible when one lives with constant threat or fear of violence. The culture must change in such a way that it will no longer tolerate the sacrifice of women's fullest potential in the service of domination and control.

Kohlenberg and Tsai (1991) note that individuals in the culture have lost contact with the consequences of their behavior. In the case of violence against women, I think that we have no real sense of what we as a people could be, or what relationships between men and women could be, if that violence were to stop. It is not enough to sit in our offices and quietly do our work, helping our clients to deal with the wounds of a lifetime. We must be active outside of that small space, working to change our culture to one in which such oppression is no longer useful and therefore does not exist.

References

American Psychiatric Press (1994). Diagnostic and statistical manual of mental disorders, Fourth Edition. Washington D.C.: American Psychiatric Association.

Bifulco, A., Brown, G. W., & Adler, Z. (1991). Early sexual abuse and clinical depression in adult life. *British Journal of Psychiatry, 159*, 115-122.

Briere, J. (1992). *Child abuse trauma: Theory and treatment of the lasting effects.* Newbury Park, CA: Sage.

Briere, J., & Runtz, M. (1987). Post sexual abuse trauma: Data and implications for clinical practice. *Journal of Interpersonal Violence, 2*, 367-379.

Briere, J., & Runtz, M. (1989). The Trauma Symptom Checklist (TSC-33). Early data on a new scale. *Journal of Interpersonal Violence, 4*, 151-163.

Briere, J., & Runtz, M. (1991). The long-term effects of sexual abuse: A review and synthesis. In J. Briere, (Ed.), *Treating victims of child sexual abuse.* San Francisco, CA: Jossey-Bass.

Briere, J., & Runtz, M. (1993). Childhood sexual abuse: Long-term sequelae and implications for psychological assessment. *Journal of Interpersonal Violence, 8*, 312-330.

Briere, J., & Zaidi, L. Y. (1989). Sexual abuse histories and sequelae in female psychiatric emergency room patients. *American Journal of Psychiatry, 146*, 1602-1606.

Browne, A., & Finkelhor, D. (1986). Impact of child sexual abuse: A review of the research. *Psychological Bulletin, 99*, 66-77.

Burnam, M. A., Stein, J. A., Golding, J. M., Siegel, J. M., Sorenson, S. B., Forsythe, A. B., & Telles, C. A. (1988). Sexual assault and mental disorders in a community population. *Journal of Consulting and Clinical Psychology*, 56, 843-850.

Clapper, R. L., & Lipsitt, L. P. (1991). A retrospective study of risk-taking and alcohol-mediated unprotected intercourse. *Journal of Substance Abuse*, 3, 91-96.

Courtois, C. C. (1988). *Healing the incest wound: Adult survivors in therapy.* New York: Norton.

Finkelhor, D., Hotaling, G., Lewis, I. A., & Smith, C. (1990). Sexual abuse in a national survey of adult men and women: Prevalence, characteristics, and risk factors. *Child Abuse & Neglect, 14*, 19-28.

Follette, V. M., Polusny, M. A., Bechtle A., & Naugle, A. E. (In press). Cumulative trauma effects: The impact of child sexual abuse, adult sexual assault, and spouse abuse. *Journal of Traumatic Stress.*

Fry, R. (1993). Adult physical illness and childhood sexual abuse. *Journal of Psychosomatic Research, 37*, 89-103.

Harter, S., Alexander, P. C., & Neimeyer, R. A. (1988). Long-term effects of incestuous child abuse in college women: Social adjustment, social cognition, and family characteristics. *Journal of Consulting and Clinical Psychology, 56*, 5-8.

Hayes, S. C. (1987). A contextual approach to therapeutic change. In N. S. Jacobson (Ed.), *Psychotherapists in clinical practice: Cognitive and behavioral perspectives.* (Pp. 327-387). New York: Guilford.

Hayes, S. C. (1992). Verbal Relations: Time and Suicide. In S. C. Hayes and L. J. Hayes (Eds.), *Understanding Verbal Relations.* (pp. 109-118). Reno: Context Press

Hayes, S. C., McCurry, S. M., Afari, N., & Wilson, K. Acceptance and Commitment Therapy. Unpublished manual.

Herman, J. L. (1981). *Father-daughter incest.* Cambridge: Harvard University Press.

Herman, J. L. (1992). *Trauma and recovery.* Basic Books.

Jackson, J. L., Calhoun, K. S., Amick, A. A., Maddever, H. M., & Habif, V. L. (1990). Young adult women who report childhood intrafamilial sexual abuse: Subsequent adjustment. *Archives of Sexual Behavior, 19*, 211-221.

Kohlenberg, R. J., & Tsai, M. (1991). *Functional analytic psychotherapy: Creating intense and curative therapeutic relationships.* New York: Plenum Press.

Linehan, M. M. (1993). *Cognitive-behavioral treatment of borderline personality disorder.* New York: Guilford.

Polusny, M. A., & Follette, V. M. (in press). Long term correlates of child sexual abuse: Theory and review of the empirical literature. *Applied and Preventive Psychology: Current Scientific Perspectives.*

Pribor, E. F., & Dinwiddie, S. H. (1992). Psychiatric correlates of incest in childhood. *American Journal of Psychiatry, 149*, 52-56.

Saunders, B. E., Villeponteaux, L. A., Lipovsky, J. A., Kilpatrick, D. G., & Veronen, L. J. (1992). Child sexual assault as a risk factor for mental health disorders among women: A community sample. *Journal of Interpersonal Violence, 7*, 189-204.

Skinner, B. F. (1974). About Behaviorism. New York: Knopf.

van der Kolk, B. A., Perry, J. C., Herman, J. L. (1991). Childhood origins of self-destructive behavior. *American Journal of Psychiatry, 148*, 1665-1671.

Wyatt, G. (1985). The sexual abuse of Afro-American and White-American women in childhood. *Child Abuse & Neglect, 9*, 507-519.

Wyatt, G. E., Guthrie, D., & Notgrass, C. M. (1992). Differential effects of women's child sexual abuse and subsequent sexual revictimization. *Journal of Consulting and Clinical Psychology, 60*, 167- 173.

Wyatt, G. E., Newcomb, M. D., & Riederle, M. H. (1993). *Sexual abuse and consensual sex: Women's developmental patterns and outcomes*. Newbury Park, CA: Sage.

Zierler, S., Feingold, L., Laufer, D., Velentgas, P., Kantrowitz-Gordon, I., & Mayer, K. (1991). Adult survivors of childhood sexual abuse and subsequent risk for HIV infection. *American Journal of Public Health, 81*, 572-575.

Discussion of Follette

Acceptance and Sexual Abuse Survivors: The Cultural and Therapeutic Context

Heidi L. Heard
University of Washington

It is difficult to imagine any other area in which acceptance has played as dramatic and controversial a role as it has played in the understanding and treatment of the sequelae of sexual abuse, and in which non-acceptance has had such devastating effects. For a significant period in the history of psychotherapy, both the general culture and the psychiatric establishment either ignored or even denied that sexual abuse, and childhood sexual abuse specifically, was as prevalent as data now suggests it is. As a result, only in recent decades have clinical researchers developed and tested treatments which attend specifically to the sequelae of sexual abuse survivors. In her chapter, Victoria Follette, one of these clinical researchers, describes her treatment, which has as a primary goal the helping of the client to achieve a comprehensive acceptance of abuse which includes acknowledging that the abuse occurred, addressing issues about ones own involvement in a non-judgemental manner, and allowing the experience of emotions and memories without inhibiting or extending them.

Although Follette's therapy focuses on the treatment of the client, we must remember that it does not occur in isolation of the broader therapeutic and cultural context. The therapist treating the client as well as the broader culture in which the client lives each have their own set of feelings, beliefs, and responses toward sexual abuse. Issues related to the treatment of sexual abuse which arise in treatment occur in these broader contexts as well. For example, the larger culture still debates whether or not abuse occurs to the degree that current data suggests, and therapist themselves can have difficulty tolerating the distress of their clients memories and emotions. The degree to which non-acceptance in the culture and/or in the therapist, influences the clients therapeutic progress remains unclear, but if we want to teach clients to accept, it seems essential to consider the ways in which we as therapists or as a culture may inhibit our clients from accepting, and may even model non-acceptance ourselves. In this discussion, I will briefly describe several of the ways in which issues that Follette addresses in her treatment of the client also exist as issues for the larger culture and the therapist.

Cultural Context

The first issue that arises for sexual abuse survivors is acceptance of the fact that they did experience sexual abuse. For many clients, and particularly in the case of childhood abuse, the acknowledgment of the abuse constitutes one of the major challenges of the treatment. Historically, the non-acceptance of the occurrence of sexual abuse has existed within both the general culture and the more specific culture of the psychiatric community. We can easily trace the controversy over the acknowledgment of the occurrence of childhood sexual abuse in the psychiatric culture to Freud's early hypothesis that many of the neuroses among his female patients were the sequelae of childhood sexual abuse. The Victorian age medical field, and perhaps Freud himself, refused to accept this hypothesis. As a result, women who described childhood sexual abuse were invalidated and further pathologized by a therapeutic culture which dismissed the descriptions as fantasy. The psychiatric culture thus created a context that would severely inhibit a client's acceptance of any experiences of sexual abuse and probably proved iatrogenic for a number of clients. It is only in the past two decades that the general and psychiatric cultures have acknowledged that childhood sexual abuse does occur with some regularity. Stories in the media about sexual abuse have become as commonplace as other forms of trauma. As the attention to and the acknowledgment of the phenomenon of sexual abuse increases, so too does the number of individuals seeking treatment, and the number of treatments available.

Despite the progress in the cultural acknowledgment of the occurrence of sexual abuse, acceptance remains a controversial issue. The proverbial pendulum has swung far in the acknowledgment of the prevalence of sexual abuse, but it may have moved too far and in only now beginning to swing in the other direction, as debates concerning false memory syndrome demonstrate. While some argue that the false memory debate provides another example of society's unwillingness to acknowledge the prevalence of sexual abuse, one may also argue that the other side has failed to accept that not every individual who seeks treatment has a history of sexual abuse. A zeitgeist has developed in some clinical settings that assumes that any client who has problems resembling those of sexually abused patients must have been sexually abused, and if the client does not recall the abuse, the memories must be repressed. Diagnoses become confused with precipitants to diagnoses. Concurrent with the increasing expectation of sexual abuse histories in these settings, clients have begun to enter therapy with the assumptions that they must have been abused, even if they have no memory of it, and that their current problems result directly from the abuse. Therapies which hold these assumptions focus on "uncovering" memories of sexual abuse to explain and to change the client's current behavior. Like Freud's search for the unconscious fantasy, therapies that search for unconscious memories are non-acceptance based approaches to treatment and may also prove invalidating and iatrogenic. Such therapies contrast sharply with Follette's emphasis on acceptance in several ways. First, while "repressed memory" therapies focus on uncovering and understanding the past, selective approach focuses on what the client is experiencing in the current moment, and how the current experiences influence behavior. Second, the uncovering approach focuses on finding certain memories (i.e., memories of abuse), while the acceptance approach of Follette focuses on helping clients to experience memories as they naturally arise, neither searching for, nor preventing, and neither adding to, nor subtracting from, those memories. Third, many of the repressed memory therapies maintain a cathartic view of the expression of inhibited emotions, while Follette's therapy employes exposure techniques.

Closely related to the issue of accepting that abuse has or has not occurred is a second issue that arises for may clients-the question of who is to blame for the abuse. Clients frequently oscillate between extremes of "It was all my fault; I'm a horrible person" and "It was all his fault; he's a horrible person. It's not my fault, there was nothing that I could do." Within this culture, blame not only assigns responsibility or causality for a behavior or event, it also makes a judgement of being "bad". When blame shifts to another person, the responsibility for the behavior, as well as the judgement of "badness" is removed from oneself. In the case of dysfunctional behavior, the individual's character traits such as laziness, selfishness, or neediness are blamed (i.e., the person is bad), unless another "cause" such as a genetic defect of a history of abuse can be found. When another cause is found, the individual is no longer either bad or responsible for the behavior. This lack of responsibility for behavior is often extended to mean lack of control over the behavior. Thus, each side of the blame dichotomy between which sexual abuse survivors oscillate has its' own costs. For example, blaming oneself may cost a sense of self-worth, self-esteem and/ or self-respect, while blaming the other may cost a sense of empowerment and control over the environment. Follette's acceptance approach could be expected to reduce the blame dichotomy through its emphasis on being non-judgmental and its focus on being effective. By teaching the client to observe instead of judge, the therapy may decrease the client's self-judgments and shame associated with low self-esteem and low self respect. The therapy teaches the client to understand the complexity of causal connections and to differentiate a statement of causality from a judgment. A non-judgmental approach may also facilitate the client's ability to maintain relationships with the perpetrator (if desired) by describing how the perpetrator can engage in harmful behavior without being a "bad" person. By focusing on being effective, the therapy may decrease the client's sense of disempowerment. The therapy redirects the client's attention away from the past, in which the client can learn to assert control in the environment. The therapy focuses on what the client can do differently now, not what he or she should have done differently in the past.

Therapeutic Context

Within the therapeutic context, the therapist's own personal feelings, beliefs, and responses, as well as any vulnerability to the cultural issues described above, may influence his or her ability to conduct effective therapy. As Follette discusses, the therapist must practice acceptance as well. She emphasizes the necessity of the therapist accepting the client as the client is, and experiencing one's own feelings about the client.

The therapist's practice of acceptance seems most essential and most difficult during the process of exposing the client to avoided emotions, a principal component of Follette's therapy. During exposure, the client learns to accept avoided emotions primarily by observing them as they arise, without inhibiting or extending them. The therapist directs the client though this process and serves as a role model by accepting the emotions as well. Exposure techniques can be rendered ineffective, however, by even the most technically competent therapist as the therapist fails to accept the client's feelings and begins to inhibit the client's feelings or attempts to insist that the client should experience particular feelings (e.g., anger toward the perpetrator). To effectively direct the client through the exposure process, the therapist must accept the client in the moment. This requires the therapist to acknowledge the client's feelings as they arise, and not according to any assumptions about which feelings should arise, and to tolerate the intensity of those feelings and to be aware in the moment of the degree to which the client can cope with exposure, and to modulate the process accordingly. The therapist also must tolerate his or her own emotional responses to the exposure process, general emotional discomfort, fears that the client mya become overwhelmed or suicidal, anger toward the perpetrator, or grief for the client's loss. The therapist must also be aware of any verbal or non-verbal communication of these feelings to the client, and to the client's response. The use of exposure techniques to enhance the client's emotional acceptance can prove very effective, but only if the therapist succeeds in accepting those same emotions.